# Ensuring Health and Income Security for an Aging Workforce

Peter P. Budetti, Richard V. Burkhauser,
Janice M. Gregory, and H. Allan Hunt
*Editors*

2001

W.E. Upjohn Institute for Employment Research
Kalamazoo, Michigan

*Ensuring Health and Income Security for an Aging Workforce* may be ordered from
W.E. Upjohn Institute for Employment Research
300 S. Westnedge Avenue
Kalamazoo, Michigan 49007–4686
(616) 343–4330

**Library of Congress Cataloging-in-Publication Data**

Ensuring health and income security for an aging workforce /
Peter P. Budetti . . . [et al], editors
p. cm.
Based on the National Academy of Social Insurance's 12th annual conference,
held Jan. 26–27, 2000 in Washington, D.C.
Includes bibliographical references and index.
ISBN 0–88099–219–0 (pbk. : alk. paper) — ISBN 0–88099–220–4
(cloth : alk. paper)
1. Middle aged persons—Employment—United States. 2. Aged—Employment—
United States. 3. Retirement—United States. 4. Social security—United States. 5.
Age and employment—United States. I. Budetti, Peter. II. National Academy of
Social Insurance (U.S.). Conference (12th : 2000 : Washington, D.C.)
HD6280 .E63 2000
331.3'94—dc21                                                    00–043889

Cover design by J.R. Underhill.
Index prepared by Leoni McVey.
Printed in the United States of America.

## NATIONAL ACADEMY OF·SOCIAL INSURANCE

The National Academy of Social Insurance (NASI) is a non-profit, nonpartisan research and education organization made up of the nation's leading experts in social insurance. Its mission is to conduct research and enhance public understanding of social insurance, to develop new leaders, and to provide a nonpartisan forum for the exchange of ideas on important issues in the field. Social Insurance encompasses broad-based systems for insuring workers and their families against economic insecurity caused by loss of income from work, as well as protecting individuals against the cost of personal health care services. The Academy's research covers Social Security, Medicare, workers' compensation, unemployment insurance, and related public and private programs.

The National Academy of Social Insurance does not lobby or take positions on policy issues.

# Contents

## Session 2  Job Loss

## Session 3  Chronic Illness and Disability

*BK Title*

# Editors' Introduction

Peter P. Budetti, Richard V. Burkhauser,
Janice M. Gregory, and H. Allan Hunt

*NIH*

The number of older workers will nearly double in the next two decades. Without immediate attention to the issues they present to public and private health and income security programs, some worker-protection programs will be strained to bursting, and policymakers will migrate from one quick-fix solution to another as they scramble to respond to gaps in coverage and benefit inequities that become more urgent as they grow larger.

Individuals and institutions concerned about preparing for the sharp increase in the number of retired individuals in the United States can turn to many volumes of excellent work that profile the characteristics and resources of present and future retirees, examine their impact on the retirement and health programs designed to support them, and suggest policy options to accommodate those programs to the future. For the next 20 years, however, those who will produce this future retirement bulge will first transform the workplace and the social insurance programs that are designed to support individuals while they are working.

In 1999, almost 23 million Americans were between ages 55 and 64. But aging members of the so-called baby-boom cohort (individuals born between 1946 and 1963) will nearly double that number in the next two decades. In 1999, the age 45–54 cohort numbered 35.3 million, and the age 35–44 cohort checked in at 44.8 million. Who are these people? What will they want? Who among them will be vulnerable? What will society ask of them? Should social insurance policies support a pro-work agenda that keeps these cohorts in the workplace longer? Or should those policies expand the income and health support programs available to older workers, even if it encourages early retirement? If so, how?

Responding to the phenomenon of an older workforce with rational policies and structurally sound programs is vitally important to both the short- and long-term economic well-being of all of us. Many older workers are at the height of their earning capabilities, but they

1

also frequently carry heavy family responsibilities and have the least ability to recoup and prepare adequately for their old age if disaster strikes. How well we respond to older workers will, to a considerable degree, dictate how much and what kind of assistance these same individuals will require when they leave the workforce.

Very little research is available to guide employers, employees, and policymakers through this period. This volume—based on the National Academy of Social Insurance's 12th annual conference, "Ensuring Health and Income Security for an Aging Workforce," which was held in Washington, D.C., on January 26–27, 2000—begins to fill that gap. The conference kicked off a multiyear, interdisciplinary study of the social insurance problems of our aging workforce.

A group of papers were commissioned by the Academy about the implications of an aging workforce for various social insurance programs in the coming decades. Those papers are presented here, together with the comments of the assigned conference reactors. While authors were offered a chance to revise their remarks, the edited papers in this volume reflect the content of the conference very well. The papers in this volume provide a foundation for discussion of the social insurance challenges affecting these older workers and the policy issues that will be raised as they move toward retirement.

A critical feature of the Academy's work is its broad approach to social policy questions. This is essential to any effort to address the impact and needs of older workers; otherwise, efforts to deal with issues and problems related to older workers that appear in one program can lead to dislocations in another program or create gaps in protection that had not been there before. For example, policies that make social security early retirement benefits less generous or that increase the age of "early" retirement will likely lead to greater use of disability programs. Policies designed to limit access to disability programs may put pressure on workers' compensation and unemployment insurance programs or may increase the number of individuals without adequate health care insurance. Hence, policymakers must consider the implications of any single policy change for the entire social safety net in order to mitigate the economic risks associated with exiting the labor force at older ages.

In the first section of this volume, four papers chart the current landscape of older workers' access to and use of health insurance, workers' compensation, unemployment compensation, and disability insurance. These examinations are then synthesized into cross-cutting themes. Subsequent sections of the book target the worker risks of job loss, chronic illness and disability, earlier (or later) retirement, and access to health care from the specific vantage point of the older worker.

## SESSION I.  CHARTING THE LANDSCAPE: WHAT RISKS DO OLDER WORKERS FACE?

Katherine Swartz and Betsey Stevenson analyze 1999 Current Population Survey data to provide a profile of health insurance coverage of current 55- to 64-year-olds.  Striking a theme that will recur in other studies, they note that increases in the fraction of individuals in this age cohort with no health coverage could have more serious short- and long-term consequences than similar gaps for younger individuals. In the short term, older workers are more likely than younger ones to need medical care, and in the long term, because they are less likely to avail themselves of preventive care services, uninsured older workers may later increase Medicare costs.  Determining the causes of coverage gaps among older workers will enable the development of better-targeted public policies to provide coverage for this group at a critical time.

John Burton and Emily Spieler examine older workers in workers' compensation programs and highlight another recurring theme: current programs often do not match the needs of older workers.  In particular, chronic impairments and disabilities common among older workers present both diagnostic and therapeutic hurdles for workers' compensation programs.  These programs have focused on traumatic injury treatment and rehabilitation.  However, many older workers are neither impairment-free nor fully disabled—they are somewhere in between. Since workers' compensation programs are relatively unique among social insurance programs in that they recognize partial disabilities, pressure on these programs may intensify as the number of aged workers increases.

Of course, as the number of older workers swells in the next decades, the number of younger workers will decrease relatively. Christopher O'Leary and Stephen Wandner call for greater understanding of the current and potential impact of unemployment insurance programs on the income security and labor force participation of older workers. They consider the labor market situation of older workers in the context of unemployment insurance policies, including the plight of older workers who move to part-time work or self-employed arrangements.

Mark Nadel examines older workers' risk of long-term disability, including circumstances under which long-term disability also leads to loss of employment and income among older workers. He also reviews systems of insurance coverage and gaps in protection of older workers with disabilities, as well as the implications for disability programs of increasing the age at which early retirement benefits are available.

Robert Haveman poses a central policy question arising from these profiles, i.e., how should social insurance policy respond to the needs of a growing group of older workers who tend to be more work-impaired than their younger peers and who face eroding personal capabilities and difficult decisions regarding transitioning into retirement? Several additional questions flow from Haveman's overarching challenge: Should public policy promote a pro-work agenda or seek to improve the adequacy of income support? How can social insurance policies simultaneously address the needs of two very different groups of older workers, one group that is generally healthy, educated, and working and a second group that has health conditions that limit their ability to work, eroding job skills, and limited education? Where can older workers get the training they need to stay current in their career or to change to a new career? What access to public income support and publicly financed health benefits should be provided to older workers who are working less than full time or in other "bridge" jobs prior to full retirement?

Session I concludes with the comments of Walter Maher and David Smith, who provide employer and union perspectives on these questions.

## SESSION II.  JOB LOSS:
## INCOME AND HEALTH COVERAGE

The use of employment-based insurance plans as the predominant source of health coverage has created a complex interaction between job status and access to health insurance.  Not all individuals or families will have the requisite employment link at all times in their lives, and not all employers will choose to offer coverage in a voluntary system.  Public programs have filled some of the inevitable gaps, but these programs are not comprehensive in their protection.  Workers and their spouses aged 65 and over, as well as those workers who become so seriously disabled that they cannot work at all, are well covered by Medicare.  Persons who are aged 65 and older, or are unable to work at all because of a disability and who are poor, are covered by Medicaid.  In addition, children are also eligible for Medicaid if their family income is not substantially over the federal poverty level.

But other non-employed groups, such as "early retirees" and individuals "between jobs" who are not sufficiently poor, are not protected by public sources, nor are many workers younger than age 65 and their families whose employers do not offer affordable coverage.  Problems of securing coverage in the private insurance market, especially for older persons or persons with chronic health conditions, are well documented.  Thus, job loss has profound implications for older workers (less than age 65) with employment-based health coverage, because they are likely to fall outside of the scope of publicly provided health coverage and may not be able to find new employment or affordable private insurance that provides adequate coverage.  This section focuses on this issue and others related to job loss at older ages.

Ann Huff Stevens and Sewin Chan assess the effects of job loss on the economic status of older workers.  Analyzing Health and Retirement Study (HRS) data on the employment history of displaced workers aged 50 and over, they identified "large and lasting effects of job loss on the future employment probabilities of older workers."  That is, workers who lose jobs at this stage of their lives are far less likely to be working at subsequent ages than their nondisplaced counterparts.  Moreover, those who do find new jobs face substantial reductions in earnings, averaging only two-thirds of what they would have made if they had not lost their previous jobs.  Finally, although the findings are less dramatic, displaced workers may use up their savings to cover lost earnings, and job loss may also lead to substantial reductions in pension benefits.

Jill Quadagno, David Macpherson, and Jennifer Reid Keene surveyed and conducted in-depth interviews with bank officers shortly after layoffs were announced following a takeover of a major West Coast bank.  Some losses in retirement benefits occurred, and younger displaced workers tended to spend down their retirement savings and assets.  But, even some of those who were retained felt they were being set up to resign rather than being offered a generous severance package.  In addition, older employees were less likely than younger ones to find new full-time jobs.  Overall, however, most workers were employed at follow-up, and there was very little disruption in their health coverage.  Thus, at least for this group of relatively well-educated and high-income workers, the effects of job loss were moderate.

Karen Pollitz reviews the effects of public policies with respect to the health and insurance status of older workers and early retirees, aged 55–64.  The health care needs of this age group are far greater than for younger individuals, but coverage opportunities may be less.  Certain specific federal policies play an important role for this age group.  COBRA continuation rights keep employment-related plans available for 1.5 years after job loss.  Medicare and Medicaid help to make up for lower rates of work-based coverage in this age group, at least for those with disabilities.  Because premiums are relatively expensive, even when people have the opportunity to buy individual insurance, other federal statutes have had uncertain or quite limited effects, and state laws and programs vary greatly in their ability to assist the near-elderly in obtaining coverage.  New legislation may be required to assure adequate coverage as the baby boom enters this age group.

This session finishes with the observations of Katherine Swartz on the job problems and health insurance access problems of aging workers.

## SESSION III.  CHRONIC ILLNESS AND DISABILITY: POLICY ISSUES FOR AN AGING WORKFORCE

Jeffrey Biddle, Leslie Boden, and Robert Reville present evidence from three states (Washington, Wisconsin and California) that income replacement programs for permanent partial disability under workers' compensation programs vary greatly, but in each case they leave workers with substantial losses.  Older workers face particular problems; they suffer more permanently disabling injuries, and even though those disabilities are partial, older workers have higher rates of injury-related non-employment.  In addition, at least for the first few years after injury, older workers recover a smaller proportion of their losses.

Richard Burkhauser, Mary Daly, and Andrew Houtenville raise an issue that becomes increasingly worrisome if the rate of disability among working-age individuals continues to grow.  They found that workers with disabilities did not do as well as other workers during the recent economic expansion, and many had their employment and earnings fall in times of expansion, not just recession.  Incomes of households with working-age individuals with disabilities either lagged behind other households or actually fell below previous levels even during the economic boom of the 1990s.  In particular, individuals with disabilities had lower levels of employment and lower annual earnings, and their households became increasingly dependent on public income transfers to sustain income.

Bruce Flynn reports on the results of a survey of disability management practices at large employers by the Washington Business Group on Health and Watson Wyatt Worldwide.  They found that employer costs of disability have leveled off, or even decreased, in the past three years.  This is largely due to market forces, but also partly to the emergence of integrated disability management programs.  The implications for older workers in the areas of health care, functional outcomes, and workplace flexibility are discussed.

Commentary by Vicki Gottlich and Patricia Nemore focused on a consumer perspective of the problems that older workers and persons with disabilities have dealing with private health insurance, Medicare, and Medicaid.  The session concludes with an overview by Barbara

Wolfe. She provides a framework for and a detailed critique of the papers presented.

## SESSION IV. IS WORKING LONGER AND RETIRING LATER POSSIBLE? IS IT DESIRABLE?

Finally, we return to the question asked by Robert Haveman in his overview: what about work at older ages? Is working longer and retiring later possible, or desirable? Gary Burtless and Joseph Quinn argue that the burden of an aging population would rise more gradually if workers delayed retirement and thereby continued contributing to the health and pension systems rather than only being beneficiaries. After a long slide, the long-term trend for earlier retirement, especially among males, seems to have halted and perhaps even reversed in the United States. Burtless and Quinn outline policies that might reinforce this nascent turnaround.

Anna Rappaport explores these policies from the very different perspective of employers, for whom retirement is defined as an employee leaving a particular employer rather than exiting the workforce completely. Employers focus on business need when structuring human resource programs, but they must also consider the constraints of public policy. She calls for additional research on the costs and benefits of employing older workers.

Glen Pransky brings a medical perspective to the question of aging and work capacity. He asks whether recent success in mortality reduction has resulted in an aging population with more morbidity, less ability to function, and thus less average work capacity at a given age; or, have gains in morbidity paralleled the gains in mortality, with a prolongation of functional capacity? He reviews the evidence and finds few broadly generalizable conclusions. Further research is needed to define and evaluate the issues.

In her commentary, Teresa Ghilarducci examines the issue of how much choice older workers should have over whether they continue to work or not. Who is to decide when enough work is enough, if not the worker him or herself? She cites falling male workforce participation rates as a demonstration of how workers have chosen to spend the increases in the nation's productive capacity. She questions whether public policy initiatives should encourage later retirement or whether alternative ways to enable worker choice should be found.

## SESSION V. FILLING GAPS IN HEALTH COVERAGE: SHARING RESPONSIBILITY AND COSTS

Len Nichols makes a strong case for public policy initiatives to assist the age 55–64 cohort with health coverage—despite their relatively high insurance coverage rate—by demonstrating, first, that their health needs and the risks they face from being uninsured are far greater than are those of younger cohorts, and second, that their numbers are rapidly expanding even as their likelihood of having employer-sponsored retiree health insurance is declining.

After examining the opportunities and limitations presented by public program and COBRA expansions, tax credits, and direct subsidies, and outlining the high financial costs of the current-nongroup market and the high political costs of trying to reform that market, he presents and simulates the costs and effects of three promising subsidy policy options. He argues that major gains can be achieved at relatively low cost by targeting those with the most pressing needs within the 55–64 age group, i.e., uncovered persons with low incomes and those whose health is fair or poor but not impaired enough to qualify for the current Medicare or Medicaid programs. Nichols concludes with a set of four principles for public policy based on the greater needs of these subgroups and the relative ease with which our society could address those needs.

Deborah Chollet examines these arguments with a critical eye. She wonders about the source of health care coverage, given experience with high-risk pools at the state level. She submits that a principal danger is to try and fix too much. Frank McArdle contributes an employer's perspective on the policy solutions of the Nichols paper. He finds merit in a defined-contribution approach to health care coverage for retirees. Diane Rowland urges that we not throw out the good in our public programs. Sometimes it is preferable to work on reforming what is "in the box" rather than going "outside the box."

## CONCLUSION

After seven years of vigorous economic growth, not only has the federal budget been balanced for the first time in decades, but we are actually rolling up sizable surpluses.  Politicians are competing over the most creative ways to invest this surplus, but it is clear that substantial reforms of our social welfare system will be required to finance the growing income and health care needs of future cohorts of older workers.  The authors in this book provide a variety of ways in which our current public and private publicly financed safety net could be reconstructed to provide this protection.

In a very real sense, the future is in our hands.  It is time for both the public and private sector to focus on the special questions, challenges, and needs of the growing population of older workers on payrolls across the land.  The papers in this volume provide a beginning for this process.  The National Academy of Social Insurance intends to pursue these issues at greater length and invites all interested parties to participate.

# Session 1
# Charting the Landscape
## What Risks Do Older Workers Face?

13-40

# Health Insurance Coverage of People in the Ten Years before Medicare Eligibility

(US 1

I 18
J 14

Katherine Swartz
*Harvard School of Public Health*

Betsey Stevenson
*Harvard University*

A decade remains before the oldest members of the baby boom generation begin to be eligible for Medicare. The potentially large effects on the economy and federal budget have made understanding this group's preretirement behavior essential. Small changes in behavior regarding the age of retirement and the preretirement use of preventive medical care could have dramatic consequences for Medicare expenditures. Thus, we need answers to questions such as, how many baby boomers will retire before the Social Security eligibility age, either by choice or because of illness? How many will be financially prepared, with health insurance as part of their preparation, to retire early? How many will have retiree health insurance benefits from a former employer and how many will be able to afford Medigap insurance to supplement Medicare?

Different subgenerations or successive five-year cohorts of baby boomers are not all going to have the same preretirement experiences as the oldest baby boomers, because the entire group was born over a nearly 20-year span between 1946 and 1963. The different subgenerations have had quite different economic experiences since reaching adulthood, and these different experiences are likely to have affected asset accumulation for retirement. However, it is likely that there are enough similarities among the subgroups to be able to gain insight into the potential behavior of at least the older half of the baby boom generation by studying the economic readiness to retire and health insurance coverage of the current cohort of 55- to 64-year-olds.

Much has been written about the retirement incentives inherent in access to employer-sponsored health insurance for retirees (e.g., Gustman and Steinmeier 1994; Karoly and Rogowski 1994; Gruber and Madrian 1995; Blau and Gilleskie 1997; Loprest 1998; Madrian and Beaulieu 1998; Johnson, Davidoff, and Perese 1999), but we know much less about the types of health insurance coverage (or lack thereof) among people who are within 10 years of becoming eligible for Medicare coverage. What we do know has come from Swartz and Moon (1986), Jensen (1992), Johnson and Crystal (1997), and Loprest and Uccello (1997). With all of the fast-paced changes occurring in health insurance coverage and premiums—and employer-sponsored retiree health insurance in particular—policymakers need to know what types of health insurance coverage are held by people who currently are 55 to 64 years of age. Understanding who has what types of health insurance now will identify the types of people who are potentially at financial risk when faced with expensive medical care needs. Further, identifying the characteristics of people who may need government assistance in obtaining health coverage prior to Medicare eligibility will help in assessing the likely costs of such a program. Finally, such knowledge will also help identify the types of people most unlikely to have employer-sponsored health benefits when they retire.

In 1999, 22.9 million Americans were ages 55 to 64, according to the March 1999 Current Population Survey (CPS). Only 16.6 percent of this age group were retired, with just over half of the retirees being 62 to 64 years of age. Two-thirds (65.6 percent) of the 55- to 64-year-olds had employer-sponsored health insurance, and another 8.4 percent had private, nongroup coverage. Just over 9 percent had some form of public health insurance (Medicare, Medicaid, a combination of Medicare and Medicaid or Medicaid and private coverage, or Champus/VA) during the year. Fifteen percent had no form of health insurance. Historically, 55- to 64-year-olds have accounted for the smallest percentage of the total population of the uninsured. For example, estimates from the March 1999 Current Population Survey (CPS), indicate that 3.434 million uninsured people (less than 8 percent of the non-elderly uninsured) were 55 to 64 years of age. This is very close to the 8.3 percent estimated from the March 1984 CPS (Sulvetta and Swartz 1986).

However, what is different between 1999 and 1984 is that the proportion of the 55- to 64-year-old cohort without any coverage has increased from 13 percent to 15 percent. In part, this increase reflects the growth since 1984 in the total percentage of the population without health insurance. The proportion of each of the younger adult-age cohorts without health insurance has also increased in the intervening 15 years (Table 1; tables start on p. 27). This implies that as all the baby boomers move through the 55- to 64-year-age range, we should anticipate higher fractions of near-retirees being uninsured.

The increase in the fraction of people approaching retirement who are without any health insurance coverage is cause for concern. As people age, they are statistically more likely to need medical care, and if they are uninsured, they are less likely to obtain preventive care. The delays in obtaining preventive care may lead to an increase in the cost of their medical care once they reach age 65 and are eligible for Medicare coverage. Thus, an increase in the average expenditure per Medicare recipient is likely just because higher percentages of younger age cohorts are uninsured prior to age 65. In turn, this suggests that projected expenditures for Medicare in the future may need to be revised upwards.

The Clinton administration has proposed (and is expected to propose again) that near-retirees who are uninsured be permitted to buy into Medicare. By providing them early Medicare coverage, there may be long-run savings stemming from obtaining timely preventive care. However, the potential for adverse selection with such a plan means that more information is needed about 55- to 64-year-olds who are uninsured in order to evaluate such a plan (Reischauer 1998; Swartz 1998).

In addition, with the corporate downsizing that has occurred in the past decade, people 55 to 64 years of age were especially likely to lose their jobs or to become self-employed as consultants or contract workers for projects of specified duration. Such workers have two federal protections that permit them to maintain insurance coverage. Under the Consolidated Omnibus Budget Reconciliation Act of 1985 (COBRA), such workers are permitted to continue their former employer-group coverage for up to 18 months so long as they pay up to 102 percent of the total premium. Further, under the Health Insurance Portability and Accountability Act of 1996 (HIPAA), workers who have had group coverage are able to convert such policies to individual coverage without fearing loss of coverage for preexisting medical conditions. Yet, neither of these acts guarantees that the premium to be paid will be low or close to what a person may have paid for group coverage. The number of 55- to 64-year-olds with nongroup coverage declined between 1998 and 1999 by 273,000 (from 9.9 percent to 8.4 percent of the age cohort). It may be that this decline is a reflection of the rising costs of individual, nongroup policies. If so, the double-digit increases in premiums that are projected for the next several years may cause further erosion in the number of 55- to 64-year-olds covered by nongroup policies.

The proportion of 55- to 64-year-olds with employer-group coverage might be expected to provide an indication of the number of people who are likely to have employer-sponsored retiree health benefits to supplement Medicare coverage once they are 65 or older. However, within the past decade, employers have been reducing retiree health benefits and often are restricting such benefits to the worker rather than the worker and dependents (GAO 1997). Consequently, while it is important to know who among the 55- to 64-year-old cohort has employer-group coverage, it is likely that having employer-sponsored coverage before retirement is no longer a strong predictor of who will have employer-sponsored health benefits when they retire.

In this paper, we present findings from an analysis of health insurance coverage among people 55 to 64 years of age in 1999—the age cohort born between 1935 and 1944, just before the baby boom began in 1946. This age cohort has been small by historical standards and has benefited financially from its relatively small size. As a result, it is not clear that its experiences with health insurance are good indicators of the experiences subsequent age cohorts will experience when they are 55 to 64. But, if we view this age cohort's experiences as the most optimistic scenarios for subsequent age cohorts, they permit policymakers to plan more realistically for the need for publicly funded or subsidized health insurance programs for near-retirees in the future. We particularly focus on the characteristics of the people who are in the major types of health insurance categories: employer-sponsored (with and without other private insurance), individual/nongroup coverage only, Medicaid, and no health insurance. Our intent is twofold: first, to identify the types of people who may not be able to afford medical care and face health risks, and second, to show how socioeconomic characteristics are related to different types of health insurance coverage.

## OVERVIEW

As noted above, there were almost 23 million people 55 to 64 years of age in 1999.[1]  This age cohort accounts for about 8.5 percent of the total U.S. population.  To place the size of this cohort in perspective, the baby boomers in 1999 were in the 35- to 44-year-old and 45- to 54-year-old cohorts, which had 44.8 million and 35.3 million people, respectively.

Table 2 shows the distribution of types of health insurance that people 55 to 64 years of age had according to the March 1999 Current Population Survey (CPS).  Two-thirds of the near-retirees have employer-sponsored health insurance (ESI) and/or individual, non-group coverage and another 8.4 percent have individual, nongroup coverage—so, three-quarters of all 55- to 64-year-olds have some type of private health insurance.  About 10 percent of the age cohort have Medicaid, Medicare, Champus/VA, or a mix of these public types of coverage and private coverage during the year.  Finally, 15 percent of the near-retirees are uninsured.  We describe the characteristics of the people who have these major types of coverage in more detail below.

In analyzing the types of characteristics that may be associated with different types of health insurance, it is useful to think about the near-retirees as being composed of two major groups.  In one group are people who are seemingly healthy, working, with higher educational levels and earning high incomes, i.e., people who are likely to work until age 65 unless they decide that they have accumulated high enough assets that they can retire early.  The second group consists of people who are less healthy, unemployed, or simply poor.  This group includes the less educated or less skilled, those forced into early retirement because of employer downsizing, and those who have had other types of bad luck (perhaps in the form of becoming widowed or divorced, having lower incomes [in part because of no longer being married], or having to leave the labor force in order to care for an ailing spouse or elderly parent).  A simple way of thinking of the two groups is to regard the first group as fortunate and the second group as unfortunate.  One might expect the fortunate group to be largely covered by private health insurance, while those less fortunate might be expected to have a greater reliance on public coverage (Medicaid, Medicare, Medicaid and Medicare, Medicaid and private coverage, or Champus/VA). As we show in the next section, both of these assumptions are true.

Although having employer-sponsored coverage prior to retirement is not a perfect predictor of retiree health insurance benefits, it is still a useful indicator. Thus, the fact that people in our first group, the fortunate near-retirees, are more likely to have employer-sponsored coverage implies that proposals to shift the age of eligibility for Medicare to match the Social Security eligibility age will disproportionately hurt people who already have problems with health insurance coverage in their near-retirement years. Further, as the life expectancy of people increases, it is likely that a significant portion of the baby boomers will face choices between working to continue their own access to health insurance and reducing work efforts in order to care for elderly parents. This is especially likely to occur for those between the ages of 62 and the age of eligibility for full Social Security benefits. Thus, the patterns of health insurance coverage of the near-retirees point to the need to determine the consequences of proposals to enable people to buy into Medicare at age 62.

## CHARACTERISTICS ASSOCIATED WITH TYPE OF HEALTH INSURANCE

Not surprisingly, the type of health insurance coverage a person has is strongly linked to the person's labor force activity (Table 3). Among 55- to 64-year-olds, there seem to be only two major labor force activities: either working or else not in the labor force (i.e., only 2 percent were either unemployed and looking for work or on lay-off). In 1999, almost three out of five 55- to 64-year-olds were working; the other 40 percent were not engaged in the workforce. Among those working, more than three-quarters were covered by employer-sponsored insurance, while among those not in the labor force, just under half had ESI.

Among the 9.2 million people who were not in the labor force, almost 90 percent provided reasons for not working (Table 4). Of those responding, almost half had retired, a third were ill or disabled and could not work, and almost a fifth worked without pay on family and home responsibilities. Among those who worked in the home without pay, 30 percent were uninsured, half had ESI, and 10 percent purchased their own nongroup coverage. Those who were retired were similar in their coverage, although there are fewer who are uninsured (17.5 percent). In sharp contrast, half of the ill and disabled had public coverage (Medicaid and/or Medicare), only a quarter had ESI, less than 8 percent had individual coverage, and 12 percent were uninsured.

Given the impact of being in the labor force on type of health insurance, it should come as no surprise that family income is a strong predictor of the type of coverage held by 55- to 64-year-olds (Table 5). Among 55- to 64-year-olds, family income is somewhat skewed: 21 percent had 1998 incomes below $20,000; 18 percent had incomes between $20,000 and $35,000; 16 percent had incomes between $35,000 and $50,000; and 45 percent had incomes at or above $50,000. Note that only when family incomes were above $20,000 do we observe at least half of the people in particular income groups with ESI, and family incomes have to exceed $35,000 before at least two-thirds of the income group has ESI.

Family income, however, can be deceptive because it is the sum of the incomes of all related people living in the same household. In the case of near-retirees, we know that living arrangements can change as an individual's financial situation changes. Thus, a widower or divorcee between the ages of 55 and 64 may find him- or herself living with adult children or with other adult relatives. In these circumstances, family income does not necessarily indicate the financial circumstances of the individual involved. Furthermore, insurance companies define "family" as including only married couples and their dependent children (or single parents and their dependent children), and therefore they do not permit elderly parents to be covered by a family policy of their adult children. Table 6 shows the insurance family unit types of 55- to 64-year-olds by whether or not the person has any type of health insurance. Clearly, any 55- to 64- year-old who is living in a nuclear family with or without children at home has the lowest probability of being without health insurance. Single adults (with or without children at home), single or married parents living with their adult children, and adults living in other arrangements with related people are more likely to be uninsured. Because one-fifth of all 55- to 64-year-olds live in households where family income is more than the person's insurance family unit (IFU) income, it is important to examine the distribution of types of health insurance that people have by their IFU income. This provides a more accurate view of the insurance coverage of near-retirees relative to their available financial resources.

As a comparison of Tables 5, 7, and 8 indicate, uninsured near-retirees are less likely to be poor than the rest of the non-elderly uninsured population. In 1998, 52 percent of uninsured 55- to 64-year-olds had family incomes below 250 percent of the poverty level, compared with 65 percent of the all the non-elderly uninsured. Although 26 percent had family incomes at or above $50,000, over a quarter of this was the result of the uninsured near-elderly living with other relatives whose income was counted as part of the person's family income. That is, of the nearly 900,000 uninsured 55- to 64-year-olds with 1998 family incomes at or above $50,000, almost a quarter of a million had "insurance family unit" incomes less than $50,000. Thus, as with all the non-elderly, near-retirees with high IFU incomes were likely to have ESI, while those with low IFU incomes were more likely to be uninsured. When we examine only Tables 7 and 8 to distinguish the near-retirees in terms of 55- to 61-year-olds and 62- to 64-year-olds, we find that at the lower IFU income levels, the older near-retirees are more likely to have public coverage than to be uninsured. This may reflect age related higher probabilities of being eligible for Medicaid and Medicare if one is disabled.

Not surprisingly, people who identify themselves as healthy are far more likely to have ESI, while almost half of those who report poor health (7.9 percent of the near-retirees) have public coverage (Table 9). Among those reporting fair health (almost 15 percent of 55- to 64-year-olds), almost half have ESI and a quarter have public coverage.

Given the differences between men and women in employment patterns and marriage status as they age, it is useful to examine the distribution of health insurance types for men and women separately. Table 10 provides an overview of the distribution of health coverage among men and women, for 55- to 61-year-olds and 62- to 64-year-olds. Women are less likely to have ESI than men in each of the age subgroups, but women are more likely to have nongroup private coverage than their male counterparts. For both age groups, women are more likely than men to be uninsured. Table 11 permits us to examine the male-female health coverage differences in terms of how marital status interacts with coverage options and decisions. Married people in all four sex/age subgroups are most likely to have ESI. Among men in both age subgroups, unmarried men are more likely to have either public coverage or no insurance. Both married and widowed women in the older age group are more likely to have nongroup coverage. This finding is consistent with the observation that women are often married to men one or more years older, and if the husband has retired or died, the woman may obtain nongroup coverage for the one to three years' time until eligible for Medicare. What is very clear from both tables is that being married is a big advantage in terms of having ESI and not being uninsured.

As with marriage, increasing levels of educational attainment raise the probability that a person will have ESI rather than have public coverage or be uninsured. Table 12 indicates the distribution of type of health insurance by educational level of near-retirees. Among the nearly 20 percent of 55- to 64-year-olds without a high school diploma, 50 percent are either uninsured or relying on public coverage, and only 40 percent have ESI. In contrast, of the 37 percent with a high school diploma, two-thirds have ESI. Among those with a college degree or post-graduate education, more than three-fourths have ESI. This pattern is not surprising, since higher levels of education allow people to choose jobs with better benefits and lower injury rates.

Finally, there are differences by race in the distribution of types of health insurance among 55- to 64-year-olds. Table 13 shows the distribution for the two age subgroups (55 to 61 and 62 to 64 years of age). Approximately two-thirds of white near-retirees have ESI and about 14 percent are uninsured. In contrast, just over half of 55- to 61-year-old blacks have ESI, and only 41.5 percent of 62 to 64 year old blacks have ESI. People in "other" racial categories (Asian, Native American, Pacific Islander, and other), who comprise 4 percent of near-retirees, are also more likely to have public coverage or no insurance at all.

In sum, near-retirees who have ESI coverage are most likely to be in higher income categories, to be married, white, in good health, and to have higher educational levels. For these people, raising the age of eligibility for Medicare to 67 is unlikely to leave them uninsured. However, for those near-retirees who are unmarried, nonwhite, in poor health, or simply have less education, raising the Medicare eligibility age is likely to exacerbate the already high percentage who are uninsured or relying on public coverage.

## RELATIVE EFFECTS OF DIFFERENT CHARACTERISTICS ON TYPE OF HEALTH INSURANCE

Examining the near-retirees' types of health insurance in terms of different characteristics does not provide us with the relative importance of each of the characteristics in predicting the type of coverage that a near-retiree may have. It is important to understand the relative effects because many of the characteristics examined in the previous section are correlated with one another (for example, education and income, or marital status and income). To estimate the relative effects of these characteristics and determine which are most important for predicting type of health coverage, we estimated a multinomial logit model with four outcomes: ESI coverage (including possibly double-coverage with nongroup), nongroup only, public coverage, and no insurance. Table 14 contains the estimated coefficients for the model with insurance family unit (IFU) income and other characteristics, along with $z$-statistics. The coefficients indicate the effect of each characteristic on the probability (relative to having ESI) of having nongroup coverage, public coverage, or no insurance. We also estimated the same model with family income substituted for IFU income. Although the overall results do not change substantially when family income is used instead of IFU income (as will be illustrated below), the model with IFU income is slightly better in terms of goodness of fit measures.

What is interesting about Table 14 is that almost all of the characteristics are statistically significant in their effect on the probability that an individual would have each of the types of coverage. However, holding all the other characteristics constant, being 55 to 61 years of age rather than 62 to 64 is significant only in predicting nongroup coverage relative to ESI, not in predicting public coverage or no insurance relative to ESI. Whether a person is a male or female also is not significant in predicting no insurance relative to ESI when all other characteristics are held constant, which is surprising given the data in Table

10. Being married (as opposed to any nonmarried marital state) is statistically significant only in predicting no insurance relative to having ESI. Whether or not a person is working is not statistically significant in predicting whether a person has nongroup private insurance relative to ESI, but if a person is working he or she is statistically significantly less likely to have public coverage or be uninsured. In contrast, being ill/disabled and unable to work or being retired and not working are both statistically significant characteristics for predicting type of health insurance. Similarly, being white (as opposed to nonwhite) is a statistically significant characteristic, making a person less likely to have either public coverage or be uninsured relative to having ESI. In general, IFU income, educational attainment, and health status are the characteristics that have the largest effects on the probabilities of having each type of coverage, which is consistent with the theme we began with, that the near-retirees consist of two distinct groups of people.

Tables 15 and 16 provide illustrations of prototypical male and female (respectively) near-retirees and their probabilities of having each of the four major types of insurance coverage. Both tables also indicate how using IFU income (rather than family income) yields somewhat different predicted probabilities of having each of the types of insurance, but does not yield different outcomes in terms of the types of insurance with the highest probability. This result is reassuring given that family income is easier to obtain than IFU income, which often involves parsing out components of family income to the separate IFUs in a household. The illustrations clearly show that having higher income, more education, and better health status increase the probability of having ESI rather than public coverage or being uninsured. Further, being ill/disabled and in poor health significantly lowers the probability of having ESI and increases the probability of having public coverage. Controlling for marital status, we find that early retirement (for reasons other than illness/disability) significantly lowers the probability of having ESI for men, but not for women. Undoubtedly, this is indicative of access to a husband's ESI coverage for women who retire early, while the reverse is less likely to be true for men.

To place the prototypical examples in perspective, Table 17 shows the distribution of near-elderly across the four types of health insurance and the proportions with various characteristics in each type. Among the people who have ESI coverage, for example, far greater proportions of the men and women are married than is true of the men and women with public coverage or no insurance at all. Similarly, the people who have ESI are far more likely to have higher levels of education than the people with public coverage or no insurance.

## CONCLUSIONS

The age cohort of 55- to 64-year-olds can be roughly divided into two groups. The fortunate group consists of people who are able to work until at least age 65; this group is more likely to have higher education and income levels, and better health, as well as employer-sponsored insurance. The unfortunate group is that who either have developed health conditions or otherwise find it difficult to continue working, and have fewer financial resources (including ESI) in the years before they reach age 65. The policy implication of this finding is that proposals to extend the age of eligibility for Medicare to match the age of eligibility for full Social Security benefits are more likely to harm the second group of near-retirees.

In terms of developing public policies to help near-retirees who do not have ESI and are uninsured, the major empirical issue is the extent to which adverse selection might occur if 55- to 64-year-olds were provided with a public program (Swartz 1998). One such option, proposed by the Clinton administration, is to permit people to purchase Medicare coverage under restricted circumstances. Creating and evaluating a demonstration program targeted at 55- to 64-year-olds to learn how severe adverse selection might be would provide the empirical evidence needed to estimate the costs of permitting early enrollment in Medicare.

Finally, people who do not have health insurance prior to reaching age 65 are less likely to have retiree health insurance benefits or to buy Medigap policies to supplement Medicare. The fact that 15 percent of people currently 55 to 64 years of age are uninsured has implications for the health needs and costs of people when they reach age 65 and begin to be covered by Medicare, but to understand why near-retirees may not have health insurance, we need analyses of longitudinal data on people 50 years of age and older. We need to understand how changes in employment, income, health status, marital status and family responsibilities over the ages of 50 to 65 affect access to health insurance for people of different educational and occupational backgrounds. If all the 55- to 64-year-olds without health insurance lost such coverage because of health problems, that would suggest a strong need for expanding Medicare. Similarly, longitudinal analyses would provide estimates of the numbers of near-retirees who stopped working in order to care for older spouses or aging parents and used up their own savings in the process. Determining why near-retirees become uninsured, as well as how many people face pressures to retire early and lose insurance coverage, would enable us to develop better-targeted public policies to help near-retirees maintain and obtain health insurance coverage.

## Notes

Partial funding for this paper was provided by the Robert Wood Johnson Foundation Grant no. 037484, which is gratefully acknowledged. The authors also thank Karen Neoh for her superb research assistance. Opinions expressed in this paper are solely those of the authors and are not necessarily those of the Robert Wood Johnson Foundation or Harvard University.

1. Data from the March 1999 Supplement to the Current Population Survey (CPS) are the basis for the estimates of the numbers of people with various types of health insurance and their socioeconomic and demographic characteristics. Analysts disagree as to whether the CPS numbers on the uninsured refer to a point in time (i.e., March of the year of the survey) or to the previous calendar year. We believe the uninsured numbers are closer to point-in-time estimates than to estimates of the number who were uninsured during all of the previous year, and therefore we refer to the year of the CPS when describing the uninsured as a particular year. See Swartz (1986) for more details.

## References

Blau, D.M., and D.B. Gilleskie. 1997. "Retiree Health Insurance and the Labor Force Behavior of Older Men in the 1990s." Working paper 5948, National Bureau of Economic Research, Cambridge, Massachusetts.

GAO. 1997. *Retiree Health Insurance: Erosion in Employer-Based Health Benefits for Early Retirees.* Government Accounting Office, GAO/HEHS-97-150, Washington, D.C.

Gruber, J., and B.C. Madrian. 1995. "Health Insurance Availability and Retirement Decision." *American Economic Review* 85(4): 938–948.

Gustman, A.L., and T.L. Steinmeier. 1994. "Employer-Provided Health Insurance and Retirement Behavior." *Industrial and Labor Relations Review* 48(1): 124–140.

Jensen, G.A. 1992. "The Dynamics of Health Insurance among the Near Elderly." *Medical Care* 30(7): 598–614.

Johnson, R.W., and S. Crystal. 1997. "Health Insurance Coverage at Midlife: Characteristics, Costs and Dynamics." *Health Care Financing and Review* 18(3): 123–148.

Johnson, R.W., A.J. Davidoff, and K. Perese. 1999. "Health Insurance Costs and Early Retirement Decisions." Working paper, The Urban Institute, Washington, D.C.

Karoly, L.A., and J.A. Rogowski. 1994. "The Effect of Access to Post-Retirement Health Insurance on the Decision to Retire Early." *Industrial and Labor Relations Review* 48(1): 103–123.

Loprest, P., and C. Uccello. 1997. "Uninsured Older Adults: Implications for Changing Medicare Eligibility." Working paper, The Urban Institute, Washington, D.C.

Loprest, P. 1998. "Retiree Health Benefits: Availability from Employers and Participation by Employees." *The Gerontologist* 38(6): 684–694.

Madrian, B.C., and N.D. Beaulieu. 1998. "Does Medicare Eligibility Affect Retirement?" In *Inquiries in the Economics of Aging*, D.A. Wise, ed. University of Chicago Press: Chicago, pp. 109–131.

Reischauer, R.D. 1998. "Medicare for the Almost Old." *The Washington Post* January 12: A17.

Sulvetta, M.B., and K. Swartz. 1986. *The Uninsured and Uncompensated Care.* National Health Policy Forum: Washington, D.C.

Swartz, K. 1986. "Interpreting the Estimates from Four National Surveys of the Number of People without Health Insurance." *Journal of Economic and Social Measurement* 14(3): 233–242.

_____. 1998. "Medicare Expansions 35 Years Later." *Inquiry* 35(1): 6–8.

Swartz, K., and M. Moon. 1986. *The Health Insurance Status of Mid-Life Women: The Problem and Options for Alleviating It.* American Association of Retired Persons: Washington, D.C.

**Table 1  Changes in the Percentage of Non-Elderly Age Cohorts without Health Insurance, 1984 and 1999**

| Cohort | Share of uninsured (%) | | Share of age cohort uninsured (%) | |
|---|---|---|---|---|
| | 1984 | 1999 | 1984 | 1999 |
| Less than 18 years | 33.0 | 25.2 | 18.6 | 15.4 |
| 18–24 years | 23.6 | 17.7 | 29.0 | 30.0 |
| 25–34 years | 17.7 | 20.8 | 15.4 | 23.7 |
| 35–44 years | 9.7 | 17.5 | 11.3 | 17.2 |
| 45–54 years | 7.7 | 10.9 | 12.0 | 13.6 |
| 55–64 years | 8.3 | 7.8 | 13.0 | 15.0 |

SOURCE: March 1984 and March 1999 Current Population Survey.

**Table 2  Distribution of Types of Health Insurance of 55- to 64-Year-Olds**

| Type of health insurance | Number (millions) | Percent |
|---|---|---|
| Private (employer-group only and employer-group + nongroup) | 15.028 | 65.6 |
| Nongroup only | 1.924 | 8.4 |
| Medicaid only | 0.724 | 3.2 |
| Medicare only | 0.760 | 3.3 |
| Medicaid and Medicare | 0.476 | 2.1 |
| Medicaid and private | 0.182 | 0.8 |
| Champus/VA | 0.349 | 1.5 |
| Not otherwise defined | 0.033 | 0.1 |
| Uninsured | 3.434 | 15.0 |
| Total | 22.909 | 100.0 |

SOURCE: March 1999 Current Population Survey.

**Table 3  Health Insurance Coverage by Labor Force Activity of 55- to 64-Year-Olds**

| Labor force activity | Private[a] (%) | Nongroup only (%) | Public[b] (%) | Uninsured (%) | Total (%) | Total number (millions) |
|---|---|---|---|---|---|---|
| Working | 77.5 | 7.3 | 2.5 | 12.7 | 100 | 13.293 |
| Unemployed | 60.5 | 7.9 | 5.9 | 25.7 | 100 | 0.338 |
| On lay-off | 78.7 | 2.4 | 2.7 | 16.2 | 100 | 0.111 |
| Not in labor force | 48.3 | 10.0 | 23.8 | 17.9 | 100 | 9.159 |

SOURCE: March 1999 Current Population Survey.
[a] "Private" includes employer-group only and employer-group + nongroup.
[b] "Public" includes Medicaid, Medicare, Medicaid + Medicare, Champus/VA, Medicaid + private, and other combinations.

**Table 4  Health Insurance Coverage by Reasons for Not Working for 8.013 Million 55- to 64-Year-Olds**

| Reason for not working | Private[a] (%) | Nongroup only (%) | Public[b] (%) | Uninsured (%) | Total (%) | Total number (millions) |
|---|---|---|---|---|---|---|
| Ill/disabled | 24.1 | 7.6 | 56.4 | 11.9 | 100 | 2.529 |
| Retired | 56.8 | 12.0 | 13.7 | 17.5 | 100 | 3.808 |
| Home/family | 49.9 | 9.9 | 10.7 | 29.5 | 100 | 1.470 |
| Other | 39.8 | —[c] | 17.5 | 42.7 | 100 | 0.206 |

SOURCE: March 1999 Current Population Survey.
[a] "Private" includes employer-group only and employer-group + nongroup.
[b] "Public" includes Medicaid, Medicare, Medicaid + Medicare, Champus/VA, Medicaid + private, and other combinations.
[c] A dash (—) indicates a sample size too small for a statistically reliable estimate.

**Table 5  Health Insurance Coverage by Family Income for
55- to 64-Year-Olds**

| Family income | Private[a] (%) | Nongroup | Public[b] | Uninsured (%) | Total (%) | Total number (millions) |
|---|---|---|---|---|---|---|
| less than $10,000 | 20.8 | 11.1 | 38.5 | 29.6 | 100 | 2.195 |
| $10,000–19,999 | 38.5 | 11.1 | 25.7 | 24.7 | 100 | 2.551 |
| $20,000–29,999 | 57.4 | 10.7 | 12.8 | 19.1 | 100 | 2.813 |
| $30,000–39,999 | 64.9 | 10.8 | 8.0 | 16.3 | 100 | 2.649 |
| $40,000–49,999 | 71.9 | 9.2 | 6.7 | 12.2 | 100 | 2.424 |
| $50,000–74,999 | 80.9 | 5.8 | 3.5 | 9.8 | 100 | 4.323 |
| $75,000–99,999 | 81.7 | 5.5 | 3.5 | 9.3 | 100 | 2.699 |
| $100,000 and more | 86.3 | 5.9 | 1.3 | 6.5 | 100 | 3.256 |

SOURCE: March 1999 Current Population Survey.
[a] "Private" includes employer-group only and employer-group plus nongroup.
[b] "Public" includes Medicaid, Medicare, Medicaid + Medicare, Champus/VA,
   Medicaid + private, and other combinations.


**Table 6  Insurance Family Unit Type in which 55- to 64-Year-Olds Live,
by Insurance Status**

| Insurance family unit type | Insured (%) | Uninsured (%) | Number (millions) | % of All 55–64 in IFU type |
|---|---|---|---|---|
| Single adult, no kids | 81.2 | 18.8 | 4.914 | 21.5 |
| Married couple, no kids | 87.8 | 12.2 | 11.412 | 49.8 |
| Married couple, kids | 89.5 | 10.5 | 1.606 | 7.0 |
| Single adult, kids | 74.0 | 26.0 | 0.298 | 1.3 |
| Single parent living with adult kids | 73.5 | 26.5 | 1.155 | 5.0 |
| Married parent living with adult kids | 85.4 | 14.6 | 2.791 | 12.2 |
| Other | 78.9 | 21.1 | 0.733 | 3.2 |
| All | 85.0 | 15.0 | 22.909 | 100 |

SOURCE: March 1999 Current Population Survey.

**Table 7  Health Insurance Coverage by IFU Income among 55- to 61-Year-Olds**

| IFU Income | Private[a] (%) | Nongroup (%) | Public[b] (%) | Uninsured (%) | Total (%) | Total number (millions) |
|---|---|---|---|---|---|---|
| Less than $10,000 | 18.3 | 11.3 | 26.7 | 33.7 | 100 | 2.157 |
| $10,000–19,999 | 41.6 | 9.2 | 21.6 | 27.6 | 100 | 1.979 |
| $20,000–29,999 | 62.3 | 10.9 | 7.6 | 19.2 | 100 | 2.016 |
| $30,000–39,999 | 72.9 | 8.1 | 5.1 | 13.9 | 100 | 1.920 |
| $40,000–49,999 | 81.2 | 7.2 | 4.2 | 7.1 | 100 | 1.605 |
| $50,000–59,999 | 84.5 | 4.9 | 2.8 | 7.8 | 100 | 1.473 |
| $60,000–69,999 | 85.7 | 5.8 | 1.7 | 6.8 | 100 | 1.154 |
| $70,000–79,999 | 85.0 | 4.8 | 2.6 | 7.6 | 100 | 0.945 |
| $80,000–89,999 | 85.6 | 3.5 | 1.9 | 9.0 | 100 | 0.792 |
| $90,000–99,999 | 85.2 | 3.2 | 4.5 | 7.1 | 100 | 0.559 |
| $100,000 and more | 89.3 | 5.5 | 0.7 | 4.3 | 100 | 2.295 |
| All | 67.6 | 7.5 | 10.0 | 14.9 | 100 | 16.923 |

SOURCE: March 1999 Current Population Survey.

[a] "Private" includes employer-group only and employer-group plus nongroup.

[b] "Public" includes Medicaid, Medicare, Medicaid + Medicare, Champus/VA, Medicaid + private, and other combinations.

**Table 8  Health Insurance Coverage by IFU Income among 62- to 64-Year-Olds**

| IFU Income | Private[a] (%) | Nongroup (%) | Public[b] (%) | Uninsured (%) | Total (%) | Total number (millions) |
|---|---|---|---|---|---|---|
| Less than $10,000 | 20.8 | 9.4 | 41.8 | 28.0 | 100 | 0.866 |
| $10,000–19,999 | 39.3 | 14.0 | 23.9 | 22.8 | 100 | 1.030 |
| $20,000–29,999 | 64.4 | 10.9 | 11.6 | 13.1 | 100 | 0.982 |
| $30,000–39,999 | 68.5 | 15.3 | 6.4 | 9.8 | 100 | 0.715 |
| $40,000–49,999 | 73.6 | 10.5 | 5.0 | 10.9 | 100 | 0.642 |
| $50,000–59,999 | 81.2 | 5.2 | 2.9 | 10.7 | 100 | 0.401 |
| $60,000–69,999 | 84.3 | 4.8 | 2.5 | 8.4 | 100 | 0.317 |
| $70,000–79,999 | 82.7 | 8.5 | 1.7 | 7.1 | 100 | 0.236 |
| $80,000–89,999 | 75.0 | 13.6 | 3.5 | 7.9 | 100 | 0.195 |
| $90,000–99,999 | 77.5 | 13.1 | 0 | 9.4 | 100 | 0.157 |
| $100,000 and more | 78.7 | 8.5 | 1.7 | 11.1 | 100 | 0.444 |
| All | 59.9 | 10.9 | 14.0 | 15.2 | 100 | 5.986 |

SOURCE: March 1999 Current Population Survey.
[a] "Private" includes employer-group only and employer-group plus nongroup.
[b] "Public" includes Medicaid, Medicare, Medicaid + Medicare, Champus/VA, Medicaid + private, and other combinations.

**Table 9  Health Insurance Coverage by Health Status among 55- to 64-Year-Olds**

| Health status | Private[a] (%) | Nongroup (%) | Public[b] (%) | Uninsured (%) | Total (%) | Total number (millions) |
|---|---|---|---|---|---|---|
| Excellent | 77.0 | 9.1 | 2.9 | 11.0 | 100 | 4.319 |
| Very good | 75.0 | 8.3 | 3.4 | 13.3 | 100 | 6.763 |
| Good | 67.1 | 8.1 | 7.4 | 17.4 | 100 | 6.629 |
| Fair | 47.9 | 9.2 | 24.5 | 18.4 | 100 | 3.383 |
| Poor | 31.2 | 6.9 | 46.4 | 15.5 | 100 | 1.816 |

SOURCE: March 1999 Current Population Survey.
[a] "Private" includes employer-group only and employer-group plus nongroup.
[b] "Public" includes Medicaid, Medicare, Medicaid + Medicare, Champus/VA, Medicaid + private, and other combinations.

**Table 10  Health Insurance Coverage, by Sex among 55- to 61-Year-Olds and 62- to 64-Year-Olds**

| Age/sex | Private[a] (%) | Nongroup (%) | Public[b] (%) | Uninsured (%) | Total (%) | Total number (millions) |
|---|---|---|---|---|---|---|
| 55–61/males | 71.6 | 6.3 | 9.2 | 12.9 | 100 | 8.180 |
| 62–64/males | 64.9 | 9.3 | 13.2 | 12.6 | 100 | 2.787 |
| 55–61/females | 63.9 | 8.7 | 10.6 | 16.8 | 100 | 8.743 |
| 62–64/females | 55.6 | 12.3 | 14.5 | 17.6 | 100 | 3.199 |

SOURCE: March 1999 Current Population Survey.

[a] "Private" includes employer-group only and employer-group plus nongroup.

[b] "Public" includes Medicaid, Medicare, Medicaid + Medicare, Champus/VA, Medicaid + private, and other combinations.

**Table 11  Type of Health Insurance among 55- to 61-Year-Olds and 62- to 64-Year-Olds by Sex and Marital Status**

| Age/sex/marital group | Private[a] (%) | Nongroup (%) | Public[b] (%) | Uninsured (%) | Total (%) | Total number (millions) |
|---|---|---|---|---|---|---|
| 55 to 61/males | | | | | | |
| Married | 74.1 | 5.6 | 10.2 | 10.1 | 100 | 6.670 |
| Widowed | 46.9 | 6.2 | 20.1 | 26.8 | 100 | 0.194 |
| Divorced | 52.9 | 5.8 | 19.2 | 22.1 | 100 | 0.995 |
| Separated | 43.6 | —[c] | — | 26.1 | 100 | 0.165 |
| Never married | 49.1 | 11.1 | 25.2 | 14.6 | 100 | 0.460 |
| 62 to 64/males | | | | | | |
| Married | 69.9 | 9.1 | 10.3 | 10.7 | 100 | 2.192 |
| Widowed | 43.0 | — | — | — | 100 | 0.114 |
| Divorced | 49.8 | 8.5 | 23.3 | 18.4 | 100 | 0.293 |
| Separated | — | — | — | — | 100 | 0.052 |
| Never married | 43.1 | — | — | 24.8 | 100 | 0.137 |
| 55 to 61/females | | | | | | |
| Married | 71.7 | 7.9 | 5.8 | 14.4 | 100 | 5.676 |
| Widowed | 45.3 | 12.3 | 19.7 | 22.7 | 100 | 0.907 |
| Divorced | 57.8 | 9.1 | 15.7 | 17.4 | 100 | 1.435 |
| Separated | 26.6 | 12.1 | 32.7 | 28.6 | 100 | 0.248 |
| Never married | 46.5 | 8.9 | 18.0 | 26.6 | 100 | 0.447 |
| 62 to 64/females | | | | | | |
| Married | 59.9 | 13.3 | 9.3 | 17.5 | 100 | 2.044 |
| Widowed | 45.2 | 12.1 | 24.4 | 18.3 | 100 | 0.580 |
| Divorced | 55.6 | 9.3 | 21.9 | 13.2 | 100 | 0.378 |
| Separated | — | — | — | — | 100 | 0.044 |
| Never married | 49.7 | — | — | 23.1 | 100 | 0.147 |

SOURCE: March 1999 Current Population Survey.

[a] "Private" includes employer-group only and employer-group + nongroup.

[b] "Public" includes Medicaid, Medicare, Medicaid + Medicare, Champus/VA, Medicaid + private, and other combinations.

[c] A dash (—) indicates a sample size too small for a statistically reliable estimate.

**Table 12  Health Insurance Coverage by Educational Attainment among 55- to 64-Year-Olds**

| Education level | Private[a] (%) | Nongroup (%) | Public[b] (%) | Uninsured (%) | Total (%) | Total number (millions) |
|---|---|---|---|---|---|---|
| Less than high school | 40.4 | 8.0 | 25.9 | 25.7 | 100 | 4.314 |
| High school diploma | 66.1 | 9.1 | 10.0 | 14.8 | 100 | 8.449 |
| Some college (1–3 yr.) | 72.3 | 8.3 | 7.5 | 11.9 | 100 | 4.943 |
| College degree | 75.7 | 8.7 | 4.5 | 11.1 | 100 | 3.035 |
| Postgraduate study | 84.4 | 6.1 | 2.5 | 7.0 | 100 | 2.168 |

SOURCE: March 1999 Current Population Survey.
[a] "Private" includes employer-group only and employer-group + nongroup.
[b] "Public" includes Medicaid, Medicare, Medicaid + Medicare, Champus/VA, Medicaid + private, and other combinations.

**Table 13  Health Insurance Coverage by Race among 55- to 61-Year-Olds and 62- to 64-Year-Olds**

| Race and age group | Private[a] (%) | Nongroup (%) | Public[b] (%) | Uninsured (%) | Total (%) | Total number (millions) |
|---|---|---|---|---|---|---|
| 55- to 61-yr.-olds | | | | | | |
| White | 69.9 | 7.9 | 8.4 | 13.8 | 100 | 14.560 |
| Black | 51.4 | 5.7 | 21.0 | 21.9 | 100 | 1.676 |
| Other | 59.7 | 5.1 | 14.4 | 20.8 | 100 | 0.687 |
| | | | | | | |
| 62- to 64-yr.-olds | | | | | | |
| White | 63.0 | 10.9 | 12.0 | 14.1 | 100 | 5.165 |
| Black | 41.5 | 9.5 | 25.7 | 23.3 | 100 | 0.609 |
| Other | 38.7 | 14.6 | 26.4 | 20.3 | 100 | 0.212 |

SOURCE: March 1999 Current Population Survey.
[a] "Private" includes employer-group only and employer-group + nongroup.
[b] "Public" includes Medicaid, Medicare, Medicaid + Medicare, Champus/VA, Medicaid + private, and other combinations.

**Table 14  Estimated Multinomial Logit Model Predicting Type of Health Insurance for 55- to 64-Year-Olds[a]**

| Characteristic | Nongroup | | Public | | No insurance | |
|---|---|---|---|---|---|---|
| | Coefficient | z-stat. | Coefficient | z-stat. | Coefficient | z-stat. |
| Age 55–61 | -0.2939 | -3.711 | 0.1091 | 1.566 | -0.1097 | -1.257 |
| Male | -0.2515 | -3.407 | -0.1089 | -1.774 | 0.1156 | 1.422 |
| High school | -0.0406 | -0.385 | -0.5955 | -7.718 | -0.5819 | -5.950 |
| Some college | -0.0582 | 0.494 | -0.6727 | -7.293 | -0.4068 | -3.412 |
| College degree | -0.0595 | 0.431 | -0.6137 | -5.479 | -0.6383 | -3.844 |
| Postgraduate | -0.2082 | -1.255 | -1.0672 | -7.239 | -1.1243 | -4.859 |
| Married | 0.1191 | 1.342 | -0.0661 | 0.923 | -0.4095 | -4.400 |
| Working | -0.0478 | -0.454 | -0.3546 | -4.418 | -1.0259 | -7.656 |
| Ill/disabled | 0.4147 | 2.471 | -0.5319 | -3.897 | 1.6035 | 11.830 |
| Retired | 0.1802 | 1.502 | -0.3972 | -4.046 | 0.4821 | 3.835 |
| White (vs. nonwhite) | 0.3987 | 3.213 | -0.1988 | -2.387 | -0.2783 | -2.668 |
| IFU income[b] | | | | | | |
| $10–19,999 | -0.8049 | -5.759 | -1.0452 | -10.005 | -0.7953 | -6.637 |
| $20–34,999 | -1.2146 | -9.169 | -1.9010 | -18.224 | -1.8870 | -14.341 |
| $35–49,999 | -1.5267 | -10.514 | -2.5968 | -21.010 | -2.3618 | -14.132 |
| $50,000 plus | -2.0712 | -14.236 | -2.7953 | -24.060 | -2.4369 | -15.299 |

(continued)

36

**Table 14 (continued)**

| Characteristic | Nongroup | | Public | | No insurance | |
|---|---|---|---|---|---|---|
| | Coefficient | z-stat. | Coefficient | z-stat. | Coefficient | z-stat. |
| Health status | | | | | | |
| Very good | -0.1771 | -1.742 | 0.0256 | 0.280 | -0.1248 | -0.742 |
| Good | -0.1630 | -1.588 | 0.1273 | 1.409 | 0.3627 | 2.363 |
| Fair | -0.0806 | -0.627 | 0.2476 | 2.290 | 0.9210 | 5.774 |
| Poor | -0.1595 | -0.866 | 0.3191 | 2.185 | 1.2437 | 7.017 |
| Constant | -0.6002 | -2.857 | 1.3315 | 8.375 | 0.1870 | 0.865 |

Unweighted N    11,128
log(likelihood)  −9050.396
Pseudo $R^2$    0.2044

SOURCE: March 1999 Current Population Survey.
[a] The coefficients indicate the affect of each characteristic on the probability of having nongroup coverage, public coverage, or no insurance relative to having employer-group coverage only and employer-group plus nongroup.
[b] IFU = insurance family unit.

**Table 15  Predicted Probabilities of Four Types of Insurance Coverage for Prototypical Men**

| Characteristics of person | Private[a] (%) | Nongroup (%) | Public[b] (%) | Uninsured |
|---|---|---|---|---|
| Using IFU income | | | | |
| 1) 55- to 61-yr-old male, married, did not complete HS, working, white, IFU income $20,000–34,999, very good health | 0.472 | 0.090 | 0.041 | 0.396 |
| 2) same as #1 except HS graduate | 0.590 | 0.108 | 0.029 | 0.273 |
| 3) same as #2 except ill/ disabled and poor health | 0.224 | 0.066 | 0.594 | 0.116 |
| 4) same as #2 except retired | 0.528 | 0.121 | 0.116 | 0.234 |
| 5) same as #2 except nonwhite | 0.571 | 0.070 | 0.037 | 0.322 |
| 6) same as #1 except 62–64 yrs of age | 0.475 | 0.121 | 0.046 | 0.357 |
| 7) same as #6 except HS graduate | 0.583 | 0.143 | 0.032 | 0.032 |
| 8) same as #7 except ill/ disabled and poor health | 0.207 | 0.082 | 0.614 | 0.097 |
| 9) same as #7 except retired | 0.512 | 0.158 | 0.126 | 0.204 |
| 10) same as #7 except nonwhite | 0.574 | 0.095 | 0.041 | 0.290 |
| | | | | |
| Using family income | | | | |
| 1) 55- to 61-yr-old male, married, did not complete HS, working, white, family income $20,000–34,999, very good health | 0.505 | 0.096 | 0.039 | 0.361 |
| 2) same as #1 except HS graduate | 0.645 | 0.108 | 0.025 | 0.222 |
| 3) same as #2 except ill/ disabled and poor health | 0.237 | 0.070 | 0.578 | 0.115 |
| 4) same as #2 except retired | 0.556 | 0.123 | 0.107 | 0.215 |
| 5) same as #2 except nonwhite | 0.605 | 0.074 | 0.035 | 0.286 |
| 6) same as #1 except 62–64 yrs of age | 0.503 | 0.129 | 0.044 | 0.324 |

(continued)

**Table 15 (continued)**

| Characteristics of person | Private[a] (%) | Nongroup (%) | Public[b] (%) | Uninsured |
|---|---|---|---|---|
| 7) same as #6 except HS graduate | 0.633 | 0.144 | 0.028 | 0.196 |
| 8) same as #7 except ill/ disabled and poor health | 0.217 | 0.088 | 0.600 | 0.095 |
| 9) same as #7 except retired | 0.537 | 0.160 | 0.116 | 0.187 |
| 10) same as #7 except nonwhite | 0.604 | 0.010 | 0.039 | 0.257 |

SOURCE: March 1999 Current Population Survey.

[a] "Private" includes employer-group only and employer-group + nongroup.

[b] "Public" includes Medicaid, Medicare, Medicaid + Medicare, Champus/VA, Medicaid + private, and other combinations.

**Table 16  Predicted Probabilities of Four Types of Insurance Coverage for Prototypical Women**

| Type of person | Private[a] (%) | Nongroup (%) | Public[b] (%) | Uninsured |
|---|---|---|---|---|
| Using IFU income | | | | |
| 1) 55- to 61-yr.-old female, some college (1–3 yr.), married, working, white, IFU income $50,000 or greater, very good health | 0.836 | 0.087 | 0.013 | 0.065 |
| 2) same as #1 except IFU income of $20,000–34,999 | 0.682 | 0.166 | 0.020 | 0.132 |
| 3) same as #2 except not married | 0.694 | 0.150 | 0.030 | 0.125 |
| 4) same as #1 except 62 to 64 yr. of age | 0.850 | 0.066 | 0.011 | 0.073 |
| 5) same as #4 except retired | 0.801 | 0.078 | 0.054 | 0.067 |
| | | | | |
| Using family income | | | | |
| 1) 55- to 61-yr.-old female, some college (1–3 yr.), married, working, white, family income $50,000 or greater, very good health | 0.832 | 0.089 | 0.012 | 0.067 |
| 2) same as #1 except family income of $20,000–34,999 | 0.687 | 0.167 | 0.022 | 0.124 |
| 3) same as #2 except not married | 0.642 | 0.164 | 0.041 | 0.153 |
| 4) same as #1 except 62 to 64 yr. of age | 0.848 | 0.067 | 0.011 | 0.075 |
| 5) same as #4 except retired | 0.785 | 0.081 | 0.054 | 0.079 |

SOURCE: March 1999 Current Population Survey.
[a] "Private" includes employer-group only and employer-group + nongroup.
[b] "Public" includes Medicaid, Medicare, Medicaid + Medicare, Champus/VA, Medicaid + private, and other combinations.

**Table 17  Proportion of People with the Listed Characteristics by Type of Health Insurance, 1999**

| Characteristic | Private[a] (%) | Nongroup (%) | Public[b] (%) | Uninsured |
|---|---|---|---|---|
| All 55- to 64-year-olds | | | | |
| Number (millions) | 15.028 | 1.924 | 2.523 | 3.434 |
| Share (%) | 65.6 | 8.4 | 11.0 | 15.0 |
| Married men (%) | 84.5 | 74.6 | 52.9 | 64.6 |
| Married women (%) | 71.9 | 62.5 | 39.6 | 58.1 |
| Less than HS education (%) | 11.6 | 17.9 | 44.3 | 32.3 |
| HS diploma (%) | 37.2 | 40.0 | 33.4 | 36.5 |
| Some college (%) | 23.8 | 21.4 | 14.8 | 17.1 |
| College degree or more (%) | 27.5 | 20.7 | 7.5 | 14.2 |
| With family income less than $50,000 (%) | 43.4 | 69.3 | 88.7 | 74.1 |
| Working (%) | 68.6 | 50.9 | 12.6 | 49.2 |
| In poor health (%) | 3.8 | 6.5 | 33.4 | 8.2 |

SOURCE: March 1999 Current Population Survey.

[a] "Private" includes employer-group only and employer-group + nongroup.

[b] "Public" includes Medicaid, Medicare, Medicaid + Medicare, Champus/VA, Medicaid + private, and other combinations.

# Workers' Compensation
# and Older Workers

(US)

John F. Burton, Jr.
*Rutgers University*

J14  I18
J28

Emily A. Spieler
*West Virginia University*

State and federal workers' compensation programs provide cash payments and medical benefits to workers disabled by work-related injuries and diseases. This chapter summarizes major issues facing workers' compensation, with a focus on aging workers. In the first section, we give an introductory overview of workers' compensation that may be most useful to those relatively unfamiliar with the program. This section includes a description of eligibility requirements, particularly the work-relatedness tests; a brief summary of the critical ways in which workers' compensation differs from other social insurance programs; and a description of recent cost trends.[1] The second section examines the particular issues of older workers relating to chronic impairment and disability, and the third discusses the problem of applying the standard of work-relatedness to chronic health conditions that do not fit easily into the traditional definitions of compensable conditions, focusing on back conditions.[2] The fourth section reviews some of the recent legislative and judicial changes that are most likely to impact older workers, particularly with regard to eligibility for benefits.

In the final section, we briefly address the following question: what are the likely effects of changes in workers' compensation programs on the adequacy of this program for older workers with work-related or work-aggravated disabilities? Our attempt to answer this question must be read with the understanding that there has been little empirical investigation of the different experiences of older and younger workers in these programs. We are thus forced to speculate, and we hope to encourage additional research that will explore this question.

Workers' compensation programs draw few overt distinctions based upon the age of the applicant for benefits. Exceptions to this general rule are discussed later in this paper.[3] Perhaps more important than overt age distinctions, however, is the inescapable fact that older workers are themselves different from younger workers: older workers are less prone to injuries resulting from traumatic events; they are more prone to impairments associated with aging, including heart disease and back conditions; they may take longer to heal and have greater impairments resulting from injuries than younger workers; and their mobility in the labor market may be more restricted than younger workers with occupational disabilities. Older workers may therefore be affected differently by certain aspects of the system. For example, because of the legal rules used to determine eligibility for workers' compensation benefits, health conditions associated with older age may be less likely to be compensated. We believe that recent developments in workers' compensation have increased the barriers to obtaining benefits for these conditions and have limited the amount of available benefits for permanent disabilities that are more common in older workers. As a result, costs of workplace injuries and diseases are likely to be shifted to other public and private programs or to the workers themselves and their families.


## OVERVIEW OF WORKERS' COMPENSATION


Unlike the civil justice system for compensation of injuries, workers' compensation is a "no-fault" system: employers are liable without regard to fault, and employees only have to prove that the injury or disease is work-related, not that the employer was negligent. Employers' liability is limited to the benefits in the program, and employees cannot (with very limited exceptions) bring a tort suit against the employer and recover for full economic losses or for nonpecuniary losses such as pain and suffering. This limited liability/no fault scheme is often described as the two sides of the workers' compensation principle.

Workers' compensation provides benefits only to workers who suffer from work-related injuries or illnesses and, in some instances, to their dependents. These benefits include medical treatment for the work-related condition; temporary total disability benefits for the period that the worker is recovering but is unable to perform his or regular job; permanent partial disability benefits to compensate for the worker's permanent loss of earnings (or, in some states, permanent level of impairment), although the worker is expected to return to active work; permanent total disability benefits for workers who are unable to work; and benefits to surviving dependents when a worker dies as a result of an occupational injury or illness.

Most employees are covered by the workers' compensation system, although in some states there are exclusions for very small employers or particular categories of workers (most commonly, agricultural and domestic employees). Persons who are not employees (e.g., independent contractors) are generally not covered. For a claim to be covered, the employee must incur medical expenses, suffer permanent impairment, or be absent from work because of a work-related health condition.

The most common type of workers' compensation claim involves an injury that requires medical treatment but no claim for cash benefits. In theory, these medical benefits are provided for the particular injury or illness for the duration of the condition, irrespective of whether the individual is working or is totally disabled. In fact, however, in cases involving more serious injuries, medical benefits may be included in cash settlements of claims, and workers may then not have medical coverage for the condition if it persists.

The most common type of claim for cash benefits is for temporary total disability benefits. Often, workers who suffer acute injuries will collect these temporary benefits for a limited period of time and then return to work. Once workers recover from the injury (reach "maximum medical improvement," or MMI) or return to work, they are no longer eligible for temporary total disability benefits. In some states, when workers return to a reduced work schedule, they may receive temporary partial disability benefits.

At the point of MMI or return to work, workers may be eligible for permanent partial disability benefits if they have a permanent impairment or suffer wage loss or loss of earning capacity as a result of the injury. Permanent partial disability (PPD) benefits are theoretically designed to replace earnings lost as a result of the permanent impairment. The expectation is that workers who receive these benefits will return to work, either at their old job or at a new one. PPD benefits are, in the aggregate, the most expensive (and most controversial) type of benefits in workers' compensation programs. Despite their expense, however, recent studies suggest that these benefits do not fully replace lost earnings for injured workers (Petersen et al. 1997; Boden and Galizzi 1999; Biddle, Boden, and Reville 2001). Permanent total disability benefits, which on average are the most expensive type of award, are rarely granted.[4]

## Eligibility for Workers' Compensation Benefits: The Work-Relatedness Test

To be compensable, a claim must relate to an injury or illness that "arises out of" and "in the course of" employment. Eligibility for workers' compensation benefits is thus tied to the work-relatedness of the health condition or disability. In most states, the employee must meet four legal tests to establish that an injury is work-related and therefore the employee is entitled to benefits:

1) there must be a <u>personal injury</u>, which in some jurisdictions is interpreted to exclude mental illnesses;

2) that results from an <u>accident</u>, which is a test normally involving two elements: the injury must be unexpected or unusual, and the injury must be traceable, within reasonable limits, to a definite time, place, and occasion;

3) that must <u>arise out of employment</u>, which means the source of the injury must be related to the job (a worker shot at work by a neighbor because of a personal quarrel is unlikely to satisfy the arising out of employment test); and

4) that must occur during the <u>course of employment</u>, which normally requires that the injury occur on the employer's premises and during working hours.

Under the traditional rule, if a worker met these four tests, then he or she was generally entitled to full cash and medical benefits, even if the medical condition was due to multiple causes. There was, in short, generally no effort to apportion causation.

These four tests are relatively easy to apply for injuries resulting from traumatic events, such as fractures or amputations resulting from malfunctioning machinery at work (which normally are compensable) or from automobile accidents (which normally are compensable if they occur as part of the job during paid time, and are generally not compensable if they occur when a worker is driving to or from work). These four tests are also relatively easy to apply to medical conditions resulting from a single cause. For example, an asbestos-exposed worker with a diagnosis of mesothelioma is likely to meet the work-relatedness test for compensation because this rare cancer is almost always associated with exposure to asbestos (although there may be other obstacles to compensability, such as the application of rules governing time limits for the filing of claims).

The tests are more difficult to apply to diseases that occur regularly in everyday life, or that have multiple causation, or that result from long-term exposures at work. Historically, the exclusion of these diseases was often based on the application of the "accident" test. Workers' compensation statutes typically now have special compensability rules for diseases, although often these contain restrictions that are not used for injuries. Occupational diseases remain largely uncompensated today, as a result of a variety of factors: 1) the "accident" test persists in some states; 2) statutes of limitations sometimes require that a claim be filed within a few years of the last exposure, and not all state systems have expanded the time limits to include diseases with long latency periods; 3) "ordinary diseases of life" are still often not compensable, even if the particular individual's disease is occupationally caused; and 4) many occupationally caused diseases are not properly diagnosed by physicians. The result of these factors is that workers' compensation often does not provide benefits for disability associated with chronic diseases that are caused by work.

In addition, there is a growing body of evidence that suggests a significant underreporting of work-related health problems to workers' compensation programs (Biddle et al. 1998; Michaels 1998; Morse et al. 1998; Pransky et al. 1999; Morse, Dillon, and Warren 2000). The underreporting is likely to be a particular problem for older workers, who are most likely to suffer the long-term effects of work exposures.

## Key Differences between Workers' Compensation and Other Major Social Insurance Programs

Several aspects of workers' compensation distinguish it from other social insurance programs in the United States. First, as noted in the prior subsection, the injury or illness must be work-related. The question of work-relatedness is a difficult one, particularly when work and nonwork factors contribute to an individual's disability. Individuals whose conditions are deemed work-related by the compensation systems will receive benefits; those whose conditions are not deemed work-related will receive no benefits.

Second, workers' compensation programs emerged in the United States about 1910, when a federal workers' compensation program for private employees would have been unconstitutional. It is therefore a state, rather than a federal, program. More accurately, it consists of over 50 programs: one for each state, plus several federal programs for federal employees, longshore workers, coal miners, and so on. Despite several attempts during the last century, federal standards for the state workers' compensation programs have never been adopted. This means both that eligibility and benefit levels vary significantly among states and that it is difficult to formulate broad conclusions regarding trends without careful study.

Third, workers' compensation provides a variety of cash benefits that do not require total and permanent disability. The duration of a worker's cash or medical benefits may range from days to a lifetime. Unlike other social programs, workers' compensation provides partial benefits that recognize that a worker's earning capacity may be reduced, but not eliminated, by the disability.

Fourth, the financing scheme for workers' compensation includes private insurers and self-insurance, as well as state run funds. Although premium rates are regulated in many states, this is nevertheless primarily a private insurance market, more similar in some respects to the health insurance market than to Social Security or unemployment insurance.

Fifth, claims for workers' compensation benefits involve a substantial amount of litigation in some jurisdictions.[5] Unlike Social Security Disability Insurance (SSDI) and Supplemental Security Income (SSI) claims, employers or their insurance carriers must pay the costs of claims, and therefore they have a strong incentive to mount a vigorous defense. Litigation tends to focus on issues of compensability, particularly work-relatedness questions, and the extent or duration of permanent disability.

Sixth, these disputed cases can be, and often are, resolved by "compromise and release agreements" that typically involve three elements: a compromise between the worker and the employer concerning the amount of benefits to be paid; the payment of the compromised amount in a lump sum; and the release of the employer from further liability for both cash and medical benefits. The terminology for compromise and release agreements varies among states: examples of alternative terms are "lump-sum settlements" and "wash-outs." It is likely that many workers use these settlements to meet immediate, rather than future, income needs.[6]

As a result of these differences, workers' compensation functions in a manner that is quite different from federal programs (e.g., Social Security), or state programs that operate with federal financing (e.g., vocational rehabilitation), or even state programs that are funded by payroll taxes and are governed by some federal guidelines (e.g., unemployment insurance).

### Financing and Cost Trends in Workers' Compensation Programs

Employers are nominally responsible for the cost of workers' compensation, although a substantial portion of the cost is shifted to employees in the form of lower wages. Insurance premiums are paid based on a percentage of payroll. Insurance rates are experience-rated and vary among firms based on the benefits paid by all the firms in the employer's industry and, for larger employers, on the amount of previous benefit payments to the firm's own employees.

In 1998, workers' compensation programs provided $41.7 billion of benefits to workers disabled by work-related injuries and diseases (Mont, Burton, and Reno 2000). Cash benefits accounted for $25.8 billion (62 percent of total benefits) and medical and rehabilitation benefits accounted for $15.9 billion (38 percent). Private carriers paid about 53 percent of these benefits, state and federal funds about 25 percent, and self-insuring employers about 22 percent. Total employers' costs were $52.1 billion in 1998. The $10.4 billion difference between total benefits and employers' costs was attributable to various factors, including administrative expenses, profits for carriers, and attorneys' fees.

Current figures do not give the full picture of the rapidly changing costs and benefits paid by workers' compensation programs over the past 15 years. In fact, conditions changed rapidly over this period, with benefits paid and employers' costs increasing rapidly from 1984 to 1991, and then declining rapidly from 1991 to 1998. From 1984 to 1991, workers' compensation benefits (cash and medical) increased from $19.7 billion to $42.2, or an average annual increase of 11.5 percent. Benefits increased from 1.21 percent of payroll in 1984 to 1.64 percent in 1991. Employers' workers' compensation costs also increased during this period, from $25.1 billion in 1984 to $55.2 billion in 1991, an average of 11.9 percent increase per year. This rapid escalation in costs far outpaced payroll growth. As a result, workers' compensation costs as a percentage of payroll increased rapidly, rising from 1.66 percent in 1984 to 2.16 percent of payroll in 1991.

Throughout the late 1980s and early 1990s, many employers and insurance carriers became concerned, if not alarmed, about these increasing costs of the workers' compensation program. One result was that employers and carriers supported a series of changes in the program that are examined later in this chapter.

These changes (or "reforms") were important factors in the trends in the aggregate benefits and costs for the workers' compensation program after 1991. Benefits paid to workers in current dollars decreased from $42.2 billion in 1991 to $41.7 billion in 1998, which represented a 0.2 percent annual rate of decrease. While benefit payments declined, employment and payroll surged in the 1990s, and so benefits as a percentage of payroll peaked at 1.66 percent of payroll in 1992 and then plummeted to a low of 1.08 percent of payroll in 1998. The multi-year decline in benefits paid relative to payroll is unprecedented in duration and magnitude since at least 1948, when the annual data from the workers' compensation programs were first published for successive years. Accompanying the slowdown or decline in benefit payments to workers was a similar development for the employers' costs of workers' compensation. The costs were $55.2 billion in 1991, increased to $60.8 billion in 1993, and then fell to $52.1 billion in 1998. Because payroll grew rapidly during the period, the employers' costs as a percentage of payroll plateaued briefly (2.16 percent of payroll in 1991 and 2.17 percent of payroll in 1993) and then spiraled down to 1.35 percent in 1998.

The sources of the rapid increases in workers' compensation benefits and costs between 1984 and 1991 and the stagnation or decline of these aggregate measures of the workers' compensation program during the 1990s are examined in Spieler and Burton (1998) and Thomason, Schmidle, and Burton (forthcoming).

## SPECIAL CONCERNS OF OLDER WORKERS

There are three relationships that are relevant to our interest in the responsiveness of the workers' compensation program to the concerns of older workers. First, what is the relationship between age and the prevalence of impairments? We use the term impairment to mean "a deviation from normal in a body part or organ system and its functioning" (American Medical Association 1993, p. 1/1). An impairment can result from an injury or an illness and can lead to the inability to perform activities of daily living (American Medical Association 1993, p. 1/1). Second, what is the relationship between age and the prevalence of disability? We use the term disability to mean reduction or "alteration of an individual's capacity to meet personal, social, or occupational demands or statutory or regulatory requirements because of an impairment" (American Medical Association 1993, p. 1/2). Our particular concern is work disability. The extent of work disability resulting from an impairment is affected by personal attributes, such as age, education, and job experience, as well as external factors, such as the state of the labor market and the extent of job modifications. Third, what is the relationship between age and the prevalence of workers' compensation benefits? Even if work disability increases with age, the compensability rules for workers' compensation may preclude some of the disabled workers from obtaining benefits.

## Age and Impairment

The relationship between age and the prevalence of impairments varies by the source or type of impairment. The frequency of work-related injuries generally declines with age; severity, however, tends to increase with age (Wegman 2000). This pattern is shown in Table 1; the frequency of work injuries is lower for workers in the 45–64 years age category than for younger workers (ages 18–24 and 25–44), while the numbers of restricted-activity days and bed days associated with work injuries are higher for workers in the 45–64 years age category than for younger workers.

While the Table 1 data show that the frequency of work injuries is lower for older workers, the data shown in Table 2 indicate that the number of chronic conditions per 1,000 persons for those 45–64 years old is considerably higher than the rate for persons aged 18–44 for several of the most common conditions, including intervertebral disc disorders, orthopedic impairments of the back, hearing impairment, and heart disease.[7] It is these "border-challenging" conditions that present the most difficult issues regarding work-relatedness for workers' compensation systems. We explore the historical treatment of one of the most common of these conditions, back injuries, in the following section.[8]

**Table 1  Numbers of Episodes of Injuries at Work and Their Consequences per 100 Persons, by Age[a]**

|  | All ages | 18–24 yr. | 25–44 yr. | 45–64 yr. |
|---|---|---|---|---|
| Episodes of persons injured | 3.9 | 5.4*[b] | 6.4 | 1.7* |
| Number of restricted-activity days associated with episodes | 91.1 | 45.4* | 100.5 | 142.5 |
| Number of bed days associated with episodes | 21.9 | 3.1* | 24.5 | 34.6 |

SOURCE: Adams, Hendershot, and Marano (1999), Tables 51, 53, and 55.
[a] Data are for the United States in 1996.
[b] An asterisk (*) means the "figure does not meet standard of reliability or precision."

**Table 2  Number of Selected[a] Reported Chronic Conditions per 1,000 Persons, by Age[b]**

| Type of chronic condition | All ages | 18–44 yr. | 45–64 yr. | 65 yr. and over |
|---|---|---|---|---|
| Arthritis | 127.3 | 50.1 | 240.1 | 482.7 |
| Intervertebral discs | 25.4 | 21.1 | 62.7 | 32.2 |
| Hearing impairment | 83.4 | 41.9 | 131.5 | 303.4 |
| Deformity or orthopedic impairment | 111.6 | 122.4 | 177.8 | 157.6 |
| Back | 64.0 | 80.6 | 102.8 | 68.7 |
| Upper extremity | 15.8 | 13.3 | 29.4 | 30.9 |
| Lower extremity | 48.0 | 43.2 | 82.5 | 72.6 |
| Heart disease | 78.2 | 39.3 | 116.4 | 268.7 |
| High blood pressure (hypertension) | 107.1 | 49.6 | 214.1 | 363.5 |
| Chronic bronchitis | 53.5 | 45.4 | 59.1 | 63.5 |
| Asthma | 55.2 | 56.9 | 48.6 | 45.5 |
| Hay fever or allergic rhinitis without asthma | 89.8 | 109.4 | 104.8 | 67.7 |
| Chronic sinusitis | 125.5 | 144.7 | 174.1 | 117.1 |

SOURCE: Adams, Hendershot, and Marano (1999), Table 57.

[a] All conditions with at least 50 chronic conditions per 1,000 persons are included in this table.

[b] Data are for the United States in 1996.

## Age and Disability

The relationship between impairment and disability is complicated because of the multiplicity of factors, including age, education, and experience, that interact with a given impairment to produce work disability. Isolating the effect of age per se on disability is especially complicated because age may be correlated with other factors, notably work experience. Berkowitz (1988) provided a good discussion of the difficulties of capturing the independent effect of age and also provided an unambiguous conclusion: age is related to disability even after controlling for the other determinants of disability.

The general relationship between age and work disability (not controlling for factors such as experience) is documented by Pransky (2001, Table 4). According to U.S. Census data from 1989, the percentage of persons who report work disability increases steadily with age. Thus, while 7.1 percent of 35- to 44-year-olds report work disability, 10.3 percent of those aged 45–54 and 22.3 percent of those aged 55–64 report they are disabled for work. Burkhauser, Daly, and Houtenville (2001, Table A2) present data from the Current Population Survey which indicate that disability is increasing over time for workers in the same age category. Thus, 6.7 percent of persons aged 35 to 44 reported they were disabled in 1999, up from 5.9 percent of persons in that age category in 1988. Similarly, 10.4 percent of persons aged 45–54 indicated they were disabled in 1999, up from 9.1 percent of persons in that age category in 1988. These and other studies clearly demonstrate a general positive relationship between age and work disability. This association is compounded and partially explained for older workers by the general decrease in labor market mobility associated with advancing age (Hirsch, Macpherson, and Hardy 2000).

### Age and Workers' Compensation

The evidence concerning the relationship between age and the receipt of workers' compensation benefits is more fragmentary and inconclusive.[9] Biddle, Boden, and Reville (2001, Tables 2, 4, and 7 and Figure 1) have provided evidence that the proportion of workers' compensation cases paying permanent partial disability benefits increases with age; that earnings losses and injury-related non-employment for workers receiving permanent partial disability benefits increase with age; and that replacement rates (workers' compensation benefits as a percent of earnings losses) decline with age. Tattrie (2000) has presented some preliminary data suggesting that a young workforce has much lower costs per claim than a middle-aged workforce, but that average costs per claim of older workers are only modestly higher those of middle-aged workers.

Both of these studies provide clues that age is an important factor in determining the award and payment of benefits, but they are more tantalizing than conclusive about the exact nature of the relationship between age and the workers' compensation program. In order to better understand the performance of workers' compensation in providing benefits to workers in different age categories, it would be useful to have data showing for various age categories the frequency of workers' compensation claims per 100,000 workers, the average benefits per claim, and the total costs of workers' compensation benefits per 100,000 workers. These data should be disaggregated not only by age but also by the nature of the impairment or medical condition causing the disability. Specifically, the data should distinguish between disability resulting from injuries and disability resulting from the chronic conditions identified in Table 2.

We are not suggesting that the patterns of workers' compensation payments for different age groups should necessarily match the patterns of impairments or work disability for these age groups. Some of the conditions showing an increasing incidence of impairments for older persons in Table 2 may reflect the pure effect of aging. Workers' compensation, with its work-related test, presumably should not have a higher incidence of conditions for older workers that are due solely to aging. Yet, conditions that are substantially aggravated by work may be more prevalent among older workers. These conditions may be of greater concern, particularly in view of the changes in compensability standards (described later) that have occurred in some states. Some of these conditions, notably disorders involving the back, have traditionally met the compensability tests for workers' compensation benefits. If the data indicate that the frequency of compensable back disorders does not increase with age, or if the overall frequency of compensable back or similar disorders is declining, the results will suggest that recent reforms of the eligibility rules for workers' compensation have had a particularly deleterious effect on older workers.

## BACKS: CASE STUDY OF A MEDICAL CONDITION WITH A HISTORICAL PROBLEM OF APPLYING THE WORK-RELATED TESTS

Work-relatedness, as we have noted, is the key to eligibility for workers' compensation benefits. The four legal tests described in the first section of this chapter are particularly difficult to apply to medical conditions resulting from multiple causes. Where impairments are caused by workplace exposures combined with personal lifestyle, aging, or hereditary factors, workers' compensation systems are confronted with a particularly challenging problem. The chronic impairments that increase with age (see Table 2) are among the conditions that are likely to fall into this category. All of these conditions can be considered "border-challenging" in the sense that they challenge the boundaries of the work-related tests for workers' compensation. Thus, a workers' compensation program is likely to have difficulty deciding whether the work-related test is met for a heart attack of a worker who is under job stress, smokes, is 55 years old, and has a family history of heart disease.

The workers' compensation programs in the various states have developed a variety of refinements to the work-related tests in order to deal with these more complex cases involving medical conditions resulting from exposures over time and/or conditions resulting from multiple causes. Back injuries provide an interesting case study. An examination of the issues pertaining to the compensability of back conditions in workers' compensation programs is instructive because of the mixed etiology of many back conditions; the relative importance of back cases in the workers' compensation program (they account for about 40 percent of all benefit payments); and the prevalence of back disorders in older workers. Burton (1992) examined the medical and legal approaches to back disorders.

### The Medical Approach

Three sources of back disorders can be distinguished from a medical standpoint. First, there are fractures and dislocations of the back. These conditions are relatively uncommon, although they can be quite serious. The common causes of fractures and dislocations are traumatic events such as direct blows and falls from heights.

Second, there are sprains and strains of the back. The back is the most frequently affected part of the body; each year nearly 1 out of 30 persons of working age experiences a strain or sprain of the back of sufficient severity to either require medical care or restricted activity. In general, strains and sprains have less serious consequences than fractures and dislocations and are likely to result from less obvious events.

Third, there are diseases of the back, in which damage to the body results from a slowly developing condition rather than from an acute traumatic event. However, the symptoms of many diseases can be precipitated by trauma. Following the approach of Kelsey (1982), diseases can be separated into those involving specific conditions of the back or neck (such as prolapsed discs, degenerated discs, and spondylolisthesis) and those of a more general nature that frequently affect the back (such as osteoarthrosis).

Prolapsed intervertebral discs (also known as herniated discs, ruptured discs, or "slipped" discs) are one of the most common sources of disability among the working-age population. At one time, physical trauma was believed to be the only cause of prolapsed discs. However, the accepted medical view now is that, although trauma is sometimes the precipitating event, many prolapsed discs occur without any antecedent trauma, and trauma is seldom the underlying cause.

Two other diseases affecting the back are disc degeneration and spondylolisthesis. A confusing matter for each of these conditions is many people with x-ray evidence of the disease have no symptoms. In addition to the diseases specifically affecting the back, there are other diseases of a general nature that can affect the back, including arthritic disorders.

Burton (1992) made four generalizations about the medical approach to back disorders.

1) Pain in the back and neck are very common problems.

2) In a large portion of cases of low back and neck pain, a definite diagnosis cannot be made. This is partially because the symptoms often are not uniquely associated with a particular disease; partially because x-ray evidence of a disorder often is associated

with no symptoms; and partially because a particular patient may have multiple disorders.

3) The contribution of the workplace to back disorders is difficult to ascertain.

4) The medical view of trauma as a cause varies among the three sources of back disorders. For a fracture or dislocation, a traumatic event normally is readily identifiable as the likely cause. For a strain or sprain, a less significant and therefore less identifiable trauma is the likely cause. For diseases, the role of trauma is much more problematic. Trauma or mechanical stress seems to be a precipitant or perhaps an aggravating factor, rather than the underlying cause for diseases affecting the back. The true culprit often is age, although factors such as hereditary disposition also may be involved.

## The Legal Approach

Backs are almost always treated as injuries rather than diseases in workers' compensation programs. Consequently, the four legal tests for a compensable injury are normally used to decide whether back injuries are work-related. The most difficult legal test for claims involving backs is the accident requirement.

There appears to be little problem with reconciling the medical knowledge concerning fractures and dislocations with the legal approach to these back disorders. There is normally an external traumatic event that causes the back problem, and the application of the accident test is no more difficult than in most workers' compensation cases. However, fractures and dislocations represent only a small proportion of the back disorders handled by workers' compensation, so there is little consolation to be derived from this congruence of the medical and legal approaches.

Among back disorders caused by disease, the legal approach makes it easier for herniated discs than for other back disorders to meet the accident test. This is largely because the law relies on an outmoded view of causation in which external trauma is assumed to be the cause of discal herniation. Probably the most serious problem with the legal approach, however, is the implicit assumption that herniated discs can be differentiated from other sources of back disorders, while medically this is often not possible.

Another aspect of the legal approach to back disorders resulting from diseases (other than herniated discs) is to hold that the accident test is met when unusual exertion is the precipitant of the back disorder but to deny compensation when there is only usual exertion. However, from the medical standpoint (aside from the few cases involving obvious trauma), there is little proof that pattern of use causes lower back disease. In fact, the conclusion that results from this review of the legal rules used to decide which back disorders are work-related (and therefore are compensable) is that these rules have little scientific validity.

While backs are the most important medical condition for which application of the work-related test causes problems, there are similar problems for other medical conditions such as heart disease, stress, and repetitive trauma, for which the etiology can involve a mixture of hereditary, degenerative, and occupational factors. The higher prevalence of these conditions in older workers poses a particular challenge for workers' compensation systems.

## CHANGING RULES IN WORKERS' COMPENSATION: RESPONSES TO THE COST INCREASES OF 1984–1991[10]

The aggregate costs of workers' compensation, like those of other social insurance programs, are primarily affected by four factors: the number of claims that are filed, the number that are approved for payment, the amount of benefits paid in approved claims, and the amount of administrative and other costs associated with the provision of benefits. Over half of the state legislatures passed major amendments to workers' compensation laws during the period 1989–1997, largely in response to organized political opposition by employers and insurers to escalating costs. During this period of retrenchment, these legislative changes (together with judicial rulings) tightened eligibility rules, lowered the amount of benefits paid on some claims, changed mechanisms and time periods for payment for permanent disabilities, instituted various health care cost containment strategies, and heightened requirements for applicants' burden of proof. This section describes some of these changes and speculates regarding the likely effects of these changes on older workers.

The specific changes in the availability of benefits vary considerably among states. Moreover, since each state's program is an interdependent system with its own history of tradeoffs among key provisions, it is important to be careful in making generalizations about trends. It is also important to note that the specific effects of these changes on older workers have not yet been subjected to careful empirical research; data based on age of applicants or beneficiaries are not generally available. It does appear quite likely, however, that many of these changes may particularly restrict the access of older workers to workers' compensation benefits. The result of these restrictions is therefore likely to be a transfer of disability costs related to occupational morbidity to other social insurance programs or directly to aging workers and their families. This is particularly true for those workers who cannot meet SSDI eligibility requirements because they are only partially disabled, but who are unable to continue to work at their regular or similar wage jobs as a result of their work-related disabilities.

## Reducing the Number of Claims in the Workers' Compensation System

The development of more restrictive rules governing eligibility for benefits has been a prevalent feature of workers' compensation changes in the 1990s.

### Limitations on coverage when the injury involves aggravation of a preexisting condition

Perhaps the most significant development for aging workers is the growing restriction on compensation for disabilities when the worker suffers from a preexisting health condition. This means that a predisposition to an injury or illness may bar a worker from receiving workers' compensation benefits for an injury or illness caused by current workplace exposures, and that the systems are tightened for those conditions that we have characterized as "border-challenging."

As noted above, under traditional workers' compensation theory, compensation did not depend on whether the worker's condition was caused, in part, by a prior injury or an underlying chronic condition.

Thus, a worker who was aging or who had some preexisting nondis-abling condition was not barred from coverage for an injury occurring at work, even if the underlying condition contributed to the occurrence of the injury or to the extent of the resulting disability. Through a variety of legislative and judicial changes, rules governing compensation for preexisting conditions or aggravation have been tightened in many jurisdictions.

Most significantly, a number of states have now limited compensation when the current injury is not the sole or major cause of the disabling condition. These limitations come in a variety of forms: requiring that work be the major or primary cause of the disability (e.g., Oregon, Florida, South Dakota, and Nevada); excluding from compensability injuries for which current work is merely the triggering factor (Missouri); and requiring that any preexisting condition be aggravated by a discrete accident, rather than chronic work exposures (Idaho). A few of these changes specifically target older workers, or the conditions that are prevalent among older workers. For example, several states now specifically exclude injuries or resulting disabilities or impairments from compensability if they are the effects of "the natural aging process" (e.g., Kentucky, Missouri, and Wyoming), and one state requires proof of a discrete injury if there is an underlying aging-related condition (New Hampshire). These changes are further strengthened both by heightened general evidentiary standards for claimants, including the requirements for "objective medical evidence" (discussed below) and by stricter rules and shorter time limits for reopening prior claims when progression of a condition occurs (e.g., West Virginia, Kentucky, Wyoming, and Idaho). These changes have resulted in the denial of claims involving cumulative trauma disorders, asthma and other respiratory conditions, low back and other musculoskeletal disorders, and so on.[11]

In Oregon, the revised rule meant that a steel worker who was predisposed to respiratory illness because of underlying airway irritation disease and who suffered from an occupationally caused lung disease was not entitled to compensation under the state workers' compensation law.[12] Subsequent developments in Oregon show the interesting underbelly of workers' compensation politics and litigation. Because the worker was foreclosed from seeking workers' compensation benefits, he was successful in maintaining a common law tort action against his employer. The Oregon legislature then responded quickly to employers' concerns about this erosion of the usual workers' compensation bar to civil actions, passing a revised state statute that extends workers' compensation exclusivity "to all injuries and to diseases, symptom complexes or similar conditions" arising out of employment "whether or not they are determined to be compensable under this chapter."[13]    Under this provision, workers with occupationally exacerbated conditions are barred from recovering benefits both under the workers' compensation program and in a civil law suit, even if the injury was due to an employer's negligence. Another worker then challenged the new statute as an unconstitutional denial of remedies; in 1997 an Oregon appellate court upheld its constitutionality.[14]    As of August 28, 2000, this case was still under consideration by the Oregon Supreme Court. Similar cases are pending in other states, including Idaho.[15]

In addition, second-injury funds (instituted initially to promote the employment of war veterans) historically provided insurance coverage for disability that resulted from the combined effects of a new injury and preexisting conditions. Over the past 20 years, costs associated with second injuries rose, and employers and insurers had little incentive to defend against claims that would be charged to these funds. These funds were generally underfunded, but reformulated accounting principles forced states to recognize the magnitude of future unfunded liabilities. In the 1990s, the private insurance industry led a lobbying campaign for the elimination of the funds. Serious underfunding, when combined with unsubstantiated arguments that disability discrimination laws have made these funds obsolete, resulted in the abolition or severe restriction of second injury funds in a number of states (e.g., Colorado, Utah, Florida, Minnesota, and New Mexico). To the extent that the disability discrimination laws do in fact result in increased hiring of previously injured workers, the elimination of the financial protection offered by second-injury funds means that employers might face increased workers' compensation liability for aggravation of old injuries or chronic conditions. With the abolition of these funds, employers have more incentive both to fight individual claims and to argue in the political arena for reduced workers' compensation coverage for injuries previously compensated by these funds.

Although these changes vary in their scope, they all have the same effect: they limit the liability of workers' compensation systems when a worker brings to his or her current employment an increased level of risk of injury or disability. The likely result may be the exclusion of claims by workers, often older workers, with preexisting chronic musculoskeletal and pulmonary conditions and underlying chronic diseases that predispose them to injury and illness caused by work.

### Procedural and evidentiary changes in claims processing that restrict compensability

More subtle, but equally restrictive, changes are occurring in the approach to the evaluation of evidence in many state workers' compensation systems. For example, statutory changes in a number of states now require that a claimant prove that his or her injury was both primarily work-related and that the resulting medical condition can be documented by "objective medical" evidence. These heightened requirements appear to be rooted both in a desire to save money and in a distrust of subjective reports of injuries by claimants. A broad requirement for objective evidence excludes from coverage those claims based upon the subjective reports of patients that cannot be substantiated by objective medical testing. Debilitating musculoskeletal injuries involving soft tissue damage and reports of pain and psychological impairment may be excluded from compensation based upon this requirement.

In addition, in some jurisdictions, claimants are being required to meet increasingly strict burdens of proof. In a landmark 1994 case under the federal black lung compensation law, the U.S. Supreme Court threw out the Department of Labor's "true doubt rule" under which the claimant won if the medical evidence offered by the claimant and the coal operator were equal in weight. The court ruled that, due to requirements in the Administrative Procedures Act, claimants must prove their cases by a "preponderance of the evidence."[16] Statutory amendments to some state statutes now require, either in all claims or for specifically delineated ones, that claimants meet this preponderance standard or, for some injuries or diseases, the even more difficult standard of "clear and convincing evidence." Because many compensation programs gave claimants the benefit of the doubt in close or marginal cases in the past, these changes could prove to be significant, particularly for workers with "border-challenging" claims.

The general tightening of eligibility and compensability standards appears to have a predictable, but difficult to document, effect on the defense of claims. All over the country, claimants and their representatives claim that workers' compensation insurance carriers are more likely to controvert or contest claims and less likely to offer what claimants view as reasonable settlements. The Workers Compensation Research Institute report regarding Massachusetts' experience supports this claim (Gardner, Telles, and Moss 1996). Similarly, a study by physicians at the Mount Sinai Center for Environmental Medicine in New York City found that 81 percent of workers diagnosed in their occupational medicine clinic with occupational cumulative trauma disorders had their claims contested or received no response from the insurance carrier when the claim was filed (Herbert, Janeway, and Schechter 1997). Thus, even in those jurisdictions that nominally compensate for these injuries, many claims go uncompensated. This trend may further magnify the statutory and judicial changes that restrict workers' access to benefits for work-related injuries.

On the other hand, the interpretation of what constitutes objective evidence, an excluded preexisting condition, or the preponderance of the evidence is ultimately up to the courts. Judicial interpretations vary and may not always prove to be as restrictive as the statutory language appears to demand.[17] It is therefore difficult to assess fully the impact of these statutory changes without further study.

### Changes in compensability rules for particular conditions

As noted above, workers' compensation systems have often failed to compensate occupational diseases. Because of changes in the state laws during the period following the 1972 report of the National Commission on State Workmen's Compensation Laws, claims for conditions involving common physical and mental complaints (such as back or other nonacute musculoskeletal injuries and mental stress) rose in many states. As we have noted, these conditions challenge the boundaries of the traditional work-relatedness test and are often caused by chronic, rather than acute, exposures at work. They sometimes also involve a higher degree of medical ambiguity than do many acute injuries, because they are not easily diagnosed using clearly objective medical tests.  In those states in which compensation for these conditions was paid, however, insurers and employers regarded them as a primary cost-driver to the system.  Perhaps not surprisingly, these types of conditions became the focus of some attempts to exclude conditions in order to limit aggregate workers' compensation costs.

The two primary areas of exclusion have been psychological injuries and cumulative trauma disorders (CTDs), also known as repetitive stress injuries.  In the case of CTDs, as the reported incidence of injuries caused by repetitive trauma skyrocketed, some state legislatures responded by tightening the eligibility standards for compensation.  This was done using a variety of mechanisms: heightened burdens of proof; more specific causation requirements; or requirements for positive findings on specific diagnostic tests.  In the most notorious case, the state supreme court in Virginia ruled that repetitive injury claims, including both carpal tunnel syndrome and noise induced hearing loss, were simply noncompensable under the language of the state workers' compensation statute.  In response to the political reaction to these decisions, the Virginia legislature amended the workers' compensation statute to provide nominal, but very narrow, coverage for these conditions.[18]  It is important to note, however, that this is not a universal trend.  The majority of states do provide some compensation for these conditions; in fact, in 1997, Oklahoma added cumulative trauma to the statutory list of terms denoting compensable injuries.

Stress and other psychological injuries present a more extreme picture.  A number of states have made claims for psychological conditions (in the absence of a physical injury) noncompensable.  In a much smaller number of states, restrictions on compensation for psychological injury even include those that develop as a result of physical injury and impairment.  These restrictions have been designed in a number of ways.  Some state laws simply now provide that purely psychological ("mental-mental") claims are noncompensable (e.g., Wyoming, Oklahoma, South Dakota, and West Virginia).  A second approach restricts the availability of compensation by imposing heightened standards of causation or increased burdens of proof.  A third approach reduces the amount of benefits: in Colorado, benefits for stress or mental injury are now limited to 12 weeks, with a maximum weekly benefit of 50 percent of the state's average weekly wage.

Several states explicitly limit mental-mental claims to situations not involving lawful personnel actions or to situations involving extraordinary or unusual circumstances (e.g., Hawaii, Connecticut, South Carolina, California, Idaho, Missouri, and New York). Psychological reactions to extremely stressful work situations that are not illegal or unusual are therefore noncompensable in these states. Thus, while psychological sequelae from a physical injury remain compensable in most jurisdictions, psychological symptomatology caused by events at work that do not involve physical injury are often no longer compensable.

The motivation for these limitations is clear. Workers' responses to physical and mental stressors at work are subject both to very individualized real responses and to serious measurement problems. The costs are therefore both potentially large and uncertain. The filing of large numbers of claims involving CTDs and stress was a relatively new phenomenon and appeared to be growing quickly in some jurisdictions. By changing the legal rules, claims are made to disappear from the workers' compensation programs. The result is that workers' compensation is eliminated as a primary payer for significant numbers of disabilities that are work-related, thereby externalizing costs from the workers' compensation system.

### Restrictions on compensability of permanent total disability cases

Workers' compensation provides benefits for both long and short-term disabilities. The political and economic pressure to reduce costs has also been directed at the actuarially defined "long tail" of workers' compensation claims—those benefits that may continue for years. Benefits for permanent disabilities, including permanent total disability, are the major cost drivers in the system. The assault on these benefits has taken two forms. First, eligibility has been restricted through the mechanisms described above and through a more direct assault on permanent total disability benefits. Second, as described in the next section, payment has been tightened on those claims that are approved.

Permanent total disability (PTD) benefits are generally paid to disabled workers for life.[19]   In view of the relatively high cost of a lifetime award, it is not surprising that state legislatures have attempted to reduce these costs. Prior to recent developments, many states had adopted the "odd-lot" doctrine, which allowed for the consideration of a claimant's age, education and skills in addition to the nature of injury in determining eligibility for benefits.  Odd-lot workers were generally older workers with a combination of health impairments and a history of working in manual industries.  This is the same population, for example, that may qualify for SSDI benefits under the more lenient provisions for workers who are over 55 years old and have limited education and a long work history in manual labor.[20]   Recently, many states have significantly restricted the use of the odd lot doctrine, most adversely affecting older workers.  In addition, some states, like Florida, now require a "catastrophic" injury before a worker can be considered for a PTD award.  Others have established impairment thresholds requiring the injury to result in a specified and very high level of functional impairment before a worker can be considered for a PTD award.  Many states have narrowed the definition of what it means to be permanently and totally disabled by abandoning the claimant's prior work as a reference point.  In Minnesota, the injured worker must be incapable of working at any occupation that produces an income; in Colorado, it is inability to earn a wage; in Oregon, a gainful occupation is defined as one that pays the minimum wage.

The results of these eligibility restrictions for PTD benefits have sometimes been startling.  For example, in West Virginia, the adoption of a threshold requirement that a claimant have at least 50 percent functional impairment (within the definition in the *Guides to the Evaluation of Permanent Impairment* [American Medical Association 1993]) resulted in a 97 percent reduction in the rate of permanent total disability awards, from 117 to 5.8 per 100,000 workers in the first two years after enactment (BNA 1997, p. 276).[21]  This spurred legislative action in 1999 that relaxed the eligibility threshold to 40 percent functional impairment.  The effects of this change have not yet been determined.

### Underfiling of claims and expansion of fraud prosecutions

State statutes during this period also expanded criminal liability for fraud.  Substantial, and perhaps excessive, media attention has been focused on claimants who are viewed as illegally seeking to obtain or extend benefits.  Often, these articles assert that large numbers of claims in workers' compensation involve fraud, resulting in a broad stigmatization of workers who file for benefits.[22]

Of course, the expansion and publicizing of fraud prosecutions of claimants deters intentionally fraudulent claims, but it also may discourage the filing of legitimate claims. Current research indicates that large numbers of workers with occupationally caused disabilities do not file claims for workers' compensation (Biddle et al. 1998; Pransky et al. 1999; Michaels 1998; Morse et al. 1998; and Morse, Dillon, and Warren 2000). The decision by a worker not to seek benefits is a complex one and has been found to be affected by the severity of the injury, the worker's level of knowledge about workers' compensation, and the worker's own fears regarding how the employer and others will react to the filing of a claim (Morse, Dillon, and Warren 2000). Older workers may have more access to alternative benefits; they are more likely to qualify for SSDI due to the consideration of age in the evaluation process and they are more likely to have vested pension benefits due to duration of employment. To the extent that other programs lack the same level of stigmatization, workers may preferentially seek these alternative benefits, thereby shifting costs from workers' compensation to these other programs.

## Reductions in the Amount Paid in Approved Claims

Reduction in the costs of approved claims is primarily being achieved through reductions in the amount that is paid for permanent disabilities. In general, weekly benefit rates have not been reduced, in large part because most states now provide that maximum weekly benefits automatically increase each year as the state's average weekly wage increases.[23]

### Reductions in payment of permanent partial disability benefits

A critical difference between workers' compensation and other social insurance programs is the availability of permanent partial disability benefits, designed to compensate the worker for loss of income resulting from the injury or illness although the worker remains active in the labor market. These benefits, which typically are the largest component of disability benefit costs, were a primary target for reform in the 1990s. These changes have particular consequence to older workers, whose injuries tend to be more severe (Wegman 2000).

Three patterns of reform are evident. First, there have been reductions in the duration or weekly amount of the PPD benefits. For example, in Connecticut, an aggregate 27 percent reduction in PPD benefits was achieved in 1993 by reducing the nominal replacement rate from 80 percent to 75 percent of spendable earnings; by reducing the duration for scheduled injuries (e.g., the number of weeks for loss of a leg was reduced from 238 to 155 weeks); and by reducing the maximum duration of nonscheduled PPD benefits from 780 to 520 weeks. Other states that curtailed the maximum number of weeks of PPD benefits include Massachusetts, Florida, and Maine. The result of these reductions is both to decrease the duration of compensation awards in the more serious cases and to reduce the value of claims when they are settled early in litigation. According to a study by the Workers Compensation Research Institute, these and related changes in Massachusetts drove the average lump sum settlement from $27,040 to $18,860 (Gardner, Telles, and Moss 1996, p. 98).

Second, there was a substantial curtailment of the wage-loss approach to calculation of benefits in the 1990s. Pennsylvania enacted legislation in 1996 that reduced the employer's responsibilities to offer an actual employment opportunity in order to avoid responsibility for wage-loss benefits. Florida had been viewed as a pioneer in 1979 when it introduced a two-track system for PPD benefits, one track for impairment benefits if the worker experienced an actual physical loss of a body member and another track that could be paid concurrently if the worker had actual earnings losses due to the injury. During the 1980s, the maximum duration for the wage-loss benefits was 525 weeks. In 1990, the maximum duration of the wage-loss benefits was seriously curtailed (which reduced the actuarial valuation of the PPD benefits by 48.4 percent). And in 1994, the impairment benefits track was eliminated, the wage-loss benefits were restricted to a few workers with very serious injuries, and the overall duration for all types of benefits in PPD cases was limited to 401 weeks. The actuarial valuation indicated these 1994 reforms reduced the Florida PPD benefits by another 16.7 percent (NCCI 2000, p. 101).

A third pattern in PPD reform in the 1990s was to move toward benefits that are primarily determined on the basis of the assessment of the extent of impairment, rather than on the basis of an evaluation of the extent of loss of earning capacity (or loss of actual earnings). The claimed rationale was that the impairment ratings were more objective and thus less prone to litigation. The switch to an impairment-only rating system was often associated with adoption of the AMA's *Guides to the Evaluation of Permanent Impairment* as the tool for assessment of impairment. The *Guides* relies primarily on purportedly objective medical testing but produces inconsistent ratings that may result in devaluation of common disabling injuries for workers. (Spieler et al. 2000) The precise effect of the *Guides'* ratings has not been studied, but claimants' advocates assert that the adoption of the impairment-only PPD system is accompanied by reductions in the amount of PPD benefits paid.

### Reductions in benefits based on receipt of other income

Significantly for older workers, many states now mandate that disability benefits be reduced by other income, most commonly Social Security Old Age benefits, or be terminated when the claimant reaches retirement age or becomes eligible to collect SSOA benefits.[24]   These offset or termination provisions, which are designed to reduce the cost of workers' compensation costs for employers, generally make no allowance for the reduction in retirement income resulting from the loss of wages associated with the disability. This means that workers who leave the workforce with reduced old age or pension benefits have their total income further reduced, often dollar for dollar, by the cuts in workers' compensation payments. These restrictions have been challenged in many states; state courts are split on whether this reduction or termination of workers' compensation benefits constitutes an unconstitutional age-based classification.[25]

### Medical Care Cost Containment

During the 1980s, workers' compensation health care continued to be paid entirely by the employer and to rely primarily on fee-for-service reimbursement arrangements with medical practitioners. During this same period, general group health insurance adopted and expanded a variety of cost containment strategies. The results of the disparate rules were that medical expenses for comparable conditions were considerably higher in workers' compensation than in the general health care system. Such disparities provided an incentive for providers to classify marginal conditions (such as backs) as work-related in order to receive higher payments.

Since about 1990, because of a perception that workers' compensation was experiencing inordinate rates of increase in health care costs, many states made changes in the health care component of their workers' compensation programs. These included the adoption of "traditional" approaches to limiting health care costs in workers' compensation (e.g., fee schedules, limits on the choice of treating physicians and on the amount or duration of health care); the introduction of managed care networks; and some movement toward "24-hour coverage" which integrated workers' compensation health care with other coverage (Burton 1997, pp. 141–48).[26] Most of these changes were designed to reduce the costs of health care delivery in workers' compensation and the cost shifting to workers' compensation from other payers. The likely results of these changes include the transfer of health care costs to the worker and to other health payers; decreases in medical costs in workers' compensation; increases in the control that the insurer or employer has over medical management; and, conversely, decreases in the worker's own control of his or her health care.

Some of these developments may have particular impact on older workers. For example, many states now restrict employees' choice of physician for both treatment and evaluation of workplace injuries, either directly or through employer-selected managed care networks.[27] In these instances, the employer-selected physician may control both treatment and assessment of the worker for continuation of weekly cash benefits. Not surprisingly, organized labor and many workers argue that restrictions on employee choice of providers have an adverse impact on the injured worker, damage the provider-patient relationship, and lead to inferior treatment and premature return to work. This may be especially true for older workers with chronic health conditions, who are required to seek treatment from employer-chosen physicians for health problems with complex etiology.

In addition, there has been considerable concern and political agitation regarding the issue of confidentiality of workers' compensation medical records. Under pressure from employers, some states have explicitly restricted the scope of confidentiality of medical records when an employee files for workers' compensation benefits, including allowing both oral and written communications between the employer or insurer and the employees' physician without a release by the employee (e.g., West Virginia) and requiring the release of all medical information relating to arguably relevant preexisting conditions (e.g., Nevada).

The effects of expansion of communication among third parties about a worker's health status have not been studied. It is however reasonable to speculate that broad elimination of medical confidentiality may have several effects. On the one hand, providing the health care provider and employer with better information may promote appropriate disability management and return to work. On the other hand, this erosion of confidentiality may discourage some workers from filing for workers' compensation benefits, particularly those with chronic health conditions who prefer not to reveal their health status to their employers. This last group of workers is likely to include an overrepresentation of older workers.

## Rise of Disability Management and Return-to-Work Programs

Like the interest in expanding return to work for SSDI/SSI recipients, there has been a significant shift to a focus on disability management and "return-to-work" programs in workers' compensation. In the past, whether a disabled worker would return to his or her old job, or to any job at all, was solely within the discretion of employers and was not viewed as the concern of workers' compensation programs. In contrast, work participation by disabled workers is now actively encouraged.

Disability management can accomplish two critical goals: it can save costs by decreasing both the length of time a worker is out of work and the higher permanent disability rating that is thought to result from longer absence from work, and it can improve quality of life for workers by increasing successful postinjury work participation. Clearly, employers and insurers are economically motivated to decrease workers' compensation liability by encouraging—or forcing—employees to return to work. Light duty programs are often designed specifically to bring workers back to work, often at temporary job assignments, after initial recovery from an occupational injury. In general, employers and insurers believe that earlier return to work will limit both the duration of temporary benefits and any psychological "overlay" which may result in increased permanent disability.

Not surprisingly, the strong economic motivation for insurers and employers to focus on rapid return to work makes many labor union officials and injured workers' groups wary of these developments. In many states, an offer of a job, even before the worker has reached maximum medical improvement after an injury, will lead to termination of temporary total disability benefits; in states that measure permanent disability based upon wage loss or loss of earning capacity, the job offer may limit permanent disability benefits as well. Not all states require that the job offered be an appropriate one that the worker can perform. Workers and their unions have charged that injured workers are asked to resume duties they are not yet physically capable of performing.

Legal changes have both supported and reflected this shift toward disability management. Some of these changes are internal to workers' compensation statutes: expanding rehabilitation opportunities, making retaliation for filing workers' compensation claims actionable, and establishing both incentives and requirements for returning an injured worker to work. Other legal developments, outside of the workers' compensation laws, have both encouraged and reinforced these trends. Most importantly, the Americans with Disabilities Act (ADA), state disability discrimination laws, and the Family and Medical Leave Act now regulate employers' treatment of injured workers. Workers with disabilities caused by work-related injuries and diseases are within the potential class of employees who receive the protection of these new laws. The ADA clearly supports the return-to-work concepts now espoused in workers' compensation.[28] However, the overall effectiveness of the ADA in promoting employment of occupationally injured workers is currently in doubt (Acemoglu and Angrist 1998; American Bar Association, Commission on Mental and Physical Disabilities 1998 and 2000; Colker 1999; DeLeire 1997).

The focus on return to work supports the decrease in the availability of permanent disability benefits. It may therefore affect older workers in two ways. First, if it results in successful extension of worklife through appropriate workplace accommodations, it will tend to expand both work earnings and retirement income levels. On the other hand, to the extent that it results in reductions in benefits without successful extensions of work, it will erode the cushion provided by workers' compensation benefits to those who face reduced earnings as a result of partial disabilities.

## EFFECTS OF WORKERS' COMPENSATION DEVELOPMENTS ON OLDER WORKERS AND OTHER SOCIAL INSURANCE PROGRAMS

The foregoing summary suggests that several factors must be considered when analyzing the adequacy of workers' compensation programs for older workers. First, workers' compensation has never provided compensation for all occupationally induced disabilities, nor has workers' compensation fully replaced lost wages when a worker is eligible for benefits. Workers' compensation is most adequate, from the standpoint of both eligibility and benefit rates, for workers who suffer short term, acute injuries. Occupational diseases, chronic conditions resulting from long-term job exposures, and conditions that are caused by multiple factors have never been fully compensated by these programs.

Second, under recent workers' compensation developments in some states, the likelihood that workers with chronic impairments will replace their lost wages through workers' compensation appears to be shrinking. The reductions are due to changes in eligibility rules, changes in the approach to permanent disability, and reductions in benefits on receipt of other old age benefits.

Third, the combined effect of the various changes in compensability of conditions will have their greatest impact on conditions that are most medically ambiguous. Musculoskeletal conditions resulting from the wearing down of a worker's body and chronic diseases such as hearing loss, arthritis, respiratory ailments, and heart disease are all more prevalent in older workers. These conditions involve questions regarding causation; all are subject to challenge based on tightened evidentiary standards; many cannot be clearly diagnosed and evaluated using "objective" medical tests; and several have been the specific target of tightened eligibility standards. Aging workers are overrepresented among people with chronic disabilities and diseases that are partially work-induced. Restrictions on compensation are therefore likely to affect older workers more adversely.

Fourth, aging workers face barriers in the labor market when they lose their jobs. The job mobility of all disabled workers is also limited. It is certainly likely that aging workers with disabilities face even greater barriers. Erosion of medical confidentiality, increases in stigmatization of workers who file for benefits, and generalized concern about labor market mobility may all act to increase the reluctance of aging workers to file claims for workers' compensation benefits, particularly if other benefits are available to cover their medical costs.

Fifth, the decline of long-tailed indemnity benefits means that workers' compensation is unlikely to be a useful source for wage and pension replacement for aging workers in the coming period. This problem is exacerbated by the practice of compromise and release, which allows for lump-sum, non-annuity payments to workers in order to end the adjudication of a claim.

Sixth, reductions in the availability of permanent disability benefits (both through eligibility and duration/amount restrictions) result in a loss of replacement income for injured workers. To the extent that this affects workers who may be eligible for SSDI or SSI, the federal programs become the primary payers for these disabilities.

Seventh, state legislatures and those who lobby for restrictions in workers' compensation benefits focus only on the costs of workers' compensation programs and not on the costs that are externalized to other programs (or to workers and their families). This means that there is little attention paid in the states to the effects of these legislative changes on other, primarily federal, benefit programs.

The implications of these factors for older workers and for other social and private insurance programs are troubling. Like other social insurance programs, workers' compensation was designed to provide protection against poverty and catastrophic losses. But more than other programs, workers' compensation was also expected to provide disabled workers with a substantial proportion of the income lost as a result of the work-related injury or illness. This latter goal is reflected in various program design elements: relatively high maximum weekly benefits, provision of partial disability benefits for people who continue to work, a benefit structure designed to replace a substantial proportion of lost earnings, and so on.  Currently, we are concerned that workers' compensation may be increasingly failing to meet both goals. Because of changes in compensability standards, workers suffering from occupationally induced morbidity may not meet the work-relatedness tests to qualify for benefits, and in a number of jurisdictions, permanent disability benefits—designed to cushion the economic impact of injuries for workers—have been significantly reduced.

As a result, workers may be less likely to be able to retain their economic status in the face of work-caused disabilities.  To some extent, other programs will fill the gap.  But many workers who are not totally disabled will face reductions in income that are not compensated.  To the extent that workers' compensation reduces the availability of benefits to workers who cannot qualify for SSDI or other benefits, the costs associated with these disabilities are transferred to the workers (and their families).  The reductions in benefits after disabled workers reach the age of 65 may mean that levels of poverty for these workers will grow, since workers' compensation benefits will no longer compensate for the reductions in pension and SSOA benefits that were caused by the reduced lifetime earnings resulting from workplace injuries.

In addition, although conclusive evidence is not available, there are some data that suggest workers turn to SSDI for income support when workers' compensation benefits are unavailable.[29]  The proportion of workers with occupationally caused disabilities may therefore rise in the DI program.  This means that the SSA expectation that workers whose disability is occupationally caused will find benefits elsewhere may be increasingly misplaced.  Similarly, the growing restrictions on both compensability and medical care are likely to transfer health care costs from workers' compensation to Medicare (if the worker qualifies for SSDI) or to Medicaid (if the worker is impoverished or does not qualify for Medicare).  From the standpoint of injured workers, the effect of this is mixed.  On the one hand, SSDI benefits tend to be lower and the disability eligibility requirements have historically been stricter than in workers' compensation programs.  On the other, applicants for DI benefits are unlikely to face equivalent resistance from employers or carriers to their claims, and once eligibility for SSDI benefits has been established, the benefits are more secure and the health care provided is more comprehensive than that available through workers' compensation.

Costs are also likely to be shifted from workers' compensation to employment-based insurance programs offered by employers. This includes short- and long-term disability and general health plans. Since the premium costs of these programs tend to be sensitive to specific employer experience, this may then encourage large employers to expand the integration of benefit and disability plans, including workers' compensation, in order to gain control over the firm's total expenditures on disability.

## CONCLUSION

In summary, the recent decline in workers' compensation costs and benefits in part reflects a decline in the adequacy and availability of these benefits. In particular, workers in the second half of their work lives are likely to be adversely affected by these declines. Although workers' compensation will continue to provide adequate compensation for acute short-term injuries, the availability of benefits for permanent disabilities, particularly those associated with aging, appears to be declining in many states. This trend is likely to shift additional economic burdens to other social and private insurance systems. To the extent that other social insurance programs fail to provide replacement of a substantial proportion of earnings lost due to partial disability, these costs are being transferred to workers and their families.

## Notes

We appreciate the assistance of several persons who provided comments or other assistance during the preparation of this chapter: Keith Bateman, Leslie Boden, Ann Clayton, Alan Ducatman, Donald Elisburg, H. Allan Hunt, William Johnson, Barbara Markiewicz, and Greg Wagner. We absolve them of responsibility for any remaining errors of fact or analysis.

1. A more extensive description of the program and additional references can be found in Spieler and Burton (1998).

2. We use the term *border-challenging* for these often chronic conditions with complex etiology, in the sense that these conditions are on the border of the traditional definitions of compensable conditions.

3. Three exceptions to the general rule are the following: 1) the doctrine of the "odd-lot" worker (which considers age as a component of evaluation of eligibility for permanent total disability benefits); 2) the reduction or termination of cash benefits when a worker receives Social Security Old Age benefits, reaches a particular age (usually 65), or is eligible for a pension or other benefits; and 3) the use of age adjustments to the ratings assigned to particular impairments (e.g., respiratory diseases and hearing loss). The first two of these exceptions are discussed in the fourth section of this chapter.

4. Countrywide data indicate there are 6,837 workers' compensation cases per 100,000 workers, of which only 7 per 100,000 workers involve permanent total disability benefits (NCCI 2000, Exhibit XII). The average total benefits per case (including cash and medical benefits) for all workers' compensation cases are $5,244, while the average total benefits for permanent total disability cases are $513,284 (NCCI 2000, Exhibit XI).

5. The Workers Compensation Research Institute (WCRI) has published a series of administrative inventories of state workers' compensation programs. One of the measures of litigiousness used in these studies is requests for workers' compensation agency intervention to resolve contested cases involving cash (or indemnity) benefits. Ballantyne and Shiman (1997, p. 75) summarized the results for 11 states the WCRI has recently studied. The low end of the range was from North Carolina, where 9 percent of indemnity claims involved a hearing request; similar results were found for Wisconsin (10 percent). States where litigation (as measured by agency intervention to resolve disputes) was most extensive were Washington (40 percent of state-fund indemnity claims involved a protest filing), Missouri (43 percent of indemnity claims involved at least one meeting at the agency), New Jersey (35 to 55 percent of indemnity claims involve one or more claim petition filings), and Illinois (68 percent of indemnity claims involved agency intervention).

6. Thomason and Burton (1993) surveyed the limited literature on the use of compromise and release agreements. One of their conclusions (p. S12) is that the evidence "suggests that claimants who settle for lump sum awards are in a more precarious financial position after their injury compared to claimants who do not settle."

7. The data in Table 2 are inconsistent with the following statement in Bernard (1997, p. B-2): "The prevalence of MSDs [musculoskeletal disorders] increases as people enter their working years. By the age of 35, most people have had their first episode of back pain . . . Once in their working years (ages 25 to 65), however, the prevalence is relatively consistent . . ."

8. Pransky (2000) provides additional evidence (in his Table 2) of "the dramatic age-related increase in prevalence of selected chronic diseases and the number of persons with . . . any limitations in ability to do usual life activities."

9. The relationship is particularly elusive because of the general underreporting of work-related health problems (discussed earlier) that are likely to be especially prevalent among older workers.

10. Much of the information in this section is drawn from Berreth (1992, 1994, 1996, 1997), Brown (1993, 1995), Tinsley (1990, 1991), and Whittington (1998, 1999, 2000).

11. In Idaho, for example, the Supreme Court has upheld denial of benefits in the following types of claims where there was a preexisting condition: carpal tunnel syndrome (*Reyes v. Kit Manufacturing Co.* [Id. 1998], *Nelson v. Ponsness-Warren IDGAS Enterprises*, 879 P.2d 592 [Id. 1994]), asthma (*Combes v. State of Idaho*, ISIF, 942 P.2d 554 [Id. 1997], second appeal pending, Idaho Supreme Court No. 25407); lumbar back pain (*Demain v. Bruce McLaughlin Logging*, 979 P.2d 655 [Id. 1999]); and flexor tenosynovitis secondary to underlying diabetes (*Nycum v. Triangle Dairy*, 712 P.2d 559 [Id. 1985]).

12. *Errand v. Cascade Steel Rolling Mills, Inc.*, 888 P.2d 544 (Or. 1995). The compensation bureau had denied him workers' compensation benefits because "his work was not the 'major cause' of his condition and, thus, he did not suffer 'compensable injury' within meaning of exclusivity provision."

13. 1996 Oregon Rev. Statutes, Title 51, Section 656.018.

14. *Smothers v. Gresham Transfer Inc.*, 941 P.2d 1065 (Or. App. 1997), appeal granted 977 P.2d 1170 (Or. Nov 24, 1998); pending as of August 28, 2000.

15. *Combes v. State of Idaho Industrial Special Indemnity Fund*, Idaho Supreme Court No. 25407; pending as of August 28, 2000.

16. *Director, OWCP v. Greenwich Collieries*, 114 S.Ct. 2251 (1994).

17. See, for example, some of the cases decided by the Oregon appellate courts under the more restrictive standards that were adopted by the legislature: *Conner v. B&S Logging*, 957 P.2d 159 (Or. App. 1998); *Beverly Enterprises v. Michl*, 945 P.2d 658 (Or. App. 1997); *SAIF Corp. v. Williamson*, 882 P.2d 621 (Or. App. 1994) (a finding of impairment may be based on a physically verifiable impairment or on the physician's evaluation of the worker's description of the pain that she is experiencing.)

18. *Stenrich Group v. Jemmott*, 467 S.E.2d 795 (Va. 1996), carpal tunnel; *Allied Fibers v. Rhodes*, as: 23 Va. 101, 474 S.E.2d 829 (Va. 1996), noise-induced hearing loss. The amended statute is Virginia Code Sec. 65.2-400(c) and 65.2-401.

19. It is important to note the following. First, PTD awards have always been relatively infrequent in workers' compensation programs (see note 4). These data may, however, be somewhat misleading, since the frequent practice of settling claims (termed compromise and release agreements or lump sum settlements) often means that awards for significant disabilities are classified as permanent partial disability benefits, even when the workers' medical and economic conditions could justify permanent total disability awards. Second, although the majority of states provide for lifetime weekly benefits, some states set a maximum period of eligibility for PTD benefits even before the recent legislative changes in these types of benefits.

20. According to §608 of the 1997 Social Security Handbook (13th ed.),
    two special provisions may establish disability for persons who are unable to
    perform any of their past relevant work.
    A. A finding of disability may be made where the individual:
       1. Has long-time work experience (35 years or more) limited to
          arduous, unskilled, physical labor; and
       2. Has little education; and
       3. Has a significant impairment that prevents performance of
          the previous kind of work; and
       4. Has not demonstrated ability to do lighter work.
    B. A finding of disability may also be made where the individual:
       1. Has no past relevant work; and
       2. Is of advanced age (55 years or older); and
       3. Has less than a high school education; and
       4. Has an impairment that is more than "not severe" (see §606).
    However, considering age, education, and work experience, a younger or bet-
    ter educated worker, or one who has transferable skills to work that could be per-
    formed despite the impairment(s), might not be considered disabled. Although
    advancing age may affect a person's capacity to work in competition with others,
    unemployment due primarily to age (i.e., employers may not wish to hire older
    workers) does not show inability to engage in substantial gainful activity by rea-
    son of a medical impairment.

21. The rate of PTD awards in West Virginia prior to the 1995 legislative amendments
    far exceeded the national average of 7 per 100,000 (NCCI 2000, Exhibit XII).
    The rate of PTD awards after the changes was below this national average. As
    discussed in note 19, these data can be somewhat misleading (Spieler 1995).

22. Burton and Thomason (1993) provided a dispassionate critique of a series of arti-
    cles in the *New York Times* that alleged there was a "vast amount of fraud" in the
    workers' compensation system.

23. In January 1990, 32 of 51 jurisdictions (including the District of Columbia) had
    maximum weekly benefits for temporary total disability that were at least 100 per-
    cent of the jurisdiction's average weekly wage; by January 1998, 34 jurisdictions
    met this standard. Again, this is not a universal development. Connecticut and
    Massachusetts cut the nominal replacement rate for temporary total disability
    benefits, and several states (including Minnesota, New Hampshire, and Texas)
    reduced the maximum number of weeks of temporary total disability benefits
    (usually to a limit of 104 weeks).

24. There are specific federal rules regarding offsets between SSDI and state workers'
    compensation systems for workers who are below the age of SSOA eligibility (see
    20 C.F.R. 404.408). In general, with the exception of some states that were
    "grandfathered," SSDI benefits are reduced based upon receipt of total benefits
    that exceed caps on income established in the Social Security Act. This is differ-
    ent from these new offset provisions, which generally provide for an automatic
    dollar for dollar reduction in workers' compensation benefits <u>after</u> the worker

becomes SSOA eligible, or which simply terminate workers' compensation benefits at age 65 without regard to the total income the retiree is receiving.

25. Cases that have held that these provisions are unconstitutional include *Golden v. Westark Community College*, 969 S.W.2d 154 (Ark. 1998); *State of West Virginia ex rel. Boan v. Richardson*, 482 S.E.2d 162 (W.Va. 1996); and *Industrial Claim Appeals Office v. Romero*, 912 P.2d 62 (Colo. 1996). Cases that have upheld these provisions include *Sasso v. Ram Property Management*, 431 So.2d 204 (Fla.Dist.Ct.App. 1983), aff'd, 452 So.2d 932 (Fla.1984); *Tobin's Case*, 675 N.E.2d 781 (Mass. 1997); and *Vogel v. Wells Fargo Guard Services*, 937 S.W.2d 856 (Tenn. 1996).

26. For a more complete discussion of medical care cost containment in workers' compensation, see Dembe (1998) and Spieler and Burton (1998).

27. A survey by the Workers Compensation Research Institute indicated that, as of 1998, workers' compensation programs in 14 states gave employees an unre-stricted initial choice of the treating provider, a number that has been cut in half in the last decade (Tanabe 1998, p. 41). Four jurisdictions required employees to select from an insurer's or employer's list of providers, and 12 required the employee to choose from within a managed care organization if one exists. The employer selects the initial treating provider in 17 states. Four other states have choice rules that vary by circumstances.

28. See particularly, EEOC Enforcement Guidance: Workers' Compensation and the Americans with Disabilities Act, Reasonable Accommodation (September 3, 1996).

29. Mont, Burton, and Reno (2000, p. 25) speculate that

> the opposite trends in workers' compensation and Social Security bene-fits during many years since the mid 1970s raise the question of whether adjustments in one program increases demands placed on the other, and vice versa. The substitutability of DI and workers' compensation for workers with severe, long-term disabilities that are, at least arguably, work-related, or might be exacerbated by the demands of work, has received little attention by researchers and is not well understood.

# References

Acemoglu, Daron, and Joshua Angrist. 1998. "Consequences of Employment Protection? The Case of the Americans with Disabilities Act." NBER working paper no. 6670, National Bureau of Economic Research, Cam-bridge, Massachusetts.

Adams P.F., G.E. Hendershot, and M.A. Marano. 1999. *Current Estimates from the National Health Interview Survey, 1996*. Vital and Health Statis-tics Series 10, Survey no. 200, National Center for Health Statistics, Hyattsville, Maryland.

American Medical Association. 1993. *Guides to the Evaluation of Permanent Impairment, Fourth edition.* Chicago, Illinois: American Medical Association.

American Bar Association, Commission on Mental and Physical Disabilities. 1998. "Study Finds Employers Win Most ADA Title I Judicial and Administrative Complaints." *Mental & Physical Disability Law Reporter* 22: 403–405.

American Bar Association, Commission on Mental and Physical Disabilities. 200. "1999 Employment Decisions Under the ADA Title 1 – Survey Update." *Mental & Physical Disability Law Reporter* 24(3): 348–350.

Ballantyne, Duncan, and Lawrence Shiman. 1997. *Revisiting Workers' Compensation in Michigan: Administrative Inventory.* Cambridge, Massachusetts: Workers Compensation Research Institute.

Berkowitz, Monroe. 1988. "Functioning Ability and Job Performance as Workers Age." In *The Older Worker*, Michael E. Borus, Herbert S. Parnes, Steven H. Sandell, and Bert Seidman, eds. Madison, Wisconsin: Industrial Relations Research Association, pp. 87–114.

Bernard, Bruce P. 1997. *Musculoskeletal Disorders and Workplace Factors.* Cincinnati, Ohio: National Institute for Occupational Safety and Health.

Berreth, Charles A. 1992. "Workers' Compensation; State Enactments in 1991." *Monthly Labor Review* 115(1): 56–63.

_____. 1994. "Workers' Compensation Laws: Significant Changes in 1993." *Monthly Labor Review* 116(1): 53–64.

_____. 1996. "Workers' Compensation Laws Enacted in 1995." *Monthly Labor Review* 118(1): 59–72.

_____. 1997. "State Workers' Compensation Legislation Enacted in 1996." *Monthly Labor Review* 119(1): 43–50.

Biddle, Jeff, Leslie I. Boden, and Robert T. Reville. 2001. "Permanent Partial Disability from Occupational Injuries: Earnings Losses and Replacement in Three States." In this volume, pp. 263–290.

Biddle, Jeff, Karen Roberts, D.D. Rosenman, and Edward M. Welch. 1998. "What Percentage of Workers with Work-Related Illnesses Receive Workers Compensation Benefits?" *Journal of Occupational & Environmental Medicine* 40(4): 325–331.

Boden, Leslie I., and Monica Galizzi. 1999. "Economic Consequences of Workplace Injuries and Illnesses: Lost Earnings and Benefit Adequacy." *American Journal of Industrial Medicine* 36(5): 487–503.

_____. 1993. "Workers' Compensation: State Enactments in 1992." *Monthly Labor Review* 116(1): 50–55.

Brown, Ruth A. 1995. "Workers' Compensation Laws: Enactments in 1994." *Monthly Labor Review* 117(1): 53–59.

BNA (Bureau of National Affairs). 1997. "Permanent Total Disability Awards Fell by 97 Percent under New Law." *BNA's Workers' Compensation Report* 8(11): 276–277.

Burkhauser, Richard V., Mary C. Daly, and Andrew J. Houtenville. 2001. "How Working-Age People with Disabilities Fared over the 1990s Business Cycle." In this volume, pp. 291–346.

Burton John F., Jr. 1992. "Compensation for Back Disorders." In *Workers' Compensation Desk Book*, John F. Burton, Jr., and Timothy P. Schmidle, eds. Horsham, Pennsylvania: LRP Publications, pp. I-123– I-128.

_____. 1997. "Workers' Compensation, Twenty-Four-Hour Coverage, and Managed Care." In *Disability: Challenges for Social Insurance, Health Care Financing, and Labor Market Policy*, Virginia P. Reno, Jerry L. Mashaw and Bill Gradison, eds. Washington, D.C.: National Academy of Social Insurance, pp. 129–149.

Burton, John F., Jr., and Terry Thomason. 1993. "Workers' Compensation Fraud: Let the Reader Beware." In *1994 Workers' Compensation Year Book*, John F. Burton, Jr. and Timothy P. Schmidle, eds. Horsham, Pennsylvania: LRP Publications, pp. I-141–I-143.

Colker, Ruth. 1999. "The Americans with Disabilities Act: A Windfall for Defendants." *Harvard Civil Rights–Civil Liberties Law Review* 34(Winter 1999): 99–162.

DeLeire, Thomas. 1997. "The Wage and Employment Effects of the Americans with Disabilities Act." Working paper, University of Chicago, Illinois.

Dembe, Allard E. 1998. "Evaluating the Impact of Managed Health Care in Workers' Compensation." In *Managed Care*, Jeffrey S. Harris, ed. Vol. 13(4) of Occupational Medicine: State-of-the-Art Reviews. Philadelphia, Pennsylvania: Hanley & Belfus, pp. 799–821.

Gardner, John A., Carol A. Telles, and Gretchen A. Moss. 1996. *The 1991 Reforms in Massachusetts: An Assessment of Impact*. Cambridge, Massachusetts: Workers Compensation Research Institute.

Herbert, Robin, K. Janeway, and C. Schechter. 1997. "Carpal Tunnel Syndrome and Workers' Compensation among an Occupational Clinic Population in New York State." *American Journal of Industrial Medicine* 35(4): 335–342.

Hirsch, Barry T., David A. Macpherson, and Melissa A. Hardy. 2000. "Occupational Age Structure and Access for Older Workers." *Industrial and Labor Relations Review* 53(3): 401–418.

Kelsey, J.L. 1982. *Epidemiology of Musculoskeletal Disorders*. New York: Oxford University Press.

Michaels, David. 1998. "Fraud in the Workers' Compensation System: Origin and Magnitude." In *Workers' Compensation*, T.L. Guidotti and

J.W.F. Cowell, eds. Vol. 3(2) of Occupational Medicine: State-of-the-Art Reviews. Philadelphia, Pennsylvania: Hanley & Belfus, pp. 439–442.

Mont, Daniel, John F. Burton, Jr., and Virginia Reno. 2000. *Workers' Compensation: Benefits, Coverage, and Costs, 1997–1998: New Estimates.* Washington, D.C.: National Academy of Social Insurance.

Morse, Tim, C. Dillon, N. Warren, C. Levenstein, and A. Warren. 1998. "The Economic and Social Consequences of Work-Related Musculoskeletal Disorders: The Connecticut Upper-Extremity Surveillance Project (CUSP)." *International Journal of Occupational and Environmental Health* 4(4): 209–216.

Morse, Tim, C. Dillon, and N. Warren. 2000. "Reporting of Musculoskeletal Disorder (MSD) to Workers' Compensation." *New Solutions* 10(3): 281–292.

National Commission on State Workmen's Compensation Laws. 1972. *The Report of the National Commission on State Workmen's Compensation Laws.* Washington, D.C.: U.S. Government Printing Office.

NCCI. 2000. *Annual Statistical Bulletin.* Boca Raton, Florida: National Council on Compensation Insurance.

Peterson, Mark, Robert Reville, Rachel Kaganoff Stern, and Peter Barth. 1997. *Compensating Permanent Workplace Injuries: A Study of California's System.* MR-920, RAND, Santa Monica, California.

Pransky, Glenn, T. Snyder, A. Dembe, and J. Himmelstein. 1999. "Under-Reporting of Work-Related Disorders in the Workplace: A Case Study and Review of the Literature." *Ergonomics* 42(1): 171–182.

Pransky, Glenn. 2001. "Living Longer, but Able to Work?" In this volume, pp. 431–438.

Spieler, Emily A. 1995. "Assessing Fairness in Workers' Compensation Reform: A Commentary on the 1995 West Virginia Workers' Compensation Legislation." *West Virginia Law Review* 98: 23–170

Spieler, Emily, and John F. Burton, Jr. 1998. "Compensation for Disabled Workers: Workers' Compensation." In *New Approaches to Disability in the Workplace*, Terry Thomason, J.F. Burton, Jr., and D.E. Hyatt, eds. Madison, Wisconsin: Industrial Relations Research Association, pp. 205–244.

Spieler, Emily, Peter Barth, John F. Burton, Jr., Jay Himmelstein, and Linda Rudolf. 2000. "Recommendations to Guide the Revision of the Guides to the Evaluation of Permanent Impairment." *Journal of the American Medical Association* 283: 519–523

Tanabe, Ramona P. 1998. *Managed Care and Medical Cost Containment in Workers' Compensation: A National Inventory, 1998–99.* Cambridge, Massachusetts: Workers Compensation Research Institute.

Tattrie, Douglas. 2000. "The Aging Workforce and Workers' Compensation." Presentation to the WCRI 2000 Annual Issues and Research Conference. Workers Compensation Research Institute, Cambridge, Massachusetts.

Thomason, Terry, and John F. Burton, Jr. 1993. "Economic Effects of Workers' Compensation in the United States: Private Insurance and the Administration of Compensation Claims." *Journal of Labor Economics* 11(1, pt. 2): S1–S37.

Thomason, Terry, Timothy Schmidle, and John F. Burton, Jr. Forthcoming. *Workers' Compensation: Benefits, Costs, and Safety under Alternative Insurance Arrangements.* Kalamazoo, Michigan: W.E. Upjohn Institute for Employment Research.

Tinsley, LaVerne C. 1990. "State Workers' Compensation: Significant Legislation in 1989." *Monthly Labor Review* 113(1): 57–63.

_____. 1991. "State Workers' Compensation: Legislation Enacted in 1990." *Monthly Labor Review* 114(1): 57–62.

Wegman, David H. 2000. "Older Workers." In *Occupational Health: Recognizing and Preventing Work-Related Disease and Injury,* Barry S. Levy and David H. Wegman, eds. Fourth ed. Philadelphia, Pennsylvania: Lippincott Williams and Wilkins, pp. 701–714.

Whittington, Glen. 1998. "Workers' Compensation Legislation Enacted in 1997." *Monthly Labor Review* 121(1): 23–28.

_____. 1999. "Workers' Compensation Legislation Enacted in 1998." *Monthly Labor Review* 115(1): 16–19.

_____. 2000. "Workers' Compensation Legislation Enacted in 1999." *Monthly Labor Review* 123(1): 20–26.

85- 133

# Unemployment Compensation and Older Workers

*Christopher J. O'Leary*
*W.E. Upjohn Institute for Employment Research*

*Stephen A. Wandner*
*U.S. Department of Labor*

Unemployment compensation in the United States is provided through a federal–state system of unemployment insurance (UI). UI provides temporary partial wage replacement to active job seekers who are involuntarily out of work. Eligibility for UI benefits and compensation levels depend on recent earnings experience, the conditions of job separation, and continuing job search activity. The amount of compensation paid for any week of joblessness can be affected by current income from other sources, including part-time work and pensions.

During the second half of the working life, decisions about the process and timing of movement toward full retirement move to the forefront. For many, the sequence is voluntary and orderly; for others, job displacement greatly disrupts plans. While UI is critical for income security of the latter group, it may also play an important role for the former.

Most economic analysis of retirement patterns has focused on the financial incentives created by public and private pension systems.[1] Quinn, Burkhauser, and Myers (1990, p. 5) pointed out that while an abrupt and complete transition from full-time work is still the most common avenue to retirement, a variety of others paths are often taken. A crucial concept in their research is that of the career job. The career job is the one in which a worker spends the bulk of his or her working life, usually working full time. If transition from the career job to retirement is not immediate, it may involve an hours reduction to part-time work on the career job. Alternatively, there may be an exit from the career job to full- or part-time work on another job, which most often is not in the same industry and occupation.

85

*Bridge employment* is what Quinn (1999) calls work between the career job and complete retirement. He estimates that a minimum of 49 percent of women and 34 percent of men engage in bridge employment and that the great majority of bridge employment involves fewer hours per week and less compensation per hour than the career job. The probability of involuntary exit from the career job later in life is high and has risen in recent years (Farber 1997). Furthermore, the chance of gaining reemployment after displacement from a career job diminishes with age (Chan and Stevens 1999).

Job and income security after age 45 and strategies for transition to retirement can be greatly influenced by the institutional arrangements of UI. Many issues at the forefront of the current UI policy debate are also issues of prime importance to those in the second half of their working life. Issues occur in all the standard areas of UI policy: coverage, eligibility, benefit adequacy, duration of benefits, work incentives, benefit financing, and interaction with other programs. We will examine issues of prime concern to older workers in these areas of UI policy after providing a brief background sketch of the labor market situation of older workers.

## BACKGROUND

Whether they can admit it to themselves or not, the second half of their working life starts by age 45 for the great majority of Americans. In this chapter, we examine the labor market and UI beneficiary experience of those aged 45 and over relative to those who are younger. The investigation is summary in nature and is meant to suggest topic areas where focused research would be valuable. We rely on published summary statistics reported in the *Handbook of U.S. Labor Statistics* (Jacobs 1999), the Social Security Administration's publication *Income of the Population 55 or Older—1996* (Social Security Administration 1998), on samples drawn for evaluation and modeling in the states of Michigan and Washington, and on unpublished data provided by the U.S. Department of Labor based on their Benefit Accuracy Measurement (BAM) system of random audits.[2]

The percentages of older workers among the labor force, the total unemployed, and the insured unemployed are reported in Table 1 for the United States in 1998; the data are based on monthly averages for the year. The table indicates that those aged 45 years and over made up one-third of the labor force, encompassed only one-fifth of those experiencing unemployment, but included one-third of all UI beneficiaries. Table 2 provides an age distribution of insured unemployment by state for 1998. Note that the retirement states Arizona and Florida reasonably mimic the national shares of UI receipt by age, whereas the District of Columbia pays a disproportionately large share to older workers, and payments are weighted heavily toward younger workers in Maryland, Oregon, and Puerto Rico. The national average numbers suggest that older workers shoulder a proportionately small share of the unemployment burden while enjoying a higher-than-average chance of receiving UI compensation while jobless and seeking work.

These summary statistics on UI recipiency for older workers are at odds with trends experienced by the work force as a whole since the state UI reforms following the 1975 and 1982 recessions. Vroman (1991) summarized research into causes of the decline in the ratio of the insured unemployment rate to the total unemployment rate (IUR/TUR). Burtless (1983) identified a raft of factors including tightened eligibility requirements, a rising level of UI exhaustions, and the introduction of income taxes on UI benefits. This last factor operates because those from higher-income households are less likely to apply for benefits. Blank and Card (1991) found the decline partly explained by tightened eligibility, but largely due to a decline in UI benefit application rates. They estimated the overall take-up rate among those eligible for UI benefits to be only about 65 percent. Corson and Nicholson (1988) identified declines in unionism and manufacturing employment as causes of a declining IUR/TUR ratio. Concerning older workers, Corson and Nicholson (1988) suggested that changed treatment of the pension benefit offset required by the federal unemployment compensation amendments of 1976 may explain part of the declining IUR/TUR. Details about the treatment of pensions in UI are provided below.

One factor that could partly explain higher recipiency rates among older unemployed workers is that a large share of older UI claimants may be dislocated workers. In employment policy and research defini-

**Table 1  Labor Force and Unemployment Concepts by Age for the United States, 1998**

|  | Total | ≤24 yr. | 25–34 yr. | 35–44 yr. | 45–54 yr. | 55–64 yr. | ≥65 yr. |
|---|---|---|---|---|---|---|---|
| Labor force[a] (000) | 137,673 | 21,894 | 32,813 | 37,536 | 28,368 | 13,215 | 3,847 |
| % of labor force |  | 15.9 | 23.8 | 27.3 | 20.6 | 9.6 | 2.8 |
| Total unemployed[b] (000) | 6,210 | 2,286 | 1,419 | 1,258 | 782 | 343 | 122 |
| % of total unemployed |  | 36.8 | 22.9 | 20.3 | 12.6 | 5.5 | 2.0 |
| % of insured unemployed[c] |  | 8.9 | 25.8 | 29.6 | 20.6 | 10.9 | 2.5 |

[a] Data from Jacobs (1999, Table 1-6).
[b] Data from Jacobs (1999, Table 1-26).
[c] Unpublished data from the U.S. Department of Labor, UI Service.  Age information not available for 1.8 percent of beneficiaries.

**Table 2  Age Distribution of the Insured Unemployed in the United States, 1998 (%)**

| State | Total no. | ≤ 24 yr. | 25–34 yr. | 35–44 yr. | 45–54 yr. | 55–64 yr. | ≥ 65 yr. | INA[a] |
|---|---|---|---|---|---|---|---|---|
| United States | 2,222,936 | 8.9 | 25.8 | 29.6 | 20.6 | 10.9 | 2.5 | 1.8 |
| Alabama | 29,151 | 10.5 | 27.2 | 29.7 | 20.1 | 10.1 | 2.2 | 0.2 |
| Alaska | 12,049 | 10.1 | 28.0 | 33.5 | 20.1 | 7.3 | 1.2 | 0.0 |
| Arizona | 19,114 | 7.1 | 25.5 | 32.3 | 22.7 | 10.7 | 1.7 | 0.0 |
| Arkansas | 25,803 | 11.5 | 28.4 | 30.6 | 18.7 | 9.0 | 1.7 | 0.0 |
| California | 372,144 | 8.6 | 26.8 | 31.3 | 20.3 | 10.4 | 2.6 | 0.0 |
| Colorado | 17,341 | 5.7 | 24.2 | 34.0 | 25.1 | 10.2 | 0.8 | 0.0 |
| Connecticut | 31,180 | 6.7 | 24.6 | 29.6 | 21.5 | 13.8 | 3.8 | 0.0 |
| Delaware | 6,266 | 8.2 | 28.4 | 32.6 | 18.9 | 8.9 | 2.4 | 0.6 |
| D.C. | 6,996 | 0.9 | 7.1 | 20.0 | 33.4 | 28.8 | 10.0 | 0.0 |
| Florida | 77,378 | 5.1 | 32.7 | 29.4 | 23.2 | 13.8 | 5.4 | 0.5 |
| Georgia | 32,709 | 7.0 | 25.3 | 28.7 | 19.4 | 9.1 | 2.0 | 8.6 |
| Hawaii | 12,555 | 6.9 | 25.5 | 29.7 | 23.1 | 11.4 | 3.5 | 0.0 |
| Idaho | 13,080 | 9.8 | 25.0 | 30.3 | 21.9 | 11.0 | 1.7 | 0.3 |
| Illinois | 103,556 | 7.7 | 27.0 | 31.7 | 20.5 | 10.4 | 2.7 | 0.0 |
| Indiana | 30,602 | 7.5 | 24.0 | 28.7 | 21.1 | 10.3 | 1.9 | 6.5 |
| Iowa | 15,792 | 9.7 | 24.9 | 30.7 | 20.8 | 11.3 | 2.5 | 0.0 |
| Kansas | 13,253 | 7.4 | 25.3 | 33.4 | 22.0 | 10.2 | 1.7 | 0.0 |
| Kentucky | 26,654 | 8.6 | 26.7 | 30.9 | 22.1 | 9.8 | 1.9 | 0.0 |

(continued)

**Table 2 (continued)**

| State | Total | ≤ 24 yr. | 25–34 yr. | 35–44 yr. | 45–54 yr. | 55–64 yr. | ≥ 65 yr. | INA[a] |
|---|---|---|---|---|---|---|---|---|
| Louisiana | 22,605 | 7.7 | 26.4 | 32.6 | 21.5 | 9.9 | 1.8 | 0.1 |
| Maine | 11,348 | 7.8 | 24.1 | 27.0 | 19.8 | 10.1 | 2.2 | 9.1 |
| Maryland | 33,912 | 18.1 | 25.8 | 27.9 | 17.1 | 8.6 | 2.5 | 0.0 |
| Massachusetts | 63,678 | 7.4 | 26.6 | 30.3 | 21.3 | 11.8 | 2.4 | 0.0 |
| Michigan | 88,770 | 9.1 | 26.8 | 31.3 | 21.3 | 9.7 | 1.9 | 0.0 |
| Minnesota | 33,105 | 9.6 | 26.2 | 30.7 | 20.8 | 10.9 | 1.9 | 0.0 |
| Mississippi | 18,669 | 9.8 | 27.1 | 31.1 | 20.6 | 10.1 | 1.4 | 0.0 |
| Missouri | 42,875 | 9.0 | 26.7 | 31.8 | 19.8 | 9.9 | 2.8 | 0.0 |
| Montana | 8,419 | 8.6 | 24.0 | 32.9 | 22.2 | 10.1 | 2.2 | 0.0 |
| Nebraska | 6,718 | 9.8 | 26.6 | 30.6 | 20.6 | 10.1 | 2.2 | 0.0 |
| Nevada | 17,531 | 6.3 | 23.6 | 30.2 | 22.7 | 12.9 | 3.9 | 0.3 |
| New Hampshire | 3,691 | 4.7 | 20.5 | 31.3 | 26.8 | 13.7 | 3.2 | 0.0 |
| New Jersey | 91,211 | 8.0 | 26.1 | 28.4 | 20.4 | 12.6 | 4.4 | 0.0 |
| New Mexico | 11,530 | 6.5 | 26.5 | 32.2 | 22.0 | 10.8 | 2.0 | 0.0 |
| New York | 169,950 | 7.3 | 21.9 | 22.6 | 16.6 | 9.8 | 3.3 | 18.6 |
| North Carolina | 47,953 | 9.2 | 27.1 | 29.9 | 20.9 | 10.5 | 2.4 | 0.0 |
| North Dakota | 3,625 | 8.5 | 24.2 | 31.1 | 21.3 | 10.8 | 2.8 | 1.3 |
| Ohio | 70,724 | 7.6 | 25.6 | 32.1 | 23.3 | 10.4 | 1.0 | 0.0 |
| Oklahoma | 12,536 | 7.1 | 24.4 | 32.1 | 22.7 | 11.3 | 2.3 | 0.0 |
| Oregon | 42,758 | 17.9 | 28.6 | 28.4 | 17.3 | 5.8 | 1.1 | 0.9 |

| | | | | | | | |
|---|---|---|---|---|---|---|---|
| Pennsylvania | 142,903 | 9.5 | 24.0 | 28.4 | 22.3 | 12.8 | 2.8 | 0.3 |
| Puerto Rico | 58,341 | 19.6 | 32.3 | 23.58 | 16.1 | 7.5 | 1.1 | 0.0 |
| Rhode Island | 13,294 | 7.3 | 24.7 | 29.3 | 21.0 | 12.8 | 4.9 | 0.0 |
| South Carolina | 24,323 | 5.4 | 19.7 | 23.8 | 17.0 | 32.3 | 1.7 | 0.0 |
| South Dakota | 2,309 | 7.7 | 18.6 | 27.6 | 23.4 | 16.8 | 5.9 | 0.0 |
| Tennessee | 41,157 | 7.9 | 24.1 | 28.4 | 22.3 | 13.0 | 4.1 | 0.3 |
| Texas | 111,624 | 9.5 | 27.9 | 31.0 | 20.8 | 9.4 | 1.5 | 0.0 |
| Utah | 9,619 | 13.8 | 28.5 | 30.0 | 19.1 | 8.1 | 0.5 | 0.0 |
| Vermont | 5,716 | 10.3 | 25.5 | 28.8 | 20.6 | 11.4 | 3.4 | 0.0 |
| Virgin Islands | 575 | 8.4 | 21.7 | 24.6 | 21.5 | 10.9 | 1.6 | 11.2 |
| Virginia | 23,737 | 6.8 | 26.0 | 32.2 | 22.9 | 10.9 | 1.0 | 0.1 |
| Washington | 72,273 | 9.0 | 27.2 | 30.9 | 31.8 | 9.6 | 1.5 | 0.1 |
| West Virginia | 16,455 | 8.2 | 25.9 | 30.5 | 24.4 | 10.6 | 0.4 | 0.0 |
| Wisconsin | 50,033 | 9.7 | 26.2 | 30.7 | 20.3 | 10.8 | 2.3 | 0.0 |
| Wyoming | 3,330 | 11.0 | 25.6 | 31.9 | 20.7 | 9.3 | 1.1 | 0.5 |

SOURCE: Unpublished U.S. Department of Labor data on claims filed for UI in the week including 12th of each month.
[a] INA = age information not available for this percentage of UI beneficiaries.

tions, dislocated workers are those with long job tenure who become permanently separated from their employer.[3] Being dislocated increases workers' chances of eligibility for UI benefits. Unfortunately, such circumstances may increase the probability of UI benefit exhaustion. Relying on data from Hipple (1999a), Table 3 shows that job dislocation increases with age; Farber (1997) found similar evidence.[4] Table 3 also shows that employment rates decline precipitously after age 54 and that the prospect of returning to full-time reemployment after displacement is 30–70 percent lower for older workers. Less than one-tenth of displaced workers under 55 years of age leave the labor force, but more than one-fourth of workers aged 55 to 64 and nearly half of those 65 and over exit. Chan and Stevens (1999) similarly found that involuntary job loss reduces reemployment chances more for older job seekers, who often make early transitions to being permanently out of the labor force (i.e., fully retired).

Unpublished data from the displaced worker survey (Hipple 1999b) revealed that while only 51 percent of all displaced workers received UI, the percentage rises as durations of unemployment increase. Three-quarters of displaced workers unemployed for five or more weeks received UI, and, among those unemployed for 15 or more weeks, the proportion rises to four-fifths. Thus, it appears that some displaced workers never file for UI benefits, as they search for jobs and become reemployed quickly; only one-fifth of displaced workers unemployed for less than five weeks collect benefits. These data also indicate that while the rate of recipiency of UI is stable among age groups around the mean of 51 percent, exhaustion rates rise sharply with age.

The path of employment and income transition from a career job to retirement income can be rocky. As shown in Table 3, displaced workers become reemployed at rapidly declining rates as they age. Older displaced workers who gain reemployment also suffer larger earnings losses. Among displaced workers aged 55 to 64, the earnings loss was 20 percent or more for 38.2 percent of those who got reemployed, while an earnings reduction of that magnitude was experienced by less than a quarter of younger displaced workers.

For those who do ultimately receive UI benefits, the Benefits Accuracy Measurement (BAM) audit data provides a picture of their characteristics.[5] Such a summary is provided in Table 4. Men tend to draw a

**Table 3 Long-Tenured Displaced Workers by Age Group, 1995–1996 (%)**

| Characteristics | 20–24 yr. | 25–34 yr. | 35–44 yr. | 45–54 yr. | 55–64 yr. | ≥65 yr. |
|---|---|---|---|---|---|---|
| Displacement rates | 1.9 | 2.9 | 3.0 | 3.0 | 3.3 | 3.5 |
| Employment status, February 1998 | | | | | | |
| Employed | Note a | 88.5 | 89.0 | 87.2 | 63.6 | 47.2 |
| Unemployed | Note a | 2.5 | 4.2 | 5.3 | 7.7 | 5.5 |
| Not in labor force | Note a | 8.6 | 6.7 | 7.5 | 28.8 | 47.3 |
| Among displaced | | | | | | |
| Reemployed full-time | 60.0 | 74.6 | 74.9 | 56.0 | 47.8 | 20.7 |
| Of those reemployed full time, % experiencing earnings loss ≥ 20% | Note a | 24.6 | 23.8 | 24.5 | 38.2 | Note a |
| UI recipiency rate | 0.30 | 0.53 | 0.51 | 0.49 | 0.53[b] | |
| UI exhaustion rate | 0.19 | 0.45 | 0.52 | 0.54 | 0.70[b] | |

SOURCE: First six rows, Hipple (1999a); last two rows, Hipple (1999b).
[a] Percentage not reported where the base is less than 75,000.
[b] Values for age 55 and over.

**Table 4 Percentage Distribution by Age of UI Beneficiary Characteristics in the United States, 1998**

| Characteristic | Total | ≤24 yr. | 25–44 yr. | 45–54 yr. | 55–64 yr. | ≥65 yr. |
|---|---|---|---|---|---|---|
| U.S. citizen | 89.5 | 90.3 | 88.8 | 90.3 | 90.3 | 94.2 |
| Gender | | | | | | |
| Male | 56.7 | 58.3 | 57.2 | 56.6 | 54.9 | 49.2 |
| Female | 43.3 | 41.7 | 42.8 | 43.4 | 45.1 | 50.8 |
| Education | | | | | | |
| No formal schooling | 0.5 | 0.1 | 0.3 | 0.7 | 1.1 | 1.9 |
| Some high school, no diploma | 20.9 | 19.6 | 19.4 | 20.4 | 27.5 | 33.1 |
| High school graduate | 42.2 | 51.1 | 42.4 | 39.2 | 42.4 | 34.8 |
| Some college, but no degree | 20.8 | 24.1 | 21.9 | 20.9 | 14.2 | 13.0 |
| Associate's degree | 4.9 | 2.4 | 5.4 | 5.5 | 3.5 | 3.2 |
| BA/BS | 8.2 | 2.6 | 8.7 | 9.1 | 7.1 | 11.4 |
| Graduate degree | 2.5 | 0.1 | 1.9 | 4.4 | 4.2 | 2.6 |
| Ethnic group | | | | | | |
| White | 63.1 | 56.8 | 59.8 | 67.4 | 74.0 | 73.8 |
| African American | 15.4 | 13.8 | 17.3 | 13.9 | 10.9 | 10.7 |
| Hispanic | 17.6 | 25.3 | 19.1 | 14.8 | 11.5 | 11.1 |
| Native American | 0.9 | 1.1 | 1.0 | 0.9 | 0.5 | 0.5 |
| Asian/Pacific | 2.9 | 2.9 | 2.7 | 3.0 | 3.2 | 3.8 |
| Last occupation | | | | | | |
| Professional | 17.5 | 7.8 | 17.2 | 20.6 | 19.8 | 17.2 |
| Clerical | 14.1 | 17.5 | 14.2 | 12.8 | 14.2 | 13.7 |

| | | | | | | |
|---|---|---|---|---|---|---|
| Sales | 5.5 | 7.1 | 5.1 | 4.9 | 6.1 | 11.2 |
| Services | 11.2 | 11.6 | 11.6 | 9.6 | 10.3 | 18.8 |
| Processing | 3.7 | 4.2 | 3.6 | 3.5 | 4.5 | 4.9 |
| Machine trades | 5.6 | 5.5 | 5.4 | 6.5 | 6.2 | 2.8 |
| Bench work | 7.0 | 6.6 | 6.7 | 7.7 | 7.8 | 6.3 |
| Structural | 17.3 | 18.0 | 18.4 | 16.6 | 15.3 | 6.8 |
| Miscellaneous | 12.2 | 14.3 | 11.9 | 12.2 | 11.5 | 14.0 |
| Agriculture/mining | 5.8 | 7.2 | 6.1 | 5.5 | 4.3 | 4.4 |
| Last industry | | | | | | |
| Agriculture/mining | 6.9 | 8.3 | 7.1 | 6.5 | 5.7 | 6.4 |
| Construction | 15.0 | 15.0 | 15.8 | 14.7 | 13.0 | 6.5 |
| Manufacturing | 21.5 | 21.0 | 20.0 | 24.6 | 24.7 | 14.1 |
| Transportation, utilities, communication | 5.1 | 3.8 | 4.9 | 5.6 | 6.2 | 5.7 |
| Trade | 16.9 | 19.7 | 16.8 | 16.1 | 15.9 | 21.2 |
| Finance/insurance/real estate | 3.7 | 1.9 | 3.8 | 3.5 | 4.3 | 5.9 |
| Services | 27.4 | 25.2 | 28.1 | 25.7 | 27.0 | 36.0 |
| Public administration | 3.2 | 4.3 | 3.1 | 3.0 | 2.6 | 4.1 |
| Other | 0.5 | 0.7 | 0.4 | 0.4 | 0.5 | 0.2 |

SOURCE: BAM data for calendar year 1998, U.S. Department of Labor.

larger share of UI benefits up until age 65.  Older beneficiaries tend to have lower levels of formal educational attainment.  Beneficiaries over age 54 are less likely to be Black or Hispanic and more likely to be White or Asian/Pacific islander.  The age distribution of the prior occupation is different for the oldest workers.  After age 64, larger shares of beneficiaries are from sales and services occupations and smaller shares are from structural occupations.  These results are consistent with a movement into bridge occupations prior to full retirement.

## COVERAGE

"The coverage provisions of state UI laws determine the employers who are liable for contributions and the workers who accrue rights under the laws" (U.S. Department of Labor 1999, p. 1-D).  Original federal requirements limited coverage to employers of 8 or more workers in each of 20 or more weeks in a year (Blaustein 1993, p. 162).  UI coverage today is nearly universal, with only four main exclusions remaining: agricultural workers, household workers, employees of religious organizations, and the self-employed (Bassi and McMurrer 1997, pp. 54–61)·

Exclusion of the self-employed is an issue of particular importance to older workers.  Table 5 indicates that 6.8 percent of all nonagricultural workers participate in self-employment, but the share rises to 10.9 percent of those aged 55 to 64 and to 17.2 percent of those aged 65 and over.  It is even more important among workers in agriculture, for whom a majority of those 45 years of age and over are self-employed.

Since the depression-era beginnings of the federal–state UI program in the United States, the self-employed have generally not been covered.  The main reason is to avoid problems of *moral hazard*.[6]  With UI for self-employment, those who would pay premiums and be eligible for benefits would also manage the risk of unemployment and make decisions about work stoppage.  In particular, there is an inability to determine whether individuals are involuntarily unemployed, to measure the economic loss of income, and to determine whether an individual is employed or unemployed for a given week.  UI is social

**Table 5  Employed and Self-Employed by Age in the United States, 1998**

| | Total | ≤24 yr. | 25–34 yr. | 35–44 yr. | 45–54 yr. | 55–64 yr. | ≥65 yr. |
|---|---|---|---|---|---|---|---|
| Employment (000) | | | | | | | |
| Total | 131,463 | 19,611 | 31,395 | 36,278 | 27,587 | 12,873 | 3,725 |
| Nonagriculture | 128,084 | 19,009 | 30,677 | 35,486 | 26,991 | 12,477 | 3,448 |
| Wage and salary | 119,019 | 18,694 | 29,146 | 32,750 | 24,565 | 11,066 | 2,800 |
| Self-employment | 8,962 | 299 | 1,513 | 2,710 | 2,403 | 1,399 | 639 |
| Nonpaid family | 103 | 16 | 18 | 26 | 23 | 12 | 9 |
| Agriculture | 3,379 | 602 | 718 | 792 | 596 | 396 | 277 |
| Wage and salary | 2,000 | 519 | 531 | 473 | 275 | 149 | 53 |
| Self-employment | 1,341 | 64 | 179 | 314 | 319 | 245 | 221 |
| Nonpaid family | 38 | 19 | 8 | 5 | 2 | 2 | 3 |
| Share of total employment in group (%) | | | | | | | |
| Nonagriculture | 97.4 | 96.9 | 97.7 | 97.8 | 97.8 | 96.9 | 92.6 |
| Wage and salary | 90.5 | 95.3 | 92.8 | 90.3 | 89.0 | 86.0 | 75.2 |
| Self-employment | 6.8 | 1.5 | 4.8 | 7.5 | 8.7 | 10.9 | 17.2 |
| Nonpaid family | 0.1 | 0.1 | 0.1 | 0.1 | 0.1 | 0.1 | 0.2 |
| Agriculture | 2.6 | 3.1 | 2.3 | 2.2 | 2.2 | 3.1 | 7.4 |
| Wage and salary | 1.5 | 2.6 | 1.7 | 1.3 | 1.0 | 1.2 | 1.4 |
| Self-employment | 1.0 | 0.3 | 0.6 | 0.9 | 1.2 | 1.9 | 5.9 |
| Nonpaid family | 0.0 | 0.1 | 0.0 | 0.0 | 0.0 | 0.0 | 0.1 |

SOURCE: *Employment and Earnings* 46(1), January 1999, Table 15.

insurance and extending coverage to the self-employed compromises the insurance nature of the program.

California is the only state that has a limited form of UI coverage for the self-employed. The California scheme operates on a fully reimbursable basis. This method of coverage has been used widely in the UI program first for governmental agencies and since 1972 for private nonprofit firms. In 1998, reimbursable benefits accounted for 5.7 percent of all payments in the federal–state system, with 42 percent of these reimbursables going to employees separated from nonprofits (U.S. Department of Labor 1998). Reimbursement may not be a particularly effective approach to UI coverage, but it is a method of avoiding the moral hazard issue by not allowing manipulation of the system for one's own benefit (Bassi and McMurrer 1997). Under the reimbursable approach, repayment is due in the calendar quarter following disbursement of benefits. Such a system would amount to short-term loans to self-employed for reintegration back to regular wage and salary employment. Feldstein and Altman (1998) suggested individual UI savings accounts that could be established with pre-tax contributions and might be particularly appropriate for the self-employed.[7]

While the UI system is not currently structured to provide temporary income replacement to the self-employed, in several states UI beneficiaries can start their own business instead of searching for wage and salary employment.[8] While they establish their self-employment activity they can receive self-employment assistance (SEA) payments in lieu of UI weekly benefits. To date, 11 states have enacted conforming state legislation.[9]

The SEA program, like similar programs in nearly 20 other OECD (Organization for Economic Co-operation and Development) nations, has been very small.[10] In 1996, no state had as many as 0.5 percent of its regular UI recipients receiving SEA payments. SEA participants are generally successful at starting up their own business; about two-thirds do so. These participants differ dramatically from other UI claimants: they are older; less likely to be a minority (particularly Hispanic); more likely to be from professional, managerial and technical occupations; have higher educational attainment; and are more likely to be dislocated workers (Vroman 1999).

When the U.S. Department of Labor began the SEA experiments in Massachusetts and Washington in the 1980s, the overrepresentation of older workers was not expected. Participating states imagined that the program would be particularly valuable for minorities and women. It did not turn out that way either in the experiments or the early program operations.[11] Rather, older permanently separated workers have found SEA to be a promising alternative, apparently because of their greater difficulty in finding wage and salary employment and because of skills acquired through years of employment.

## ELIGIBILITY—INITIAL AND CONTINUING

As stated in the introduction to this chapter, eligibility for UI benefits depends on recent earnings experience, the conditions of job separation, and continuing job search activity. Rules regarding recent earnings activity call for checking for sufficient prior labor force attachment in UI-covered work.[12] Essentially these rules ensure that UI premiums have been paid before compensation is granted. Earnings are considered for a base period consisting of four calendar quarters, which are usually the first four of the previous five completed quarters for administrative practicality.[13] Table 1 showed that workers aged 45 and over make up only one-fifth of the unemployed, but they total more than one-third of all the UI beneficiaries. This suggests that a high proportion of unemployed older workers had sufficient prior earnings to qualify for UI benefits.

The conditions of job separation were set to minimize insurance problems of moral hazard by essentially ensuring that the separation was involuntary and primarily due to lack of work, not due to controllable factors such as a quit, a collective bargaining dispute, or discharge for misconduct. Joblessness is compensable in all states for voluntary separations for good cause, which may include 1) sexual harassment, 2) illness, 3) leaving to accept other work, 4) joining the armed forces, or 5) compulsory retirement (Nicholson 1997, p. 103). The last of these is of interest to older workers. As Quinn (1999) pointed out, mandatory retirement was outlawed entirely in 1986. Workers dismissed for reason of age have been illegally discharged and are therefore entitled to UI benefits, with the separating employer liable for benefit charges.

The final requirements for jobless benefits are known as continuing eligibility conditions. These are set to ensure continuing labor force attachment. They are of two types: job search requirements and limits on refusing suitable work. The job search rules are known as "able, available, and actively seeking work" requirements. Administration of these rules is more art than science.[14]

Job search requirements are not imposed on beneficiaries who are still waiting to be recalled by the employer liable for benefit charges. One of the original aims of UI was to prevent the dispersal of the experienced workers for an enterprise. Employers may temporarily furlough workers and promise the employment security agency that the workers will be recalled to their old jobs. Using the BAM data, Table 6 summarizes the recall status of UI beneficiaries by age, as well as the age distribution of various work search requirements. Workers aged 45 and over are more likely to be on recall status during their period of UI benefit receipt, and the proportion awaiting recall appears to increase with age. Direct data on work search requirements suggest that the rate of job attachment among UI beneficiaries increases with age, and, as a result, there is a slight downward trend with age in required work search.

The UI system was designed to operate for full-time, permanently attached members of the labor force. Both initial and continuing UI benefit eligibility issues are raised when part-time employment is considered. As seen in Table 7, relative to those aged 25 to 54, part-time work is popular among both younger and older workers. For those aged 55 and over, more than one-quarter of all workers were employed part-time in 1998. Furthermore, over 30 percent of unemployed job seekers aged 55 and over were seeking part-time employment.

We now consider two questions concerning part-time work and initial UI eligibility, and then two different questions about part-time work and continuing eligibility.

A) If a part-time job is lost and the job seeker is without work, are prior earnings and hours sufficient to qualify for benefits?

The crux of this issue is the current use and measurement of monetary eligibility for UI using a measure of quarterly or annual wages. Such measures have traditionally been used by state UI programs to measure labor force attachment. The Advi-

**Table 6 Return-to-Work Issues for UI Beneficiaries by Age Group (%)**

| Issue | Total | ≤24 yr. | 25–44 yr. | 45–54 yr. | 55–64 yr. | ≥65 yr. |
|---|---|---|---|---|---|---|
| Recall status | | | | | | |
| No recall | 65.0 | 63.2 | 66.1 | 64.8 | 62.5 | 56.3 |
| Definite recall | 9.7 | 6.7 | 9.5 | 10.3 | 11.1 | 13.8 |
| Indefinite recall | 20.4 | 24.8 | 19.4 | 20.5 | 21.0 | 24.4 |
| N/A (partial) | 4.9 | 5.3 | 5.0 | 4.4 | 5.4 | 5.5 |
| Work search requirement | | | | | | |
| No WS requirement | 9.3 | 11.0 | 9.1 | 8.8 | 9.7 | 10.0 |
| WS required | 70.0 | 71.4 | 70.4 | 69.6 | 68.3 | 68.2 |
| WS temporarily suspended | 1.0 | 1.2 | 1.0 | 0.8 | 0.9 | 0.3 |
| Union deferral | 5.0 | 2.2 | 4.6 | 6.4 | 6.2 | 3.0 |
| Job attached | 12.8 | 11.1 | 12.7 | 12.6 | 13.6 | 17.2 |
| Other deferral | 2.0 | 3.2 | 2.1 | 1.8 | 1.3 | 1.2 |
| Registered with a private employment agency | 4.0 | 3.4 | 4.1 | 4.5 | 3.4 | 1.6 |

SOURCE: Unpublished Benefit Accuracy Measurement (BAM) data for calendar year 1998, U.S. Department of Labor.

**Table 7  Employed and Unemployed Full-Time and Part-Time by Age in the United States, 1998**

| Employment status | Total | ≤24 yr. | 25–54 yr. | ≥55 yr. |
|---|---|---|---|---|
| Total employment (000) | 131,463 | 19,611 | 95,259 | 16,597 |
| Full-time | 108,202 | 11,593 | 84,274 | 12,336 |
| Part-time | 23,261 | 8,016 | 10,985 | 4,261 |
| Total unemployment (000) | 6,209 | 2,286 | 3,45 | 464 |
| Seeking full-time work | 4,916 | 1,494 | 3,097 | 325 |
| Seeking part-time work | 1,293 | 792 | 362 | 139 |
| % of total employment | | | | |
| Full-time | 82.3 | 59.1 | 88.5 | 74.3 |
| Part-time | 17.7 | 40.9 | 11.5 | 25.7 |
| % of total unemployment | | | | |
| Seeking full-time work | 79.2 | 65.4 | 89.5 | 70.0 |
| Seeking part-time work | 20.8 | 34.6 | 10.5 | 30.0 |

SOURCE: *Employment and Earnings* 46(1), January 1999, Table 8.

sory Council on Unemployment Compensation (ACUC 1996) addressed this issue for both part-time and low-wage workers. States examine earnings and hours in a base period that consists of four calendar quarters to see if UI claimants can demonstrate labor force attachment. In many states, someone working either half-time at the state average covered wage or full-time at the state minimum wage would not qualify for UI benefits. The Advisory Council on Unemployment Compensation (ACUC 1996, p. 20) recommended that "each state should set its law so that its base period earnings requirements do not exceed 800 times the state's minimum hourly wage, and so that its high quarter earnings requirements do not exceed one-quarter of that amount." The intent of the ACUC was to improve the likelihood that part-time and low-wage workers who work at least 40 percent of the work year would be able to collect UI.

B) If two or more part-time jobs were held and one is lost, is there eligibility for UI benefits?

Eligibility is possible in many states, but the answer depends on the level of prior income and current income. All states will

pay a weekly UI benefit to claimants with sufficient prior earnings if current weekly income drops to a low but positive level.
Most states have a lump sum earnings disregard.  There are 11
states which have both a disregard and a benefit reduction tax
rate on earnings.

In 1994–1995, a field experiment was conducted in Washington
state to evaluate whether liberalizing the benefit reduction formula
would increase work effort.[15]  The control group of 208,818 UI beneficiaries from that experiment provides some insight into earnings by
older workers while in claims status.  For the control group, under
then-existing Washington state law, the earnings disregard was $5 per
week and benefits were reduced by 75 percent of weekly earnings
above $5.  As shown in Table 8, workers 45 years of age and older
tended to have more weeks with a UI payment and more weeks with
reported earnings and a UI payment.  Note that this pattern is most
exaggerated for the oldest group of workers (those 65 years of age and
over), who also had a significantly lower average weekly benefit
amount.

C) Will a beneficiary lose UI eligibility for refusing a new job
   because it is full-time rather than part-time?
      State UI laws would generally disqualify beneficiaries from
   the receipt of benefits.  The beneficiary would lose eligibility for
   refusing suitable work, provided that the available job was in the
   usual occupation and paid a wage close to that paid for recent
   similar work.  Thus, the UI program continues to expect that the
   norm for labor force participation is full-time employment and
   that only job seekers for such jobs should continue to receive UI.

D) Will a beneficiary lose UI eligibility for refusing a new job
   because the hours of work would conflict with required hours on
   a currently held part-time job?
      State rules would suspend UI benefit eligibility for failing to
   satisfy the availability requirement for job search.  Current UI
   eligibility rules are based on the assumption that people leave
   full-time work and seek return to full-time work.

Thus, all part-time workers experience severe difficulty when they
apply to receive benefits.  Even if they succeed in initially receiving

**Table 8  Part-Time Earnings and UI Benefits in Washington State, 1994–95**

| Earnings/benefits | Mean | ≤24 yr. | 25–34 yr. | 35–44 yr. | 45–54 yr. | 55–64 yr. | ≥65 yr. |
|---|---|---|---|---|---|---|---|
| Earnings when on UI claim ($) | 1,218 | 443 | 967 | 1,485 | 1,766 | 1,853 | 1,133 |
| UI amount received ($) | 2,731 | 1,583 | 2,596 | 3,050 | 3,316 | 3,320 | 2,724 |
| UI when earning ($) | 184 | 96 | 167 | 212 | 233 | 230 | 196 |
| UI when not earning ($) | 2,547 | 1,486 | 2,429 | 2,839 | 3,083 | 3,090 | 2,529 |
| % of UI dollars | | | | | | | |
| When earning | 6.7 | 6.1 | 6.4 | 7.0 | 7.0 | 6.9 | 7.2 |
| When not earning | 93.3 | 93.9 | 93.6 | 93.1 | 93.0 | 93.1 | 92.8 |
| Weeks with UI receipt | 13.4 | 10.2 | 13.0 | 14.1 | 15.0 | 15.9 | 17.6 |
| Weeks UI when earning | 1.8 | 1.1 | 1.6 | 1.9 | 2.2 | 2.4 | 2.7 |
| Weeks UI when not earning | 11.7 | 9.1 | 11.4 | 12.2 | 12.8 | 13.5 | 14.9 |
| % of weeks with UI | | | | | | | |
| When earning | 13.1 | 10.9 | 12.1 | 13.7 | 14.6 | 14.9 | 15.3 |
| When not earning | 86.9 | 89.0 | 87.9 | 86.3 | 85.5 | 85.1 | 84.7 |
| Weekly benefit amount ($) | 214 | 154 | 210 | 234 | 239 | 235 | 169 |
| Base period earnings ($) | 17,110 | 10,357 | 15,878 | 19,419 | 20,876 | 20,873 | 13,585 |
| High quarter earnings ($) | 6,237 | 4,005 | 5,833 | 7,006 | 7,496 | 7,427 | 4,917 |
| Sample size | | 32,176 | 69,216 | 58,367 | 33,429 | 13,655 | 1,975 |

benefits, they are in danger of loss of benefits if they are not prepared to accept a full-time job.  Since they participate in part-time work at a greater rate than others, older workers are particularly disadvantaged from receiving UI by these eligibility rules.

## ADEQUACY OF BENEFITS

Unemployment insurance provides temporary partial wage replacement to active job-seekers who are involuntarily out of work. The level of the weekly benefit amount (WBA) is directly related to the prior level of earnings.  Having a wage-related benefit reinforces the concept that unemployment insurance is an earned right, based on contributions required by law to be paid by the worker's employer as "insurance premiums" against the risk of unemployment.  The wage-related benefit is intended neither to improve a prior low standard of living nor to support a sumptuous living standard created by a high income.  Because UI is a social insurance program with the fundamental social aim of preventing wide-spread poverty, all states impose UI maximum benefit rates to spread benefits as widely as is practical.

The adequacy of the WBA in performing the income maintenance function can be gauged by the percentage of lost income which benefits replace (i.e., the replacement rate).  Since the beginning of the federal–state UI program in the United States, there has been general acceptance of the idea that the weekly benefit should replace one-half of the worker's lost weekly wages (O'Leary and Rubin 1997, pp. 166–169). More broadly, adequacy depends on how well UI benefits help to maintain usual levels of household expenditure.  We will briefly examine both of these concepts for older workers.  Naturally, the latter considers all sources of income while out of work, including dissaving, pensions, and other household members.  To understand the role of UI in supporting income security of older workers, it is important to clearly understand the interaction of pensions and UI.  We give special attention to this topic.

As shown in Table 9, the weekly benefit amount (WBA) for UI claimants rises steadily with age up until age 65.  While the WBA averaged $202 in 1998 across all age groups, it averaged only $157 for

**Table 9 Benefit and Earnings Measures for UI Beneficiaries in the United States by Age Group, 1998**

| Measure | Total | ≤24 yr. | 25–4 yr. | 45–54 yr. | 55–64 yr. | ≥65 yr. |
|---|---|---|---|---|---|---|
| Weekly benefit amount (WBA) ($) | 202 | 157 | 201 | 215 | 216 | 174 |
| Normal hourly wage ($) | 12.14 | 8.69 | 11.72 | 13.76 | 13.68 | 11.50 |
| Lowest acceptable hourly wage[a] ($) | 10.28 | 7.38 | 9.96 | 11.48 | 11.55 | 10.17 |
| Reservation wage/normal wage (%) | 88.0 | 90.1 | 88.2 | 86.5 | 88.0 | 91.1 |
| Base period wages (BPW) ($, 000) | 20.0 | 12.1 | 19.2 | 23.8 | 23.4 | 15.7 |
| High quarter wages (HQW) ($, 000) | 6.6 | 4.2 | 6.4 | 7.9 | 7.6 | 5.5 |
| HQW÷BPW (%) | 38.8 | 41.5 | 38.9 | 37.9 | 37.6 | 40.6 |
| Base period weeks worked | 41.1 | 38.8 | 41.2 | 41.2 | 41.5 | 41.1 |
| Average weekly wage[b] (AWW) ($) | 487 | 312 | 466 | 578 | 564 | 382 |
| Replacement ratio, WBA÷AWW (%) | 41.5 | 50.3 | 43.1 | 37.2 | 38.3 | 45.6 |

SOURCE: Unpublished Benefit Accuracy Measurement (BAM) data for calendar year 1998, U.S. Department of Labor.
[a] Also called the "reservation wage."
[b] Average weekly wage is computed as base period wages divided by base period weeks worked.

workers aged 24 or less and reached $216 for workers aged 55 to 64. The average WBA for workers 65 and over was only $174. The decline for these oldest workers most likely is related to the fact that workers aged 65 and over often move into lower-wage bridge employment as they near full retirement age (Quinn 1999). As shown in Table 9, the normal hourly wage for the 65-and-over group is appreciably lower than that for the 55-to-64 age cohort. This dip translates into a dip in the base period wage rate, since base period weeks worked are on a par with those of younger age groups.

A common summary measure of UI benefit adequacy is the wage replacement ratio. While this gross average ratio of mean WBA to mean weekly earnings is a crude measure of adequacy with well documented deficiencies, it is a commonly used measure.[16] By this measure, Table 9 suggests that UI wage replacement tends to decline with age until after age 64. Meeting the UI benefit adequacy standard of one-half wage replacement may actually mean beneficiaries are receiving more than half of potential future wages. This is most likely true for displaced workers, who gain reemployment at average wages 20 percent below prior levels and suffer greater wage reductions if they are forced to find work in a new industry or occupation.[17] Even if not displaced, it may be true for many older workers who voluntarily seek bridge employment after job separation later in their careers. Quinn (1999) points out that bridge employment is usually for fewer hours if in the same occupation and for lower wages if in a different occupation than the career job.

The receipt of pension income had no effect on weekly UI benefit payments until the advent of federal rules applied for special extended benefits that were authorized during the 1961 recession. In response to these recessionary rules, the states experimented with alternative treatment of pension income by UI beneficiaries. Merrill Murray (1967) investigated the question, "Should pensioners receive unemployment compensation?" based on a collection of 12 state studies of practices and effects. He argued that there should be no reduction in UI benefits because of pension receipt, that UI is social insurance based on prior work experience that should be paid with dignity and dispatch to eligible claimants with no means test applied. Furthermore, he asserted that the state studies showed pensioners who were UI beneficiaries were not becoming wealthy from "double dipping." He wrote that "the chief reason that pensioners work or seek work is economic necessity. Pensions are, in most instances, insufficient to provide even a modest but adequate income" (Murray 1967, p. 37).

Nonetheless, 1976 federal UI amendments (Public Law 94-566) required a dollar-for-dollar reduction of UI payments against any governmental or other pension, retirement or retired pay, annuity, or any other similar periodic payment which is based on the previous work of such individual (U.S. Department of Labor 1999, p. 4–19). The rule applies only to payments from plans established by the base period or UI chargeable employer. States may disregard pension income if established by other than a base period employer, except that Social Security and Railroad Retirement benefits reduce UI dollar-for-dollar regardless of when entitlement was established. Also, states are permitted to reduce UI by less than each dollar of pension income if an employee's own contributions helped establish the pension benefit.

Currently among the 53 state UI programs, 38 prorate UI benefit reductions for employee contributions to pension plans, and 28 states disregard benefits received from pensions established outside of the base period. In recent years, states have experienced administrative difficulty when pension accumulations in employer-established defined contribution plans (401k) are rolled over into individual retirement accounts (IRA). Since the IRA may have been previously established with direct personal contributions, the state faces a complex problem determining the proportion of IRA distributions to disregard. The problem is further complicated when it is recognized that 401k type funds may include both employer and employee contributions.

To understand the importance of UI in maintaining living standards for older workers, consider the percentage of aged household units with income from various sources. Table 10 shows that the proportion having income from earnings declines with age. For the three age groups 55–61, 62–64, and 65 plus, the respective percentages with earnings were 80, 63, and 21; conversely for the same three groups, the percentages with retirement income were 27, 63 and 93, respectively. A uniform 61–63 percent had asset income, and a uniform 6 percent had income from public assistance. UI benefits were received by 6 percent of the 55-to-61-year-old group, by 3 percent of those 62–64, and by only 1 percent of those 65 or over. Table 11 considers the same three age groups and shows that the majority of aggregate income

**Table 10  Percent of Aged Units[a] with Money Income from Various Sources by Age in the United States, 1996**

| Sources | 55–61 yr. | 62–64 yr. | ≥65 yr. |
|---|---|---|---|
| Earnings | 80 | 63 | 21 |
| Wages and salaries | 77 | 59 | 18 |
| Self-employment income | 12 | 10 | 4 |
| Retirement benefits | 27 | 63 | 93 |
| Social security (SS) | 13 | 53 | 91 |
| Benefits other than SS | 18 | 33 | 41 |
| Income from assets | 63 | 61 | 63 |
| Veterans benefits | 2 | 4 | 5 |
| UI benefits | 6 | 3 | 1 |
| Workers' compensation | 2 | 2 | 1 |
| Public assistance | 6 | 6 | 6 |
| Personal contributions | 2 | 2 | 1 |
| Number of aged units (in thousands) | 10,821 | 3,951 | 24,553 |

SOURCE:  Social Security Administration (1998), Table I.1.
[a] An aged unit is either a married couple living together or a nonmarried person.

**Table 11  Aggregate Income of Aged Units[a] by Source of Income and Age in the United States, 1996**

| | 55–61 yr. | 62–64 yr. | ≥65 yr. |
|---|---|---|---|
| % of money income from | | | |
| Earnings | 80.3 | 61.6 | 20.0 |
| Retirement benefits | 8.7 | 25.6 | 58.8 |
| Income from assets | 8.2 | 9.7 | 18.0 |
| Public assistance | 0.7 | 0.8 | 0.8 |
| Other | 2.1 | 2.2 | 2.3 |
| Number of aged units (000s) | 10,821 | 3,951 | 24,553 |

SOURCE: Social Security Administration (1998), Table I.1.
[a] An aged unit is either a married couple living together or a nonmarried person.

comes from earnings and retirement benefits, with the latter most important for the oldest group. The bulk of remaining income is provided from assets, less than 1 percent from public assistance and approximately 2 percent from other sources, including personal contributions and UI.

Only a small fraction of older citizens receive UI, and in total it amounts to a small proportion of their aggregate income. An important question regards the role of UI in maintaining living standards for older workers who do receive UI: would their economic position be dramatically altered if UI benefits were not provided? These questions were exhaustively examined by Daniel Hamermesh. The following are some of his main findings which anticipate effects of the 1976 UI reforms (Hamermesh 1980, pp. 83–84).

- Unemployment insurance equalizes the distribution of income among older workers compared to what it would be in the absence of UI benefit payments.

- Dollar-for-dollar reduction of UI for receipt of private or public pension income would reduce UI payments by more than 25 percent among workers aged 59–64 and by over 40 percent among workers aged 61–66. Because older Americans generally have lower incomes, this increases the income gap between older workers and others.

- Within the population of households headed by older workers, instituting the pension offset will increase income equality. This is because the majority of those receiving both pension and UI benefits are in the upper deciles of the income distribution for the older population. These households also have a greater ability to maintain consumption during periods of unemployment.

- Among older UI recipients, about half have access to past savings or borrowing in sufficient amounts such that the pension offset would not cause hardship. Families without the capacity to borrow when the head is unemployed cut back mostly on consumption of luxury goods.

- The availability of UI benefits neither induces older workers to remain in the labor force, nor does it facilitate quicker exit from the labor force. However, UI functions as an income transfer to workers who have made the decision to retire.

The social insurance aspect of UI explains the presence of maximum and minimum weekly benefit amounts (WBAs).[18]   States impose maximum WBAs because the aim is to prevent widespread descent into poverty, not to perfectly smooth consumption for high wage earners.[19]   The minimum WBA is probably of more concern to older workers, many of whom are involved in part-time and low-wage work. WBA minimums are set in part to relieve the administrative burden of processing weekly payments smaller than some reasonable amount, but the minimum WBA often replaces more than half of lost wages because of the social adequacy requirement to provide at least a modicum of cash income.[20]   If UI system changes meant to broaden recipiency by low-wage and part-time workers are considered, investigation of minimum WBA policy is needed.

## DURATION OF BENEFITS

In the absence of severe economic conditions which trigger benefit payments of extended duration, the maximum entitled duration of UI benefits is 26 weeks in all but two states.[21]   Based on the Benefits Accuracy Measurement (BAM) data, the average duration of benefits across all age groups is 15.9 weeks, with the average duration increasing steadily with age (Table 12).[22]   Benefit durations for workers 24 years of age or less averaged 14.7 weeks; the average duration increased with each age group and reached 16.7 weeks for workers 65 years of age or older.[23]

In recent years, some countries experiencing severe labor surplus conditions have added a feature to unemployment compensation which is targeted to older workers and is intended to provide income payments as a bridge to private and/or public pension income receipt.  In 1976, the Netherlands began paying benefits through age 65 to persons exhausting regular entitlement at age 60 or over; in 1981, the U.K. extended the duration and increased the benefit rate for long-term recipients aged 60 and over; in the mid 1980s, Germany increased the maximum duration of benefits from 12 to 32 months for those aged 54 and over (Blackwell, Okba, and Casey 1995, p. 84).  Such early retire-

112

**Table 12  Outcomes Observed for UI beneficiaries in the Benefits Accuracy Measurement Audit Data**

| Outcome | Total | ≤24 yr. | 25–44 yr. | 45–54 yr. | 55–64 yr. | ≥65 yr. |
|---|---|---|---|---|---|---|
| Weekly benefit amount ($) | 202 | 157 | 201 | 215 | 216 | 174 |
| Duration of benefits (weeks)[a] | 15.9 | 14.7 | 15.7 | 16.3 | 16.6 | 16.7 |
| Entitlement based on earnings in more than one state[b] (%) | 2.9 | 4.0 | 2.9 | 3.1 | 2.2 | 1.2 |
| Outcomes during the key week: | | | | | | |
| Earnings reported ($) | 12.2 | 11.0 | 12.6 | 12.0 | 11.5 | 10.4 |
| Benefit reduced because of earnings ($) | 10.8 | 7.6 | 11.4 | 11.1 | 10.4 | 6.4 |
| Other income reported ($) | 1.6 | 0.4 | 0.8 | 0.8 | 4.4 | 18.6 |
| Benefit reduced because of other income ($) | 1.4 | 0.4 | 0.8 | 0.8 | 3.8 | 14.3 |

SOURCE: Unpublished Benefit Accuracy Measurement (BAM) data for calendar year 1998, U.S. Department of Labor.
[a] The duration of benefits is measured from the Benefit Year Beginning (BYB) date to the key week. The *key week* is the week in which a payment was sampled for the BAM data.
[b] Called a combined wage claim.

ment uses of unemployment compensation also became a popular tool for supporting the transition to a competitive labor market in the formerly planned economies of eastern and central Europe. For example, in Hungary, where full public pension payments may begin at age 60 for men and 55 for women, early retirement unemployment compensation payments were offered at even younger ages beginning in 1991.[24] Within the past 15 years, additional countries have relaxed work search rules for older workers, thereby permitting longer benefit durations.[25]

Given the tight labor market conditions in the United States at the beginning of the twenty-first century, it is unlikely that UI program features intended to remove workers from the labor force will be considered in the near future. The pattern of full- and part-time work by older UI beneficiaries suggests a desire for prolonged labor force attachment and greater flexibility in choosing employment and income sources. In addition to recognizing the importance of work transitions between career and bridge jobs and from bridge jobs to full retirement, switches between bridge jobs should be accommodated. Flexibility in UI benefit duration, wage replacement, initial entitlement, and continuing entitlement are all elements in shaping a decision context to encourage continued labor market involvement by older workers.

## WORK INCENTIVES

In providing partial wage replacement, the UI system has the potential of prolonging spells of unemployment. Several economists following Feldstein (1974) have reported evidence suggesting that UI lengthens jobless spells beyond what would occur in the absence of UI compensation. Decker (1997) summarizes estimates of how the entitled duration of benefits and the rate of wage replacement affect the length of joblessness.[26] None of the previous research has reported how these effects of UI vary by age.

Two opposite solutions have been tried to solve this principal-agent work-incentive problem. Traditional policy has been to monitor work search, while positive reemployment incentives were evaluated through field experiments in the 1980s.

To ensure continuing labor force attachment by beneficiaries and to guard against avoidable joblessness, work search requirements have been part of continuing eligibility rules since the inception of UI. In terms of carrot-and-stick incentives, work search rules represent the stick. The stringency and enforcement of such rules has varied greatly across the states, and the majority of benefit overpayment errors have been traced to improper application of work search rules.[27]

Work search rules of varying stringency were evaluated in a field experiment conducted in Tacoma, Washington, in 1986–1987. Johnson and Klepinger (1991, 1994) found that eliminating the work test would greatly lengthen the duration of UI benefit receipt. They also found that requiring attendance at a job search workshop four weeks after the claim and an in-person eligibility review interview halfway through the entitled duration of benefits would measurably reduce UI benefit receipt. A subgroup analysis of impacts by age found that those under 25 and those 55 and over behaved similarly to each other and somewhat differently from other age groups. Both groups increased UI receipt by the most of all age groups when the work search test was relaxed (about 3.3 weeks more for both groups), and both reduced UI receipt by the least of all age groups when the work test was strengthened (about –0.4 weeks for both groups). The work test appears to be particularly effective in changing the work search behavior of older workers.

In the 1980s, inadequate forward financing of UI benefits, combined with political efforts to restrain tax increases, led to the exploration of new means for dealing with work disincentive problems while retaining the income maintenance function of UI. A variety of new initiatives were tested as field experiments, with the UI reemployment bonus gaining considerable attention.

Decker and O'Leary (1992, 1995) examined the effect of offering cash bonus payments to UI beneficiaries who return to work quickly in Pennsylvania and Washington. Across the two experiments, the average bonus offer of about 4 weeks of benefits for return to work within about 10 weeks shortened UI benefit receipt by just under half a week.

A subgroup analysis by age for the Pennsylvania experiment suggested that the bonus impact decreased with age and had virtually no impact on those over age 55; the Washington results suggested a generally opposite pattern, with older beneficiaries responding more strongly.[28]  However, in Washington, workers aged over 45 had an appreciably smaller response to the biggest bonus offer, which had the largest overall effects.  In a pooled analysis of Pennsylvania and Washington data, bonus impacts were virtually identical across the three age groups: under 35, 35 to 54, and 55 plus.[29]  Age is neither a legal nor an effective characteristic on which to target reemployment bonus offers; however, recent research suggests that bonus offers targeted to those most likely to exhaust benefits may be more cost-effective.[30]

## FINANCING  BENEFITS AND POTENTIAL NEW LEGISLATION

UI is social insurance; it is neither private insurance nor social welfare.[31]  Social insurance embodies incentive aspects found in private insurance contracts and eligibility and benefit features required by considerations of social adequacy.  Key features which distinguish UI as insurance are related to the financing provisions.  UI benefits are financed by employers through experience-rated payroll taxes.[32]  Experience rating means that employer UI tax rates increase with their experience in laying off workers who subsequently draw UI benefits.[33]

When the federal–state UI system was established by the Social Security Act of 1935, the experience rating of employer UI taxes greatly helped make the program acceptable to employers.  It was reasoned that allocating benefit costs to businesses responsible for unemployment benefit claims would make UI consistent with the free market system.  The costs of the goods and services produced by insured workers would thus reflect the costs of any UI benefits paid to them.

Experience rating results in employer involvement in initial eligibility determination and reduces the risk of moral hazard.  The United States is the only nation in the world which finances unemployment compensation benefits with experience-rated taxes.[34]  It is the main cause of business–labor involvement in the system, but experience rating ensures that UI will not become a dole on a par with social assistance.  No stigma attaches to the receipt of UI, "which provides compensation for wage loss as a matter of right with dignity and dispatch."[35]

Limitations of state UI tax systems mean that benefits are not always completely charged back to prior employers. Tannenwald and O'Leary (1997) identified a number of factors which interrupt the operation of perfect experience rating: maximum and minimum tax rates, limits on the taxable payroll, time lags, and exclusions.[36] Among the exclusions are state contributions to extended benefits, benefits paid to former employees of bankrupt firms, and dependents allowances. Benefit payments which are not charged back to prior employers are said to be socialized. They are paid for by tax features that are usually not experience-rated, but instead are collected as a fixed percentage of the taxable payrolls at UI covered employers.

For 65 years, the experience-rated UI tax system has operated to finance hundreds of billions of dollars in UI benefits. Except for occasional and temporary loans to the states, the basic system has operated independent of general tax revenues. The federal/state UI system currently holds in excess of $50 billion in the Unemployment Trust Fund (UTF) and has annual revenues and benefit payments of about $20 billion (U.S. Department of Labor 1999). Since the Unified Budget Act (UBA) of 1969, money held in the UTF is accounted for in the annual budget of the United States government (West and Hildebrand 1997, p. 575). From the time of UBA enactment through 1997, the federal government experienced annual budget deficits; in these years, the UTF surplus was hoarded to improve federal unified budget reports. The current federal government budget surplus and projections for future surplus budgets have raised policy interest in expanded uses of UTF money.

A particular policy concern of the Clinton administration has been the decline in the ratio of the insured to the total unemployment rate (IUR/TUR), that is, the decline in the recipiency ratio. This decline threatens both the aggregate adequacy of income replacement and the built-in stabilizer function of the UI benefit system for the macro-economy.

We have recognized that displaced older workers have difficulty gaining reemployment at wages which match their career jobs and that voluntary transition from career jobs is often done gradually by a shift to part-time work on the career job, or to a bridge job which usually pays substantially less per hour of work. Late in life, workers make transitions from career jobs to bridge jobs, between bridge jobs, sometimes back to career jobs, and eventually to full retirement with income from pensions and assets. What improvements in the federal/state UI system would best facilitate these transitions, and what would be their financing implications?

Changes in UI eligibility rules to accommodate workers in low-wage labor markets and workers with preferences for part-time work could be financed within the current experience rating framework.[37] As recommended by the ACUC (1996), permitting initial eligibility for those working at least 800 hours in the base period, regardless of base period wages, would benefit the low-wage group. Changing continuing eligibility requirements concerning the refusal of suitable work to include not only customary wage and occupation, but also customary hours per week, is a practical solution. These expansions would impose UI tax cost increases on employers in low-wage industries such as retail and hospitality, who customarily pay UI taxes at the minimum rate. However, such increases would be shared in part by employees through moderation in wage increases, and UI tax subsidies flowing from these industries to high-wage, high-layoff industries such as construction and manufacturing would diminish.

Some other UI-related policy accommodations to older workers, which may be tempting given federal budget surplus projections and the aim of broadening UI recipiency, would most certainly be financed from socialized rather than experience-rated taxes. Dependents' allowances are financed by socialized taxes because they stretch the social insurance standard, which sets a weekly maximum on partial income replacement because of the aim to prevent a desent into poverty. While not relevant to older workers, in the spring of 1999, President Clinton announced his desire to use the UI system to provide "Birth and Adoption Unemployment Compensation." Such a program would most certainly be financed by socialized UI taxes.[38] A similar financing scheme would be most natural for extensions of UI more relevant to older workers, such as paying health insurance premiums for the unemployed or providing early retirement unemployment compensation payments to support transition to pension income.[39]

## INTERACTION WITH OTHER
## EMPLOYMENT PROGRAMS

While discussing the adequacy of UI for older workers, we described the interaction between UI and Social Security retirement payments: federal law requires that UI benefits be reduced by one dollar for each dollar of Social Security benefits received. In this section of the chapter, we examine UI interactions with other employment programs which may be of relevance for older workers.

The strongest linkage between UI and Employment Service (ES) programs is provided through the work test for continuing UI eligibility. Many state UI laws require registration with and active use of ES services to maintain established UI benefit entitlement. For a variety of reasons, including the fact that UI payment errors have often been due to improper application of statutory work search rules, many states have relaxed their work test.[40] These changes have weakened the link between UI and ES.

The UI-ES linkage was renewed and strengthened in 1993 by federal legislation creating the Worker Profiling and Reemployment Services (WPRS) system. The legislation required states to establish procedures for early identification of UI beneficiaries most likely to exhaust their UI benefit entitlement and to refer these persons quickly to special reemployment services. State UI and ES agencies were identified as key partners in the WPRS, and Job Training Partnership Act (JTPA) service delivery agencies were encouraged to cooperate and provide reemployment services, particularly for their Economic Dislocation and Worker Adjustment Assistance (EDWAA) Act clients.

Most states choose to implement the WPRS system using a statistical profiling model. The U.S. Department of Labor developed a prototype statistical model and provided training to the states in how to adapt principles of the prototype for their own uses. To examine the model's sensitivity, the preliminary prototype prepared by the U.S. Department of Labor included an age variable to help predict the likelihood of UI benefit exhaustion. This variable and certain others, however, are prohibited by federal civil rights legislation and were excluded from the final model recommended by the Department of Labor. Nonetheless, an analysis was conducted to determine the impact of dropping the prohibited variables. In the case of age, it was found that even though age was a significant variable, the effect of the age variable was largely accounted for by the variable for tenure on the prior job, which was adopted in the final model (Wandner 1998).

Table 13 presents predicted and actual UI benefit exhaustion rates by age group, computed on a sample of beneficiaries drawn in Michigan before the WPRS was implemented. This sample was used to estimate the Michigan WPRS profiling model (Eberts and O'Leary 1996). Because of the civil rights prohibition, age was not included in the logit models estimated to predict UI benefit exhaustion in Michigan. The table shows that the actual UI exhaustion rate for beneficiaries aged 65 and over is appreciably higher than for other age groups and that the Michigan model predicts a modestly higher exhaustion rate for that group. However, the actual exhaustion rate for all the age groups less than 65 is nearly uniform, ranging between 21 and 25 percent. The Michigan profiling model was estimated using nonlinear methods and predicts the likelihood of exhaustion to increase exponentially with age. This pattern was most likely captured by the tenure variable. The model indirectly identifies those permanently separated from their employer and industry, because they are likely to be long-term UI beneficiaries. Research by Chan and Stevens (1999) and others suggests that unemployed older workers have a greater risk of prolonged jobless spells. Data are not available on the age distribution of those referred to WPRS job search workshops, but it is likely to include older workers in high proportion to their numbers in UI benefit receipt. It should be mentioned that both program staff and participants have responded very positively to the special services given those profiled and referred by the WPRS system (Dickinson, Decker, and Kreutzer 1999).

In addition to the WPRS system, several other global changes are now altering the way that UI interacts with other employment programs and the way that clients interact with UI. The local administration of UI is rapidly changing from conducting in-person interviews to taking claims by telephone. The new telephone systems are being used for the filing of both new initial claims and continuing claims. Less and less do unemployed workers wait in line at a UI claims center. Unless older workers are either called in to attend a job search workshop because of the WPRS or called to attend an eligibility review interview to go over their job search efforts and plans, they may never

**Table 13 Predicted and Actual UI Benefit Exhaustion Rates by Age in Michigan, 1994**

| Measure | ≤24 yr. | 25–34 yr. | 35–44 yr. | 45–54 yr. | 55–64 yr. | ≥65 yr. |
|---|---|---|---|---|---|---|
| Predicted UI exhaustion rate | 0.187 | 0.208 | 0.217 | 0.231 | 0.231 | 0.273 |
| Actual UI exhaustion rate | 0.244 | 0.226 | 0.212 | 0.225 | 0.250 | 0.370 |
| Sample size | 21,855 | 62,687 | 59,808 | 35,947 | 17,104 | 3,068 |

SOURCE: For the control group used to develop the Michigan Worker Profiling and Reemployment Services model (Eberts and O'Leary 1996).

enter a physical location for UI services. By 1998, half or more of continued claims in 35 states were taken by telephone (24 states took more than three-quarters of these claims by telephone). Furthermore, 11 states took about half or more of their initial claims by telephone.[41] This move to telephone claims is now accelerating.

Sweeping change in the public reemployment services landscape is coming soon because of requirements of the Workforce Investment Act (WIA) of 1998. This law requires that public one-stop career centers be established in local areas to deliver a coordinated package of reemployment services including UI, ES, skill retraining, and referral to other employment programs. While UI is a required partner at one-stop career centers, the trend toward telephone claims suggests that it may be present simply as a telephone on the wall over which UI claims can be made.

By July 2000, when WIA becomes operational nationally, an older worker reaching a one-stop career center in most areas will find a different mix of training and employment services than has been offered under JTPA. Under WIA, there is a more structured approach to the provision of services. It is expected that all individuals entering a one-stop career center will first be offered core services that will consist of self-service and modest staff-assisted services. Only if these core services do not suffice will the individual be offered intensive services which will involve greater staff assistance. Skill training will be offered only after other avenues to employment have been exhausted. It is expected that training will be provided to a smaller proportion of clients than under JTPA.

Under JTPA, most of the services received by older workers were from two special programs, the Senior Community Service Employment Program and Services for Older Workers (JTPA Title II, Section 204(D)). Older workers usually did not participate in regular JTPA programs for disadvantaged adults. Older workers were greatly under represented in their receipt of service under the program for disadvantaged adults (Title IIA). Workers 45 years of age and over amounted to about 45 percent of the eligible population in program year 1995, but those 45 and over received only 13 percent of services. Notably, those aged 55 and over received only 2 percent. For the dislocated worker program (Title III), workers 45 years of age and over were proportionally represented, being about one-third of both the eligible and service receiving populations (Poulos and Nightengale 1997).

The aim of new one-stop career centers under the Workforce Investment Act (WIA) is to attempt to serve all workers who seek assistance. No single group is targeted for services under WIA; instead, a wide variety of services can be accessed by all workers.

Under the JTPA program, services for older workers were specified under Section 204(D), and section 202(c)(1)(D) required that 5 percent of the federal allocation to states had to be used for these older worker services. No similar provision exists under the WIA to differentiate older workers from other adults. On the other hand, in the establishment of the one-stop delivery system under WIA, there are a number of required partners and programs. Some activities provided by the Older Americans Act of 1965 are part of the required partnerships.[42] The result is that older workers will have certain activities available under WIA, but these activities will not have special funding. Older workers will be treated differently, but they will be subject to the same funding constraints and have the same availability of services as any other adult worker when entering a one-stop career center.[43]

There is a separate employment program funded by the federal government for older workers. The Senior Community Service Program provides part-time employment, at least 20 hours per week, in community service activities for older workers. This program is funded by an annual federal appropriation. Strong congressional support has resulted in a stable funding level for this program in recent years. Congress appropriated $440.2 million for the program in the 1998 and 1999 fiscal year budgets and has appropriated the same amount for the year 2000, which will be the first year of full operation under WIA.

## TOPICS FOR FUTURE POLICY ANALYSIS AND RESEARCH

In studying economic security for older workers, considerable attention should be given to unemployment insurance (UI) as a source of income security and as a potential influence on work incentives.

Current policy reviews, such as the one by the Committee for Economic Development (1999), which have explored how the private sector can make better use of older workers in the labor force, consider the impact of governmental policy with respect to Social Security and Medicare on older workers, but they do not address the important role of UI.

Previous policy analysis and research which does examine UI and older workers has tended to be based on an earlier and more simplistic model. It was a model of a single transition near the end of the working life: a one-step move from full-time work in a career job to full retirement. That model is rapidly being replaced by one involving a chain of employment transitions: from career job to bridge job, between bridge jobs, perhaps back from a bridge job to a career job, and finally a gradual movement into full retirement.

New research should address how UI influences the choice and timing of the wide variety of labor market transitions which happen in the second half of the working life. Many older workers are already electing to work rather than retire and to remain in their current communities rather than to move to retirement communities. This trend is likely to continue strongly in the future. In particular, the role of part-time work and self-employment are likely to be very important in the future. A recent survey sponsored by the American Association of Retired Persons (AARP) found that four-fifths of all workers born between 1946 and 1964, the "baby boomers," intend to continue working after retirement: 58 percent in part-time employment; 5 percent in full-time employment "doing something different"; and 17 percent in self-employment (Roper Starch 1999).

Demographic patterns in United States labor markets at the start of the twenty-first century suggest that it would be wise to investigate and develop policies to encourage the continued labor market participation of older workers. Employer groups are increasingly concerned about maintaining labor market participation of older workers, given the smaller cohorts that will follow. They want the supply of skilled labor that older workers embody available for productive use. The new study by the Committee on Economic Development (1999), entitled "New Opportunities for Older Workers," is really about what employers and, to a lesser extent, government can do to retain and hire older workers. This study seems to focus more on the basic decision to work or not, rather than the ongoing decisions that older workers continually need to make about what type of employment to pursue and what to do if a given job ends. More attention needs to be paid to the impact of UI as a source of income and as an influence on work incentives for older workers.

Changes in UI rules concerning initial eligibility, continuing eligibility, wage replacement, and partial benefits should all be examined to evaluate effects on the likely employment patterns of older workers. Particular attention should be given to UI features affecting the choice of self-employment, part-time work, seasonal work, and agricultural jobs.

The financing consequences of possible UI program changes should also be estimated, as should the macroeconomic impact of broadening recipiency. UI program features that would promote flexible and extended labor force participation by older workers should also enrich the employment choice environment for other workers. Therefore, it would be useful to examine the impact of such program changes on UI as a built in stabilizer of aggregate expenditure.

The UI program has an impact on whether workers choose to work or to enjoy leisure. The potential impact of policy change in the areas outlined would probably have a greater impact on the behavior of older workers than on that of younger workers, who are strongly attached to the labor force. As our society tries to retain older workers in the labor force, we need to look closely at the current and potential role of UI.

## Notes

The opinions expressed are our own and do not necessarily reflect the position of either the W.E. Upjohn Institute for Employment Research or the U.S. Department of Labor. We thank Erich Larisch, Joe Quinn, Burman Skrable, Tom Stengle, Tom West, and Steve Woodbury for useful contributions. Any errors are our responsibility.

1. Burtless (1999) summarizes retirement trends and the economic research focusing on retirement incentives.
2. Methods for collection and use of the Benefits Accuracy Measurement (BAM) data is given in U.S. Department of Labor (1996). BAM samples are drawn weekly in the 50 states, Puerto Rico and the District of Columbia. Procedures are designed to ensure that each sample is representative of paid claims in the state that week.

3. Policy definitions are given in the Economic Dislocation and Worker Adjustment Assistance (EDWAA) Act of 1988. These definitions largely carried over to the Workforce Investment Act (WIA) of 1998. An overview of research applications of this concept are given in Leigh (1990).

4. Hipple's (1999a) data is from the Displaced Worker survey, which is conducted every two years by the Bureau of Labor Statistics to provide information on the number and characteristics of persons who have been displaced from their jobs over the past three years. Based on a supplement to the February 1998 Current Population Survey, the latest study is for the period 1995–1996. It reveals that between 1995 and 1996, 2.2 million workers aged 20 years or older lost jobs they had held for three or more years due to the plant or company closing or moving; positions or shifts being abolished; or the employer not having enough work for them to do. The data show that during the 1990s there was a steady decline in the displacement rate of long-term workers from 3.9 percent in 1991–1992, to 3.3 percent in 1993–1994, to 2.9 percent in 1995–1996.

5. The BAM data are used to assess the accuracy of UI benefit payments by selecting key weeks of benefit payments. Beneficiaries who have long durations of UI benefit receipt have a higher probability of being selected for the weekly BAM samples.

6. The problem of moral hazard is present when the insured can affect the chance of experiencing the unfavorable outcome insured against, without being observed by the insurer. In unemployment insurance, moral hazard is present if a worker can affect the chance of being unemployed while not being detected by the state unemployment agency. The state agency will disqualify UI beneficiaries when a job separation or continuing joblessness is determined to be avoidable.

7. For older workers, an appealing feature of Feldstein and Altman's (1998) proposal is that borrowing from the government takes place when accounts are exhausted, and "negative account balances are forgiven at retirement age."

8. A temporary UI self-employment program was established in 1993 as part of the North American Free Trade Act (NAFTA). Federal legislation in 1998 permanently gave states the option to provide self-employment assistance with UI trust fund money.

9. The 11 states are California, Connecticut, Delaware, Maine, Maryland, Minnesota, New Jersey, New York, Oregon, Pennsylvania, and Rhode Island. Among these, Connecticut, Minnesota, and Rhode Island have not yet implemented their programs.

10. Wandner (1992) provided an overview of the international experience. He also summarized the two U.S. experiments which predated the NAFTA authorizing legislation.

11. About the experiments, see Benus, Wood, and Grover (1994); about the programs, see Vroman (1999).

12. In many states there is also a requirement that a certain number of hours must have been worked in the reference period called the *base year*.

13. Following a 1994 decision by the U.S. Court of Appeals in the Seventh Circuit case of Pennington versus Didrickson, many states have implemented alternate benefit year (ABY) rules which consider income and hours in the four most recent calendar quarters if eligibility is not established using the standard rule. The Advisory Council on Unemployment Compensation (ACUC 1996, p. 19) endorsed general adoption of ABY rules.

14. Anderson (1997) examined state rules and practices in administering continuing UI eligibility.

15. O'Leary (1997) found that liberalizing the benefit reduction formula increased earnings reported to the employment security department but did not increase work effort.

16. O'Leary (1998, pp. 66–71) discussed the deficiencies of such aggregate average measures.

17. See the estimates of Jacobson, LaLonde, and Sullivan (1993).

18. A thorough discussion of these matters is provided by O'Leary and Rubin (1997, pp. 194–199).

19. The Advisory Council on Unemployment Compensation (ACUC 1996) recommended a federal standard requiring the maximum weekly benefit amount to equal two-thirds of the statewide average weekly wage, so as to allow a majority of covered workers to receive at least 50 percent wage replacement.

20. A 1962 Department of Labor recommendation urged that the minimum "be related to the weekly wages of the lowest wage group in the state for which the unemployment insurance program is considered appropriate" (U.S. Department of Labor 1962).

21. Both Massachusetts and Washington offer regular benefit durations as long as 30 weeks. Woodbury and Rubin (1997) provided an exhaustive review and critique of UI extended benefit programs.

22. The Benefit Accuracy Measurement (BAM) data measures the duration of benefits from the beginning date of a worker's benefit year—the date at which they established their eligibility for benefits—until the date when that worker's claim was investigated (the *key week*).

23. These duration estimates underestimate claimant duration because the data is censored. The claimant's benefit history is measured up until the BAM key week is selected but not after.

24. In Hungary, the unemployment compensation financing system partially subsidized early retirement payments for surplus workers in struggling enterprises and fully paid such benefits when the enterprise was bankrupt (O'Leary 1995, p. 732).

25. Australia in 1987, Belgium in 1985, and New Zealand in 1992 either eliminated or greatly relaxed the work search requirement for older unemployment compensation beneficiaries (Blackwell, Okba, and Casey 1995, p. 85).

26. Lengthening the entitled duration of benefits by one week is estimated to lengthen joblessness by between 0.1 and 0.5 weeks, while a 10 percent increase in the wage replacement rate is estimated to increase the joblessness by between 0.3 and 1.5 weeks.

27. Burgess and Kingston (1987, p. 235) cited "difficulty in monitoring claimant compliance with weekly eligibility criteria" as a prime cause for UI payment errors associated with the work test.

28. Impact analyses by age for the Pennsylvania experiment are reported by Corson et al. (1992, p. 111), while those for Washington are reported by Spiegelman, O'Leary, and Kline (1992, p. 127).

29. Decker and O'Leary (1992, p. 54) reported impact estimates by age group for a pooled Pennsylvania and Washington sample while controlling for the interaction of age with other factors.

30. Recent research suggests that when a low bonus amount with a long benefit duration is targeted to those most likely to exhaust benefits (displaced workers), it appears to be cost-effective (O'Leary, Decker, and Wandner 1998).

31. These arguments are developed more completely by Blaustein, O'Leary, and Wandner (1997, pp. 11–17).

32. Employees make small direct contributions in Alaska, New Jersey, and Pennsylvania, but it has been estimated by Anderson and Meyer (1995) that employer UI taxes are partly paid by workers who contribute to the system through accepting lower wages.

33. Principles of experience rating UI taxes are explained in Tannenwald and O'Leary (1997). Estimates of the degree of experience rating among states are provided by Tannenwald, O'Leary, and Huang (1999).

34. The Netherlands and Poland have considered adopting experience rating of unemployment compensation taxes. Countries outside of the United States often levy employer and employee contributions with rates set on a socialized basis to cover recent benefit payments. Unemployment compensation payments often are subsidized by central government general revenues; occasionally this is the only source of financing.

35. Blaustein (1993), p. 47, from a statement of UI objectives issued by the U.S. Department of Labor, Bureau of Employment Security, in 1955.

36. For example, when an employer's UI tax rate is at the maximum of the range, additional UI benefit charges do not change the tax rate on wages. Tannenwald and O'Leary (1997) explained that, in such circumstances, subsidies flow from other employers.

37. These and related issues are discussed in a broader context by O'Leary and Wandner (1997, pp. 714–716). Other policies to increase UI recipiency, such as broadening coverage to seasonal workers and employees of small farms, are to a lesser degree important to older workers, but could also be financed within the experience rating framework.

38. The proposed rule for Birth and Adoption Unemployment Compensation allows states to determine whether the benefits would be experience-rated or socialized (*Federal Register* 64, no. 232, pp. 67971–67979). Pear (1999) described the political dispute over President Clinton's plan to pay cash benefits to those on parental leave from the unemployment trust fund.

39. In 1995, President Clinton "mentioned finding some way to help workers who lose their jobs keep their health insurance while they look for work. Under federal law they can continue their policy for a year and a half by paying 102 percent of the combined employer-employee premium, but many cannot afford to do so. Clinton favors some form of subsidy to help them" (Rich 1995). On December 17, 1999, the Ticket to Work and Work Incentive Improvement Act (Public Law 106-170) was enacted; it allows the extension of Medicare for those on Social Security Disability Insurance and Medicaid for those on Social Security Income after recipients earnings rise above a given level.
40. Burgess and Kingston (1987) identify the work test as a main source of UI overpayments, citing the complexity of the ES-UI monitoring as part of the problem.
41. Based on state UI Benefits Accuracy Measurement (BAM) data for 1998.
42. WIA section 121(b)(1)(B)(vi).
43. A training and technical assistance guide has been developed for providing special services for older workers under the Workforce Investment Act.

# References

ACUC (Advisory Council on Unemployment Compensation). 1996. *Collected Findings and Recommendations: 1994–1996*. Washington, D.C.: U.S. Department of Labor.

Anderson, Patricia M. 1997. "Continuing Eligibility: Current Labor Market Attachment." In *Unemployment Insurance in the United States: Analysis of Policy Issues*, Christopher J. O'Leary and Stephen A. Wandner, eds. Kalamazoo, Michigan: W.E. Upjohn Institute for Employment Research, pp. 125–161.

Anderson, Patricia M., and Bruce D. Meyer. 1995. "The Incidence of the Unemployment Insurance Payroll Tax." In *Advisory Council on Unemployment Compensation: Background Papers, Volume II*. Washington, D.C.: U.S. Department of Labor, pp. P-1 to P-25, July.

Bassi, Laurie, and Daniel P. McMurrer. 1997. "Coverage and Recipiency." In *Unemployment Insurance in the United States: Analysis of Policy Issues*, Christopher J. O'Leary and Stephen A. Wandner, eds. Kalamazoo, Michigan: W.E. Upjohn Institute for Employment Research, pp. 51–89.

Benus, Jacob, Michelle L. Wood, and Neelima Grover. 1994. "Self-Employment as a Reemployment Option: Demonstration Results and National Legislation." Unemployment Insurance Occasional Paper 94-3, U.S. Department of Labor, Employment and Training Administration.

Blackwell, John, Mahrez Okba, and Bernard Casey. 1995. *The Transition from Work to Retirement*. Paris: Organization for Economic Co-operation and Development.

Blank, Rebecca, and David Card. 1991. "Recent Trends in Insured and Uninsured Unemployment: Is There an Explanation?" *Quarterly Journal of Economics* 106(4): 1157–1189.

Blaustein, Saul J. 1993. *Unemployment Insurance in the United States: The First Half Century*. Kalamazoo, Michigan: W.E. Upjohn Institute for Employment Research.

Blaustein, Saul J., Christopher J. O'Leary, and Stephen A. Wandner. 1997. "Policy Issues: An Overview." In *Unemployment Insurance in the United States: Analysis of Policy Issues*, Christopher J. O'Leary and Stephen A. Wandner, eds. Kalamazoo, Michigan: W.E. Upjohn Institute for Employment Research, pp. 1–49.

Burgess, Paul L., and Jerry L. Kingston. 1987. *An Incentives Approach to Improving the Unemployment Compensation System*. Kalamazoo, Michigan: W.E. Upjohn Institute for Employment Research.

Burtless, Gary. 1999. "An Economic View of Retirement." In *Behavioral Dimensions of Retirement Economics*, Henry J. Aaron, ed. Washington, D.C.: Brookings Institution Press and Russell Sage Foundation.

_____. 1983. "Why is Insured Unemployment So Low?" Brookings Papers on Economic Activity no. 1: 225–253.

Chan, Sewin, and Ann Huff Stevens. 1999. "Job Loss and Retirement Behavior of Older Men." Working paper no. 6920, National Bureau of Economic Research, Cambridge, Massachusetts.

Committee for Economic Development. 1999. *New Opportunities for Older Workers*. Washington, D.C.: Committee for Economic Development.

Corson, Walter, and Walter Nicholson. 1988. "An Examination of Declining UI Claims during the 1980s." Unemployment Insurance Occasional Paper 88-3, Unemployment Insurance Service, Employment and Training Administration, U.S. Department of Labor, Washington, D.C.

Corson, Walter, Paul Decker, Shari Dunstan, and Stuart Kerachsky. 1992. "Pennsylvania Reemployment Bonus Demonstration: Final Report." Unemployment Insurance Occasional Paper 92-1, U.S. Department of Labor, Employment and Training Administration.

Decker, Paul T. 1997. "Work Incentives and Disincentives." In *Unemployment Insurance in the United States: Analysis of Policy Issues*, Christopher J. O'Leary and Stephen A. Wandner, eds. Kalamazoo, Michigan: W.E. Upjohn Institute for Employment Research, pp. 285–320.

Decker, Paul T., and Christopher J. O'Leary. 1995. "Evaluating Pooled Evidence from the Reemployment Bonus Experiments." *Journal of Human Resources* 30(3): 534–550.

_____. 1992. "An Analysis of Pooled Evidence from the Pennsylvania and Washington Reemployment Bonus Demonstrations." Unemployment Insurance Occasional Paper 92-7, Employment and Training Administration, U.S. Department of Labor, Washington, D.C..

Dickinson, Katherine P., Paul T. Decker, and Suzanne D. Kreutzer. 1999. *Evaluation of Worker Profiling and Reemployment Services Systems: Summary of Findings.* Menlo Park, California: Social Policy Research Associates.

Eberts, Randall W., and Christopher J. O'Leary. 1996. "Design of the Worker Profiling and Reemployment Services System and Evaluation in Michigan." Working paper no. 95-41, W.E. Upjohn Institute for Employment Research, Kalamazoo, Michigan.

Farber, Henry. 1997. "The Changing Face of Job Loss in the United States, 1981-1995." *Brookings Papers on Economic Activity: Microeconomics*, pp. 55-128.

Feldstein, Martin, and Daniel Altman. 1998. "Unemployment Insurance Savings Accounts." Working paper no. 6860, National Bureau of Economic Research, Cambridge, Massachusetts.

Feldstein, Martin S. 1974. "Unemployment Compensation: Adverse Incentives and Distributional Anomalies." *National Tax Journal* 27: 231–44.

Hamermesh, Daniel S. 1980. *Unemployment Insurance and the Older American.* Kalamazoo, Michigan: W.E. Upjohn Institute for Employment Research.

Jacobs, Eva E., ed. 1999. *Handbook of U.S. Labor Statistics.* Third edition. Lanham, Maryland: Bernan Press.

Hipple, Steven. 1999a. "Worker Displacement in the Mid-1990s." *Monthly Labor Review* 122(7): 15–32.

_____. 1999b. Unpublished tables from the Bureau of Labor Statistics' 1995–1996 Displaced Worker Survey.

Jacobson, Louis S., Robert J. LaLonde, and Daniel G. Sullivan. 1993. "Earnings Losses of Displaced Workers." *American Economic Review* 83(4): 685–709.

Johnson, Terry R., and Daniel H. Klepinger. 1994. "Experimental Evidence on Unemployment Insurance Work-Search Policies." *Journal of Human Resources* 29(3): 695–715.

_____. 1991. "Evaluation of the Impacts of the Washington Alternative Work Search Experiment." Unemployment Insurance Occasional Paper

91-4, Unemployment Insurance Service, Employment and Training Administration, U.S. Department of Labor, Washington, D.C.

Leigh, Duane E. 1990. *Does Training Work for Displaced Workers? A Survey of Existing Evidence.* Kalamazoo, Michigan: W.E. Upjohn Institute for Employment Research.

Murray, Merrill G. 1967. *Should Pensioners Receive Unemployment Compensation?* Kalamazoo, Michigan: W.E. Upjohn Institute for Employment Research.

Nicholson, Walter. 1997. "Initial Eligibility for Unemployment Compensation." In *Unemployment Insurance in the United States: Analysis of Policy Issues,* Christopher J. O'Leary and Stephen A. Wandner, eds. Kalamazoo, Michigan: W.E. Upjohn Institute for Employment Research, pp. 91–123.

O'Leary, Christopher J. 1998. "The Adequacy of Unemployment Insurance Benefits." In *Research in Employment Policy,* Volume 1, Laurie J. Bassi and Stephen A. Woodbury, eds. Stamford, Connecticut: JAI Press, pp. 63–110.

_____. 1997. *Unemployment Insurance Earnings Deduction Project: Final Report.* Olympia, Washington: Washington State Employment Security Department.

_____. 1995. "Performance Indicators: A Management Tool for Active Labour Programmes in Hungary and Poland." *International Labour Review* 134(6): 729–751.

O'Leary, Christopher J., Paul T. Decker, an d Stephen A. Wandner. 1998. "Reemployment Bonuses and Profiling." Working paper no. 98-51, W.E. Upjohn Institute for Employment Research, Kalamazoo, Michigan.

O'Leary, Christopher J. and Murray A. Rubin. 1997. "Adequacy of the Weekly Benefit Amount." In *Unemployment Insurance in the United States: Analysis of Policy Issues,* Christopher J. O'Leary and Stephen A. Wandner, eds. Kalamazoo, Michigan: W.E. Upjohn Institute for Employment Research, pp. 163–176.

O'Leary, Christopher J., and Stephen A. Wandner. 1997. "Summing Up: Achievements, Problems, and Prospects." In *Unemployment Insurance in the United States: Analysis of Policy Issues,* Christopher J. O'Leary and Stephen A. Wandner, eds. Kalamazoo, Michigan: W.E. Upjohn Institute for Employment Research, pp. 669–722.

Pear, Robert. 1999. "Dispute over Plan to Use Jobless Aid for Parental Leave." *New York Times,* November 8.

Poulos, Stacey, and Demetra Nightengale. 1997. *The Aging Baby Boom: Implications for Employment and Training Programs.* Washington: D.C.: The Urban Institute.

Quinn, Joseph. 1999. "New Paths to Retirement." In *Forecasting Retirement Needs and Retirement Wealth, Brett Hammond*, Olivia Mitchell and Anna Rappaport, eds. Philadelphia: University of Pennsylvania Press.

Quinn, Joseph F., Richard V. Burkhauser, and Daniel A. Myers. 1990. *Passing the Torch: The Influence of Economic Incentives on Work and Retirement.* Kalamazoo, Michigan: W.E. Upjohn Institute for Employment Research.

Rich, Spencer. 1995. "Clinton Offers a Limited Version of Health Reform." *Washington Post*, January 26.

Roper Starch. 1999. *Baby Boomers Envision Their Retirement: An AARP Segmentation Analysis.* New York: Roper Starch Worldwide Inc.

Social Security Administration. 1998. *Income of the population 55 or older, 1996.* Office of Research, Evaluation and Statistics, SSA Publication no. 13-11871, April.

Spiegelman, Robert G., Christopher J. O'Leary, and Kenneth J. Kline. 1992. "The Washington Reemployment Bonus Experiment Final Report." Unemployment Insurance Occasional Paper 92-6, U.S. Department of Labor, Employment and Training Administration.

Tannenwald, Robert, and Christopher J. O'Leary. 1997. "Unemployment Insurance Reform in New England: Options and Considerations." *New England Economic Review* (May/June): 3-22.

Tannenwald, Robert, Christopher J. O'Leary, and Wei-Jang Huang. 1999. "New Ways of Evaluating State Unemployment Insurance." *New England Economic Review* (March/April): 15-40.

U.S. Department of Labor. 1962. *Unemployment Insurance Legislative Policy, Recommendations for State Legislation 1962.* Washington D.C.: Bureau of Employment Security, no. U-212a, p. 11.

_____. 1996. *Unemployment Insurance Benefit Accuracy Measurement, 1995 Annual Report.* Washington, D.C.: Unemployment Insurance Service, Employment and Training Administration.

_____. 1998. *Unemployment Insurance Financial Data.* Employment and Training Administration Handbook no. 394. Washington, D.C.: Unemployment Insurance Service, Employment and Training Administration.

_____. 1999. *Comparison of State Unemployment Insurance Laws.* Washington, D.C.: Unemployment Insurance Service, Employment and Training Administration.

Vroman, Wayne. 1999. "Self-Employment Assistance (SEA) Program: Report to Congress." Unemployment Insurance Occasional Paper 99-5, Unemployment Insurance Service, Employment and Training Administration, U.S. Department of Labor, Washington, D.C.

_____. 1991. "Why the Decline in Unemployment Insurance Claims?" *Challenge* (September-October): 55–58.

Wandner, Stephen A. 1992. "Self Employment Programs for Unemployed Workers." Unemployment Insurance Occasional Paper 92-2, Unemployment Insurance Service, Employment and Training Administration, U.S. Department of Labor, Washington, D.C.

_____. 1998. "Worker Profiling and Reemployment Services in the United States." In *Early Identification of Jobseekers at Risk of Long-Term Unemployment: The Role of Profiling.* Paris: Organization for Economic Cooperation and Development.

West, Thomas E., and Gerard Hildebrand. 1997. "Federal–state Regulations." In *Unemployment Insurance in the United States: Analysis of Policy Issues*, Christopher J. O'Leary and Stephen A. Wandner, eds. Kalamazoo, Michigan: W.E. Upjohn Institute for Employment Research, pp. 545–598.

Woodbury, Stephen A., and Murray Rubin. 1997. "The Duration of Benefits." In *Unemployment Insurance in the United States: Analysis of Policy Issues*, Christopher J. O'Leary and Stephen A. Wandner, eds. Kalamazoo, Michigan: W.E. Upjohn Institute for Employment Research, pp. 211–283.

# Getting Older in the 21st Century (US)

## The Risks and Consequences of Disability

Mark V. Nadel
*Social Security Administration*

Among the fearful risks facing workers as they get older, disability looms large. As insurance salespeople never tire of telling us, for younger workers the risk of disability is greater than the risk of death. It is a risk that is somewhat mitigated in that some workers can start drawing pensions before they are in their mid sixties and nearly all workers have been able to draw Social Security early retirement benefits starting at age 62. Yet, until reaching the age where retirement income is available, workers confront an increased risk of disability as they age. In light of the gradual increase in the normal retirement age that began in January 2000 and concomitant diminution in early retirement benefits, the risk to older workers of becoming disabled is a particularly timely issue. We are concerned about two groups of older workers: those in what is commonly regarded as the latter years of "normal employment age" (ages 55 to 64) who will be affected by changes in the Early Retirement Age benefits and those 65 and older who will be affected by current and proposed changes in the normal retirement age.

This chapter has four objectives. The first is to examine older workers' risk of disability, primarily the long-term disability that may limit or end employment for the rest of a worker's life. The second is to examine the risk of loss of employment resulting from disability and the characteristics of workers that affect that employment risk. While impairment does not necessarily equate to a loss of employment, being able to overcome the impairment and work by no means guarantees that anyone will give the older worker a job. Moreover, even with the same impairment, different individuals have very different risks of losing employment or income. Third, I examine the systems of insurance coverage against those risks; who is insured, by whom, and how adequately? Last, I consider the public policy implications of older workers' risk of disability, in particular the implications for proposals to raise the retirement age. In this chapter, the term *impairment* is used to mean diminished physical or mental health; *disability* refers to an impairment that results in loss of employment or serious reduction in income.

## THE RISK OF DISABILITY

As we get older, we confront a greater risk of becoming disabled. Almost one quarter of older Americans report that they have a significant disability that affects their ability to work. Data from the 1995 National Health Interview Survey (NHIS) show that 15.7 percent of individuals aged 55 to 64 reported that they were unable to work due to a disability. An additional 7 percent report that they are limited in their work activity by a disability. In contrast, 7.9 percent of the 45- to 54-year-old age group reported inability to work, but about the same proportion (6.5 percent) reported limitations in work.

It should be noted at the outset that these data, while the best available, should still be viewed with caution. The findings are based on self-reported assessments, and it is likely that some unknown number of respondents prefer to ascribe their lack of work to a disability than to the less socially acceptable reason that they just do not want to work any more. If such fudging overstates the true state of disability, there is also a countervailing trend. Almost one million 55- to 64-year-olds who report that they have no disability simultaneously report that they are unable to work due to health reasons. This may be due to some people having an acute but temporary problem, and it probably includes a number of mentally ill individuals.

We will soon have a much better assessment of the prevalence of health impairments in the population. The Social Security Administration (SSA) is embarking on an ambitious survey of disability status and functioning in the population that will provide an estimate of the number of people in the population who are severely disabled enough to qualify for Social Security Disability Insurance (SSDI) benefits.[1]

## Trends

The current prevalence of disability tells us just part of the story. Ideally, we would want to know what this portends for older workers in the future, and the best way to forecast the future is to examine recent trends in disability.

From the time that the 1983 amendments enacting changes in the normal retirement age were passed, there was concern that longer life spans did not necessarily translate into longer work life. An important article by Ernest Gruenberg advanced the argument that recent medical successes in postponing death only resulted in the prolongation of sickness (Gruenberg 1977). That concern was underscored by subsequent studies that pointed to evidence of deteriorating health and disability status among the older working-age population from the late 1960s through the 1970s. More recently, however, the data show a very different picture. Crimmins, Reynolds, and Saito (1999), using data from the National Health Interview Survey, analyzed trends in work ability and work limitations during the period 1982 to 1993 for the 50- to 69-year-old population. They found that in the later years of that period, both men and women older than the age of 61 are less likely to report inability to work. The size of the annual average decline in inability to work ranged from 40 to 70 percent for men and 50 to 70 percent for women. This improvement is also seen in older individuals.

Given the increase in the normal retirement age, disability trends for individuals older than 65 are also relevant. The trend toward better health is manifest for that group as well. For the 12 years between 1982 to 1994, analyses of the National Long Term Care Survey (NLTCS) data have shown that the fraction of the 65- to 74-year-old population that is not chronically disabled grew by 2.6 percentage points, from 85.9 to 88.5 percent, and the fraction of the 75- to 84-year-olds not chronically disabled grew by 5.4 percentage points (Manton, Corder, and Stallard 1997). These findings support the idea that as the health and ability to work among older and younger retirement-age workers improve, increasing the age of full eligibility for Social Security will not be as detrimental to older workers as some have argued.

However, the effect of health status is more complex than a simple snapshot of point-in-time impairment would indicate. A recent analysis of the longitudinal Health and Retirement Survey found that it is not just poor health, but rapid declines in health ("health shocks") that explain retirement behavior. What we don't know is whether the proportion of workers affected by the onset of such health shocks is also declining. Presumably, those who do retire early due to such health issues would be disproportionately affected by increasing the retirement age.

In summary, while becoming older increases the risk of disability, the situation for workers is better than it was. Living longer does not necessarily mean living sicker, and in the aggregate, the possibility of longer work lives is somewhat less constrained by health concerns than was true a generation ago (Bound et al. 1999).

## International Perspectives

The decline in disability in the United States has also been seen in other industrial countries. Waidmann and Manton (1998) reviewed studies from 10 industrial countries and found that these nations also recently experienced moderate to large declines in chronic disability in the elderly. For example, Canadian studies have shown there was a significant increase in life expectancy free of severe disability for both males and females at age 65 from 1986 to 1991. In Great Britain, analyses of Britain's three General Household Surveys in 1976, 1981, and 1985 found an improvement over time in the expectation of life without disability in for 65- and 75-year-olds. Also, in Italy, the Netherlands, and for females in Switzerland, there were relative increases in disability-free life expectancy (DFLE) over the respective time periods.

The reasons behind the improvement are hinted at by findings in France, where disability-free life expectancy at birth increased significantly for both males and females from 1981 to 1991. For individuals 65 and older, DFLE also increased sizably in absolute and relative terms for both males and females. Robine, Morrniche, and Sermet (1998) assessed whether declines in disability were due to delayed onset of morbidity or improved management of potentially disabling conditions once they exist. The results showed that the prevalence of potentially disabling conditions rose significantly between 1980 and 1991. However, the propensity of those having these conditions to report themselves disabled fell (Robine, Mormiche, and Sermet 1998). These findings, Waidmann and Manton argued, suggest the possibility that the treatment or management of diseases has improved or that rehabilitation rates have increased.

## Trends and Projections in the SSDI Program

As I discuss in more detail below, self-reported impairments are a far cry from qualifying for SSDI. Nonetheless, Social Security disability awards seem to reinforce the findings of the recent survey research. This can be seen by looking at the percentage of older workers who are awarded disability benefits at different time periods. In 1975, among 55- to 59-year-olds, the disability incidence rate (i.e., the proportion of workers in that age range who were determined to be disabled by Social Security) was 2.1 percent; by 1997, the percentage had declined to 1.4 percent. More notably, the incidence among workers aged 60–64 declined from 2.9 to 1.6 percent (Social Security Administration 1999). This decline may be due largely to the trend toward early retirement, but the administrative data do not reveal the extent to which older workers in declining health opt for early retirement in lieu of applying for DI benefits. However, an analysis of HRS data by Burkhauser, Couch, and Phillips (1996) found that the men who retired early (at age 62) do not significantly differ in the prevalence of health limitations from those who wait. While they caution that this does not mean that health is unimportant, the finding at least casts some doubt on the assumption that raising the retirement age will automatically cause a proportional response in DI applications.

While trends in self-reported impairments for older workers and DI award incidence rates show a slight decline, Social Security actuarial estimates project an increase in the proportion of the workforce on the rolls. This is not in contradiction to the improving health trends. Rather, it is a reflection of the greater trend of the aging of the population as the baby boom bulges through middle age. An increasing proportion of the population will be in the over-50 age range, with its higher disability incidence rates. The Social Security Actuary's intermediate projections of the disability insurance incidence rate in 2008 is 5.9 per thousand, compared with 4.7 per thousand in 1998. The estimate takes into account the increase in the normal retirement age, with its consequent incentive for workers over 62 to seek to get on the SSDI rolls.

## Who Gets Impaired and How?

As we contemplate the possible effects of current and potential increases in retirement age, we can get a more complete understanding of the consequences by getting behind the aggregate figures and examining the disability status of different subgroups in the population. It is useful to consider the categories of disabilities affecting older workers and how disabilities are distributed across subgroups of older workers.

Not only are older workers more likely to be impaired, but the nature of the probable impairments also change over the lifespan. Figures 1, 2, and 3 show the prevalence of the three largest categories of disability among different age groups (Social Security Administration 1998, p. 219). Not surprisingly, the prevalence of musculoskeletal and circulatory disorders rise dramatically with age. Mental disorders do not necessarily decrease with age in the population. Rather, the decreasing proportion in that category for older workers reflects the growth in mental impairment SSDI allowances for younger age workers and the consequent larger numbers of younger works in that category.

Age is not the only demographic characteristic for which disability varies. Numerous studies have documented differences in health status among racial and ethnic groups across the life cycle in the United States. For example, compared with whites, African Americans report higher rates of hypertension, diabetes, and arthritis, while Hispanics report higher rates of hypertension and diabetes and a lower rate of heart conditions (Kington and Smith 1997). Obviously, socioeconomic status must be considered in assessing the independent effect of race. In fact, Kington and Smith demonstrated that socioeconomic status plays a significant role in explaining racial and ethnic differences in the ability to function once a person has a chronic illness, but it plays a relatively minor role in explaining differences in the prevalence of chronic disease. This seems to suggest that lower socioeconomic status may lead to poorer outcomes once a disease develops because of such factors as reduced access to health care services.

Race and ethnicity are also related to employment. Crimmins, Reynolds, and Saito (1999) found that relative to non-Hispanic whites, African Americans are more than twice as likely to report inability to work. Even looking across people with the same education levels (i.e.,

**Figure 1  Distribution of SSDI Beneficiaries with Musculoskeletal System Diseases by Age**

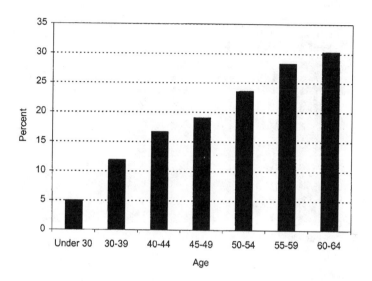

**Figure 2  Distribution of SSDI Beneficiaries with Circulatory System Diseases by Age**

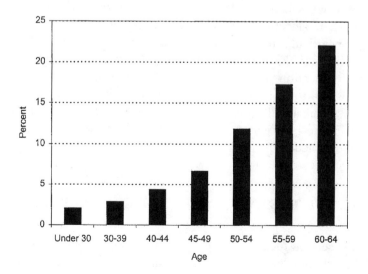

**Figure 3  Distribution of SSDI Beneficiaries with Mental Disorders by Age**

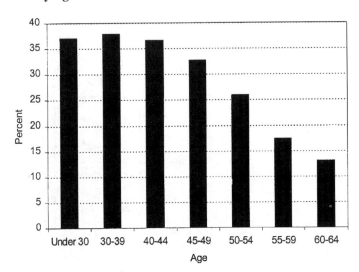

controlling for education), being African American increases the likelihood of being unable to work by about half.  Similarly, Hispanics are about one and a half times more likely than non-Hispanic whites to have work disability; however, Hispanics' relative likelihood of being unable to work is about 25 percent less than that of non-Hispanic whites when education is controlled.  For example, looking at the age group of particular interest, their logistic regression estimated that the probability of being unable to work among 62-year-old men with 10 years of education was 26.1 for African Americans, 18.4 for whites, and only 14.4 for Hispanics.  The pattern is similar for women.

These data are also mirrored by the composition of SSDI rolls.  As seen in Figure 4, African Americans are at higher risk of being severely enough disabled to qualify for SSDI.[2]

## AGING AND THE EMPLOYMENT RISKS OF IMPAIRMENT

This section focuses on the economic risk of disability in general and the risk to older workers in particular.  Age clearly has an effect on

**Figure 4  Race/Ethnic Representation of 55- to 57-Year-Olds in DI and General Populations**

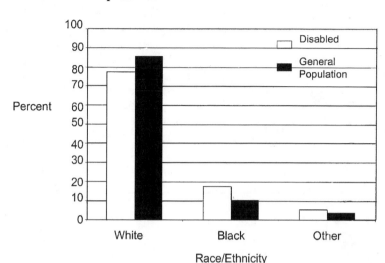

SOURCE: Table 5.A1, *Social Security Bulletin, Annual Statistical Supplement 1998*, p. 185. Data for General Population: Table No. 22, *Resident Population, by Race and Single Years of Age: 1997*, U.S. Bureau of the Census.

gaining and sustaining employment. Not only are older workers more likely to get DI benefits, data from Social Security's New Beneficiary Survey show that, once on the rolls, older beneficiaries have a lower tendency to return to work; once working they have a higher tendency also to stop working (Hennessey 1997, p. 16). Age by itself, of course, is not the only factor limiting an individual's ability to work in the economy. Similarly, a medical impairment, by itself, does not necessarily limit an individual's ability to work in the economy. Rather, the ability to work is a function of individual factors and factors in the environment. Figure 5 presents a simple model of the process. The following discussion gets below the aggregate data on disability and focuses on factors that either mitigate or exacerbate the risk of loss of employment once impairment has occurred.

**Figure 5   Factors Affecting Employability**

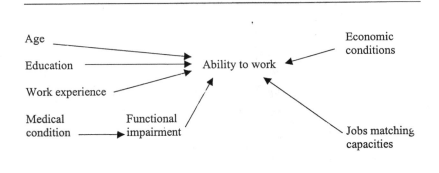

SOURCE: Adapted from Curtis et al. (1998).

## The Impact of Underlying Economic Conditions

Whether a medical impairment becomes a cause of unemployment is affected substantially by economic factors. First, economic incentives play a critical role in the decisions of people with disabilities to participate in the labor force or to seek disability benefits. An individual's decision to apply for benefits is influenced by a variety of such factors. Examples of these factors might include the availability of potential sources of other income such as pensions or savings, the availability of health insurance and noncash benefits, and the costs associated with the application process (Stapleton et al. 1998).

Secondly, underlying economic conditions affect the economic risk of disability for workers who are already out of the labor force or who are laid off. Rupp and Stapleton (1995) summarized the results of numerous econometric studies estimating the effect of the business cycle on Disability Insurance (DI) applications, awards, and caseloads. The results varied in magnitude across these studies but remained consistent in direction. The authors reported strong results in two studies they conducted. The first study analyzed DI applications and awards using 1988–1992 data; the second looked at DI initial determinations and initial allowance rates using 1988–1993 data. Stronger effects were found for applications. Specifically, they found that a 1-percentage-point increase in the unemployment rate resulted in a 4 percent growth in DI applications.

Similarly we would expect that disability insurance applications should fall when the economy rebounds from a recession. In fact, the DI application rate growth declined from a peak of 13.2 percent in 1991 to 2.7 percent in 1994, as the economy rebounded from the recession. These results suggest that the labor market affects the number of workers applying for SSDI, but note that this evidence covers only a relatively short period of time, and the DI application rate, just as the DI approval rate, is also affected by changes in SSA policy and implementation practices. Nonetheless, it seems reasonable to infer that workers with disabilities would be more likely to seek SSDI benefits when they have fewer alternatives in the economy.

Recent evidence indicates that the economic risk of disability does not occur only during economic downturns but is present even when the economy is robust. Burkhauser et al. (1999) evaluated how the 1990s business cycle impacted working-age disabled people. As expected, they were able to quantitatively demonstrate the disproportionately negative impact the downturns in the business cycle had on people with disabilities relative to those without disabilities. What is more disturbing, however, is that employment and labor earning of individuals with disabilities declined over the entire 1990 business cycle, although less so in recovery than in recession.

**Mitigating Factors**

Although aging does increase the risk of disability, and the economy (expressed by the unemployment rate) can affect workers positively or negatively, there are a number of factors for the individual and for society that mitigate the economic risk of impairment for at least a segment of the workforce. For the individual, these factors might include employer accommodations, a supportive family, and good medical care. In the aggregate, two factors of particular importance are the changing nature of work and educational attainment.

## The changing nature of work

Whether a particular impairment results in loss of employment depends largely on the kind of work one is doing when disabled and the kind of jobs that are available. This relationship, in turn, depends on broader trends affecting the physical nature of work. The replacement of high-paying manufacturing jobs with relatively low-paying service sector jobs is seen by many as an important factor in DI application and award growth. Rupp and Stapleton (1995) suggested that in the short-run this trend may increase the DI application rate, as workers with disabilities who lose their manufacturing jobs may not find new work in the service sector and then apply for disability benefits. In the long run, however, it is thought the effect might be to reduce the number of applications, because service sector workers are less susceptible to disabling injuries and illnesses. Rupp and Stapleton suggested that these long-run effects may vary across different impairment groups. For example, workers with physical impairments would be less likely to require DI benefits, while those with mental impairments would be more likely to do so. If they are correct, another correlate of this difference is that as work requires greater cognitive skills, those with mental impairments will be less likely to retain or gain employment due to a lack of skill match. At the same time, those with physical impairments but lacking requisite cognitive skills for other reasons will also be less likely to be employed because of a decline in jobs requiring only physical exertion.

## The importance of education

It has become a cliché to report that both income and likelihood of employment are positively related to levels of education—but, like many clichés, it is true. The current economy requires higher-skilled workers, and while there is an undersupply of more-skilled workers, there is an oversupply of less-skilled workers (Bassi, Benson, and Cheney 1996). Accordingly, among the general population, the jobless rate is directly related to education. For example, the unemployment rate of men who were not high school graduates was 61 percent higher than those who were. Similarly, those whose education stopped at high school graduation had a jobless rate 26 percent higher than those who had been to college (Bureau of Labor Statistics 1998).

The data on the relationship between education, disability, and employment (while controlling for other factors) is more scant (Curtis et al. 1998). Nonetheless, there have been studies that point to the importance of education in allowing persons with disabilities to continue working. For example, two-thirds of the relative reduction in inability to work over the time period analyzed by Crimmins, Reynolds, and Saito (1999) was accounted for by the higher education level of the older age cohort in the most recent time period studied. Similarly, education level is a factor positively associated with those on DI going back to work (Hennessey and Muller 1995).

The good news here is that the educational level of the population has been rising. In 1969, 36 percent of the 35- to 45-year-old age cohort had less than a high school degree. In 1994, only 12 percent of this cohort had so limited an education. Similarly, the percentage of that age group having college degrees has doubled to 27 percent (Friedland and Summer 1999).

## INSURANCE COVERAGE FOR THE RISK OF DISABILITY

When the onset or worsening of an impairment results in the inability to work, workers may be covered by a combination of public and private benefit plans. Workers generally are covered by Social Security disability programs, workers compensation, and, to a much more limited extent, private disability insurance.

The first issue to raise in considering disability coverage is one of scope. Far fewer individuals receive any disability insurance income, public or private, than have self-reported work impairments. Using data from the 1994 National Health Interview Survey on Disability, Adler (1997) found that while 16.9 million working-age adults reported having a work disability, only 9.1 million received benefits from any disability program. Many of the respondents with self-reported disabilities may have only short-term disabilities or may be overstating their condition, but we simply do not yet know how many are in those categories and how many are have serious need for assistance but lack benefits.

## The Protection Offered by Social Security Disability Insurance

Old Age, Survivors, and Disability Insurance (OASDI) is the broadest protection available for workers who become disabled, and it is the only disability insurance that the vast majority of Americans have. In 1998, 133.4 million workers were insured for DI benefits. To be disability-insured, workers over age 31 must have worked 5 of the last 10 years immediately preceding their period of disability.[3] As of 1997, 80 percent of the working-age population was SSDI insured, but the smaller proportion of younger workers who are covered lower this percentage. As a result of the exclusion of some categories of workers (such as domestics and most government workers) from Social Security in the earlier years of the program, the percentage of covered workers also trails off slightly starting with the age 50–54 cohort (Figure 6). This is especially true for women, probably because they were disproportionately out of the labor force earlier in their lives or exempt as teachers (i.e., employees of local governments).

**Figure 6  Age Groups that Are SSDI Insured (estimated)**

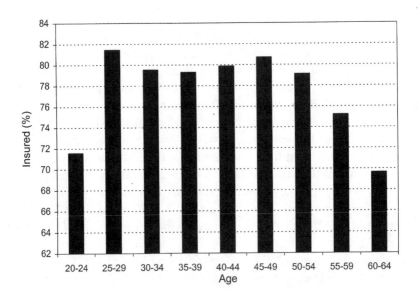

SOURCE: *Social Security Bulletin, Annual Statistical Supplement, 1998*, p. 181.

While most workers are covered by Social Security, the extent to which the SSDI program actually provides benefits in case of serious impairment is limited by two factors: the criteria for receiving benefits and the amount of those benefits relative to previous earnings.

The criteria for being awarded SSDI benefits are very stringent. The law defines disability as the inability to engage in any "substantial gainful activity" by reason of any medically determinable physical or mental impairment(s) which can be expected to result in death or which has lasted or can be expected to last for a continuous period of not less than 12 months. Moreover, SSDI benefits generally do not begin until five months after the onset of the disability. Many more individuals apply for DI benefits than actually receive them. At latest count, approximately 49 percent of applicants are ultimately awarded benefits either initially or through the final administrative appeal.

Once awarded, the SSDI benefit amount, like retirement benefits, is related to earnings, but is also progressive. That is, the more you have earned, the more you get in benefits, but lower-wage workers receive an amount that represents a higher proportion of the predisability earnings than higher-wage workers. The benefits and replacement rate for a 50-year-old worker at different income levels is shown in Table 1. Note that individuals on SSDI may earn up to $700 per month and not lose any benefits. Benefits are generally also paid to spouses when there is a dependent child and also to those children. In 1997, those benefits averaged $178 to wives and $129 to husbands. Children received an average of $195 ($292 if they were also disabled).

**Table 1   Earnings Replacement Rates for Steady Workers Entitled to SSDI (1998)[a]**

| Variable \ Earnings level | Low | Average | High | Maximum |
|---|---|---|---|---|
| 1997 Earnings ($) | 12,342 | 27,426 | 43,882 | 65,400 |
| Annual benefit[b] ($) | 7,060 | 11,629 | 15,446 | 17,920 |
| Replacement rate (%) | 57.2 | 42.4 | 35.2 | 27.4 |

[a] For a 50-year-old worker at four levels of covered earnings.

[b] Shown for illustrative purposes. Benefits are paid on a monthly basis.

## Accounting for Age

The connection between age and disability is inherent in the Social Security Disability program. The initial cash benefit program established in the Social Security Amendments of 1956 provided benefits only for disabled insured workers who were between the ages of 50 and 65. The House Ways and Means Committee Report on the legislation stated

> retirement protection for the 70 million workers under old-age and survivors insurance is incomplete because it does not now provide a lower retirement age for those who are demonstrably retired by reason of a permanent and total disability. We recommend the closing of this serious gap in the old-age and survivors insurance system by providing for the payment of retirement benefits at age 50 to those regular workers who are forced into premature retirement because of disability.

Thus, disability insurance was conceived of as a necessary early retirement program for older workers.

In 1960, Congress removed the minimum age requirement of 50 years for disability insurance beneficiaries. Nonetheless, the Social Security Administration considers age to be a significant factor in the disability decision process. It is not that age makes an individual more disabled; rather, the agency's assumption is that people in the latter stages of work life who have impairments are less likely to be able to adjust to new employment opportunities. To understand the place that age plays in disability determination, it is useful to review briefly how SSA determines that an individual is disabled for purposes of receiving SSDI. SSA uses a five-step sequential evaluation process (Figure 7).

It is at step five—determining whether there are other jobs the individual can perform—that age comes into account, as required by the Social Security Act. For younger persons (under age 50), SSA does not consider that age will seriously affect one's ability to adapt to a new work situation. Social Security regulations state that "if you are closely approaching advanced age (50–54) we will consider that your age, along with a severe impairment and limited work experience, may seriously affect your ability to adjust to a significant number of jobs in the national economy." "Advanced age" (55 or over) is that point

**Figure 7  Social Security Sequential Disability Decision-Making Process**

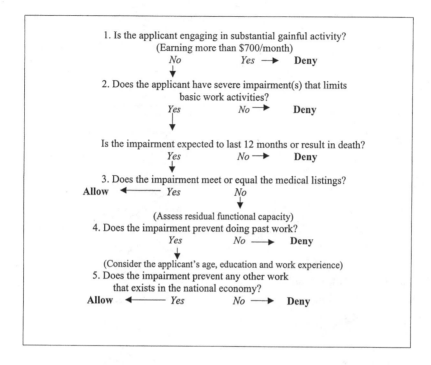

where SSA regards age as significantly affecting a person's ability to perform substantial gainful activity.

Both the increasing numbers of workers in the older age ranges and the impact of the easing of standards for them in step five can be seen in the proportion of persons who successfully apply for DI benefits (Table 2).

## The Protection Offered by Supplemental Security Income

As the name implies, the Supplemental Security Income (SSI) program supplements the coverage provided by SSDI. As a means-tested program, it does so in two ways. First, it provides disability benefits to individuals who are not covered by SSDI. For individuals who meet the low income and assets test, the sequential evaluation to determine whether they are disabled for Social Security purposes is the same as it

**Table 2  SSDI Awards and Applications by Age, 1997[a]**

| Age range | Applications filed | Awards | Applications allowed (%) |
|-----------|-------------------|--------|--------------------------|
| 30–39 | 209,355 | 70,735 | 34 |
| 40–49 | 283,343 | 116,438 | 41 |
| 50–59 | 320,861 | 195,883 | 61 |

SOURCE: Social Security Administration unpublished data.
[a] Both applications and awards are the total of first-time and reapplications.

is for SSDI.  Secondly, even for individuals who are receiving SSDI but whose benefits are very low (currently below $500 a month), SSI provides supplemental coverage with a total benefit somewhat higher than $500 a month.  Last year, 5.3 million persons received SSI on the basis of a disability.[4]  Currently, out of 6.3 million SSDI beneficiaries, 1.6 million receive SSI as well.  In addition to federal benefits, 44 states also provide additional benefits.  Unlike SSDI, every dollar of earnings after the first $65 a month results in a 50-cent reduction in SSI benefits.

## The Increased Retirement Age

In reviewing Social Security coverage for disability, we cannot look only at the DI and SSI programs.  Medicare and retirement benefits must also be considered as part of the protection available to workers who become disabled.

Medicare is provided to persons who have received SSDI benefits for two years.  While health insurance is obviously an important issue for any adult, it is particularly important for persons with disabilities because there is substantial evidence that they are at greater risk for additional health complications (Marge 1998).  Individuals who get SSI benefits then get Medicaid immediately rather than having to wait for Medicare.  Medicaid, ironically, can be more useful to these individuals because, unlike Medicare, it provides prescription drug coverage.

Social Security retirement benefits are also closely linked to workers' financial status if they become disabled.  Workers on DI automatically transition to retirement benefits upon reaching 65 years of age, but that retirement age is gradually increasing to 67. To the extent that individuals retire early due to poor health, the current increase in the normal retirement age and the eventual reduction in the amount of benefits from 80 to 70 percent of normal retirement for those workers who retire at 62 is an incentive for more workers to seek SSDI. The amount of SSDI benefits would be comparable to their normal retirement benefit. If they can get SSDI, they then convert at the normal retirement age to whatever their full Social Security retirement benefit would be and never suffer a reduction in benefits. GAO (1999) argued that while future increases in the retirement age would result in net trust fund savings, there would be some increase in disability insurance payments. However, for workers who were in poor health but could not meet the strict disability standards of SSDI, they would either have to continue to work until normal retirement age or accept a reduced retirement benefit. In short, the Social Security retirement age affects how workers mitigate the risk of disability as they age.

However, the relationship between health and retirement plans may not be as simple as is sometimes assumed. As noted above, HRS data indicate that the men who retired early (at age 62) do not significantly differ in the prevalence of health limitations from those who wait (Burkhauser, Couch, and Phillips 1996). The Congressional Budget Office (1999) also found that only 8 percent of men and 11 percent of women who took early retirement had non-Social Security income below the poverty line and a work-related disability. This may suggest that only a small proportion of early retirees are rendered extremely dependent on early Social Security benefits retirement by virtue of both disability and income.

**Insuring against Workplace Injury—Workers Compensation**

While the Social Security Disability Insurance system covers workers with severe disabilities regardless of how they developed those disabilities, workers' compensation (WC) insurance is a nearly universal system to provide reimbursement of wages and expenses for workers who become disabled as a result of their job. WC will be discussed only briefly here.

Private insurance companies provide WC insurance, but it is not an entirely private system. Employers are generally required to provide the insurance, but its existence also protects employers from legal liability. WC began in the early 1900s and now has separate programs for each of the 50 states and the District of Columbia. Since the basic goal of WC is to restore workers to their previous abilities, the programs strongly emphasize rehabilitation. WC is fully funded by employers. Benefits include a weekly amount until maximum medical improvement has been realized, with payments thereafter based on the degree of disability; medical care is also covered. Benefit payments, which include both cash payments and medical care, totaled $42.4 billion in 1996.

### Insuring against Disability—Private Plans

While Social Security provides financial protection for workers who become severely disabled over the long term and workers compensation provides coverage for those who become injured or sick on the job, private disability insurance falls between these systems. It should be noted at the outset that private plans are not independent of Social Security; they developed in a climate that already included Social Security and other public benefits. The private plans assumed the existence of Social Security and generally are tailored to integrate with it, by offsetting their benefits by the amount of Social Security benefits. Private disability plans are broadly divided into two categories, short-term and long-term, but beyond that there is great variety and no standard terminology.

The definitions of disability within the types of plans vary to some extent, but they generally share major characteristics. Short-term plans typically cover impairments that are judged to prevent employees from engaging in their usual occupation. They generally pick up workers after sick pay is exhausted, although the plan may be in lieu of sick pay. Benefit periods generally range from 30 days to six months. Nearly all employees who end up getting short-term benefits return to work within two months. Others may, if they are covered, "graduate" to long-term disability coverage. Generally, long-term plans are more restrictive, particularly after the first two years. While they initially provide payments for employees unable to perform their usual occupation, after two years the definition usually requires the employee to be unable to perform any occupation. The earnings replacement rate of these long-term plans is about 60 percent, up to a contractual maximum dollar amount. However, this generally includes any SSDI payments.

Private plans provide a useful measure of protection. The problem is that relatively few workers are covered. According to Bureau of Labor Statistics data, about 40 percent of full-time workers have short-term policies, and about one-third of workers have employer-provided long-term policies. As shown in Figure 8, workers in smaller firms are less likely to have long-term policies. Note that blue-collar workers in all categories of employers are the least likely to have long-term disability insurance. That is, workers in the most arduous occupations are least likely to be covered.

Individually purchased disability plans are also available, but we were unable to obtain data on participation rates for such plans. They are, however, mostly limited to highly compensated employees or self-employed individuals. These plans may replace up to 80 percent of earnings, though more typical replacement rates are 60–70 percent. Often these plans do not offset payments by the amount of Social Security benefits.

**Figure 8  Employees with Long-Term Disability Insurance**

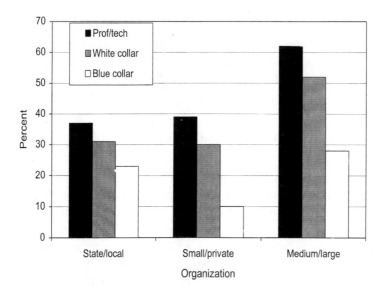

SOURCE: Bureau of Labor Statistics 1997 Employee Benefits Survey.

As with individual and small-group health insurance, the disability income insurance market is heavily underwritten. The workers we are concerned about here, with their greater risk of disability, would likely be deemed uninsurable or face extremely high premium payments. Thus for most workers, especially most blue-collar and small-firm employees, Social Security is the only game in town.

The extent of coverage and the resulting economic risk of disability-related employment loss can be put in perspective by comparison with other countries, even though comparisons are inexact due to broader definitions of disability in other nations and the use of disability rolls to cover more general unemployment. First, a higher proportion of the working-age population is receiving disability insurance benefits in most European countries. Second, the economic well-being of men with disabilities in the United States is often not equal to their counterparts in those other countries. Burkhauser and Daly (1998) made this point by comparing the experience of U.S. and German men. Using cross-sectional data, they found that the average-income German who has a disability lives in a household which has an income that is virtually the same as that of the average German without a disability. In contrast, the income gap in the United States between those with and without disabilities is approximately 25 percent. Additionally, in Germany the pre-tax and transfer income (composed largely of own wage earnings) of men with disabilities is nearly 80 percent of that of men without disabilities, whereas in the United States the pre-tax and transfer income gap for men is almost 35 percent.

## CONCLUSION AND POLICY ISSUES

Older may be wiser, but it often is also weaker. For the individual, the story is mixed. While any given individual is far more likely to be impaired in the second half of work life than in the first, the good news is that that individual is likely to be somewhat healthier than his counterpart of 20 years ago. For the social insurance system, however, the improvements in health and functioning are still going to be trumped by increased number of people in their late fifties and early sixties. It could have been worse, but demographic factors still present three key policy problems having to do with distributional issues.

The first problem is that health status is not randomly distributed in the population. Minorities and those with low educational levels are more likely to have impairments affecting their employment. Whatever the covariance and root causes of the unequal health status of minorities, under present trends, minorities will constitute a disproportionate number of those with health impairments at the same time that they are becoming a larger proportion of the general population.

The second problem is that the impact of disability on employment is concentrated. Those with higher educational status are both less likely to need to leave a job due to impairment and more likely to regain employment after losing it because of disability. This factor also reinforces the problem facing minority groups.

Finally, just as workers are admonished to have private pensions and savings in addition to Social Security (completing the famous three-legged stool), SSDI provides a benefit level that does not hold workers harmless in the event of disability. The replacement rate is less than 50 percent for most workers. However, while most people have at least short legs on their stool for retirement, a similar supplement to Social Security Disability Insurance is generally not available. We do not know the size of the assets of SSDI beneficiaries, but since their average income tends to be low, it is very unlikely that their savings are of much help when they become disabled. Similarly, private long-term disability insurance covers only about one-third of workers. Like employer-provided health insurance, it tends to be offered to workers who are already better off. In short, the health risk to the older population is not randomly distributed, and the consequences of impairment add additional risk to traditionally disadvantaged groups.

In addition to the aging baby boomers, the other contextual issue for assessing disability is the currently scheduled and potential increases in the retirement age. While we know that many people prefer to take Social Security retirement benefits at age 62, raising that age will not affect as high a proportion of workers with impairments as would have been true 20 years ago. Nonetheless, that trend will be scant comfort to those who seek to retire early for health reasons but whose impairments do not meet SSDI criteria. We are still learning more about their numbers and characteristics, but suffice it to say for now that there will be groups that will be worse off if they must defer retirement beyond the current early retirement age or take further reductions in retirement benefits.

The current policy response to the increased prevalence of disability among older workers is to make it relatively easier for older workers to be awarded SSDI.  To the extent that workers are required to work longer to receive retirement benefits, additional options may be considered.  These would include modifying (i.e., easing) the sequential evaluation system for older workers, allowing a partial disability benefit for older workers, or lowering the Medicare eligibility age to reduce health costs for workers forced to retire on reduced benefits.  These are all expensive propositions, but nonetheless, the impact on older workers in fragile health must be considered as we examine policy options to improve the solvency of the system.

## Notes

Mark V. Nadel is Associate Commissioner, Office of Disability and Income Assistance Policy, Social Security Administration.  This paper was written with the assistance of Stephane Philogene.  Howard Bradley also provided useful help.  I appreciate comments from Jane Ross, Eli Donkar, Kalman Rupp, and Michael Marge.  The views expressed in this paper are entirely my own and do not necessarily represent the position of the Social Security Administration.

1.  The National Study of Health and Activity will do medical examinations and functional assessments and collect other data from a sample of 5,500 working-age individuals, most of whom will have been previously screened to get a sample of individuals with some degree of impairment.  SSA disability examiners will determine whether individuals not now on the roles would qualify for benefits on the basis of impairment.

2.  The disability and survivors insurance features of Social Security are particularly important to blacks.  While a smaller proportion of all black beneficiaries receive retirement benefits than do whites, a larger proportion of black beneficiaries receive DI benefits than do whites (25 percent for blacks compared to 12 percent for whites).  See Hendley and Bilimoria (1999).

3.  To be insured for DI, workers under age 65 must 1) be fully insured and 2) have recent covered earnings, as follows.  Workers age 31 and over must have covered earnings in at least 20 of their last 40 quarters ending with the quarter in which the worker became disabled.  Workers who become disabled before age 31 may meet an alternative to the 20/40 test: younger workers must have quarters of coverage equal to at least half of the quarters in the period between the quarter of attain-

ment of age 21 and the quarter of onset of disability. (Any odd number of quarters in that period is rounded off by one.) Even the youngest workers, however, must have a minimum of 6 quarters. Workers who meet statutory blindness requirements need only be fully insured and need not meet the second requirements for recent earnings.

4. SSI can also be paid, if the low income and asset test is met, to the aged (65+) and to children with disabilities.

# References

Adler, Michelle. 1997. *Analysis of the Disability Survey.* Department of Health and Human Services, ASPE Research Notes, Vol. 16.

Bassi, Laurie, George Benson, and Scott Cheney. 1996. "The Top Ten Trends." *Training and Development,* Nov.

Bound, John, Michael Schoenbaum, Todd Stinebrickner, and Timothy Waidmann. 1999. "The Dynamic Effects of Health on the Labor Force Transitions of Older Workers." *Labour Economics* 6: 179–202.

Bureau of Labor Statistics. 1998. News release. Washington, D.C.: U.S. Department of Labor, http://stats.bls.gov/news.release/hsgec.t02htm (accessed December 1999).

Burkhauser, Richard V., Kenneth A. Couch, and John W. Phillips. 1996. "Who Takes Early Social Security Benefits? The Economic and Health Characteristics of Early Beneficiaries." *The Gerontologist* 36(6): 789–799.

Burkhauser, Richard V., Mary C. Daly, and Andrew J. Houtenville. 1999. "How Working-Age People with Disabilities Fared over the 1990s Business Cycle." Paper presented at the 1999 Association for Public Policy and Management Annual Research Conference held in Washington, D.C., November 4–6.

Burkhauser, Richard V., and Mary C. Daly. 1998. "Disability and Work: The Experiences of American and German Men." *FRBSF Economic Review 1998*, no. 2: 17–29.

Crimmins, Eileen M., Sandra L. Reynolds, and Yasuhiko Saito. 1999. "Trends in Health and Ability to Work among the Older Working-Age Population." *Journal of Gerontology* 54B(1): S31–S40.

Curtis, Glenn, Robert Garian, Ihor Gawdiak, David Osborne, and Eric Solsten. 1998. *Vocational Factors in the Social Security Disability Decision Process: A Review of the Literature.* Library of Congress Federal Research Division, Washington, D.C., pp. 107–121.

Friedland, Robert, and Laura Summer. 1999. *Demography Is Not Destiny.* Washington, D.C.: National Academy on an Aging Society, p. 30.

General Accounting Office. 1999. *Social Security Reform: Implications of Raising the Retirement Age*. Report no. HEHS-99-112. Washington, D.C.: U.S. Government Printing Office

Gruenberg, Ernest M. 1977. "The Failures of Success." *Milbank Memorial Fund Quarterly* 55(1):3–24.

Hendley, Alexa, and Natasha Bilimoria. 1999. "Minorities and Social Security: An Analysis of Racial and Ethnic Differences in the Current Program." *Social Security Bulletin* 62(2): 59–64.

Hennessey, John. 1997. "Factors Affecting the Work Efforts of Disabled-Worker Beneficiaries." *Social Security Bulletin*. 60(3): 3–20.

Hennessey, John, and L. Scott Muller. 1995. "The Effect of Vocational Rehabilitation and Work Incentives on Helping the Disabled-Worker Beneficiary Back to Work." *Social Security Bulletin* 58(1): 15–28.

Kington, Raynard S., and James P. Smith. 1997. Socioeconomic Status and Racial and Ethnic Differences in Functional Status Associated with Chronic Diseases. *American Journal of Public Health* 87(5): 805–810.

Manton, Kenneth, Larry Corder, and Eric Stallard, 1997. "Chronic Disability Trends in Elderly United States Populations: 1982–1994." *Proceedings of the National Academy of Sciences* 94: 2593–2598.

Marge, Michael. 1998. *Healthy People 2010 Disability Objectives: Private Sector and Consumer Perspectives*. Syracuse, New York: American Association on Health and Disability.

Robine, J.M., P. Mormiche, and C. Sermet. 1998. "Examination of the Causes and Mechanisms of the Increase in Disability Free Life Expectancy." *Journal of Aging and Health* 10(2): 171–191.

Rupp, Kalman, and David Stapleton. 1995. "Determinants of the Growth in the Social Security Administration's Disability Programs: An Overview." *Social Security Bulletin* 58(4): 43–70.

Social Security Administration. 1998. *Social Security Bulletin*, Annual Statistical Supplement, 1998. Washington, D.C.: U.S. Government Printing Office.

_____. 1999. *Social Security Disability Insurance Program Worker Experience*. Office of the Chief Actuary, SSA Publication no. 11-11543.

Stapleton, David, Kevin Coleman, Kimberly Dietrich, Gina Livermore, and the Lewin Group, 1998. "Empirical Analyses of DI and SSI Application and Award Growth." In *Growth in Disability Benefits*, Kalman Rupp and David C. Stapleton, eds. Kalamazoo, Michigan: W.E. Upjohn Institute for Employment Research, pp. 31–79.

U.S. Congressional Budget Office. 1999. *Raising the Earliest Eligibility Age for Social Security Benefits*. Washington, D.C.: U.S. Government Printing Office, p. 20.

Waidmann, Timothy A., and Kenneth G. Manton. 1998. *International Evidence on Disability Trends among the Elderly.* Report prepared under contract DHHS-100-97-0010 for the Office of Disability and Long Term Care Policy. U.S. Department of Health and Human Services, Washington, D.C.

Yelin, Edward. 1998. "Comments on Chapter 2," In *Growth in Disability Benefits*, Kalman Rupp and David C. Stapleton, eds. Kalamazoo, Michigan: W.E. Upjohn Institute for Employment Research, pp. 93–97.

Yelin, Edward H., and Patricia P. Katz 1994. "Labor Force Trends of Persons with and without Disabilities." *Monthly Labor Review* 117(10): 36–42.

# Social Insurance and the Older Worker

## An Overview

Robert Haveman
*University of Wisconsin–Madison*

## INTRODUCTION: OLDER WORKERS AND PUBLIC POLICY TOWARD THEM

Older workers—those older than, say, 45 years, but younger than the normal retirement age—face a set of constraints on their activities that increases economic insecurity and vulnerability. An increasing proportion of these older workers experience eroding strength and health, and many of them are perceived by both their employers and their younger worker peers as "long in the tooth," or "over the hill." Often these perceptions guide employer and public decisions, and these lead to both higher rates of job loss among older workers, and feelings of economic insecurity.

This set of circumstances is undeniable and is a normal accompaniment of the aging process. However, it is these circumstances that account for the relatively high incidence of reliance by older workers on the nation's social insurance system. The preceding chapters have taken apart the social insurance system for older workers and focused on four policy areas of special concern to them: health and health insurance, Social Security Disability Insurance (SSDI), workers' compensation, and unemployment compensation (UI). Interestingly, none of the conference presentations dealt with the Social Security Retirement or Medicare programs, which are, in fact, the two largest programs affecting older workers.

There is one overarching national policy issue that is central to the situation of older workers:

How should social insurance policy respond to the needs of a growing group of older workers who tend to be less strong and healthy than their younger peers and who face eroding personal capabilities and difficult decisions regarding phasing into retirement?

Should we be promoting a pro-work agenda for older U.S. citizens by, for example, reducing the bite of pension plans that discourage continued work or by changing the employer culture regarding older workers, or by modifying public benefit programs and public regulations that inhibit flexible work arrangements? Or should we be seeking to improve the adequacy of income support arrangements for these workers as they phase into retirement given existing institutions and incentives?

## SOME BASIC CHARACTERISTICS OF OLDER WORKERS

Before discussing this public policy issue, it is important to recognize several basic attributes of the older worker population. First, older workers (those aged 45 to 65) are one-third of the workforce, one-fifth of the unemployed, and one-third of the insured unemployed. Hence, relative to younger workers, they shoulder a smaller burden of unemployment and reap a larger share of UI benefits.[1]

Second, on average and relative to the remainder of the workforce, older workers have less education, fewer skills, and less flexibility in changing responsibilities and accepting new challenges. There are fewer minorities among them. They earn higher wages than the remainder of the workforce, even though a larger proportion of them are in poor health. These higher wages, of course, are related to their longer job tenure.

Third, the males in the group of 45- to 65-year-olds have shown a rapid increase in the willingness to stop regular employment and accept retirement.[2] On the other hand, women in this age group appear to have an increasing propensity to engage in formal work.

Fourth, today's cohort of older workers will live longer than prior cohorts of older workers. As a result, today's cohort has more years of expected retirement ahead of them than did prior older worker cohorts.[3]

Americans now measure retirement in decades rather than years. As a result, this cohort is under more social pressure to remain active in the labor market than prior cohorts. Perhaps as a result of this increasing social pressure, today's older workers confront a general public that believes that access to support from both private and public programs should be more difficult and that the support provided should be less generous than it in fact is.

A final characteristic of today's older workers is that they can be roughly allocated to two groups, with quite different policy implications.[4] The first and largest group is generally healthy, educated, working, and tends to be white. For them, the primary issue is the difficult set of decisions regarding the phasing into retirement and the lifestyle to be adopted in retirement. For a sizable (and growing) proportion of these older workers, increasing years of work will be desirable.

The second group of older workers consists of those with health problems[5] or with few years of schooling; minorities are prevalent in this group. These workers tend to be marginal to the labor market, and for them, the issue is the adequacy of support programs and access to economic and health care resources. Except for the small proportion of totally disabled workers among this population, SSDI is likely to be unavailable to them. Moreover, early retirement benefits have eroded, and unemployment compensation provides only temporary help if permanent loss of a regular full time job occurs. For many of these more-marginal older workers, policy changes enacted over the past few decades have caused economic hardship. This situation is not likely to improve for subsequent cohorts of older workers.

## OLDER WORKERS AND ECONOMIC SELF-SUFFICIENCY

The case for social insurance rests on the inability of the private market to adequately protect individuals (and hence society) against risk and uncertainty and on the need to assure an acceptable minimum living standard for all citizens. Hence, designing social insurance programs to meet the needs of older workers requires that the economic status and vulnerability of older workers be understood. Consider the following generalizations regarding the economic well-being of the population of older workers.

A primary problem for the group of regular workers who are employees stems from the higher costs faced by employers in providing them health insurance coverage and retirement pensions.[6] As a result, when pressures to reduce costs due to competition or declining demand are encountered, employers are less likely to retain older workers than young workers with the same sets of skills and competencies. Hence, job displacement for older workers is substantially more likely than it is for equivalent young workers.[7] Moreover, older workers are less likely to be reemployed full-time if they are displaced.[8] It follows that such displaced older workers who draw UI benefits are more likely to exhaust their benefits than are younger workers.[9]

Relative to younger workers, the population of older workers is more likely to be self-employed; 10 percent of older workers are self-employed compared with but 4 percent of younger workers. Relying on the prospects of an individual enterprise for income is risky, as the failure rate for single proprietorships is substantially higher than for larger enterprises (notwithstanding the relatively high prevalence of legal and medical professionals in the population of self-employed workers).

If they are working and are not self-employed, older workers are more likely to be employed part-time than are younger workers. As a result, they are less likely to be eligible for unemployment insurance benefits if they lose their jobs, as UI covers only full time, regular employees. Many of these part-time workers will be engaging in "bridge employment," which typically carries less compensation and fewer benefits than regular employment.[10] Many of these bridge worker-retirees have been displaced from their regular jobs and have exhausted their unemployment insurance benefits.

If they are not working—most likely a result of taking early retirement—they will be dependent on income from a combination of private pensions and early-retirement Social Security benefits. While about one-half of the group of older workers is covered by employer-supported pensions, this proportion is shrinking over time. Moreover, those who are covered with defined-benefit plans face eroding real benefits.

However, on average, these older workers have higher wage rates than younger workers, primarily because of longer job tenures. Moreover, they typically have fewer family responsibilities than do younger workers.

Further, these older workers are more likely to have employer-sponsored health insurance and less likely to be uninsured than are equivalent younger workers,[11] although the percentage with employer-sponsored health insurance has been decreasing.

Finally, if they are severely disabled, older workers are more likely to receive SSDI benefits than equivalent younger workers, and once on the disability benefit roles they are less likely to leave.

Given this profile, overall and on average it is hard to make the case that older workers as a group are a particularly vulnerable segment of American society. While they appear to face substantially higher risks of job loss, part-time work, and exclusion from some social insurance benefits, the average older worker starts from a higher earnings and income base than does the average younger worker and is less likely to be without health insurance and private pension coverage.

To find real vulnerability, we need to dig deeper into this population. In fact, such digging will reveal that second group of particularly vulnerable older workers emphasized by Kathy Swartz—namely, those with low education, few skills and minority status. Moreover, even among this group, all marginal to the labor force, true vulnerability is found by digging deeper still, to locate those with ill health, those with ill spouses, and those who have experienced job loss or perhaps the loss of a spouse. Although people with these characteristics tend to be at the bottom of any larger population grouping with which one begins, the policy implications are quite different for those at the bottom end of the distribution of the older worker group because of their age.

## SELF-SUFFICIENCY IMPLICATIONS OF
## RECENT SOCIAL POLICY CHANGES

As economic and political changes have occurred over the past decade or so, there have been a number of developments that have affected the self-sufficiency of the group of older workers, and more particularly that of the most vulnerable among them.  In the following pages, I will flag some of these developments but will not document the details of each.

Perhaps the most significant development for older workers has been the substantial increase in cost consciousness that has affected most firms, especially those enterprises confronting increasingly severe international competition.  Because of the higher costs of employing older workers—both higher wage costs as well as higher benefit costs—they have been the first to have experienced job loss and, for many, unplanned early retirement.  Those older workers who retained their jobs have experienced the stress that accompanies decreased job security.

This same concern for employment costs has led to an erosion of employer-sponsored health insurance coverage among older workers.  For those remaining covered, the private sector plans have tended to shift from defined-benefit to defined-contribution plans.  Although this shift has increased work incentives among those covered, it has also reduced the adequacy of expected pension benefits.  For many older workers, this trend has increased the perceived need to postpone retirement and to continue to work.

In addition to these changes, the brunt of which have tended to fall on the most vulnerable group of older workers, there has also been a downward trend in real wage rates for unskilled labor since the early 1970s.  In relative terms, the wage rate gap between skilled and unskilled workers has increased during this period, resulting in increased inequality and a perception by older unskilled workers that they have been left behind in the process of economic growth.[12]  This focus on gaps, however, masks the absolute deterioration of earnings for those workers with few skills or low education; since the early 1970s, the real hourly wage rate for a man with a high school degree (but no more education) has fallen by about 35 percent.

However, and to some extent offsetting these changes, there has been a substantial decrease over time in the physical demands associated with work; remaining employed today typically requires more mental and less physical effort than it did a few decades ago.  Indeed, a survey taken in 1950 inquired as to whether workers were in "physically demanding" jobs, and about 20 percent of this older-worker group answered "yes."[13]  Today, only about 7 percent of older workers answer this question affirmatively. When this shift is combined with increasing average education levels of older workers, it enables some of them to remain in the workforce longer, and with less effort, than was the case a few decades ago.

Simultaneous with these demand-side changes in employment and wages and the decrease in the physical demands of work have been changes in social policy that have affected older workers. Perhaps the most visible change has been the legislated increase in the Social Security full-benefit retirement age and the increase in the penalty for taking early retirement.[14] These changes embody the social decision that working lives should be extended and retirement pushed further up the age distribution.[15]

There have also been a large series of rule changes in workers' compensation that have reduced access and compensation if disabled. The background paper on workers' compensation by John Burton and Emily Spieler emphasizes that, while few were watching, legislation and judicial rulings since 1989 have substantially restricted the accessibility and generosity of workers' compensation benefits. Eligibility has been tightened. Benefits have been lowered. Payment mechanisms have been made more restrictive and health costs more tightly controlled.[16] As a result of these changes, health-related costs have been increasingly shifted to recipients and their families or to other programs such as SSDI and away from employers. An increased burden of proof has been imposed on covered workers. All of these changes have tended to fall most heavily on older workers.[17]

Finally, there is the more recent development that colors all discussions of the economic self-sufficiency of all worker groups, namely, eight years of sustained prosperity. Clearly the prosperity of this period has benefited nearly all groups, in part through its promotion of both the demand for and supply of labor.[18] Moreover, this development has resulted in a run up in asset values for some, but not all. While both of these developments have made the future less uncertain for some older workers, there has been a disturbing increase in disparities in both wealth holdings and earnings over time. Moreover, while the prosperity has opened up additional options for phased retirement for some older workers, it has imposed increased work demands and pressures on those who continue to work full time.

## POLICY ISSUES REGARDING OLDER WORKERS

The economic and policy developments mentioned in the previous section raise several important issues that the nation should address in terms of its treatment of older workers. The chapters of this book all fasten on the following overarching policy issue:

> Should the nation's major social insurance programs be restructured to provide a more adequate safety net, or should they be redesigned to increase work incentives for older workers? Or, should policy changes seek to accomplish both objectives?

Nestled in this issue are a number of important subquestions:[19]

- Should public regulations inhibiting flexible work arrangements be redesigned so as to increase the availability of this option?

- In the face of apparent reluctance by employers to provide training for older workers,[20] should training opportunities for retooling or moving to bridge jobs be supported by public money?

- In the face of large disincentives for continued work beyond some early eligibility retirement age in numerous private pension arrangements,[21] and the apparent reluctance of employers to change plans that contain these disincentives, should public regulations designed to encourage the restructuring of private pension arrangements so as to increase incentives for continued work be implemented?

- Finally, should access to income support and benefits while working less than full time or not working at all be expanded?

At any time, including the present, there are numerous policy proposals on the nation's table that address these questions. While some of these proposals seek to increase the adequacy of programs targeted on older workers, others stress work-continuation goals. The following menu is designed to set the stage for the subsequent discussions of numerous policy suggestions that were presented at the conference and are contained in this volume.

## Social Security Retirement

In addition to the now-resolved issue regarding the elimination or reduction of the earnings test, there have also been proposals to increase the normal retirement age still further, and perhaps to increase the early retirement age along with it. Like the elimination of the earnings test, both of these measures would promote work continuation. Consistent with this thrust, there has been little discussion of increased adequacy in benefit payments.

## Medicare

Should we allow workers to buy into Medicare at age 62—a recent proposal from the administration—or should we restrict Medicare coverage to receipt of full retirement benefits given an increasing retirement age? The first of these options aids vulnerable older workers, but it clearly contains troublesome problems of adverse selection. The second option promotes continued work, but it simultaneously imposes costs on vulnerable older workers.

On another front, should we return the employer-as-first-payer provision in Medicare to its 1982 standard, a standard that reduced health insurance costs for employers, and hence, is a pro-work policy? Or do the costs in reduced health care coverage and adequacy override the pro-work gains?

## Social Security Disability Insurance

For SSDI, should we adopt some subset of the several proposed reforms designed to promote work? These proposals include a supplemental EITC for SSDI recipients, allowing Medicare access to older workers who leave SSDI (with perhaps an earnings-conditioned premium), and the provision of vouchers for training for existing SSDI recipients? Again, all of these are pro-work. We could also consider changes in the benefit structure that would increase the adequacy of income support to the most vulnerable older workers.

### Unemployment Compensation

Currently, self-employed and part-time workers are excluded from the UI program, and that imposes a relative hardship on them; should these workers be integrated into the unemployment insurance system? For example, should we reduce the required hours of work in the base period for initial eligibility? Such a change would encourage flexible and partial retirement and facilitate the move from full work to retirement.

As an alternative, should we support tax-preferred savings accounts for older workers as a means to encourage a flexible move from full work to retirement? Should UI be used to support health insurance premiums, an adequacy concern? Still further, should the work option in UI be expanded to include more choice such as bridge jobs?[22]

In terms of adequacy, should the minimum benefit award be expanded? This award is targeted on older workers and, in particular, vulnerable older workers. Should we increase the benefit duration for the group of older workers? Or, should a self-employment assistance program with the UI system be expanded (a change that would also be pro-work)?

### Workers' Compensation

One hardly knows what to say about workers' compensation, given its diversity among the 50 states. Should there be some attempt to systematize workers' compensation coverage, eligibility, and benefits? Should there be efforts to reverse the reduced access and generosity of workers' compensation that has occurred since the late 1980s?

## CONCLUSION

These, then, form the major policy suggestions that one finds in this book and that were talked about by participants in the NASI conference. We hope that the information regarding the composition and self-sufficiency of older workers, how they are and have been treated by our institutions and policies, and how they could be treated by policy changes, sets the stage for the more in-depth analysis in subsequent chapters of this volume.

# Notes

1. See O'Leary and Wandner (2001).
2. There is evidence that this trend has slowed, or disappeared, in recent years. See Quinn (1999).
3. In 1965, an older worker who reached age 65 could expect 13 years of retirement. Today, such a worker can expect 18 years. See Gendell (1998).
4. This point was emphasized by Katherine Swartz in her discussion of health and health insurance for older workers (Swartz 2001).
5. Although about 25 percent of those aged 55 to 64 have some work limitation, the prevalence of ill health appears to be decreasing over time. While health problems are more prevalent among older workers than in the remainder of the workforce, conditional on having a problem, it is more likely to be age-related and less traumatic. Their health problems tend to be from exposure to adverse environments over time, stem from multiple causes, have long latency periods, and not be directly job-related. Because these health problems tend not to be directly job-related, establishing eligibility for work-related support such as workers' compensation is often difficult. Because these health problems are unlikely to be totally disabling, establishing eligibility for SSDI is also more difficult. See Nadel (2001) and Burton and Spieler (2001).
6. One study suggests that health insurance costs are twice as high for males over 50 than for male workers aged less than 50 (Clark 1994).
7. The displacement rate for older workers is about 3.5 percent, relative to a 2.5 percent rate for younger workers (O'Leary and Wandner 2001).
8. Indeed, the reemployment rate for displaced older workers displaced is about 50 percent, compared with a 70 percent reemployment rate for younger workers (O'Leary and Wandner 2001).
9. Sixty percent of displaced older workers exhaust their benefits compared with 40 percent for younger workers (O'Leary and Wandner 2000).
10. One survey found that 49 percent of men and 34 percent of women over 55 were "bridge, partial retirement" workers (Quinn 1999).
11. About 80 percent of older workers aged 55 to 65 are covered by employer sponsored health insurance; only about 15 percent of this group is uninsured. See Swartz (2001) and Committee for Economic Development (1999).
12. The earnings premium received by a college graduate, relative to a worker with a high school degree or less, increased from about 30 percent in the 1970s to over 60 percent by the early 1990s.
13. From C. Eugene Steurele, Rich Johnson, and Chris Spiro, The Urban Institute, 1998; cited in Committee for Economic Development (1999).

14. The legislative change in early retirement benefits increased the penalty for early retirement from 20 percent of the primary insurance amount to 30 percent. See Committee for Economic Development (1999).

15. In fact, these changes have also improved the neutrality of the Social Security system. An interesting question with respect to these legislated changes is whether they will lead to increased prevalence of disability claims among future older workers and an increase in SSDI applications.

16. An example of this trend is the adoption by workers' compensation plans in several states of the requirement that employer's physicians make the final determination regarding the work-related nature of injuries and illnesses and hence coverage by workers' compensation plans.

17. It should be noted that the incentives designed to increase the employment of workers with disabilities implicit in the Americans with Disabilities Act tend to be offset by the pattern of reduced coverage of these workers by both the UI and the workers' compensation programs.

18. A recent study concluded that, if the unemployment rate were 4 percent, about 18 percent of older workers who lose their jobs would retire; however, if the unemployment rate were 8 percent, retirement would be chosen by about 44 percent of older worker job losers. See Sandell and Baldwin (1990).

19. At the time of the Academy Conference, one of these sub-questions was, Should the earnings test in Social Security be relaxed or eliminated so as to promote continued work by retirement benefit recipients? Congress and the President have now acted positively on this issue, and this anti-work continuation measure has become a relic of the past.

20. In a recent survey of employers, 19 percent of younger workers report having been given training; 13 percent of older workers so report (Amirault 1992).

21. In some private pension plans now, there is an implicit tax of up to 50 percent on continued work beyond some early eligibility retirement date. One study of about 1000 private pension plans found that working beyond the early retirement eligibility date typically implied sizable reductions in lifetime benefits, ranging up to 30 percent (Kotlikoff and Wise 1989).

22. One possibility would be to ease the policy of denying benefits if full-time work is available but not taken for older workers. This denial of benefits policy imposes a relative hardship on older workers.

# References

Amirault, Thomas. 1992. "Training to Qualify for Jobs and Improve Skills." *Monthly Labor Review* 115(9): 31–36.

Burton, John F., and Emily A. Spieler. 2001. "Workers' Compensation and Older Workers." In this volume, pp. 41–83.

Committee for Economic Development. 1999. *New Opportunities for Older Workers.* Washington, D.C.  Available at http://www.ced.org/projects/older.htm (accessed August 2000).

Clark, Robert.  1994. "Employment Costs and the Older Worker."  AARP working paper no. 9412, AARP, Washington, D.C.

Gendell, Murray.  1998.  "Trends in Retirement Age in Four Countries, 1965–1995." *Monthly Labor Review* 121(8): 20–30.

Kotlikoff, Laurence J., and David A. Wise.  1989.  *The Wage Carrot and the Pension Stick.*  Kalamazoo, Michigan: W.E. Upjohn Institute for Employment Research.

Nadel, Mark V.  2001.  "Getting Older in the 21st Century: Will the Boomers Discover Disability?"  In this volume, pp. 135–161.

O'Leary, Christopher J., and Stephen A. Wandner.  2000.  "Unemployment Compensation and Older Workers."  In this volume, pp. 85–133.

Quinn, Joseph F.  1999.  "New Paths to Retirement."  In *Forecasting Retirement Needs and Retirement Wealth*, P. Brett Hammond, Olivia S. Mitchell, and Anna M. Rappaport, eds.  Philadelphia: University of Pennsylvania Press, pp. 13–32.

Sandell, Steven H., and Stephen E. Baldwin.  1990.  "Older Workers and Employment Shifts: Policy Responses to Displacement."  In *The Aging of the American Workforce: Problems, Programs, Policies,* Irving Bluestone, Rhonda J.V. Montgomery, and John D. Owen, eds.  Detroit: Wayne State University Press.

Swartz, Katherine, and Betsey Stevenson.  2001.  "Health Insurance Coverage of People in the Ten Years before Medicare Eligibility."  In this volume, pp. 13–40.

*Charting the Landscape:*

# Commentary

Walter B. Maher
*DaimlerChrysler Corporation*

Well, good morning, and congratulations on making it here. I'm
Wally Maher. I'm with DaimlerChrysler Corporation and I want to
first really congratulate the Academy on the initiative it's taken to
tackle this problem. It's a very real problem. I've been asked to comment on the various background papers from the perspective of an
employer. As the background papers and the summary that you just
heard reflect, for many employers, including my company, there is considerable linkage between the public and private plans covering health
care, pension, and disability benefits. And for this reason, a major benefit of the Academy effort will be to help assure that these linkages are
understood by policymakers, lest anyone believe that you can cut back
on one without impacting the other.

As I begin this morning, I'm sure that—and if it isn't, it should be
clear to all of you—that my company and my industry is not your typical U.S. employer relative to the types of benefit plans that we offer.
First, the great majority of our employees are represented by a union,
the UAW, and notwithstanding the fine and substantial efforts of the
organizing staffs of the AFL-CIO member unions, this is not true of
most U.S. employers. Second—and not totally divorced from the
first—is the fact that we provide comprehensive benefits for our
employees and retirees that relate to the subject of this conference:
health care, pension, disability, and life insurance.

Third, my company and our industry—and this may come as a surprise to some of you—is in the relatively early stage of a massive number of retirements and related hiring, based largely on the fact that we
had a large hiring binge in the mid to late 1960s. So we at my company, and I'm fairly sure that this is true of GM and Ford, are actually
witnessing the start of a reduction in the average age of our workforce,
and I'm sure that this phenomenon is being experienced by some of the
larger auto supply firms with similar benefit structures. Finally, it is
very clear that there are many companies with an aging workforce that
do not provide the health and disability benefits that we do, and it is

here where the risks that the Academy is studying can be most profound.

The reason I wanted to point these facts out is that I believe they tend to validate the data that was portrayed particularly in the paper by Katherine Swartz, which shows that there is progressively less insurance coverage among the various baby-boomer cohorts that are moving through the system and approaching retirement age. I believe that this could reflect both the then-current trend towards less unionization of workplaces and the shift in U.S. employment away from traditional manufacturing jobs.

Now, despite what I said about the fact that we have at my company an average age that is starting to decline, we still have many older employees, and I do want to discuss the major challenges that we face to assure that these workers continue to have productive jobs and that we're able to reduce the cost associated with having disabled workers. I also wish to discuss the fact that while the benefit programs we have in place are not representative of the employer population generally, there are indeed many employers with similar plans, and these employee protections could well be jeopardized by ill-conceived public policies.

Let me first discuss the major challenges that my company is confronting as we face the reality of an older workforce. First, it has become very clear that there is a priority in designing jobs in a way to reduce the risk of injury. It has been established in our industry that standardized work practices are critical to injury prevention. Second is training: you can have all the standardized work practices in the world, but unless workers are adequately trained to perform the job as designed, you're not going to avoid the risk of injury. Third, we have to have adequate supervision. Finally, in addition to these core requirements, we've also found that it's been quite helpful to have available for employees wellness programs and other information so that they understand the value of healthy lifestyles.

Now, if all that fails, another challenge is to have the resources at hand to retrain workers to be able to perform jobs that are compatible with their physical limitations. And since I brought up the subject of retraining, I should point out that this is an issue which I personally believe as a country we would be well served to focus more attention on, specifically the need to have adequate programs in place to assist workers who are unable to perform the jobs that they currently have and who have lost their jobs as a result. Now this could be the result of disability or it could also be the result of the continued globalization of the economy. In either case, just as my company has an interest in having all of our employees working productively, the country has a similar interest in having every American living as productive a life as possible. The private sector has lots of experience in, and understands the value of, retraining, and we would hope that more and more of that filters into the public sector, because retraining truly can open new horizons for workers.

Now what about some of the other concerns that I mentioned? First—as I mentioned earlier and as you just heard in the summary and in the background papers—there are many employers that don't provide the level of benefits that we do, and my concern is that despite the continued and sustained level of prosperity that we've enjoyed here in the United States, there are many employers that still do not provide even a basic level of health benefits for their employees, not to mention short- and long-term disability benefits or a pension plan with a PTD component.

What are some of the reasons for this? First, of course, they're not required to by law. Second, they may not be able to afford it. And third, they may not have to in order to attract employees. And this is particularly true for lower-paid and lower-skilled jobs, and I frankly don't see this changing. One reason it's unlikely to change is the ever-increasing cost of health benefits. In this regard, it's been pretty evident that health benefits are particularly cost-sensitive, and that's why most employees today find themselves in some form of managed-care plan and why many employers offer only HMOs—because that's all they can afford.

So a concern I have is what do you think will happen if, as a result of increased regulations, health premiums rise even faster? Or, more daunting, if the eligibility age for Medicare is increased to 67 or 70? In my judgment, you can bet that fewer employers will offer health benefits. If the Medicare eligibility age is increased, the cost of health benefits for workers who elect to continue working until 67 or 70 will rise sharply, and the incidence of employer-provided retiree health benefits will continue to plummet. The same will be true for lesser provided benefits like disability plans.

I continue to wince every time I hear the proposal to increase the Medicare eligibility age to 67 described as one merely intended to bring Medicare eligibility in sync with Social Security. I mean, while numerically this is correct, there is one fundamental, compelling difference which argues against using this analogy. It's the fact that today, given the existing, steadily increasing eligibility age for full Social Security benefits, if any American chooses to remain in the workforce beyond age 65, so as not to experience a reduction in Social Security benefits, that American is assured at the very least of getting cash wages from an employer equal to the minimum wage, and in most cases substantially more. However, that same employee has zero assurance of getting any health benefits from the employer. And in lieu of that, if they tread out into the private insurance market to buy a policy for the employee and a spouse at age 65 or 66, you can imagine the portion of the person's take home pay that that premium would represent. So that's the reason that I tend to wince about that when I hear that analogy used.

Now clearly, is the Medicare program a perfect program? No. Is it in need of reform? Yes. Does it have to more resemble the type of plans that employees have available today, including structures to help retard cost increases? Yes. Do benefits have to be modernized? Yes. But as we embrace and try to craft those reform strategies, we have to endeavor not to adopt reforms that will exacerbate the problems of the uninsured.

I would be remiss if I didn't point out that the biggest challenge we confront is to assure that any actions we take to address the problems of an aging society are consistent with maintaining a strong economy. As the background papers made clear, as the U.S. unemployment rate increases, the incidence of disability increases geometrically. Further, having a strong economy and the resulting surpluses could eliminate at least one of the barriers for improving many social programs designed to assist the elderly, the ill and disabled. So there's a compelling reason to keep U.S. employers competitive in the global economy and to keep good paying jobs here in the United States, both of which are essential ingredients for a strong economy.

I bring this up because it should be recognized that if we, in an effort to moderate the cost of public safety-net programs, shift costs to employers or otherwise pass laws which have the same effect and unreasonably increase labor costs, there will be two inevitable results, neither of which is good for workers or the economy. While employers like us and those in our industry are unlikely to cancel our benefit plans, there could be some impact on overall compensation plans; or worse, if we become less competitive, employment opportunities could stall. Again, neither of those is good news. Worse, however, is that many employers could just drop or substantially diminish their benefit plans, and new employers would be less likely to implement them in the first place. Again, neither is good news for workers.

As the cost of health and disability benefits continues to increase, in part due to an older workforce, it's important to recognize that employers do need some flexibility to manage their health and disability benefit programs, including the cost of workers' compensation, to keep them more affordable. We can't forget the fact that, under the current laws of this country, the provision of benefit programs, including health and disability benefits, is voluntary, and if employers drop their coverage, the cost shifting that results from a diminishing number of employers providing benefits will continue to grow.

In conclusion, I believe it is possible for employers to maintain programs which are sensitive to the needs of an older workforce and to act reasonably to keep the costs of these programs in line. I also believe that as a nation we are prosperous enough to have safety-net programs to meet the needs of an aging society. I hope that we are able to pursue both paths in a way that continues to provide a strong economy and good job opportunities here in the United States.

Thank you.

Charting the Landscape:

# Commentary

(USI

J26 J14

J52

David A. Smith
*AFL–CIO*

Good morning. As I was walking in this morning I was reminded that—the time must have been 1978 or 1979, and I was due at a meeting here. I was teaching at the University of Massachusetts at that point, got on a plane in a blizzard in Boston, and the plane landed at National just like it was supposed to. I got on the subway and got to my meeting. Seven or eight people were supposed to be there, all of whom lived in the District, none of whom made it. You're to be congratulated for your perseverance this morning.

Let me begin by echoing something that Wally said. The Academy is to be not only congratulated, but encouraged to do more. All four papers deal with pressing issues. They deal with them intelligently. They pose a compelling agenda and raise questions in an enormously thoughtful way. Bob's summary and discussion of cross-cutting issues highlighted that. He also made my job of trying to respond either more difficult or easier, depending on which way you think about it.

Let me make five points; none of them will come as a surprise because of the extraordinary good work that went into the preparation for this panel. First, Bob noted, and I think we need to underscore, the enormous asymmetry in both circumstance and access to benefits among older workers, whether it's the asymmetry in health status, the asymmetry that results from different employment relationships which in turn create an asymmetry with access to the public side of the program, and most importantly (as I'll come back to and as Wally mentioned), asymmetry in access to employer-provided benefits, particularly for workers who've left their permanent attachment to the workforce.

The difference between a unionized DaimlerChrysler employee and her access to an employer-provided benefit system in the early years of her retirement or the late years of her working life and the access that most workers (sadly, a growing proportion of workers) have to those supports is enormous. There is a clear racial dimension to this asymmetry, and increasingly, I think we'll find that there's a gender dimension to it as well; and, of course, it is attenuated by differences in health status. We have to pay an enormous amount of attention to that, and Bob framed—and I think purposefully—Bob framed a question in an either/or fashion. He framed it as, should we be encouraging work, or should we be improving the adequacy of the public safety net and social insurance systems or should we be doing both?

I think the asymmetry argument (among others, but powerfully) leads you (or me, at least) to the answer that I suspect Bob wanted us all to come to: obviously, both. There are good reasons; first, but not only, labor market reasons. The fulfillment of older workers' hopes for the shape of their own lives and the increase in longevity argue that we ought to be trying to encourage work and we ought to remove perversities from both the public and private benefit systems that discourage work or inappropriately tax it. But we don't all come to that moment in our lives similarly situated. Many of us come to that moment more dependent on the safety net and the social insurance system. We find it badly structured and in many cases quantitatively insufficient, and we need to be strengthening it as well. So there is not a simple answer to the work-or-safety-net question, and we won't do ourselves a service by trying to answer Bob's question in any way except "both."

Let me make a third point, which builds on something that Wally said and try to put a sharper point on it. The employer-based, collectively bargained system, as you all know, is eroding. And Wally made a point which I think sort of helps us understand this in a deeper way. It's eroding even more dramatically than aggregate data show, and more than we often think because the workers covered by it are older. They are older than the average worker. Just as Chrysler faces a shift down the demographic ladder, as a huge cohort of older workers retire, we took a look at union retirements—anticipated retirements of all organized workers in the first decade of this century—and it's a 45 degree line going up the graph. We are going to find an enormous increase in the retirement of represented workers in the next decade, and that means we are also going to see an enormous decrease in the number of workers who are represented in places where employer-provided benefits are the norm. While some firms, like Chrysler, will be replacing those workers, the covered share, all else being equal, will continue to decrease, and decrease very dramatically through about

2018, when we'll begin to see the same phenomenon among our members of a substantial increase in younger workers.

That ought to make us enormously careful, for exactly the reasons that Wally mentioned about tinkering with the existing apparatus in ways that make it more difficult to access. The number and share of rehires who are going to need it will increase; the number of people who are going to come into their early retirement years or their late work years without the protections that have allowed some to suggest increasing the retirement age will also increase; and we, therefore, must be enormously cautious, particularly about Medicare eligibility.

Let me make a fourth point that I've talked about a little bit, and Bob mentioned it particularly in terms of older workers. Do we need to modify the public side of the safety net to take account of changing employment relationships? The answer is obviously yes, but I caution against thinking that that's a problem which we can isolate to older workers. The number of people entering the labor force in some sort of nonstandard arrangement—contract work, temporary work, serial employment—is increasing (sharply in some sectors of the economy). And, the number of part-time workers is already large; it isn't increasing, but is already a big chunk of the labor force. None of our systems of social insurance adequately reflect the changing nature of our employment relationships. It may be a particularly acute problem in the short run for older workers, but it is a problem that isn't limited to that part of the population. I underscore that for reasons that you all know well—both employer preference and to a large extent the consequences of the maturation of the entry of women into the labor force— these nonstandard arrangements are unlikely to go away. Even with the relatively strong—enormously strong, in fact—employment growth over the last three years, the rate of increase in nonstandard attachment has continued to accelerate. We should expect that to continue.

Let me just make one last comment provoked by something that Wally said, which is the issue of training. We do a terrible job. Chrysler, AT&T, a handful of other corporations do a decent job, but as a society we do an enormously inadequate job of providing training for people during their working lives. We don't spend enough money. We spend about 1 percent of payroll. We skew it up the income ladder. We devote 7 or 8 times as many training dollars (private training dollars) to managers as we do to front-line workers, and we provide almost no training at the bottom of the labor market where folks are most mobile. This is a problem that will haunt us for the productivity reasons that Wally mentioned, but also for the demographic reasons that we have both talked about. We are going to be replacing a significant share of the American workforce over the next decade, and we will have systematically underinvested in those replacements.

Thank you very much.

# Session 2
# Job Loss
## Income and Health Coverage

(US)

# The Effects of Job Loss on Older Workers

## Employment, Earnings, and Wealth

J14
J31
J64 J63
J32 I31

Sewin Chan
*Rutgers University*

Ann Huff Stevens
*Yale University*

The impact of job loss on an older worker's economic well-being is likely to be substantial, with the displacement affecting both subsequent employment patterns and financial resources available before and after retirement. This paper uses data from the Health and Retirement Study (HRS) to examine employment, earnings, and wealth changes that follow involuntary job loss among workers aged 50 and over.

We find that job loss leads to very long spells of non-employment, with large differences in the employment rates of displaced and nondisplaced workers lasting for more than five years. In addition, the earnings of those who do return to work are dramatically reduced over the remaining years of the working life. Even six years after job loss, earnings are significantly below those of similar, nondisplaced individuals. Although employment-based pensions are not typically lost with displacement, account balances and expected annual pension benefits may be somewhat diminished. Among displaced men, nonhousing-related asset holdings also tend to fall after a job loss.

These results are particularly pertinent in light of the disproportionate increase in job loss rates among older workers during the last recession (Farber 1997). While job loss rates for all age groups have subsequently declined, the aging of the workforce in the United States makes it important to better document and understand the effects on older workers.

## THE DATA

To examine job loss and its effects on earnings, assets, pensions, and employment, we used publicly available data from the first three waves of the Health and Retirement Study (HRS), which were conducted in 1992, 1994, and 1996. We include all men and women aged 50 and over as of 1992 who remain in the survey at least through the second wave.

We identified and followed job loss among older workers in the HRS using the extensive information on earnings and employment collected at each wave, including information on job changes that took place between the waves. We also used information collected at the initial survey wave on up to two previous jobs. First, for those working at the wave 1 survey date, we used information on their current earnings and employment characteristics; for those who are not working at wave 1, we used information on their previous job, including when and why it ended and their final earnings. Second, all individuals at wave 1 (employed or not) were asked to provide information on their most recent previous job that lasted at least five years, thus giving us retrospective data on relatively long-term jobs that ended prior to wave 1. In subsequent waves of the HRS, employed individuals were asked whether they hold the same job as in the previous wave; if not, the reason for leaving was ascertained. Non-employed individuals were also asked about what happened to their last job. All of this employment information enabled us to construct a continuous series of monthly indicators, designating each individual as working or not in each month from 1992 through the final survey date in 1996.

Based on these jobs that end before or during the course of the three waves, we defined as our sample of "displaced" workers those who respond that their job ended when either 1) the "business closed" or 2) they were "laid off or let go." While the second part of this definition may include some individuals fired for cause, we included them for consistency with many recent definitions of displaced workers and to include individuals who have been "downsized."[1] Thus, our sample of job losses consists of reported displacements from long-term jobs ending prior to wave 1, jobs held immediately prior to becoming non-employed at the wave 1 survey date, (up to two) jobs ending between waves 1 and 2, and (up to two) jobs ending between waves 2 and 3.

For each of the jobs documented in the HRS, information was also collected on pension eligibility, structure, and benefit amounts. Employer-matched pension-provider data have been gathered as part of the HRS and used recently by several researchers.[2] We note however, that we are relying on self-reported pension information from the three surveys, because the matched pension file provides details for a single point in time only (wave 1). Given that our interest is in how pensions change with displacement, we had to use the self-reported longitudinal data. While concerns have been raised regarding the accuracy and completeness of self-reported pensions in the HRS (see Gustman and Steinmeier 1999), it is the only available source of detailed longitudinal data on private pension wealth and eligibility rules among older workers.

Additional information was collected from the HRS surveys regarding health status and demographic information, as well as income and assets. Summary statistics for men and women by their displacement status are shown in Appendix Table 1.

## EMPLOYMENT

We analyzed the probability and timing of returning to work, as well as the durability of postdisplacement employment, by estimating hazard models both for entering and exiting employment. The estimated transition rates are then used to describe the employment patterns of displaced workers following an involuntary job loss.[3] The full details of this estimation strategy and the results are discussed in Chan and Stevens (forthcoming).

First, we estimated the probability that a non-employed individual returns to work in a given month, controlling for individual characteristics, whether the worker is non-employed due to a recent job displacement, and the length of the current spell of non-employment. This provided us with an estimate of how many displaced workers return to employment and how quickly they do so.[4]

Second, we examined the persistence of postdisplacement employment for older workers who return to work by estimating the probability of leaving employment, again, controlling for demographic characteristics and whether the individual has experienced a job loss in the recent past.[5] This allowed us to consider whether displaced individuals are more or less likely to leave employment than are comparable individuals who have not been displaced. If postdisplacement jobs offer lower wages or other less desirable job characteristics or represent poor matches between workers and firms, we would expect recently displaced workers to leave employment at a higher rate.

To understand the total impact of displacement on employment among older workers, we calculated the employment rates implied by the estimated coefficients of the transition probability models. In each month, the coefficients from the entry-to-work model along with an individual's characteristics tell us the probability that a non-employed individual returns to work. Once a displaced individual does return to work, the coefficients from the model for exiting employment tell us the probability of leaving the workforce. Using the estimated transition probabilities in this way, we produced a series of monthly employment patterns over several years for workers who are displaced at a given age and for comparable workers who are employed and not displaced at that age.

Results from the probit estimation of transition probabilities from non-employment to employment and from employment to non-employment are shown in Table 1. Although our main focus will be on the employment rates implied by these transition probabilities, we briefly summarize the key results from the hazard models. The rates at which older workers return to work implied by these coefficients are fairly low, ranging up to 8 percent per month. For non-employed men and women in their fifties, the variables for a prior job loss are positive and statistically significant, indicating that displaced workers in their fifties return to the workforce more quickly than similar workers who are not employed for reasons other than displacement. This is not surprising, since many of the nondisplaced have retired voluntarily. For workers in their sixties, however, displaced and nondisplaced individuals return to work at similar rates. For example, a married, recently displaced man aged 55, with a high school education and in excellent health, has roughly a 5 percent probability of returning to the

**Table 1 Entry to Work and Exit from Work Probabilities[a]**

| Characteristic | Entry to work | | Exit from work | |
|---|---|---|---|---|
| Dependent variable | Men | Women | Men | Women |
| Intercept | -1.553 (0.108)[b] | -1.600 (0.093) | -2.503 (0.055) | -2.442 (0.061) |
| Age: 55 | -0.019 (0.077) | 0.040 (0.059) | 0.069 (0.041) | 0.058 (0.038) |
| 56 to 60 | -0.060 (0.048) | -0.053 (0.038) | 0.046 (0.026) | -0.002 (0.027) |
| 61 | -0.209 (0.080) | -0.272 (0.068) | 0.142 (0.043) | 0.121 (0.042) |
| 62 | -0.262 (0.086) | -0.333 (0.081) | 0.460 (0.041) | 0.387 (0.043) |
| 63 | -0.289 (0.092) | -0.171 (0.085) | 0.417 (0.047) | 0.328 (0.055) |
| 64 | -0.305 (0.111) | -0.233 (0.130) | 0.234 (0.063) | 0.338 (0.076) |
| 65 | -0.145 (0.104) | -0.624 (0.311) | 0.469 (0.060) | 0.682 (0.092) |
| 66+ | -0.300 (0.076) | -0.181 (0.149) | 0.299 (0.044) | 0.205 (0.126) |
| 1993 | -0.036 (0.074) | -0.021 (0.062) | -0.070 (0.039) | -0.013 (0.041) |
| 1994 | 0.107 (0.072) | 0.072 (0.061) | -0.031 (0.039) | 0.027 (0.041) |
| 1995 | -0.388 (0.082) | -0.386 (0.071) | -0.263 (0.043) | -0.140 (0.044) |
| 1996 | -0.397 (0.091) | -0.406 (0.083) | -0.132 (0.045) | 0.008 (0.046) |
| Married | 0.019 (0.045) | -0.145 (0.037) | -0.123 (0.025) | 0.014 (0.024) |
| Disability | -0.167 (0.048) | -0.179 (0.044) | 0.139 (0.028) | 0.165 (0.032) |
| Physical health | -0.089 (0.018) | -0.070 (0.016) | 0.054 (0.010) | 0.048 (0.012) |
| White | 0.001 (0.044) | 0.014 (0.041) | -0.005 (0.025) | -0.004 (0.028) |
| High school graduate | 0.035 (0.046) | 0.016 (0.041) | 0.030 (0.025) | -0.064 (0.030) |
| Some college | 0.175 (0.051) | 0.042 (0.048) | 0.023 (0.028) | -0.071 (0.034) |

(continued)

**Table 1 (continued)**

| Dependent variable | Entry to work | | Exit from work | |
|---|---|---|---|---|
| Characteristic | Men | Women | Men | Women |
| College graduate | 0.047 (0.052) | -0.009 (0.056) | -0.017 (0.028) | -0.054 (0.037) |
| Months not working | -0.032 (0.004) | -0.013 (0.002) | | |
| (Months not working)$^2$ | 3.72E-04 (6.72E-05) | 7.25E-05 (1.33E-05) | | |
| (Months not working)$^3$ | -1.60E-06 (3.72E-07) | -1.52E-07 (3.76E-08) | | |
| (Months not working)$^4$ | 1.80E-09 (4.82E-10) | 1.05E-10 (3.30E-11) | | |
| Prior job loss | 0.240 (0.068) | 0.308 (0.060) | 0.256 (0.054) | 0.143 (0.060) |
| × age 62(+) | -0.510 (0.215) | -0.018 (0.106) | -0.224 (0.101) | -0.237 (0.134) |
| × Age 63 | -0.124 (0.172) | | -0.292 (0.133) | -0.417 (0.199) |
| × Age 64 | -0.104 (0.189) | | -0.034 (0.157) | -0.741 (0.339) |
| × Age 65(+) | -0.446 (0.245) | | -0.243 (0.184) | -0.190 (0.274) |
| × Age 66 + | 0.137 (0.121) | | -0.113 (0.105) | |
| × Months not working | 0.007 (0.006) | -0.009 (0.003) | | |
| × (Months not working)$^2$ | -1.56E-04 (8.24E-05) | 7.26E-05 (3.25E-05) | | |
| × 12–23 months working | | | 0.119 (0.074) | -0.070 (0.088) |
| × 24–35 months working | | | 0.066 (0.082) | 0.057 (0.093) |
| × 36–47 months working | | | -0.149 (0.097) | 0.076 (0.102) |
| × 48–59 months working | | | -0.107 (0.098) | -0.298 (0.150) |
| × 60+ months working | | | -0.309 (0.072) | -0.134 (0.089) |

[a] Coefficients from probit discrete hazard model.
[b] Standard errors in parentheses.

workforce each month. A similar nondisplaced man has only about a 2 percent chance of returning to work each month. Differences between displaced and nondisplaced women are similar in magnitude.

The probability of exiting employment also depends on a worker's displacement experience. The coefficient for a prior job loss in the model for leaving employment is positive and statistically significant, indicating that individuals with a previous job loss are more likely to leave employment than similar nondisplaced individuals. Thus, even after returning to work, recently displaced individuals are less likely than others to remain employed at each subsequent age.

Other individual characteristics have the expected effects on entry into and exit from the workforce. Poor health and disabilities reduce the probability of returning to work and increase the likelihood of leaving the workforce. There are no statistically significant effects of race or education for men or women. Married women are much less likely to go back to work, and married men are less likely to leave employment.

To better summarize the employment patterns of displaced and nondisplaced workers, charts A and B of Figure 1 show the probability of employment over the next 10 years for two groups of workers: individuals displaced at age 55 and individuals working and not displaced at age 55. Charts C and D repeat the analysis for men and women displaced and working as of age 60. These take into account both the rates at which workers return to work and the predicted rates at which they subsequently leave the workforce.

Focusing first on the workers losing jobs at age 55, the fraction working in each month initially rises quickly but flattens out after approximately three years. One year after the job loss, 50 percent of displaced men and 46 percent of displaced women are working, compared with 95 and 92 percent of men and women who were working as of age 55. After two years, 61 and 55 percent of displaced men and women are back at work, compared with 91 and 88 percent of the nondisplaced group. This employment gap is due both to the initial period of unemployment and to postdisplacement employment instability among those reemployed. For example, taking the entry rates alone would imply that 74 percent of displaced men return to work by two years after displacement. Once we consider subsequent exit behavior, however, employment rates fall to 61 percent. These results also high-

## Figure 1  Fraction Employed by Displacement Status at Age 55 and 60

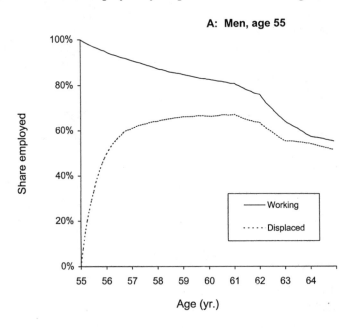

A:  Men, age 55

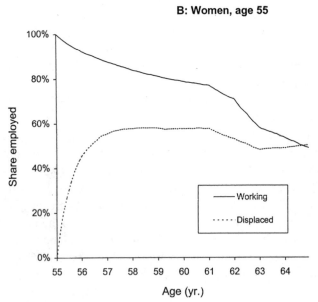

B: Women, age 55

**Figure 1 (continued)**

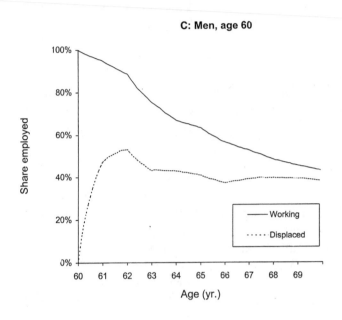

C: Men, age 60

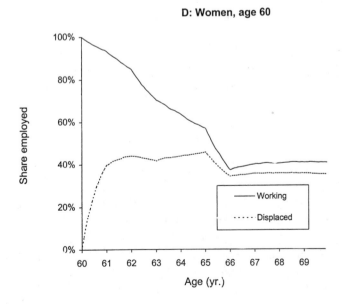

D: Women, age 60

light the long-term nature of the impact of displacement on the employment rates of older workers. It takes at least seven years after a job loss for the employment rates of displaced and nondisplaced workers to converge to within 10 percentage points of each other. Only when the nondisplaced workers begin to retire more rapidly, at age 62, does the employment gap narrow substantially.

The monthly employment probabilities following displacement or work at age 60 are similar to the results at age 55. The main difference is that the fraction of those working at age 60 who are still working in each subsequent month declines more rapidly as this cohort moves through ages of much higher retirement probabilities. The older displaced workers, however, also return to work more slowly, and so there remains a significant gap in the employment rates of the two groups.

These results suggest that workers who have lost jobs in the later portion of their careers have substantially different employment and retirement patterns throughout their fifties and sixties. One concern, however, is whether the results can be correctly interpreted as the impact of displacement, or whether they instead reflect worker heterogeneity that is correlated with job loss probabilities. We have tried including several additional controls for potential unobserved differences that could bias our findings. Including controls for predisplacement wages, pension eligibility, assets, and retirement expectations had virtually no effect on our estimated employment patterns. Moreover, when we limited the sample of displaced workers to those losing jobs only through plant or business closings (which may be more exogenous with respect to worker characteristics than layoffs), we also obtained very similar results.

## EARNINGS

For displaced workers who do return to work, we next examine the earnings on postdisplacement jobs. Many researchers have documented the large earnings reductions that accompany job loss for workers of all ages.[6] Older workers may face particularly large earnings reductions because they are likely to have been with their previous employers for many years and may have large stocks of firm-specific skills that are rendered useless by displacement. To measure the effects of job loss on earnings, we followed many recent studies and estimated fixed-effects regressions to control for both observable and unobservable worker characteristics that might be correlated with displacement probabilities. The results, shown in Table 2, use all wage observations from 1980 and later.[7] Earnings reported from jobs starting or ending prior to 1980 were eliminated because of concerns about the accuracy of retrospective information from more than a decade earlier. The dependent variable is the log of annual salary based on full-year full-time work: individuals were asked how much they earn on a given job, and these reports were converted to earnings on an annual basis.

**Table 2  Earnings Effects of Displacement (fixed-effects estimates)[a]**

| Characteristic | log(annual full-time earnings)[b] | |
| --- | --- | --- |
| | Men | Women |
| 1 year prior to displacement | -0.041 | -0.119 |
| | (0.033)[c] | (0.029) |
| 1 year after displacement | -0.392 | -0.388 |
| | (0.050) | (0.045) |
| 2 years after displacement | -0.349 | -0.361 |
| | (0.059) | (0.054) |
| 3 years after displacement | -0.327 | -0.348 |
| | (0.062) | (0.059) |
| 4 years after displacement | -0.311 | -0.300 |
| | (0.066) | (0.058) |
| 5 years after displacement | -0.316 | -0.280 |
| | (0.069) | (0.064) |
| 6 or more years after displacement | -0.262 | -0.336 |
| | (0.058) | (0.052) |
| After displacement × <3 years predisplacement tenure | 0.108 | 0.230 |
| | (0.061) | (0.058) |
| After displacement × >10 years of predisplacement tenure | -0.040 | -0.057 |
| | (0.047) | (0.046) |

[a] Additional controls: year dummies and quartic in age.
[b] Dependent variable.
[c] Standard errors are in parentheses.

Among our sample of older workers, the earnings reductions associated with job loss are large and persistent, in line with much previous research on the effects of displacement. In the year before job loss, our estimates indicate a 4 percent earnings reduction for men and an 11 percent reduction for women.[8] Such predisplacement earnings reductions have been found by many other authors. We have also included a control for two years before job loss but found this had no significant impact and, so we restricted the effect of two or more years prior to job loss to be zero. Following job loss, there is a 32 percent reduction in earnings for both men and women, much of which persists for several years. Six or more years after job loss, displaced men and women face earnings reductions of 23 and 29 percent, respectively. These effects, of course, are estimated only for individuals who are reemployed following displacement. It is very likely that these results overstate the wage opportunities available to a typical displaced worker, because those who are not reemployed may receive lower wage offers and have generally worse postdisplacement earnings opportunities.

We also interacted the postdisplacement earnings reduction with workers' predisplacement job tenure, which may serve as a proxy for the amount of specific human capital or the quality of the job match that has been lost. The main effects shown in the table are for the omitted category of workers with between 3 and 10 years of predisplacement job tenure. Average tenure prior to displacement in this sample is approximately 11 years. We find that the effect of job loss on earnings increases with predisplacement tenure. Individuals with fewer than three years of predisplacement tenure are estimated to face significantly lower earnings losses than those with higher predisplacement job tenure.

## WEALTH

We next consider the effects of job loss on older workers' holdings of wealth, including both pension and nonpension assets. We begin by exploring the effects of job loss on pension eligibility and benefit levels. The first question that arises is whether older workers who lose jobs typically retain pension benefits from their previous employers. If workers are not fully vested, the loss of a job might also result in the loss of future pension benefits. Given that all workers in our sample are at least 50 years of age, and on average have relatively high tenure with their predisplacement employers, we expect the complete loss of pension benefits with job loss to be relatively rare. Most of the workers losing jobs are already vested in their pension plans or have accumulated defined-contribution accounts that can be moved to a new employer or rolled over into an IRA.

This is confirmed in Table 3, which tabulates answers to the question "What happened to the pension associated with your previous job?" that was asked of all recent job-changers, whether the change was voluntary or involuntary. Fewer than 3 percent of displaced workers with defined-contribution (DC) plans on the previous job, and less

**Table 3  Pensions from Previous Jobs (%)[a]**

| Plan/status[b] | No displacement | Displacement |
|---|---|---|
| DB plan on previous job | | |
| Receiving benefits now | 51.0 | 33.2 |
| Will receive benefits in future | 20.9 | 42.7 |
| Rolled over to IRA | 1.1 | 1.3 |
| Received cash settlement | 19.7 | 18.9 |
| Lost pension | 9.0 | 5.5 |
| Number of observations | 2214 | 597 |
| DC plan on previous job | | |
| Transferred to a new employer | 9.7 | 6.2 |
| Rolled over to IRA | 17.8 | 24.2 |
| Left in account to accumulate | 27.4 | 34.8 |
| Converted to annuity | 4.9 | 2.2 |
| Received cash settlement | 28.8 | 25.8 |
| Lost pension | 3.0 | 2.5 |
| Unknown/other | 7.6 | 3.8 |
| Number of observations | 822 | 322 |

[a] Percentages do not sum to 100 because multiple responses were allowed (but were rare) and because of rounding.
[b] DB = defined-benefit; DC = defined-contribution.

than 6 percent of those with defined-benefit (DB) plans report that they completely lost pension accounts, benefits, or eligibility along with the job loss. Slightly more of those voluntarily changing or leaving jobs report losing pensions. Among those with DB pension accounts, 43 percent report that, despite having lost the job, they expect to receive pension benefits sometime in the future. An additional 33 percent of job losers are currently receiving benefits from their previous employers' DB plans. As might be expected, those with DC accounts generally retain their pension rights in some form after losing jobs. Sixty-five percent of displaced workers with DC accounts on the previous job either leave their accounts to continue accumulating, transfer them to a new employer, or roll them over into an IRA. A substantial fraction of displaced workers (19 percent of those with DB plans and 26 percent of those with DC plans) also report receiving cash settlements for their prior job pensions.

Because we did not find that pension plans are frequently lost with displacement, in the remainder of this analysis we focus on changes in pension wealth following job loss, conditional on having some pension plan prior to the job loss. Since displaced workers may have (at a minimum) several years in which they do not have a pension plan with their current employer, one possible effect of displacement may be to reduce the total amount accumulated in defined-contribution accounts. At the very least, employers will not be contributing to these accounts in the years following job loss. In addition, the lengthy spells of non-employment and reduced earnings that follow job loss may mean that individuals are more likely to withdraw funds from DC accounts. As a result, we should expect total pension wealth held in DC accounts to be reduced by displacement.

To explore this hypothesis, the first column of Table 4 shows results from regressions of the natural logarithm of the total amount accumulated in workers' DC accounts on indicators for before and after job loss.[9] We also controlled for age, health, education, race and calendar year. We used only the initial postdisplacement observation for each person because displaced individuals are only asked about account balances in the survey immediately after the job ended; in subsequent waves we cannot trace withdrawals or additions to these accounts.[10] Men with DC accounts in the years prior to job loss have roughly the same accumulated wealth in pension accounts as men who will not lose jobs. In the years after job loss, the estimated coefficient is –0.497, suggesting a reduction in DC account balances of 39 percent. Prior to job loss, women who are eventually displaced have DC accounts that are approximately 10 percent above those of nondisplaced women, although this difference is not statistically different from zero. After job loss, displaced women have account balances that are approximately 15 percent below those of nondisplaced women. The difference between the variables for prior to displacement and after displacement is statistically significant for men but not for women. Men who lose jobs face substantial reductions in their defined-contribution pension accounts, but there is no evidence of statistically significant reductions in these pension holdings for women who are displaced.

We also estimated fixed-effects regressions of DC account balances on job loss indicators. These specifications use the within-person variation in pension balances from before to after job loss to estimate an effect of displacement on account holdings. Including a person-specific fixed-effect in the regressions means that we are using only individuals who are observed both before and after job loss to identify the effect of job loss on pension wealth, rather than estimating average effects for before and after job loss and relying on the difference as our measure of displacement's impact. The fixed-effects results for DC account balances are similar to those estimated by ordinary least squares regressions. There is a sizable impact of displacement among men (a coefficient of –0.44, or a 36 percent reduction) and no statistically significant effect for women.

The effect of job loss on defined-benefit pension plans is more difficult to anticipate. We know that workers rarely report losing eligibility for such pension plans completely, but the effects on benefit amounts are less obvious. One possibility is that displacement may result in workers being eligible for some benefits from their previous employer, but not at the "optimal" or wealth-maximizing age. That is, a worker who loses a job at age 55 may be eligible to collect some pension benefits from the employer from whom she has separated, but would have been eligible for higher benefits if she had remained with the employer to age 62 or 65.

Examination of individual records for displaced workers who reported DB pension plans prior to job loss suggests that displacement

**Table 4  Effects of Displacement on Pensions and Assets**

| Dependent variable/Sample<br>Characteristic | log(total DC account)<br>Has DC plan | | log(expected annual DB benefit)<br>Has DB plan | | log(nonhousing assets)<br>All | |
|---|---|---|---|---|---|---|
| | OLS | Fixed-effects | OLS | Fixed-effects | OLS | Fixed-effects |
| **Men** | | | | | | |
| Prior to displacement | 0.015 | —[a] | -0.113 | — | -0.282 | — |
| | (0.147)[b] | | (0.087) | | (0.087) | |
| After displacement | -0.497 | -0.445 | -0.446 | -0.033 | -0.439 | -0.094 |
| | (0.155) | (0.217) | (0.060) | (0.057) | (0.059) | (0.055) |
| Number of observations | 2,058 | 2,058 | 5,601 | 5,601 | 2,279 | 12,279 |
| **Women** | | | | | | |
| Prior to displacement | 0.103 | — | -0.194 | — | -0.211 | — |
| | (0.184) | | (0.173) | | (0.102) | |
| After displacement | -0.162 | 0.132 | -0.569 | -0.285 | -0.267 | -0.054 |
| | (0.141) | (0.236) | (0.101) | (0.103) | (0.062) | (0.060) |
| Number of observations | 1,719 | 1,719 | 2,839 | 2,839 | 12,814 | 12,814 |

[a] A dash (—) indicates that the variables were not included in the fixed-effect regressions.
[b] Standard errors in parentheses.

results in both changes in the age at which pension benefits are received and changes in the amounts of these benefits. Prior to job loss, for example, a worker may report an expected annual pension benefit of $20,000 that can be received no earlier than age 62. After displacement, the same worker reports that he is currently receiving pension benefits from the previous job (despite being younger than age 62), but the annual benefit amount is smaller than that expected before displacement. Partial or reduced pension benefits may be offered as a form of severance package for workers displaced prior to reaching the "normal" eligibility age. Alternatively, Gustman and Steinmeier (1999) report that individuals in the HRS appear to be quite uninformed with respect to early eligibility ages for employer pension benefits, and thus it is not surprising that displaced individuals seem to receive benefits despite being younger than their self-reported eligibility age.

To understand the effect of job loss on benefits available from DB pensions, we estimated regressions of the log of current or future annual pension benefit amounts on job loss indicators for the sample of individuals reporting DB pension plans; the results are reported in the middle columns of Table 4. Men who will be displaced in a future year have expected annual pension benefits that are approximately 10 percent lower than those of similar workers who will not be displaced. In the years after job loss, annual benefits are reduced further. Men have benefit amounts in the years after job loss that are 36 percent lower than those of nondisplaced men. Women face similar reductions in annual benefit amounts. Prior to displacement, women have benefits that are 17 percent below the benefits of women who are not displaced; after job loss, displaced women report benefits that are 43 percent below those of nondisplaced women. Again, taking the difference from before to after displacement as our measure of displacement's impact, men and women are estimated to lose 30 and 32 percent of their annual benefit amounts.

The fixed-effects results for defined-benefit pensions paint a somewhat different picture. For women, the fixed-effects results are similar to the OLS results, suggesting a reduction in pension benefits of 24 percent. Among men, however, the fixed-effects results show no evidence of reductions in pension benefits. The fact that the results for men are not robust to the inclusion of individual fixed effects suggests that the benefit reductions reported here should be viewed cautiously. Work by Haider and Stephens (1999) using employer-provided pension data from the HRS points to modest negative effects of displacement on pension wealth.

These findings suggest that job loss may significantly reduce pension wealth, particularly for those with defined-contribution accounts, and for women with defined-benefit accounts. Some additional caveats should also be mentioned here. First, because we are using self-reported pension data, it is possible that displaced workers may know more (or less) about their actual pension coverage and wealth than the comparison groups.[11] If this knowledge is correlated with job loss, it could bias our estimates of displacement effects on pensions. Second, if job loss results in pension wealth being transferred to savings accounts or IRAs, the above calculations could overstate the loss in total wealth since they include only DB plans or DC accounts. To examine this issue and to further our understanding of the overall effect of job loss on older workers' economic well-being, we next examined the effects of job loss on workers' asset holdings, including IRAs and other potential retirement savings.

The final columns of Table 4 show the effect of job loss on the log of nonhousing assets in the three waves.[12] The drawback of using the log specification here is that we must eliminate individuals who report zero or negative values of nonhousing assets (roughly 10 percent of men and 15 percent of women).[13] As expected, displacement reduces nonhousing wealth, although the estimates are not statistically significant for women.[14] The coefficients on the variable indicating workers prior to job loss shows that there are large differences in nonhousing (nonpension) asset levels prior to any displacement. For women, there is not a statistically significant difference between the pre- and postdisplacement coefficients, so we cannot reject the hypothesis that displacement has no effect on their nonhousing asset holdings. The fixed-effects results for women are consistent with this finding. Because many women in our sample are not the primary earners in their household, displacement among older women may have a relatively small impact on household-level asset holdings.

For men, the coefficient for after job loss is statistically different from the predisplacement control and implies that the displacement of older men reduces nonhousing asset levels by approximately 15 percent. Fixed-effects results for men show a slightly smaller effect of displacement on nonhousing wealth that is significant at the 10 percent level. This is consistent with recent evidence reported by Gruber (1999) for younger workers. He finds that wealth holdings decline substantially with realized unemployment durations. Because older displaced workers typically have much longer spells of non-employment than younger displaced workers, it is not surprising that we find significant wealth reductions. As shown above, far less than half of older displaced workers have returned to work within one year, and it appears that private wealth holdings may provide a mechanism for replacing lost earnings in the short run.

## CONCLUSIONS

Our findings point to large and lasting effects of job loss on the future employment probabilities of older workers. Two years after a job loss at age 55, just 61 and 55 percent of men and women are employed, compared with employment rates of more than 80 percent among nondisplaced men and women who were working at age 55. Even four years after job loss, there is a gap in employment rates of approximately 20 percent between the displaced and nondisplaced groups. These long-term employment effects of displacement come as the result of both the rates of return to employment after displacement and elevated rates of exit from postdisplacement jobs.

The earnings of individuals who return to work following job loss are also dramatically affected. Immediately after displacement, earnings are only two-thirds of their expected value had the job loss not occurred. Even six years after the job loss, displaced men and women face earnings reductions of more than 20 percent.

Our findings with respect to pension and nonpension wealth are less stark. Most displaced workers over the age of 50 do not lose pension eligibility or benefits with displacement, and many of them begin to receive benefits immediately from their future employer, expect benefits at a later date, or receive a cash settlement. Nevertheless, we do find some evidence of possible reductions in the amount of defined-benefit pension payouts and in defined-contribution account balances.

Finally, for men, there is evidence that nonpension asset holdings are reduced following displacement.

The long spells of non-employment, large earnings reductions, and perhaps some reductions in pension and nonpension wealth point to significant costs of job loss for workers in their fifties and sixties. Even if these workers were well prepared for retirement prior to a job loss, changes in earnings and wealth associated with displacement may significantly reduce the private resources available to them during retirement. Our future research will focus on understanding how shocks to earnings and asset holdings such as those following job loss may affect the behavior and welfare of these workers as they consider retirement.

## Notes

The authors gratefully acknowledge financial support from the National Science Foundation, grants 9905275 and 9907824.

1. Other possible responses to the question regarding how the previous job ended include "quit," "retired," "temporary layoff," and "wanted a better job."
2. See Gustman and Steinmeier (1998), McGarry and Davenport (1997), and Venti and Wise (1998), among others.
3. Blau (1994) and Peracchi and Welch (1994) similarly focused on transition probabilities between different employment states for older workers.
4. Specifically, the probability $h^n$ of making a transition from nonwork to work in each month, given that the individual is not currently working, is represented with a standard probit functional form ($\Phi$ is the standard cumulative normal distribution):

    $$h_{it}^n = \Phi(y_{it}),$$

    where $y_{it} = f^n(\text{Age}_{it}, X_{it}, \text{Months-not-working}_{it}, \text{Prior-job-loss}_{it})$.

    That is, the hazard $h_{it}^n$ gives the probability that nonworking individual $i$ returns to work in month $t$, conditional on age, other individual characteristics ($X$), months since the individual last worked, and whether the individual has lost a job in the recent past. We can interpret $y_{it}$ as an underlying latent variable that takes a value greater than zero if a transition from nonwork to work occurs. Interactions between the variables Age, $X$, Months-not-working, and Prior-job-loss are included in the $f^n$ function.
5. This second hazard is of the form:

    $$h_{it}^w = \Phi(z_{it})$$

    where $z_{it} = f^w(\text{Age}_{it}, X_{it}, \text{Prior-job-loss}_{it})$. This gives the probability that working individual $i$ makes a work to nonwork transition in month $t$, conditional on age, other control variables $X$, and Prior-job-loss status.

6. See, for example, Ruhm (1991), Jacobson, LaLonde, and Sullivan (1993), Stevens (1997), and Schoeni and Dardia (1997).

7. We obtain similar results using a balanced sample in which each individual contributes four wage observations to the sample, one in each survey wave and one from a long-term job prior to wave 1.

8. In Table 2, the dependent variable is in log form and the percentage effect is given by $e^\beta - 1$, where $\beta$ is the estimated coefficient on the dummy variable of interest.

9. Individuals who claim to have a defined-contribution plan but have missing values for the amount held in the account were dropped from the sample.

10. These data limitations are thoroughly discussed in Uccello and Perese (1999).

11. In future work, we can explore this issue by utilizing restricted-access employer reports of pension plans. While these are currently available only for wave 1, we can at least make comparisons at wave 1 between nondisplaced workers, those displaced prior to wave 1, and those who will lose jobs after wave 1.

12. We have also examined total assets, including the value of housing, and several other subsets of the wealth variables. We find that housing does not respond to job loss, and so we focus on nonhousing-related assets.

13. We have examined the effect of job loss on the level of assets for those individuals who start out with zero or negative assets and found no statistically significant effects. The log specification results in a substantially better fit than a specification using asset levels.

14. Couch and Gallo (1998) have also examined asset changes using data from the first two waves of the HRS. They found reductions in nonhousing net worth of roughly 20 to 30 percent following displacement, although the effects are also not always statistically significant.

# References

Blau, David M. 1994. "Labor Force Dynamics of Older Men." *Econometrica* 62: 117–156.

Chan, Sewin, and Ann Huff Stevens. Forthcoming. "Job Loss and Employment Patterns of Older Workers." *Journal of Labor Economics*.

Couch, Kenneth, and William Gallo. 1998. "Earnings and Asset Losses of Older Displaced Workers." Photocopy. University of Connecticut.

Farber, Henry. 1997. "The Changing Face of Job Loss in the United States, 1981–1995." *Brookings Papers on Economic Activity, Microeconomics*: 55–128.

Gruber, Jonathan. 1999. "The Wealth of the Unemployed: Adequacy and Implications for Unemployment Insurance." Working paper no. 7348, National Bureau of Economic Research, Cambridge, Massachusetts.

Gustman, Alan L., and Thomas L. Steinmeier. 1998. "Effects of Pensions on Savings: Analysis with Data from the Health and Retirement Study."

Working paper no. 6681, National Bureau of Economic Research, Cambridge, Massachusetts.

———. 1999. "What People Don't Know about Their Pensions and Social Security: An Analysis using Linked Data from the Health and Retirement Study." Working paper no. 7368, National Bureau of Economic Research, Cambridge, Massachusetts.

Haider, Steven, and Melvin Stephens. 1999. "The Impact of Displacement for Older Workers." Photocopy. RAND Corporation, Santa Monica, California.

Jacobson, Louis, Robert LaLonde, and Daniel Sullivan. 1993. *The Costs of Worker Dislocation*. Kalamazoo, Michigan: W.E. Upjohn Institute for Employment Research.

McGarry, Kathleen, and Andrew Davenport. 1997. "Pensions and the Distribution of Wealth." Working paper no. 6171, National Bureau of Economic Research, Cambridge, Massachusetts.

Peracchi, Franco, and Finis Welch. 1994. "Trends in Labor Force Transitions of Older Men and Women." *Journal of Labor Economics* 12: 210–242.

Ruhm, Christopher. 1991. "Are Workers Permanently Scarred by Job Displacements?" *American Economic Review* 81: 319–324.

Schoeni, Robert, and Michael Dardia. 1997. "Wage Losses of Displaced Workers in the 1990s." Photocopy, RAND Corporation.

Stevens, Ann Huff. 1997. "Persistent Effects of Job Displacement: The Importance of Multiple Job Losses." *Journal of Labor Economics* 15: 165–188.

Uccello, Cori, and Kevin Perese. 1999. *Wealth Accumulation in the Health and Retirement Study: The Importance of Including Pension Wealth*. Urban Institute report, Washington, D.C.

Venti, Steven F., and David A. Wise. 1998. "The Cause of Wealth Dispersion at Retirement: Choice or Chance?" *American Economic Review* 88(2): 185–191.

**Appendix Table 1 Sample Means by Displacement Status**

| Characteristic | Men | | | Women | | |
|---|---|---|---|---|---|---|
| | Not displaced | Prior to displacement | After displacement | Not displaced | Prior to displacement | After displacement |
| Age | 58.4 | 57.1 | 58.5 | 55.9 | 56 | 56.8 |
| % Working | 76 | 92 | 58 | 66 | 86 | 45 |
| Education (yr.) | 12.3 | 12.1 | 11.9 | 12.3 | 11.9 | 11.8 |
| Health (1=excellent, 5=poor) | 2.5 | 2.4 | 2.5 | 2.5 | 2.4 | 2.5 |
| Annual earnings ($) | 35,086 | 31,641 | 29,737 | 19,976 | 17,404 | 15,996 |
| % with private pension | 66 | 65 | 60 | 46 | 41 | 34 |
| % of workers with pension from current job | 57 | 48 | 36 | 53 | 37 | 27 |
| DC account balances[a] ($) | | | | | | |
| mean | 123,260 | 71,555 | 55,152 | 70,894 | 30,747 | 21,399 |
| median | 40,000 | 31,000 | 27,500 | 15,000 | 11,000 | 7,100 |
| DB expected annual benefits[a] ($) | | | | | | |
| mean | 22,272 | 20,332 | 13,343 | 16,139 | 11,792 | 6,536 |
| median | 16,320 | 15,600 | 9,600 | 9,600 | 8,880 | 2,940 |
| Nonhousing assets ($) | | | | | | |
| mean | 204,256 | 120,129 | 131,429 | 172,520 | 111,662 | 132,547 |
| median | 55,000 | 35,500 | 31,775 | 39,931 | 28,000 | 23,000 |

[a] Among workers with this type of pension.

# The Effect of a Job Loss on the Employment Experience, Benefits, and Retirement Savings of Bank Officers

Jill S. Quadagno
David A. Macpherson
Jennifer Reid Keene
*Florida State University*

J14
G21 J26
J64
M52 J63

Although the financial consequences of the wave of mergers and acquisitions between large corporations in the 1990s have been well documented, the human costs in the form of downsizing and job losses are often ignored. The problems associated with the loss of a job may appear less compelling in the current prosperous economic environment, when workers who lose their jobs have a good chance of finding new employment. Yet there are longer-term risks that may not be visible until workers who have experienced a series of job losses reach retirement age. In this chapter, we document the effect of job loss on the employment experiences, benefits, and retirement savings of former officers of First Interstate Bank, who were among 7,500 bank employees who lost their jobs following the 1996 merger with Wells Fargo Bank. This case study of banking employees provides a detailed account of the life course consequences of job loss among employees in a service sector industry where the rate of job loss has increased in the 1990s (Farber 1997) and who face different risks and different opportunities than the blue-collar job losers of the 1980s.

## TRENDS IN JOB LOSS

### The Distribution of Job Loss

During the 1980s job loss was greatest in the manufacturing sector (Gordon 1996). Blue-collar workers still make up a majority of displaced workers, but there has been an increase in job loss among service-sector workers, who comprise over 75 percent of the workforce in the United States (U.S. Bureau of Labor Statistics 1995). The first to lose their jobs in the service sector were lower-level employees. For example, Sears automated many of its customer service operations and eliminated 21,000 positions between 1990 and 1993 (Marks 1994). Recent mergers have eliminated jobs at all levels. The job losers of the 1990s are more educated and older than those of the 1980s. College graduates are now most likely to have a job loss because their job was abolished. In fact, the most dramatic increase in job loss rates has occurred among managers (Farber 1996, p. 16).

### The Consequences of Job Loss

The effect of a job loss varies depending on the age of the worker. Younger workers are more likely than older workers to report experiencing a job loss, but older workers, particularly those 55 years and older, have a more difficult time finding new employment. Older workers are also less likely than younger workers to find employment at previous wage levels (EBRI 1997b, p. 9; Ruhm 1989). Older workers may have a difficult time with job searches because their skills have become obsolete or because of discrimination by employers (Mor-Barak and Tynan 1993).

Workers are currently saving only 35 percent of what they will require to maintain their preretirement lifestyle through retirement, even though they have more opportunities than ever to save for retirement (Bernheim 1997). One factor that reduces retirement saving is the loss of a job. Workers who experience a prolonged job search may be forced to deplete their personal savings and their retirement funds to pay for basic living expenses for themselves and their families (Newman 1989). Many retirement plans provide for the distribution of the individual's accrued vested benefits in a lump sum payment when service with the employer is terminated. Although workers are allowed to preserve their retirement savings after a job loss by "rolling over" the account balance into an IRA or into a new employer's plan, most employees who receive a lump sum payment spend it rather than saving it for retirement. One study found that only 28 percent of workers who received lump sum payments rolled them over into tax-qualified savings plans (Basset, Fleming, and Rodriguez 1996). Other research indicates that fewer than half of all workers who receive a lump-sum distribution roll over any portion of it (EBRI 1997b, p. 13). One might expect older workers to be savers, but only one-third of workers over age 55 who receive a lump-sum distribution invest that money in a retirement annuity or savings account (Salisbury 1993). Results from the Health and Retirement Survey demonstrate a similar pattern: only 25 percent of older workers (45–54) saved a defined-benefit (DB) plan distribution, and fewer than half saved a defined-contribution (DC) plan distribution (Korczyk 1996). Overall, spenders are more likely than savers to be younger, as well as less educated, female, low-paid, and African American (Salisbury 1998; Hardy and Shuey in press). It seems likely that displaced workers who are insecure about their immediate financial futures may choose not to roll over their lump retirement fund but rather keep it available during the period of unemployment (EBRIb 1997, p. 13). While such a decision makes sense as a short-term hedge against uncertainty, it is likely to have long-term consequences in the form of lower retirement income.

## Job Loss and Health Insurance

The health care system in the United States is employer-based (Harrington Meyer, and Pavalko 1996). Individuals with full-time, year-round jobs are the most likely to have health benefits. In 1996, 64 percent of Americans were covered by employer-provided plans either directly through their employer or indirectly as a dependent (EBRI 1997a); 75.9 percent of individuals in families headed by full-year, full-time workers were covered by employer-provided health insurance, compared with 38.2 percent of individuals in families headed by other workers and 18.6 percent of individuals in families headed by nonworkers (EBRI 1997a, p. 7).

Because the majority of American families depend on employers for health benefits, the loss of a job has significant implications for health care coverage. According to the Current Population Survey, just over half (50.3 percent) of workers who were displaced in the period from 1993 to 1995 had health insurance at the job they lost. Of those displaced workers who were still unemployed in 1996, only 37.3 percent now had health insurance (EBRI 1997b, p. 11).

## Job Loss in the Banking Industry

The banking industry provides a useful case for studying the long-term consequences of job loss in the service sector because of heavy rates of job loss resulting from a series of mergers and takeovers that began in the 1980s as a consequence of deregulation. Unlike most other industrialized nations, which have fewer than 1,000 commercial banks, the United States lacks a national banking system in which a few banks have branches throughout the country. In 1993, there were more than 12,000 commercial banks, 2,000 savings and loans, and 16,000 credit unions in the United States. In contrast, only 3,000 banks serve the entire European community; Japan has only 170 commercial banks (Marks 1994). The presence of so many banks reflects the effect of federal regulations, which until recently have restricted the ability of these financial institutions to open branches (Mishkin 1994).

During the 1980s deregulation allowed bank holding companies headquartered in one state to purchase banks in another state. Recent changes in banking regulation allow banks to operate branches across state lines. A few large banks have taken advantage of the opportunities opened by deregulation to engage in an aggressive series of takeovers to eliminate competition and expand their asset holdings. Industry experts predict that the banking system will consolidate to only 2,000 early in the twenty-first century (Zey 1993).

Each merger has resulted in job losses among employees at all levels, from bank tellers to bank officers. Along with declines in employment has come a paring of employee benefits. In some cases, workers have become ineligible for any benefits. For example, during a period of restructuring, the Bank of America cut the hours of the bottom of its workforce (the low-paid full-time tellers) to 19 hours a week, making them ineligible for fringe benefits (Marks 1994). Another component of the fringe benefit strategy has been ending the "paternalism" of defined-benefit pension plans. For example, J.P. Morgan and Company changed its benefit package from a defined-benefit plan to a defined-contribution plan. Similarly, following its 1988 merger, the Bank of America eliminated its defined-benefit plan and installed a defined-contribution plan.

## DESCRIPTION OF THE STUDY

In 1997, the ninth largest bank in the United States was Wells Fargo. Wells Fargo achieved its position in the banking industry as a result of an acquisition campaign, which began when Wells Fargo bought National Corporation and Crocker Bank ($19.2 billion in assets) in 1986. Then, in 1987, it purchased the personal trust businesses of Bank of America, and in 1988, the Barclay's Bank of California ($1.3 billion in assets). In 1989, Wells Fargo reached a cooperative agreement with the Hong Kong and Shanghai Banking Corp. Ltd. According to the agreement, HSBC would service the overseas banking needs of Wells Fargo customers, while Wells Fargo handled HSBC's retail customers in California. A new bank jointly owned by the two companies would provide trade, finance, and international banking services. That same year Wells Fargo also purchased the Bank of Paradise ($61 million in assets) and its three branches in California, as well as five other smaller California banks and their subsidiaries (*Wells Fargo Today*: www.Wellsfargo.com, February 27, 1996). On January 23, 1996, Wells Fargo announced plans to purchase First Interstate Bancorp (FIB) at a purchase price of $11 billion.

On April 1, 1996, the date the merger took effect, over 1,700 First Interstate employees were notified that their positions would be eliminated. On April 18, Wells Fargo announced it would close 25 branches throughout Orange County in Los Angeles and lay off 187 branch employees. Statewide, the bank closed 260 branches and laid off another 2,000 branch employees. By the end of 1996, another 7,200 First Interstate employees lost their jobs through attrition and further layoffs (Wells Fargo, 1996c).

In April 1996, we mailed a short survey to 5,326 officers at FIB immediately after the first round of layoffs was announced. We obtained the work addresses of the officers from the 1995 company phone book provided by a FIB officer. A letter accompanying the survey explained the objectives of the project and asked the workers to fill out the form and return it. The main purpose of the first survey was to obtain basic demographic data and the home addresses and telephone numbers of the First Interstate employees. A total of 1,006 surveys were returned, for a response rate of 19 percent. The actual response rate is likely higher than 19 percent: we estimate that at least 1,000 workers did not receive the survey because they were dismissed or left FIB before the survey arrived.

The mail survey was followed by in-depth telephone interviews with 20 randomly selected respondents. The telephone interviews provided background information on how FIB employees were notified about the merger, what options FIB and Wells Fargo were offering to employees, and how employees responded to the threatened layoff.

A second survey was mailed in mid October 1996 to the homes of all individuals who had responded to wave 1 and who agreed to participate in follow-up interviews. The survey included questions on current employment status, previous employment history, savings behavior, health, and family finances. Respondents were also asked to complete a financial statement concerning current salary, salary while a FIB employee, receipt of a severance package, and severance package expenditures. A total of 750 workers completed both the first and second surveys. In addition to the mail survey, another 32 in-depth telephone interviews were conducted. One year after the merger, we mailed a third survey as a follow-up to survey 2. By wave 3, we had lost 222 subjects to attrition, leaving a sample of 528.

Table 1 presents the descriptive characteristics of the respondents at wave 3. They ranged in age from 25 to 66. Forty percent were 45 or older, 36 percent were 37 to 44, and 24 percent were younger than 37. Forty-five percent were male and 55 percent were female, a distribution that reflects the feminization of the banking industry (Rich 1995). Eighty-seven percent were white, 3.8 percent of Hispanic origin, 2.8 percent African American, and 2 percent "other." A substantial fraction of the former First Interstate Bank managers were well educated. Over 63 percent of the officers had graduated from college, including one-

**Table 1  Percentage of Respondents by Employment Status at Wells Fargo and Select Demographic Characteristics**

|  | Left WF | Retained by WF | Total |
|---|---|---|---|
| Age |  |  |  |
| 36 or younger | 17.07 | 6.75 | 23.83 |
| 37 to 44 | 24.77 | 10.88 | 35.65 |
| 45 or older | 30.39 | 10.13 | 40.53 |
| Total | 72.23 | 27.77 | 100.00 |
| Gender |  |  |  |
| Male | 32.15 | 13.08 | 45.23 |
| Female | 40.00 | 14.77 | 54.77 |
| Total | 72.15 | 27.85 | 100.00 |
| Marital status |  |  |  |
| Single | 22.24 | 6.73 | 28.95 |
| Married | 49.91 | 21.12 | 71.03 |
| Total | 72.15 | 27.85 | 100.00 |
| Salary at wave 3 |  |  |  |
| < $45,000 | 26.64 | 12.36 | 39.00 |
| $45,000–$64,999 | 21.81 | 8.11 | 29.92 |
| > $65,000 | 24.13 | 6.95 | 31.08 |
| Total | 72.59 | 27.41 | 100.00 |
| Education |  |  |  |
| Some college or less | 25.75 | 10.90 | 36.65 |
| College | 23.12 | 8.46 | 31.58 |
| Graduate school | 23.50 | 8.27 | 31.77 |
| Total | 72.37 | 27.63 | 100.00 |
| Race |  |  |  |
| White | 63.23 | 24.20 | 87.43 |
| African American | 1.88 | 0.94 | 2.81 |
| Asian | 3.38 | 0.56 | 3.94 |
| Hispanic | 2.06 | 1.69 | 3.75 |
| Native American, Other | 1.50 | 0.56 | 2.06 |
| Total | 72.05 | 27.95 | 100.00 |

third who had some graduate education; fewer than 10 percent had only a high school diploma. Salaries were well above median income. About one-third earned more than $65,000 per year and nearly two-thirds earned more than $45,000 annually.


## RESULTS

### The Effect of a Job Loss on Employment

At the wave 1 timepoint, 360 of the respondents had been laid off, 482 were told they would be employed in a new job with Wells Fargo, and 264 did not yet know whether they would be laid off. At wave 3, nearly half (46 percent) had been retained by Wells Fargo, over one-third (36 percent) were now employed elsewhere, 7 percent were unemployed, and 11 percent had left the labor force. Among respondents who had been laid off, older employees were less likely than the youngest employees to be employed full-time (63 percent versus 80 percent) and more likely to be employed part-time, unemployed, or out of the labor force entirely (Figure 1).

In the open-ended interviews, many older workers expressed feelings of insecurity about their jobs. Some who were retained by Wells Fargo felt that they were not terminated because Wells Fargo feared an age discrimination suit. As Sandra Shanahan explained, "The job was given to me because of my age. I'm 58 and one-half. And its temporary. Originally, I was going to be terminated. It's a good job. I think they gave me a job because of a lawsuit. I don't think it will last beyond the first quarter of next year. I'm too young to retire but too old to get another job."

Older workers who were retained by Wells Fargo also felt they were being given difficult assignments to push them to retire. In response to the question, "Do you feel you were placed in a dead-end job?", 18 percent of younger and middle-aged workers, but 24 percent of older workers, said "Yes." John Cole, a 56-year-old project analyst, had worked for FIB for 20 years. He was targeted for a layoff until he questioned the company's age bias. As he explained, "Like so many 50+ employees, I have been removed from a line position in favor of

**Figure 1  Employment Status of Leavers by Age**

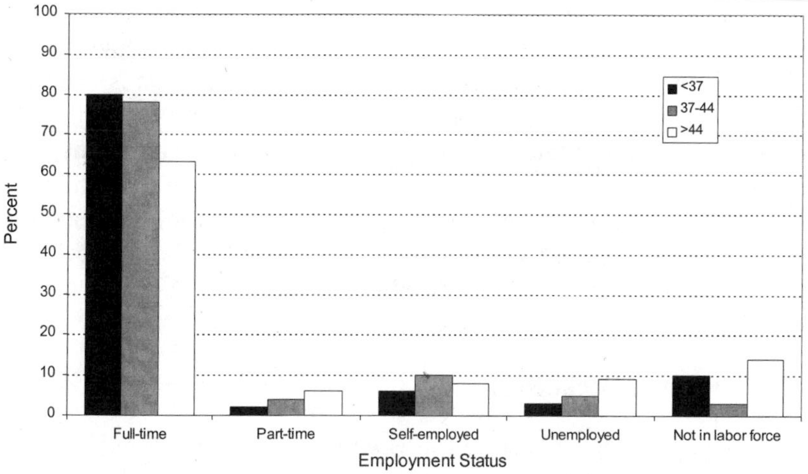

younger, less-qualified, lower-pay employees." He had been a team leader with six people reporting to him. When new management came in, they got rid of the team leaders and gave them impossible goals. John got put on special projects that were a dead end. When he complained, he was told there was nothing he could do. Then the bank proposed a program that would add years of service toward his retirement benefit if he would retire early. He was told, "Just to help you make your decision, just to let you know, by the end of the year your job will be eliminated." Four people were told that, all four over 50.

By contrast, the merger provided an opportunity for 32-year-old Thomas Chan to change jobs, something he had planned to do anyway. This was his first job. When he graduated college, he saw his classmates taking temporary jobs but decided he wanted more stability in his life. "Now," he cynically explained, "every job is a temporary job. There are people who believe in company loyalty. If you do a good job, you will be rewarded. It hasn't worked for me." Thomas became an auditor for FIB in asset-based lending, then transferred to the real estate department, doing budgets and forecasting. Before the merger was announced, he was planning to quit anyway because he doesn't like being office-based, so the severance package was a windfall for him. A Berkeley graduate with foreign language skills, he has been offered a new position with San Wah Bank, a subsidiary of a Japanese parent bank, in international banking. He will get a raise on this new job and can pursue his interest in business prospects overseas. For Thomas, the merger was "a blessing in disguise," yet he is cautious about his future. He won't take just any job. He needs to figure out what he can do best with his time. "The question is, are you flexible enough to change? Being flexible is pretty important. You have to keep pace or strike out on your own. I can't work for somebody the rest of my life. I don't want my future to depend on how other's see me." So maybe he'll work for San Wah or maybe he'll open a restaurant.

### The Severance Package

When the merger occurred, FIB employees were offered a generous severance package by industry standards. Terminated FIB employees were eligible for a severance package of one month of separation pay for each year of service. Vice presidents were guaranteed one year of severance pay, regardless of years of service, and senior vice presidents were guaranteed two years of severance pay. Terminated employees had the choice of taking the severance package as monthly salary or as a lump sum (Wells Fargo 1996a). Those who took the salary continuation plan also received health insurance for up to two years and continued 401(k) benefits. However, terminated employees who found a new job had to take a lump-sum package. Anyone who quit voluntarily lost all rights to severance pay, as did those who were fired for poor performance.

Because of the generosity of the severance package, employees jockeyed to be terminated without quitting. As one woman explained about two of her co-workers, one aged 47 and the other 48, "They had high salaries, they wanted the severance package. They were connected and could get it." Her own situation was more precarious. She feared she might be fired because a recently diagnosed illness had made work more difficult for her:

> If I'm terminated because of lack of performance, then there would be no severance package. There are many people who have gotten attorneys for one reason or another . . . When all this

started, at the beginning of the year the merger was announced, we all knew. I became very ill this year. I was diagnosed with epilepsy . . . In the meanwhile, I've lost no time off from work. I spent three days in the hospital but I didn't tell my employer. The minute I tell them, they say there is an expectation that you fulfill it or you leave. I'm tired all the time. I have to go home from work and lie down. They haven't given out that many severance packages. They've done little groups at a time so it doesn't get in the newspaper. I do know people who got it. It's managers who make 80 grand a year. They know someone in the hierarchy.

Seventy-seven percent of the terminated respondents received a severance package. Older managers were more likely than younger respondents to receive a severance package. Eighty-four percent of older workers received some severance pay, compared with 80 percent of the middle group and only 66 percent of the youngest officers. Some received just a few weeks of salary, while long-term employees or high-ranking officers received more than 200 percent of their former salary. Not surprisingly, the older officers had larger severance packages than younger respondents, no doubt because of their longer tenure at First Interstate as well as their higher salary levels and higher positions. Nearly 35 percent of workers 45 or older received a severance package that was 200 percent or more of their previous salary.

One year after the layoff, some of the former FIB employees had saved their severance packages while others had spent it all and also dipped into personal savings. The likelihood of saving varied by age. Half of the younger respondents spent their entire severance package, but 70 percent of both middle-aged and older workers saved their severance package (Figure 2).

### The Effect of Job Loss on Pension Benefits

FIB had provided three retirement plans for its employees. The first was a defined-benefit plan open to employees with at least five years of service. The benefit amount was based on age, average yearly salary, and years of service. Regular retirement began at age 65 and early retirement at 55, with an early retirement penalty of 68.5 percent of the full benefit (First Interstate Bancorp 1995).

**Figure 2  Percent Who Saved Severance Package by Age**

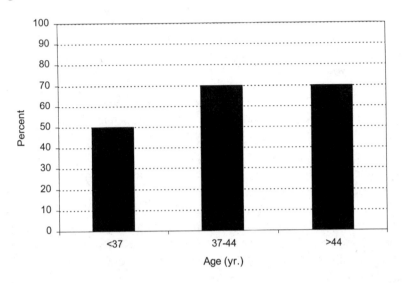

FIB employees who had been employed for five years also could contribute to a defined-contribution (401k-type) plan (First Interstate Bancorp 1993). In addition, the FirstMatch Long-Term Savings Plan was introduced in 1979. FirstMatch allowed all employees who had completed at least one year of service to contribute up to 16 percent of salary with a maximum of $9,500 (according to federal regulations at that time). First Interstate matched 6 percent of these contributions and 10 percent were not matched. The matched portion of the contribution included $1 of base pay contributed by the company for every $2 contributed by the worker. Wells Fargo had terminated its own defined-benefit pension in 1984 but it did have a defined-contribution plan. Employees who were offered jobs with Wells Fargo received a lump sum that they could convert from FirstMatch to the Wells Fargo 401(k) plan (Wells Fargo 1996a).

The company's share of pension contributions was invested in First Interstate Bancorp common stock. Laid-off workers who were vested received two-thirds of a share of Wells Fargo stock for every share of First Interstate common stock owned, the same arrangement provided for all First Interstate shareholders. However, employees were not fully vested in the company's contributions to the plan until they had been contributing for a minimum of four years. Thus, any employee who had worked for FIB for less than four years lost a portion of the company's match, with the amount of loss decreasing for longer-tenure workers.

Under the terms of the merger agreement, laid-off FIB employees who had up to nine years of service when their severance payments ended could begin receiving a pension at age 65. Those with 10 or more years of service could begin receiving a pension at age 55. However, the period in which they were receiving severance pay would not count toward "years of service" for the defined-benefit plan. Thus, although workers who were not offered jobs with Wells Fargo retained their eligibility for the First Interstate defined-benefit pension, they stood to lose the years of benefit accrual while they were receiving severance pay plus the cost of any additional years out of the labor market. The loss of pension income was the hidden price of the merger.

## The Effect of Job Loss on Retirement Savings

The layoff reduced the retirement savings of the young and middle-aged respondents, but not that of the older respondents. As Figure 3 shows, the median retirement savings of younger workers who kept their jobs was $40,000, compared with only $30,000 for leavers. There was an even greater disparity in retirement savings among workers aged 37 to 44, with stayers having $102,000 in retirement savings compared with only $70,000 for leavers. This trend was reversed among former FIB employees age 45 or over, with median retirement savings being higher among leavers ($273,000) than stayers ($259,000). Apparently the older group used their generous severance package to augment their retirement savings.

How did the spenders spend their money? A very few former FIB employees chose to spend their savings to pursue new opportunities or different life course paths. One young man opened his own business. One woman quit her job and used her retirement package to stay home and take care of her baby. She hoped to rebuild her retirement funds soon. Most, however, were forced to spend their retirement assets. Bruce Winters, a 43-year-old African American, got his first job in the banking industry in 1970. After working for 18 years for the Bank of

**Figure 3  Median Retirement Savings by Age**

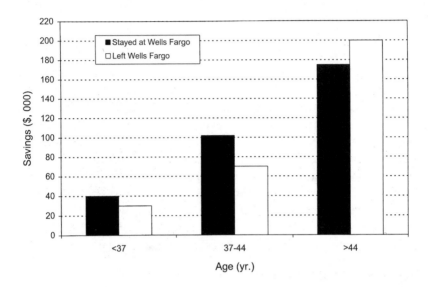

America, he lost his job in a 1988 merger.  When he left the Bank of America, he received two checks.  One was the lump-sum value of his defined-benefit pension, the other his severance pay.  He was out of work for six months.  During that period of unemployment, he depleted all his savings, including his children's college tuition.

Bruce finally found a position with First Chicago bank and moved to Los Angeles.  That was a costly move in terms of housing.  He sold for $400,000 the home he had purchased in the Bay area for $200,000, a nice profit, and then bought a new home in Los Angeles for the same price, around $400,000.  However, he financed his new home at a higher interest rate and, because the new home was assessed at the higher value, his taxes increased.  As a result, his house payments in Los Angeles were much higher than they had been, and he had the additional expense of moving costs.  Then First Chicago was bought out and he lost his job again.  He was fortunate to find a new job at First Interstate after being out of work for only three months.  He was employed for five years at First Interstate.  Now he is unemployed again and starting a job search.  He worries that if he has to sell his home and move again, he will lose money because housing values in his neighborhood have declined.  Each position he has had represents a step back in terms of financial security, because he has been unable to replace his lost savings.  His youngest child will start college next year, and he worries about how he will pay for her education.

Thirty-five-year-old Hosanna Batista tells a similar story.  She experienced her second lay-off when Wells Fargo bought out First Interstate.  She had been employed at her previous job for 10 years when she was laid off.  She was unemployed for nine and a half months.  During that period she wiped out her savings, her 401k, her IRAs, and had to pay a tax penalty.  She is still trying recover financially from the first layoff experience and will only receive two months' salary as severance pay because she has only been employed by First Interstate for two years.

By contrast, the merger has provided an opportunity for 48-year-old Mitchell Freeman to increase his retirement savings and make an attractive life change.  "I look at it as a golden opportunity, because I'm young enough and strong enough to do something else.  The merger allowed for a wonderful severance package."  He doubled his salary at his new job as president of a food distribution company.  It also was a boon to Bruce Bloom.  Bruce managed a team of technical people who rapidly found new jobs rapidly in the Phoenix area.  He had been employed by First Interstate for 26 years there and was anticipating the merger.  Now he hoped to use his past teaching experience to find a job teaching business.  He currently has $125,000 in a 401k plus a defined-benefit plan that will pay him $2,040 at age 65.  He will receive two years' severance, which he will take as salary and work on a contract basis.  He plans to be debt free by then, with his mortgage paid off.  Others among his co-workers fared even better.  Among the top tier of vice presidents in his group, 13 received three years' salary plus three years of bonuses, which he called a "golden parachute."

## The Effect of Job Loss on Health Insurance

Since most workers have health insurance through their jobs, the loss of a job poses the risk of the loss of health insurance as well.  Among the employees in this study, however, health insurance coverage was virtually unaffected by the merger.  One year after the merger,

98 percent of the leavers had health insurance coverage. Those who stayed with Wells Fargo were covered by their employer. All those who received the severance package as salary continuation had health insurance benefits. Among respondents who elected to receive the severance package as a lump-sum benefit, some purchased COBRA continuation coverage and others had coverage through a spouse or from a new job.

## CONCLUSION

The stream of mergers in the 1990s is just one component of a larger pattern associated with the mobility of the workforce in the United States, as employers increased their use of contingent, temporary, and part-time work arrangements (Mishel and Bernstein 1994). In 1991, more than half of all employees had less than five years of tenure with their current employer (Korczyk 1996). The question that remains unanswered is how the increasingly transitory nature of the employment relationship affects benefits, particularly retirement plan vesting, pension portability, and continuity of health care coverage (EBRI 1997b, p. 3).

Most research indicates that a job loss poses a greater risk to an older worker than to a younger worker. Older workers often take longer to find a new job and are more likely to experience a drop in salary when they do (Ruhm 1989). Older workers with long tenure at a firm may have expected to retire gracefully, only to find themselves pushed into early retirement in the wake of a merger. The degree of choice workers have, as well as the amount of preparation and planning, are important predictors of how they experience the transition to retirement, as well as their satisfaction with the outcome (Hardy and Quadagno 1995). Unplanned retirement may create emotional anxiety and make the transition more difficult. Older workers who spend their retirement savings during a period of unemployment also have little opportunity to rebuild their portfolios. Older workers who lose their jobs also might lose their health insurance and have to purchase expensive private policies, or worse, find themselves uninsurable. Then they have to pay for health care out of pocket or forego needed exams and procedures.

The banking officers in this study lost their jobs under optimal conditions. As a group, they were well educated and well paid. Most rapidly found new jobs, their health insurance was not interrupted, and many received a generous severance package. Many older workers took advantage of this opportunity to increase their retirement savings, but a substantial portion of the youngest group of employees spent a considerable share of their retirement savings and assets. Unlike workers of previous generations who believed in the permanence of the employer/employee attachment, younger workers seem to hold fewer expectations that they will have lifetime employment. This conclusion is indicated by the fact that younger workers are less likely than older workers to participate in their employer's pension plan, which suggests that they do not view their jobs as long term. Yet what this study shows is that even if younger workers don't expect long tenure with a single employer, job turnover does pose a long-term threat to their economic security in terms of lost retirement savings.

# References

Bassett, William, Michael Fleming and Anthony Rodriguez. 1996. "How Workers Use 401(k) Plans: The Participation, Contribution and Withdrawal Decisions." Working paper, Brown University and the Federal Reserve Bank of New York.

Bernheim, B.D. 1997. *The 1996 Merrill Lynch Baby Boom Retirement Index.* New York: Merrill Lynch.

EBRI. 1997a. *Sources of Health Insurance and Characteristics of the Uninsured: Analysis of the March 1997 Current Population Survey.* EBRI Issue Brief no. 192. Washington D.C.: Employee Benefit Research Institute.

_____. 1997b. *Worker Displacement, 1993–1995: Demographics and Implications.* EBRI Issue Brief no. 186. Washington D.C.: Employee Benefit Research Institute.

Farber, Henry. 1993. "The Incidence and Costs of Job Loss: 1982–91." *Brookings Papers on Economic Activity: Microeconomics* 1:73–132.

_____. 1996. "The Changing Face of Job Loss in the United States, 1981–1993." Working paper no. 360, Industrial Relations Section, Princeton University, March.

————. 1997. "The Changing Face of Job Loss in the United States, 1981–1995." Working paper no. 382, Industrial Relations Section, Princeton University, June, 1997.

First Interstate Bancorp. 1993. *Employee Savings Plan of First Interstate Bancorp FirstMatch.* Los Angeles: First Interstate Bancorp, November 12.

————. 1995. *A Guide to Your Employee Benefits at FirstInterstate Bancorp.* Los Angeles: First Interstate Bancorp.

Gordon, David. 1996. *Fat and Mean: The Corporate Squeeze of Working Americans and the Myth of Managerial Downsizing.* New York: Free Press.

Hardy, Melissa, and Jill Quadagno. 1995. "Satisfaction with Early Retirement: Making Choices in the Auto Industry." *Journals of Gerontology: Social Sciences* 50: S217–S228.

Hardy, Melissa, and Kim Shuey. In press. "Pension Decision in a Changing Economy: Gender, Structure and Choice." *Journal of Gerontology.*

Korczyk, Sophie. 1996. *Pre-retirement Pension Distributions in the Health and Retirement Survey.* AARP Public Policy Institute no. 9606. Washington, D.C.: AARP.

Marks, Mitchell Lee. 1994. *From Turmoil to Triumph: New Life after Mergers, Acquisitions and Downsizing.* New York: Lexington Books.

Meyer, Madonna Harrington, and Eliza K. Pavalko. 1996. "Family, Work, and Access to Health Insurance among Mature Women." *Journal of Health and Social Behavior* 37: 311–325.

Mishel, Lawrence, and Jared Bernstein. 1994. *The State of Working America: 1994–1995.* Economic Policy Institute Series. Armonk: M.E. Sharpe.

Mishkin, Frederic S. 1994. *The Economics of Money, Banking, and Financial Markets.* Reading, Massachusetts: Addison-Wesley.

Mor-Barak, M., and Tynan, M. 1993. "Older Workers and the Workplace: A New Challenge for Occupational Social Work." *Social Work* 38: 45–55.

Newman, Katherine S. 1989. *Falling from Grace: The Experience of Downward Mobility in the American Middle Class.* New York: Vintage Books.

Rich, Brian L. 1995. "Explaining Feminization in the U.S. Banking Industry, 1940–1980: Human Capital, Dual Labor Markets, or Gender Queuing?" *Sociological Perspectives* 38: 357–380.

Ruhm, Christopher. 1989. "Why Older Americans Stop Working." *The Gerontologist* 29: 294–300.

Salisbury, Dallas. 1993. "Policy Implications of Changes in Employer Benefit Protection." In *Pensions in a Changing Economy*, Richard Burkhauser and Dallas Salisbury, eds. Washington, D.C.: National Academy on Aging, pp. 41–58.

_____. 1998. "What Can the Employment Sector Do for Retirement Security? Lessons of History." In *Resecuring Social Security and Medicare*, Judith Gonyea, ed. Washington, D.C.: Gerontological Society, pp. 53–60.

U.S. Bureau of Labor Statistics. 1995. *Employment, Hours and Earnings*. Washington, D.C.: U.S. Government Printing Office.

Wells Fargo. 1996a. "Company Separation Pay Plan." *1996 Benefits Book*. March 14, 1996.

_____. 1996b. "Wells Fargo and First Interstate to Merge." Press release, January 24.

_____. 1996c. "Wells Fargo Completes Acquisition of First Interstate Bancorp." Press release, April 1.

Zey, Mary. 1993. *Banking on Fraud*. New York: Aldine deGruyter.

# Extending Health Insurance Coverage for Older Workers and Early Retirees

(US)

## How Well Have Public Policies Worked?

J4
J26
I18
I11   G22

Karen Pollitz

*Georgetown University*

Our voluntary system of health insurance, regulated by a patchwork of federal and state laws, leaves many gaps for older Americans. There are gaps of access—that is, coverage can be denied or made more difficult to obtain specifically because of a person's advancing age and declining health. There also are gaps of affordability faced by uninsured Americans of all ages who have low incomes and who simply cannot afford the cost of health insurance.

This chapter does not attempt to measure the prevalence of problems of access and affordability faced by older Americans. Such problems are a distinct possibility for older Americans, and when they do arise, they can have tragic results. Many of us take comfort in the conventional wisdom that the uninsured do, eventually, somehow, obtain the health care they need. This conventional wisdom is wrong.

The American College of Physicians–American Society of Internal Medicine recently compiled and summarized the findings of over 100 scientific studies documenting that "lack of health insurance is not simply an inconvenience . . . [It] is a public health risk that results in poorer health and earlier death" (ACPI–ASIM 1999). Mortality and morbidity are higher among the uninsured. People who lack coverage delay or forego care and medications that they need, but cannot afford. They suffer greater complications and unnecessary hospitalizations when manageable health conditions go untreated. Cancer is detected at later stages, diminishing treatment options and the chances for survival. And the uninsured who manage to get hospital care nevertheless are much more likely to die than are people who are privately insured.

This mounting evidence notwithstanding, we do not have a guarantee of health security in America for people under the age of 65. Instead we have adopted a patchwork of public policies, federal and state, that seem to help some people in some circumstances and leave gaps in assistance for others. This chapter examines the health and insurance status of older workers and early retirees, aged 55–64. It reviews the menu of public policies we have adopted to promote access to and affordability of coverage. It concludes that some of these public policies have added tangible protections for the near-elderly, while others have not, and that significant gaps in health security remain for older workers and early retirees in the United States.

## HEALTH STATUS AND COVERAGE OF THE NEAR-ELDERLY

A recent report to the Congress by the General Accounting Office documented the health status and the health insurance status of Americans between the ages of 55 and 64. Relative to other non-elderly Americans, people between these ages have the highest rate of health insurance coverage. In 1996, 13.8 percent of this near-elderly age cohort were uninsured, compared with almost 18 percent of all non-elderly Americans. Further, health coverage for the near-elderly has remained relatively stable over time, while the proportion of uninsured has climbed steadily for younger age groups (GAO 1998, p. 38).

The near-elderly's relative advantage in health insurance status should not, however, necessarily be viewed as a health security success story. It may well be that because their need for health insurance coverage is so pressing that people in this age bracket will tolerate higher expenses, job lock, deferred retirement, or other inconveniences or hardships in order to maintain coverage. Indeed, researchers at the Urban Institute who studied how health insurance needs are factored into retirement decisions found that both the availability and affordability of coverage were important considerations that shape people's plans for retirement (Loprest and Zedlewski 1998).

This finding is not at all surprising, given the health care needs of the near-elderly. Advancing age tends to bring a decline in health status. Less than half of the near-elderly report themselves to be in excellent health, compared with almost three-quarters of 25- to 34-year-olds. Almost one-quarter of the elderly report themselves to be in poor health, compared with 6 percent of 25- to 34-year-olds (GAO 1998, pp. 27–29). The incidence of serious and chronic health conditions is far more prevalent among the near-elderly than among younger people. Ironically, the onset of these health conditions, which make the need for health coverage more pressing, also makes the near-elderly more "uninsurable" (Table 1).

The near-elderly, like other Americans, rely primarily on employer-sponsored insurance (ESI) for their health coverage. Two-thirds of people aged 55–64 have employer-based health coverage. ESI is more common among the near-elderly who work full time, but early retirement does not necessarily mean the loss of ESI. Almost half of the near-elderly who do not work have employer-based coverage, through a working or retired spouse, through their own employer-spon-

**Table 1  Number of Health Conditions per 1000 People among Four Age Groups**

| Condition | 25–34 yr. | 35–44 yr. | 45–54 yr. | 55–64 yr. |
|---|---|---|---|---|
| Arthritis | 41.19 | 79.85 | 174.48 | 294.75 |
| Cataract | 3.42 | 3.21 | 5.85 | 33.73 |
| Cerebrovascular disease | 1.98 | 3.30 | 11.62 | 27.73 |
| Diabetes | 9.35 | 20.17 | 46.74 | 86.09 |
| Gallbladder disease | 6.34 | 3.04 | 5.49 | 11.17 |
| Glaucoma | 1.95 | 5.30 | 7.63 | 17.70 |
| Ischemic heart disease | 2.71 | 7.90 | 29.23 | 72.30 |
| Heart rhythm disorders | 21.75 | 30.43 | 38.82 | 53.25 |
| Other heart disease | 3.62 | 7.88 | 19.35 | 36.47 |
| Hernia | 7.40 | 17.06 | 25.27 | 39.80 |
| Hypertension | 40.42 | 82.45 | 176.21 | 285.88 |
| Ulcer | 19.45 | 22.79 | 17.26 | 36.01 |
| Varicose veins | 19.82 | 31.00 | 42.07 | 62.57 |

SOURCE: GAO 1998, p. 30. Data derived from the NCHS 1994 Health Interview Survey.

sored retirement health benefits, or through COBRA. Even so, the rate of ESI coverage is lower for the near-elderly than for most younger people. As a result, the near-elderly today rely disproportionately on individually purchased health insurance coverage and on Medicare. This is especially the case for the oldest near-elderly, i.e., between the ages of 62 and 64 (Table 2).

Trends suggest this reliance on individual coverage and public programs may increase over time. In particular, the prevalence of employer-sponsored retiree health benefits has declined over the past decade and shows evidence of continuing to do so. Fewer employers are offering such benefits to retirees and, among those that do, eligibility standards and required retiree contributions are becoming more stringent (McArdle et al. 1999). People who retire without employer-sponsored health benefits before the age of Medicare eligibility are more likely to be uninsured (Table 2).

**Table 2  Percentage of Insured and Uninsured Individuals by Source of Insurance and Age Group, 1996**

| Age group | Employer-based coverage | Individual | Medicare | Medicaid | Military/ veteran | Uninsured |
|---|---|---|---|---|---|---|
| 25–34 | 65.1 | 4.0 | 0.9 | 6.2 | 1.5 | 22.3 |
| 35–44 | 71.0 | 4.6 | 1.4 | 5.3 | 1.3 | 16.3 |
| 45–54 | 73.7 | 5.3 | 2.0 | 3.7 | 1.6 | 13.7 |
| 55–64 | 65.3 | 8.6 | 5.9 | 4.4 | 1.9 | 13.8 |
| Near-elderly subgroups | | | | | | |
| 55–61 | 67.4 | 8.0 | 4.9 | 4.6 | 1.9 | 13.2 |
| 62–64 | 59.6 | 10.1 | 8.5 | 4.0 | 2.1 | 15.5 |
| Work full time | 81.3 | 7.4 | 0.2 | 0.7 | 1.4 | 9.0 |
| Not working | 46.1 | 8.1 | 15.2 | 10.1 | 2.3 | 18.2 |

GAO 1998, pp. 40, 41, 44.

# WHAT PUBLIC POLICIES HAVE BEEN ADOPTED TO PROMOTE HEALTH INSURANCE ACCESS AND AFFORDABILITY?

Private health insurance markets tend to distinguish customers based on their health and risk status, and they sell (or renew) coverage accordingly. Low-cost, low-risk customers are the most profitable, and insurers will try to attract them—and discourage high-cost, high-risk customers—through their medical underwriting practices, benefit design, and premium pricing. Left unregulated, these practices make it more difficult for the near-elderly to obtain health insurance and leave them vulnerable to losing the coverage they have as they age and as health declines. Risk segmentation and selection practices are less of a threat to a near-elderly person in large group coverage (where the impact of any one person on an entire group's premium will be less) but become more so as group size declines. Access and affordability are most problematic in the individual market, where an older person with preexisting health conditions is unlikely to find standard coverage at standard rates and may find it unavailable at any price.

Over the past 15 years, states and the federal government have enacted health insurance reform laws to curb risk segmentation and selection practices. How well these policies have improved protections for older workers and early retirees depends on the type of health coverage and where it is obtained.

## Access to Group Coverage

### COBRA[1]

As noted above, early retirees depend primarily on employer-sponsored health insurance for their coverage. When retirement health benefits are not offered, many early retirees have the option under COBRA of remaining in their former group plan for a limited time. Assuming for a moment that an early retiree may be leaving work because of health problems, this option becomes especially important. It allows people not only to remain covered, but to keep their current policy—with its covered benefits and providers—on which they already depend.

COBRA requires some group health plans to offer temporary continuation of coverage for people who would otherwise lose it due to a qualifying event. A recent study estimates that at any time, some 4.7 million people rely on COBRA for their health coverage (Levitt and Gabel et al. 1999).

Workers and their dependents qualify for COBRA continuation coverage when employment ends due to retirement, voluntary separation, layoff, or when eligibility for health benefits ends due to a reduction in hours worked. COBRA continuation coverage resulting from these qualifying events can last up to 18 months. In some cases, when a disability causes the end of employment or reduction in hours worked, COBRA continuation can extend an additional 11 months.

Dependents also qualify for continuation coverage when they become divorced or widowed from a covered worker, when they age out of dependent status, or when the covered worker relinquishes coverage upon reaching Medicare eligibility. Under these qualifying events, COBRA continuation can last up to 36 months. Each covered worker and dependent has an independent right to elect COBRA. Continuation coverage must be the same as that offered to active workers.

COBRA's protections have limits. First, certain changes can operate to cut short COBRA continuation coverage. COBRA coverage ends when the employer ceases to offer health benefits to active workers. If an older worker retires involuntarily, for example, when a firm goes out of business, there may no longer be a health plan in which to continue. COBRA also ends if a covered person moves out of their COBRA health plan's service area. Early retirees who are "snow birds" need to consider whether they can use their COBRA coverage if they move.

Second, COBRA applies to group health plans offered by employers with 20 or more workers. People separating from coverage sponsored by smaller firms don't have federal COBRA protections. However, 38 states have enacted "mini-COBRA" laws requiring continuation coverage under small-employer plans for fewer than 20 workers. Some of these state laws mirror federal COBRA protections. Others offer shorter periods of continuation coverage (e.g., three to six months).

Finally, individuals electing COBRA must pay the full premium, including the portion formerly contributed by the employer, plus an administrative charge of up to 2 percent. While COBRA's guarantee of access to group rates generally makes coverage more affordable than it would otherwise be in the nongroup market, the sticker shock of losing the employer's premium subsidy can be considerable. In general, about one in five people eligible for COBRA coverage elect it. This election rate increases with age, however; reaching 38 percent for those age 61 or older (Flynn 1992 and Loprest 1997, as cited in GAO 1998, p. 89). One study suggests that COBRA election is very high (up to 75 percent) among early retirees who have no other coverage options (Gruber and Madrian 1993, as cited in GAO 1998, p. 89)

On average, 61- to 64-year-olds who elect COBRA remain in that coverage for 12 months (Flynn 1992, as cited in GAO 1998). This suggests COBRA may be an important bridge helping early retirees to remain covered until Medicare eligibility begins.

### HIPAA

Another potentially important contribution to the health security of the near-elderly—when they are covered under group health plans— was made by the Health Insurance Portability and Accountability Act of 1996, or HIPAA.[2] HIPAA established national standards to protect access to group health coverage. These national standards apply to all group health plans sponsored by employers with two or more workers. They include

- Nondiscrimination: Employers and group insurance carriers may not set rules for group members' eligibility for health coverage based on any health status–related factor. Nor can plans and carriers vary benefits or premium contributions for enrollees based on health status–related factors. These factors include medical history, claims experience, evidence of insurability, and genetic information.

- Limits on preexisting condition exclusions: No group health plan can impose a preexisting condition exclusion period longer than 12 months (or 18 months for late enrollees). HIPAA defines a preexisting condition as one for which diagnosis, medical advice, care, or treatment was actually recommended or received in the six-month period immediately preceding enrollment in the group plan.

- Portability:  HIPAA limits the repeated imposition of preexisting condition exclusion periods by group health plans by requiring that persons get credit for qualifying prior coverage.  Most prior coverage (including group and individual coverage, Medicare, and Medicaid) is creditable as long as it was not interrupted by a lapse of more than 63 days in a row.

- Special enrollment periods:  All group health plans must offer individuals who previously declined coverage a special opportunity of at least 30 days to enroll in group coverage when their insurance or family status changes.  For example, special enrollment periods must be offered to people when they marry or have a child, or when they lose other coverage due to a change in jobs or expiration of COBRA benefits.  Enrollment during these special periods is not considered a late enrollment.

- Certificates:  So people can document their coverage history, HIPAA requires health plans and carriers to issue certificates of creditable coverage.  Certificates must describe the content and length of coverage and must be issued automatically when coverage ends.  Certificates also must be provided at other times on request.

Older workers and early retirees are more likely to rely on HIPAA group health plan protections, given their poorer health status.  Though not prevalent in group health plans prior to HIPAA, lifetime exclusions of preexisting conditions were not unheard of.  HIPAA limits on such exclusion periods could be important to older workers and early retirees.  HIPAA requirements for portability and special enrollment periods can help people manage the transitions of work and family status that arise increasingly in this age group.

Enactment of this federal law was an important contribution because these protections were not applicable in all states and all health plans before 1996.  Prior to HIPAA, states had been active in enacting similar reforms in their small group markets.  State reforms varied widely and often were not as comprehensive as the federal law required (Pollitz et al. 1999; Institute for Health Policy Solutions 1998).  Only a handful of states applied insurance reforms in the large group market and, of course, no states could regulate coverage under self-insured employer plans.  Thus, the enactment of HIPAA expanded legal protections for all Americans in group health plans. Older workers and early retirees who maintain group coverage and who need to switch between group health plans can be assured of more consistent and comprehensive protections no matter where they live or what level of government regulates their group coverage.

### State insurance reforms beyond HIPAA

Some states have gone beyond the national floor of group health protections guaranteed by HIPAA. These additional state protections may be most helpful for older workers or early retirees who decide to establish their own business or who work for very small firms. Because these protections vary so widely, however, it is important for older workers and early retirees to familiarize themselves with the laws in their own state.

Fifteen states (Arizona, Colorado, Connecticut, Delaware, Florida, Maine, Maryland, Massachusetts, New Hampshire, New Mexico, North Carolina, Rhode Island, South Carolina, Vermont, and Washington) have applied some or all of their group market reforms to the self-employed or groups of one. In Arizona, Colorado, North Carolina, and Rhode Island, the self-employed are guaranteed access only to certain small-group policies; they are not guaranteed the issuance of all products as HIPAA requires for groups of 20–50. In Maryland, the self-employed are guaranteed access to small-group policies only during semiannual open seasons. In New Mexico, the self-employed can be considered a group if they buy family coverage, but only through the state's small-employer purchasing alliance. In South Carolina, spouses who work together in a family-owned business can be considered a group of two. For older workers who leave a job to set up their own business, these state reforms can be very helpful.

Most states also have gone beyond HIPAA's requirements to establish rating limits in their small-group markets. It is in small groups that one older worker's age or poor health may have a more tangible impact on the entire group's premium. State small-group rating reforms also vary considerably. Two states (New York and Vermont) require pure community rating, under which neither the age nor the health status of workers may cause a small group's premium to vary. Ten states require modified community rating, which permits no premium variation due to health status but allows variation based on other demographic factors such as age. In three states (Hawaii, Michigan, and Pennsylvania), community-rated coverage is available only through certain carriers. Thirty-one states impose rate bands that allow limited rate variation based on health status, as well as variations based on age and other demographic factors. Two states (Arizona and New Mexico) require modified community rating for some small-group products and rate bands for others. Virginia imposes rate bands on only two products sold to only certain small groups. Only Illinois and the District of Columbia have no small group rating restrictions at all (Pollitz et al. 1998).

## Affordability of Group Coverage

In addition to guaranteeing access to group coverage that is offered by employers, federal law does provide one protection that may improve the affordability of health coverage for some older workers and early retirees in limited circumstances.

The Family and Medical Leave Act (FMLA) was passed in 1993 primarily to help workers balance the needs of job and family.[3] It may also provide important, though short-lived, assistance to older workers who leave the workforce involuntarily due to illness or to care for a sick relative.

The FMLA guarantees up to 12 weeks of job-protected leave for workers when they become ill or disabled or when they need to care for a newborn or for a sick or disabled family member. The law guarantees only unpaid leave, although people must be allowed to draw sick pay, vacation pay, or disability income insurance benefits they have accrued. The law also requires employers to continue health benefits during leave. Unlike HIPAA and COBRA, therefore, the FMLA does provide for a subsidy to make group coverage affordable.

According to the Bipartisan Commission on Family and Medical Leave, family leave to care for a seriously ill family member and medical leave for one's own health accounts for almost 80 percent of all leave taken by employees. When surveyed about their future need for family and medical leave, about 40 percent of employees responded that they expect to need such leave within the next five years. The most frequently cited reason was to care for a seriously ill parent. While the length of leave varies depending on the reason for taking leave, the median length for all leave-takers is 10 days. Eighty-four percent of people taking leave return to work, 10 percent remain on leave, and only 6 percent do not return to work (Bipartisan Commission on Family and Medical Leave 1996).

The FMLA can offer some early retirees a brief bridge of affordable health coverage before they move on to COBRA or other group or individual insurance. However, because the law only applies to firms with 50 or more employees, because the benefit guarantees are so time limited, and because it is structured primarily to be a reform to help people return to work, it is unlikely that FMLA health coverage provides much of a lifeline to very many individuals.

## Access to Individual Coverage

As noted above, the near-elderly rely more heavily on nongroup coverage than do younger people. Reliance on individual coverage may increase if current trends toward declining employer-sponsored retirement health benefits continue. Individual insurance markets are much less tightly regulated than group markets, and the near-elderly will tend to be vulnerable purchasers of coverage in individual markets.

Individual insurance markets are characterized by the aggressiveness of their carriers' underwriting practices. Where such practices are not regulated, individual market insurers may deny coverage altogether to an applicant determined to be a bad risk. Insurers also may sell coverage that temporarily or permanently excludes coverage for a health condition or an entire body part or system. In addition, they may charge higher (substandard) premiums based on an applicant's health status. Premiums may be further increased, typically by a factor of three or higher for people in their early 60s, due to age and other demographic factors (Chollet and Kirk 1998, p. 44). For older workers and early retirees who need to buy insurance on their own, these underwriting and rating practices can pose substantial barriers to access. Consider the story of one 52-year-old woman who recently "retired" to Florida.

> We moved to Florida with insurance [under my husband's COBRA plan] and tried to buy individual coverage. [I] was turned down by no less than 5 companies because of a preexisting

condition that was corrected 30 years ago! Was told by BC/BS of
Florida to get a job or get arrested. Since I don't like stripes, I
took a job. Since my husband and I had just retired from New
York, I was not amused, but I am now insured. Our concern now,
is what . . . will [happen] . . . to us AFTER COBRA! My husband
is going to be 62 in 1/00! I've found many of my neighbors in our
new community have the same problem. We all didn't come with
"retirement insurance" from our companies, and due to some
minor problems (i.e., heel spurs) many have returned to work
because they cannot get insurance here![4]

Federal health reforms have done little to improve this situation,
though some states have acted to secure access to coverage for the
near-elderly and other individuals.

### HIPAA

While HIPAA added significantly to people's legal protections
under group health plans, it added little to their protections when buying individual coverage. Whether this result was intended is hard to
know. On the one hand, early retirees and older workers leaving group
coverage to set up their own businesses were typical of the people Congress sought to help through HIPAA. On the other, as an incremental
reform, HIPAA was limited and incomplete by design. Congress also
was especially deferential to the goal of state flexibility when it drafted
HIPAA's individual-market provisions. The combination of HIPAA's
small reform increment and great state flexibility left people in the
individual market with little more real protection under the new federal
law than they had before.

HIPAA contained two key protections in the individual market.
First, it required all coverage, including individual policies, to be guaranteed renewable. That is, carriers are prohibited from canceling or
refusing to renew coverage due to advancing age or declining health.
Second, HIPAA contains "portability" protections for people leaving
group coverage to buy individual insurance when they have maintained
a substantial and continuous coverage history. These people, called
*federally eligible individuals*, must have had at least 18 months of continuous coverage that was not interrupted by a lapse of more than 63
days in a row. Their most recent day of coverage must have been under
a group health plan, and they must have elected and exhausted any

available COBRA continuation benefits.  Once people become federally eligible, they must purchase individual coverage within 63 days.
HIPAA guarantees federally eligible people access to all policies sold
in the individual market.  States can adopt an alternative mechanism for
guaranteeing access to health coverage for federally eligible individuals, and 39 states did so.

HIPAA lacked one key protection for people buying individual
coverage: rating limits.  Consequently, while all individual policies are
now guaranteed renewable in all states, nothing in federal law prohibits
insurers from raising renewal rates so high as to deter people from continuing their coverage.  Only where states had already acted to limit
this practice do people have such protections.

The lack of rating protections also made hollow HIPAA's right of
guaranteed issue to private individual coverage.  Eleven states and the
District of Columbia adopted this new guaranteed issue protection for
their federally eligible residents.  None of these dozen jurisdictions
have individual market rating reforms, however.[5]  Consequently, policies sold to federally eligible individuals in these areas are priced as
high as 400 to 600 percent of standard rates (Scanlon 1998).

In the 39 alternative-mechanism states, people do have some rating
limits but few new access protections.  HIPAA's requirements were so
flexible that all but a few states simply made minor adjustments to the
reforms they had previously enacted.  As a result, most people in these
states have the same or similar right of access to individual coverage
after HIPAA as they did before (Pollitz et al. 1999).

In summary, where HIPAA granted a new access protection for
people in the individual market, it was rendered almost meaningless
because the lack of rating reforms let carriers deter access by changing
prohibitive premiums.  And, where HIPAA deferred to states in designing individual market access protections, most states decided to keep
reforms they already had in place.  The result for older workers and
early retirees is that coverage options remain about the same.

### State-legislated protections

For the near-elderly, then, like other Americans, access to individual market coverage remains a function of health status and geography.
Some states offer greater access protections than others.  The woman
quoted above who retired to Florida might have found it easier to

obtain individual coverage had she moved to one of the other states described below.

Access to all individual market policies is guaranteed for all residents in six states.  In all of these states, individual policies must be priced according to community rating or modified community rating (Figure 1).

In five other states, all residents are guaranteed access to at least some products sold by some carriers (for example, a Blue Cross/Blue Shield plan).  One of these states does not limit rates that can be charged for these policies (Figure 2).

Seven jurisdictions require periodic open seasons during which residents are guaranteed access to some or all individual market products (for example, some states require HMOs to conduct annual open enrollment periods.)  Rating protections exist in only four of these seven states (Figure 3).

Other states have enacted access protections in the individual market to people who were previously insured.  Residents in six states have broader portability rights than under HIPAA.  For example, residents in these states typically are guaranteed access to some or all individual coverage whenever they switch health plans, not just when they switch from group to individual coverage as HIPAA permits.  Often only several months to one year of prior coverage is required to gain such portability rights.  Again, however, rating protections are only applied in five of the six states (Figure 4).

In 31 states, early retirees and other leaving group coverage are guaranteed conversion rights, meaning their group carrier must issue them an individual policy regardless of health status.  Only 10 of these states limit premiums that can be charged for conversion coverage.  In the other 21 states, conversion rights tend to be hollow (Figure 5).

## Affordability of Individual Coverage

In addition to guaranteeing access to coverage, a few states offer subsidies for private individual coverage purchased by low-income residents.  These programs, funded with state-only dollars, tend to be fairly small.  Health Access New Jersey, for example, subsidizes the purchase of commercial health insurance by people under age 65 having family incomes below 150 percent of the poverty level.  The pro-

**Figure 1  States that Require Guaranteed Issue of All Individual Market Policies at Community Rates to All Residents**

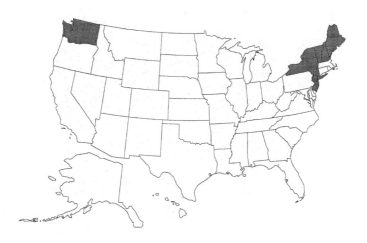

**Figure 2  States Where All Residents are Guaranteed Issue of Some Individual Products**

*no rating limits apply

**Figure 3  States Requiring Open Season Enrollment for Some or All Individual Market Policies**

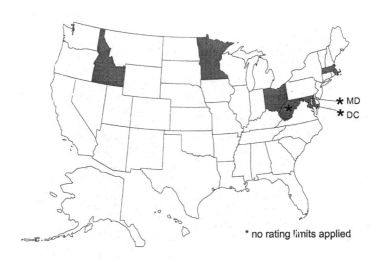

★ MD
★ DC

* no rating limits applied

**Figure 4  States with Portability Protections for Previously Insured Residents that are Greater than HIPAA Requires**

★ RI

*no rating limits apply

**Figure 5  States Requiring Conversion Rights for Individuals Leaving Group Coverage**

\* no rating limits apply

gram had over 14,000 enrollees in 1997.   In Massachusetts, the Medical Security Plan makes subsidized coverage available to people under age 65 having family incomes below 200 percent of the poverty level.  This program also provides partial premium subsidies for COBRA continuation coverage for families with incomes below 400 percent of the poverty level.  Over 15,000 Massachusetts residents participated in this program in 1997 (Summer 1998).

## Public Coverage Options

Public coverage options tend to offer both access and affordability. Eligibility under these programs, even entitlements, is limited, so older workers and early retirees may not always be eligible.

### Federal initiatives

Coverage under the federal Medicare program is only available to people before the age of 65 if they are disabled or suffer from end-stage renal disease. As noted earlier, about 6 percent of people aged 55–64 qualify for Medicare coverage this way.

Medicaid also offers coverage to certain low-income people who become disabled and can no longer work. In the closing days of 1999, Congress enacted the Work Incentives Improvement Act to expand access to Medicare and Medicaid for some disabled individuals who want to return to work.[6] People under age 65 who have left the workforce because of a disability may now have the option of returning to work because of the enactment of this law. It gives states the option to permit working individuals with a medically improved disability to buy into Medicaid and to eliminate income, asset, and resource limitations for those workers who do. It also provides $400 million for demonstration programs and incentive grants to states to encourage the expansion of these Medicaid buy-in options. In addition, the law permits disabled Medicare beneficiaries who return to work to continue their Medicare coverage for six and one-half years, which is significantly longer than the current 24 months. This extension of health coverage through public plans may address a key cause of involuntary retirement and enable more people to return to work without jeopardizing their health insurance.

Medicare and Medicaid eligibility have not yet been changed to extend coverage for non-disabled older workers who prefer to take early retirement. In 1997, President Clinton proposed legislation to establish a Medicare buy-in option at actuarially neutral premiums for certain people between the ages of 55 and 64, but it was not enacted.

### State programs offering subsidized coverage

A number of states have used Medicaid 1115 waivers to make low-income uninsured adults eligible for Medicaid coverage. For example, Hawaii's Quest program offers subsidized coverage for low-income uninsured individuals under age 65 with incomes below 300 percent of the poverty level. MinnesotaCare offers limited benefit coverage at discounted premiums for adults under 175 percent of poverty and for parents of minor children with family incomes below 275 percent of poverty (Summer 1998).

Washington offers subsidized public coverage funded entirely with state money. The Basic Health Plan offers comprehensive coverage for a sliding scale premium based on income. Residents with gross monthly income up to about $2300 (for a family of 3) could qualify for eligibility in 1999. Approximately 128,000 residents were enrolled at the end of last year (Washington State Health Care Authority 1999).

### State high-risk pools

Twenty-five states have high-risk pools to guarantee access to coverage for the medically uninsurable. Most of these state pools operate with limited funding, however, and enrollment in all but a few is very small (under a few thousand individuals). For older workers and early retirees, the access guarantee offered by many state high-risk pools might seem particularly incomplete. All state high-risk pools price premiums using age rating. Premiums for a 64-year-old range from two to five times higher than those charged for a 24-year-old. Depending on the state and benefit package, it is not uncommon for the near-elderly to face premiums in excess of $500/month under high-risk pools. A number of state high-risk pools have other shortcomings. Covered benefits under seven state high-risk pools are subject to significant limitations (such as an annual cap of $75,000 on covered services in California). Six state high-risk pools set premiums at 200 percent of standard rates before adjustments for age and other demographic factors are applied. Two states cap enrollment under their high-risk pools, and so deny access to coverage for the uninsurable when state funding runs short.[7] However, two states (Connecticut and Wisconsin) do offer premium subsidies through their high-risk pools (Pollitz et al. 1998; Communicating for Agriculture 1999).


## CONCLUSION

As Americans age, their need for health insurance grows but, coverage opportunities may decline. People leaving the workforce need both access to health insurance coverage and the means to pay for it. The erosion of employer-provided retirement coverage may make both access and affordability more problematic in the future, and as the baby-boom generation ages, these problems will be faced by greater numbers of people.

Some federal efforts to promote health insurance access have been significant. The enactment of COBRA and HIPAA group market reforms in particular have created a floor of protections, though limited in scope, that people can count on no matter where they live. The near-elderly, most of whom are covered by employer-sponsored health insurance, are among those whose access protections have been enhanced as a result.

Older workers and early retirees do rely disproportionately on individual coverage. In these health insurance markets, their age and higher risk status threatens their access to coverage. HIPAA did not add significantly to individual market protections, however, so people's coverage options were left pretty much unchanged.

Neither of these federal reforms provide subsidies, which are key to the low-income uninsured gaining private coverage. One recent federal initiative did improve access and affordability of public coverage for those disabled older retirees who qualify for Medicare or Medicaid and who may wish to return to work. Federal policy has not changed public coverage options for nondisabled older workers and retirees.

Some states continue to try to fill some of the gaps in access and affordability left by limited federal reforms. However, state efforts are limited, too, and their success varies. For older Americans, especially those who relocate later in life only to find themselves covered by a new and different set of rules, this patchwork of state rules and protections may seem particularly unreliable and confusing. Without the enactment of more sweeping federal reforms, it seems likely that there will continue to be no guarantee of health care access or affordability for the near-elderly.

## Notes

1. COBRA stands for the Consolidated Omnibus Budget Reconciliation Act of 1985. Among other things, this law amended ERISA to require temporary group health continuation coverage. COBRA amendments to ERISA are found at 29 U.S.C. 1161 et. seq.
2. P.L. 104-191.
3. P.L. 103-3.
4. This comment was left anonymously by a visitor to Georgetown's Health Insurance Consumer Guide home page, www.georgetown.edu/research/ihcrp/hippa. October 1999.

5. The state of Maryland does limit rates that can be charged only for certain policies sold to federally eligible individuals.
6. P.L. 106-170.
7. In Illinois, where the high-risk pool is part of the state's alternative mechanism under HIPAA, the enrollment cap may not be applied to people who are federally eligible.

# References

ACP–ASIM. 1999. *No Health Insurance? It's Enough to Make You Sick—Scientific Research Linking the Lack of Health Coverage to Poor Health.* Foreword by Whitney W. Addington, M.D., F.A.C.P. American College of Physicians–American Society of Internal Medicine, Philadelphia, Pennsylvania, 29 pp. Available at http://www.acponline.org/uninsured/lack-contents.htm (June 2000).

Bipartisan Commission on Family and Medical Leave. 1996. *A Workable Balance: Report to Congress on Family and Medical Leave Policies.* U.S. Department of Labor, April 30.

Chollet, Deborah J., and Adele M. Kirk. 1998. *Understanding Individual Health Insurance Markets.* Prepared for the Henry J. Kaiser Family Foundation, March.

Communicating for Agriculture. 1999. *Comprehensive Health Insurance for High-Risk Individuals, A State-By-State Analysis.* 13th ed. Fergus Falls, Minnesota: Communicating for Agriculture, Inc.

Institute for Health and Policy Solutions. 1998. *Baseline Information for Evaluating the Implementation of HIPAA: Final Report.* (Unpublished report for RAND.)

Flynn, Patrice. 1992. "Employment-Based Health Insurance under COBRA Continuation Rules." In *Health Benefits and the Workforce*, Washington, D.C.: U.S. Department of Labor.

Gruber, Jonathan, and Brigitte C. Madrian. 1993. *Health Insurance and Early Retirement: Evidence from the Availability of COBRA Coverage.* Working paper no. 4594, National Bureau of Economic Research, Cambridge, Massachusetts.

Levitt, Larry, and Jon R. Gabel. 1999. *Employer Health Benefits, 1999 Annual Survey.* The Henry J. Kaiser Family Foundation and Health Research and Educational Trust, Menlo Park, California.

Loprest, Pamela. 1997. *Retiree Health Benefits: Availability from Employers and Participation by Employees.* The Urban Institute, Washington D.C., October.

Loprest, Pamela J., and Sheila R. Zedlewski. 1998 (revised). *Health Insurance Coverage Transitions of Older Americans.* The Urban Institute, Washington, D.C., original dated May 30, 1997.

McArdle, Frank, Steve Coppock, Dale Yamamoto, and Andrew Zebrak. 1999. *Retiree Health Coverage: Recent Trends and Employer Perspectives on Future Benefits.* Prepared for the Henry J. Kaiser Family Foundation, October.

Pollitz, Karen, and Nicole Tapay, Lauren Ewers Polite, and Jalena Curtis. 1998. *Consumer's Guides to Getting and Keeping Health Insurance:* Institute for Health Care Research and Policy, Georgetown University, Washington, D.C. Guides for 50 states and the District of Columbia are available on the Internet at http://www.georgetown.edu/research/ihcrp/hipaa as of June 2000.

Pollitz, Karen, Nicole Tapay, Elizabeth Hadley, and Jalena Specht. 1999. "Monitoring the Implementation of Kassebaum-Kennedy by the States and Federal Government." Unpublished work supported by a grant from the Robert Wood Johnson Foundation, ID # 031425. Institute for Health Care Research and Policy, Georgetown University, Washington, D.C.

Scanlon, William J. 1999. "Health Insurance Standards: Implications of New Federal Law for Consumers, Insurers, Regulators." March 19th testimony before the Committee on Labor and Human Resources, United States Senate. GAO/T-HEHS-98-114.

Summer, Laura. 1998. *State-Subsidized Health Insurance Programs for Low Income Residents: Program Structure, Administration, and Costs.* Prepared for the Commonwealth Fund. Washington, D.C.: American Academy on Aging, April.

U.S. General Accounting Office. 1998. *Private Health Insurance: Declining Employer Coverage May Affect Access for 55- to 64-Year-Olds.* U.S. General Accounting Office report AAO/HEHS-98-133, June.

Washington State Health Care Authority. 1999. *Basic Health, Frequently Asked Questions.* Olympia, Washington.

# Commentary

Katherine Swartz
*Harvard School of Public Health*

I thought maybe that cold air was supposed to make us more cognizant of what it's like to be one of the unfortunates. I've been asked to pinch-hit as a discussant on these three papers, so let me try to do a reasonable job here I want to focus my comments more about the aspect that Karen just talked about, the dynamic issues involved with job loss, income, and health insurance coverage. That is to say, if we start with a job loss, that increases the probability (as Ann was describing) that a person will have a subsequent job loss, and all of this has ripple effects on a person's pension, the ability to save (and therefore what kinds of nonpension savings a person has when starting retirement), and on health insurance. These papers highlight the dynamic issues that are involved here. We have unemployment spells, spells without health insurance, and spells that are short-lived (we hope) of having poor health.

The first comment I want to make has to do with the bank merger case study. I found this especially interesting because many people who lose jobs in these huge bank mergers are lower-wage, less-educated groups of workers. Judging by the response rates to the study's survey, however, the study has respondents who happen to be older workers who were better educated and had higher incomes when they lost their jobs.

I happen to live in Boston now, and as some of you know, Boston (and New England) has been experiencing bank mergers recently. I can tell you from colleagues and friends that the recent Bank Boston merger with Fleet Bank targeted older employees for severance. They've been provided with very generous severance packages—in part because of their long tenure with the banks—so that the bank would not be sued for the age discrimination that Jill talks about in her paper. Her discussion of this issue resonated with what I am observing in Boston.

However, what I found distressing about this case study is that I'm seeing similar subtleties at work now in other types of firms and not just banks. For example, we now see changes in job descriptions that are intended to drive workers from their jobs. Changes such as requiring a worker to know how to use a new computer system or a new accounting system are not uncommon. At the same time, employers are not doing enough of the training, which Wally Maher and Dave Smith talked about earlier, that would enable workers to learn the new systems. This situation then leads to what appears to be a voluntary change of job, so you have a voluntary spell without a job. Or is this really a "push and shove" and an involuntary job change? The interpretation, of course, has impacts on the kinds of health insurance one may have, what happens to one's pensions, and what happens to one's current income and ability to save.

I find all of this quite chilling. It leads again to the comment that Burt Seidman raised earlier about some kind of balance being needed between flexibility for employers in terms of their employee labor costs and protections for workers. Employers do need flexibility with labor; as we have seen in Western Europe, employers complain vociferously about all of their labor costs tied up with fringe benefits. On the other hand, there is a need for employee protections, particularly for workers 50 and older, who face higher probabilities of chronic health problems and demands to care for aging parents. Right now, we have a 10-year demographic trough in terms of the people who are 55 to 64 years old, but I can assure you—being on the leading edge of the baby boom, as are many of you in this room—we haven't seen anything yet in terms of the needs for employee protections. I suspect, since the baby boomers have led the way on a lot of things over the last 50 years, we will be heard on this issue as well.

The second point I want to make has to do with the effects of job losses on incomes and pensions. The finding that Ann and her coauthor have that earnings are significantly lower after a job loss (between a quarter to a third less) is incredibly important for those of us who are studying the issue of job loss among older workers. It means that not only are such workers' earnings less, but so is their ability to save money for retirement to round out Social Security and for any health care costs that they're going to have to incur once they are 65 and older.

Also, the finding that pensions are no longer so connected to particular employers really does alter the incentives to retire or not and to change jobs. These changed incentives may increase the probability of having a spell without health insurance; I found that quite interesting and would like to see it explored further.

My third set of comments relate to the loss of jobs and the effect on health insurance coverage. I'll spend more time on this area since my own research has focused on health insurance. We're primarily talking here about the effects of an involuntary loss of a job. That's why my earlier point about how much of job changing or job loss is involuntary versus voluntary is really important to know. People who are married and who voluntarily switch jobs are very likely to be relying on a spouse as a source of access to health insurance. We know that losing a job does not necessarily cause loss of health insurance, because frequently job losers or job changers are covered by health insurance from their spouse.

However, if a person is not married (and in my paper I show that the "unfortunates" are much less likely to be married), then clearly losing a job increases the probability of having a spell without health insurance, or it increases the probability of using up a great deal of one's savings to be able to purchase some type of nongroup health insurance policy. In addition, if a person has any type of preexisting health condition that he/she knows about or is concerned about because of a familial history, then being in a spell without a job and without health insurance is very scary. The health condition may crop up suddenly and an individual may not have the money to pay for care. Older workers also fear that they are less likely to gain a new job because a potential employer may say, "Well, you look like you're a little older and even though I worry about age discrimination, I'll just say that the other person was more qualified for that job." We ought to be worried about these subtle effects related to preexisting health conditions and what they do for employment and health coverage.

A third point about job changes and health insurance (as Karen aptly describes) is that COBRA is not as helpful as it's cracked up to be. A person has to work for an employer with at least 20 employees to even be covered by COBRA. A person also has to have an employer that offers health care coverage. Thus, if an employer goes bankrupt and the business folds, so a worker loses his or her job, the workers do not have access to the former employer's health insurance. A person also needs to have a lot of money to retain coverage under COBRA, because 102 percent of a premium is a lot of money, especially if a former employer offers generous coverage that costs $4,000 or more annually.

Another issue with COBRA is that people are often misled about their eligibility at a time when they're most vulnerable. COBRA is available not just for people who lose a job voluntarily or involuntarily; it's also there for 36 months for people who, through divorce or the death of a spouse, lose their access to the employer-sponsored coverage they have had. Those of you who have been through such circumstances know that's a particularly vulnerable period of time, and yet, a person has only 30 days to decide to continue coverage under COBRA.

So, COBRA is not all its cracked up to be, and as Karen pointed out, HIPAA also does not provide much protection for people. It doesn't prevent insurers from increasing premiums when a person changes from group coverage to nongroup coverage. There's nothing in HIPAA that says that the insurance company can't set whatever premium it deems appropriate. Although HIPAA did help place a floor on the protections that individuals have when they shift from a group policy to a nongroup policy, it is still the case that the states have the right to regulate the nongroup, individual insurance market. These markets are not competitive in terms of premium competition. Rather, they are competitive in the way that the insurers go about selecting who they want to cover and who they want to stay far away from. One group that insurers particularly want to stay far away from is anybody over the age of 50. They can do this by setting high premiums, say, $15,000 to $20,000 a year, and most people then say, "I can't afford that." So technically, while older people may not be denied a policy, they really are not offered a policy.

Let me add one other observation about the difficulties faced by older people in trying to purchase affordable nongroup health insurance policies. This relates to the web site Karen mentioned: I am struck by the fact that it is very difficult to find a high-deductible insurance policy. This is also true if you have access to insurance through employer groups. I cannot get a high-deductible policy, and my husband's employer does not offer a high-deductible insurance policy. Most people whom I've asked cannot get a high-deductible insurance policy from where they work. If you go into the nongroup market and try to buy a high-deductible, catastrophic policy, I suspect that you will find enormous difficulty because insurers are immediately suspicious.

Somebody who wants a high-deductible policy knows something—adverse selection is the issue.  Insurers fear that you know that you have cancer or some kind of cardiovascular problem and you're expecting to use medical care in excess of $10,000 a year.

All of which brings me back to where I started—the dynamic aspects of income, pensions, and health insurance facing people who lose jobs, particularly people who are older than 50 or in the 55- to 64-year-old group that we're talking about in this conference.  The issue that we really have to be thinking hard about is how do we develop public policies to help people during these spells or periods of time when they are experiencing loss of a job, loss of health insurance, loss of income—without at the same time increasing the moral hazard incentives for somebody voluntarily to enter a spell without a job.  I am very concerned about unintentionally creating incentives, then, for an employer to feel that somebody who is 55 to 64 years of age is expendable because a public safety net exists that will catch a person shoved from a job.  How do we put in place public policies that help older workers in spells without jobs without at the same time increasing incentives for more people to enter these spells?

# Session 3
# Chronic Illness and Disability
## Policy Issues for an Aging Workforce

# Permanent Partial Disability from Occupational Injuries

(US)

## Earnings Losses and Replacement in Three States

Jeff E. Biddle
*Michigan State University*

Leslie I. Boden
*Boston University*

Robert T. Reville
*RAND*

J28

J31

Many older workers develop disabling health conditions or suffer disabling injuries. The labor-market consequences of disability can include job loss, reduced income, earlier retirement, and greater reliance on private and social insurance systems to provide income security. One important source of disability is work-related illness and injury. In this chapter, we examine the labor-market consequences of work-related disabling injuries and their relation to the age of the injured in three states: California, Wisconsin, and Washington. We also report estimates of the adequacy of income benefits received for these injuries from workers' compensation.

Earnings losses and related labor-market consequences result from workplace injuries in a number of ways. Most workers who suffer workplace injuries have temporary disabilities: complete recovery from the injury is expected, though some time out of work to recover is often needed, resulting in lost earnings. During that time out of work, workers qualify for temporary disability benefits from workers' compensation, which replaces some of the earnings loss. In some cases, a workplace injury results in a permanent impairment or loss of physical or mental health. This permanent impairment may result in permanent loss of earning capacity and therefore of actual earnings. The permanent impairments incurred on the job do not typically result in the level of disability that qualifies for SSDI or SSI benefits. Still, income security is often threatened, and the onset of retirement may be substantially hastened by workplace injury and illness.

A considerable amount is spent compensating workers with permanent disabilities from workplace injuries. In California, permanent partial disability (PPD) income benefits for workers' compensation paid in 1997 totaled $1.1 billion, which is more than the total amount paid for the higher number of temporary disabilities. As we will discuss below, this $1.1 billion is only a fraction of the lost earnings of these injured workers. The remaining burden is shouldered by the workers and their families, as well as by other private and social insurance programs.

As the workforce ages, the issue of permanently disabling workplace injuries potentially becomes more significant. While the probability of a workplace injury decreases with age, according to Mitchell (1988), the probability of disabling injuries (and death) increases with age. Recovery from injury often takes longer and is less complete for older workers (Chirikos and Nestel 1989).

This chapter examines the losses experienced by workers with permanent disabilities in three states and compares the adequacy of compensation received from the states' workers' compensation systems. We present evidence that older workers suffer proportionately more injuries with permanently disabling consequences and that the losses suffered by older workers are greater, on average, than those of younger workers. We also find that injury-related non-employment is higher among older workers. Moreover, the older workers in states we have studied appear to recover a smaller proportion of their losses from workers' compensation than do other injured workers.

The data we present come from recent estimates of lost earnings of injured or ill workers in three states: Washington (Biddle 1998), Wisconsin (Boden and Galizzi 1999) and California (Peterson et al. 1997; Reville 1999). We summarize these recent studies and report new information about lost earnings from workplace injuries. The estimates we present use administrative data on workers' compensation claims linked to longitudinal earnings data to directly estimate the earnings losses of injured or ill workers. They follow in the tradition of earlier "wage loss studies" by Johnson, Cullinan, and Curington (1978) and Berkowitz and Burton (1987). Both of these studies linked claims data to Social Security earnings records.

We begin with a brief description of workers' compensation permanent disability benefits in California, Washington, and Wisconsin. We then present the methodology used to derive estimates of injury-related lost earnings. Next, we describe lost earnings in the three states and how these losses are related to the age of injured workers. Finally, we review estimates of adequacy of workers' compensation benefits and discuss implications for the income security of older workers.

## COMPENSATION FOR PERMANENT PARTIAL DISABILITY

Workers' compensation is a state-based administrative system that provides benefits to workers injured on the job without regard to fault. The benefits are set by formulas that differ from state to state. In California, Wisconsin, and Washington, as in many other states, both temporary total disability (TTD) benefits and permanent partial disability (PPD) benefits are paid. TTD benefits are intended to provide income support during recovery. PPD benefits are intended to compensate workers for the losses associated with a permanently disabling workplace injury.

Setting compensation levels for TTD benefits is relatively straightforward. The goal is income replacement during recovery. Typically, the benefit amount is set at a level lower than the preinjury wage (often two-thirds) to provide the worker with an incentive to maintain safety in the workplace and to return to work when recovery is complete.[1] If injured workers receive temporary disability benefits for all eligible workplace injuries and if these benefits are paid for the full duration of injury-related lost work time, evaluating the adequacy of temporary disability income replacement is straightforward, since it is set by formula. The actual time out of work is usually relatively short—days instead of weeks.

Setting the benefit level and schedule of payments for permanent disability benefits is considerably more difficult. Unlike TTD benefits, PPD benefits are intended to compensate for current <u>and future</u> lost earnings capacity. The administrative burden and adverse incentive effects of a system that pays injured workers as the losses are experienced (referred to as a *wage loss system*) are regarded in most states as prohibitive. For this reason, most states (including the three states compared in this study) set the benefit level for permanent disabilities prospectively. Formulas are often complex, and the basis of PPD benefits varies from state to state. No states have set the benefit levels or the schedule of payments for PPD benefits with empirical knowledge of the economic consequences of disabling workplace injuries. For this reason, the extent to which PPD benefits achieve the goal of income replacement is unknown.

We compare estimates of the adequacy of income benefits in three states (California, Wisconsin, and Washington). The approaches adopted in these three states to compensating workers with permanently disabling injuries are described below. For a discussion of the method of calculating permanent disabilities benefits in every state, see Barth and Niss (1999).

To estimate the impact of disability from occupational injuries, we estimate the losses experienced by injured workers over the years after the injury in each of the three states.[2] The estimation of losses requires comparing postinjury earnings to a counterfactual: earnings for the same individual while uninjured. Let $y_t^I$ represent the earnings while injured, where I denotes "injured" and the subscript $t$ denotes time from the injury. Let the counterfactual earnings be represented by $y_t^U$, where U denotes "uninjured." For any individual, the undiscounted earnings loss between the time of injury, which we will denote $t = 0$, and some future date, $T$, is

**Eq. 1**   $$\text{earnings loss} = \sum_{t=0}^{T} \left( y_t^U - y_t^I \right)$$

In the next section, we will describe the estimation of earnings losses, which is complicated by the need to estimate the counterfactual $y_t^U$.

To compare the adequacy of benefits across states, we also estimate the fraction of earnings loss that is replaced by benefits for the
average PPD case, i.e., the replacement rate:

**Eq. 2**   replacement rate $= \dfrac{\text{benefits}}{\text{earnings loss}}$

## THE ESTIMATION OF LOSSES

We report the estimates of earnings losses for PPD cases from
Reville (1999), Boden and Galizzi (1999), and Biddle (1998). The
results have been updated in some cases (for instance with a longer
period of postinjury earnings for California than in Reville [1999]), and
the analyses have been modified to make estimates as comparable as
possible. However, due to data limitations in each state, the comparison groups available and therefore the approaches adopted to estimating losses in those papers and among states in this paper are different.
In particular, in each state, a different control group is used. In this
section, we describe the statistical problem raised by the estimation of
losses and the solution adopted in each of the three states. In future
work, we plan to obtain more comprehensive databases in each of these
states (and in several others) in order to compare losses among states
using identical methods.

The statistical problem in the estimation of earnings losses arises
from the unobservability of the counterfactual $y_t^U$ in Eq. 1. If we
could observe both injured and uninjured earnings for every injured
worker, estimating earnings loss would be straightforward and given
by Eq. 1. However, $y_t^U$ cannot be observed, and an estimate, $\hat{y}_t^U$ must
be constructed.

At an administrative level, workers' compensation programs must
also estimate $y_t^U$ when setting benefits, and typically they use the preinjury earnings. However, particularly for estimating the long-term
consequences of permanent disabilities, the preinjury wage is not a sat-
isfactory proxy. First, without the injury, the worker may have experienced wage growth over time, which the preinjury earnings will not
measure. Second, if the injury had not occurred, it is possible that the

injured worker would have been unemployed or exited the workforce for different reasons. It is not appropriate to assume that they would have earned the preinjury earnings in every postinjury earnings period.

Instead of using preinjury earnings, we estimate uninjured earnings in the postinjury period using the earnings of a comparison (control) group. This approach draws its inspiration from the training program evaluation literature (Dehejia and Wahba 1996; Heckman and Hotz 1989; Holland 1986; LaLonde 1986). The control group comprises workers who were similar to the injured workers with respect to demographic and economic characteristics but who did not experience a workplace injury during the time period under examination.[3]

Biddle (1998) and Boden and Galizzi (1999) as well as the estimates from Washington and Wisconsin reported below, each used workers with minor injuries as comparison groups. To correct for observed differences between injured workers and controls, a fixed-effect earnings regression model is estimated. Reville (1999) and our estimates for California (reported below) used uninjured workers at the same firm as controls. Observed differences are corrected for using a case-control matching methodology. In the remainder of this section, we describe the particular estimation approach and the data used for each state.

### Washington and Wisconsin

In Biddle (1998) and Boden and Galizzi (1999), as well as in the Washington and Wisconsin estimates reported below, $\hat{y}_t^U$ is estimated from the earnings of workers with minor workplace injuries. The minor injuries used in the Washington study resulted in less than three days out of work and no permanent disability benefits (referred to as medical-only cases). The Wisconsin minor injuries resulted in 8 to 10 days out of work and no permanent disability benefits. In both states, earnings regressions were estimated using longitudinal data on real quarterly earnings for a pooled sample of controls and injured workers. Independent variables included age in the quarter of observation and calendar year and quarter dummies to control for business cycle effects common to the earnings of all workers. Also, pre- and postinjury earnings were allowed to follow different trends depending on the severity of the injury. [5]

The regression coefficients were used to project what the earnings of the injured worker would have been in the quarter of injury and the postinjury quarters, using that worker's estimated fixed effect and the coefficients estimated for the comparison group. The earnings loss estimate for each postinjury quarter was set equal to this earnings projection minus the actual earnings of the injured worker. Quarterly earnings loss estimates for the quarter of injury and 14 subsequent quarters were then discounted at a 2.3 percent rate[5] and summed to produce a single loss figure.

To check the quality of the control group, the preinjury earnings of the controls and the injured workers were compared in both Washington and Wisconsin. In Wisconsin, preinjury differences in quarterly earnings growth[6] between the controls and injured workers were small (under $8) and statistically insignificant (Boden and Galizzi 1999); in Washington, the difference was about $17 per quarter.

In Washington, the claims data are from the Washington Department of Labor and Industries and consist of a sample of workers' compensation injuries from July 1993 to June 1994. The sample includes 8769 medical-only cases and 34,618 workers receiving income benefits (TTD and PPD). The claims data are linked to 21 quarterly reports on earnings provided by employers in the state to the Washington Employment Security Department.[7] The earnings are from six quarters before to 14 quarters after the injury. The Wisconsin claims data provided by the Wisconsin Division of Workers' Compensation are from 1989 and 1990. They are linked to 24 quarterly earnings reports from the Wisconsin Division of Employment Security, ranging from 8 quarters before to as long as 18 quarters after the injury. The sample consists of 6,416 short-term injuries and 47,889 longer-term injuries and injuries involving PPD benefits.

## California

Reville (1999)[8] and the estimates reported below for California used uninjured workers as controls. Each injured worker was matched to up to 10 uninjured workers at the same employer with earnings approximately equal to the preinjury earnings for the injured worker. The mean difference in earnings between the injured and control workers in the quarters after injury was then used to estimate losses.[9] An estimate of cumulative earnings loss is calculated by summing over time for every worker the earnings loss in every quarter, discounted (at 2.3 percent) to the quarter of injury.

As in Washington and Wisconsin, to test for the quality of the controls, Reville (1999) compared the preinjury earnings of the injured workers to the comparison workers over the years prior to injury. Controls were matched to injured workers based on the four quarters prior to the injury. Eight additional quarters before the first four quarters prior are available for testing the controls. The match was found to be very close, with an average quarterly difference in earnings of only $28, less than 2 percent of the difference found in the quarters following injury.[10]

The claims data are from the California Workers' Compensation Insurance Rating Bureau and consist of workers' compensation PPD claims from injuries during 1993 at insured firms.[11] The data are matched to quarterly earnings data from the fourth quarter of 1989 through the second quarter of 1998 from the California Employment Development Department. Data on 8,107 claims are matched to earnings data for 28,862 uninjured workers.

## PERMANENT PARTIAL DISABILITY BENEFITS IN THREE STATES

The amount paid for temporary disability benefits differs among states. There are, however, only a few dimensions along which temporary disability benefits vary. Benefits are set as a fraction of the preinjury wage, where the fraction varies among states. There are also different maximum and minimum benefits, waiting periods, and maximum numbers of weeks. Most states use the pretax wage as a basis for temporary disability benefits. However, because workers' compensation benefits are not taxed, other states base their benefits on "spendable earnings," which are meant to approximate after-tax earnings. The rules governing temporary disability payments in the three states we examine are summarized in Table 1.

Differences among states in permanent disability benefits are harder to categorize along a few dimensions. This reflects the com-

## Table 1  Summary of Income Benefits in California, Wisconsin, and Washington

### California 1993 income benefits

| | |
|---|---|
| TTD weekly amount | 2/3 preinjury pretax wage to maximum of $336 |
| TTD waiting period | 3 days |
| PPD weekly amount | 2/3 preinjury pretax wage to maximum |
| PPD weekly benefit maximum | Maximum: $140 (ratings under 25) $148 (earnings 25 and above) |
| Weeks of PPD benefits | Vary by rating: |
| | 25th percentile: 24 weeks |
| | 50th percentile: 50 weeks |
| | 75th percentile: 96 weeks |
| | 99th percentile: 426 weeks plus life pension |
| Other income benefit: | |
| Vocational rehabilitation maintenance | 2/3 preinjury pretax wage to maximum of $246 |

### Wisconsin 1989–90 income benefits

| | |
|---|---|
| TTD payment amounts | 2/3 preinjury pretax wage to maximum of $363 (1989) or $388 (1990) |
| TTD waiting period | 3 days (7-day retroactive period) |
| PTD weekly amount | 2/3 preinjury pretax wage to maximum of $125 (1989) or $131 (1990) |
| Weeks of PPD benefits | 10 weeks per percentage point |
| Lump-sum payments of unaccrued benefits generally not allowed. | 25th percentile: 13 weeks |
| | 50th percentile: 28 weeks |
| | 75th percentile: 60 weeks |
| | 99th percentile: 526 weeks |
| Other income benefit: | |
| Vocational rehabilitation maintenance | 2/3 preinjury pretax wage to maximum of $363 (1989) or $388 (1990) |

(continued)

**Table 1 (continued)**

| Washington 1993–94 income benefits | |
|---|---|
| TTD payment amounts | From 60% to 75% of preinjury pretax wage, depending on marital status and number of dependents; maximum of $2216 per month paid in bimonthly installments |
| TTD waiting period | 3 days |
| PPD payment methods | Total awards based on schedule of injuries and/ or percentage disability rating system. If total award exceeds $6600 dollars, monthly payments are made according to TTD payment schedule until full award is paid. |
| Other income benefit: | |
| Vocational rehabilitation maintenance | Ordinary TTD benefits can be received during participation in approved VR program. |

plexity of the problem of setting higher benefits for people with greater disability based on comparing individuals with different injuries.[12] In most states, there are "schedules" that set dollar amounts for particular injuries (such as $27,813 for the loss of a thumb in Washington in 1997), though the schedules differ among states and the ranking of injuries is sometimes reversed in different states. Most states also use some kind of rating system that ranks different injuries on a scale of 1 to 100 depending upon physician impairment ratings or ratings derived from medical descriptions of impairments (such as the fraction of range of motion that is lost in the shoulder).[13]  These rating systems are used either for all injuries, as in California, or only for unscheduled injuries. Like the schedules, these rating systems rank different injuries, and the relative ranking of particular injuries in different rating systems can vary. Some states pay different amounts depending upon whether you have returned to work or returned to the at-injury employer. In addition, there are differences in weekly amounts and in the number of weeks that benefits are paid.

In the remainder of this section, we describe more fully the rules determining the size of permanent benefits payments in each of the three states being examined and present some descriptive statistics on the fraction of claims with permanent disabilities.

## Washington

In Washington, there are statutorily determined PPD award amounts for a list of specified injuries to scheduled body parts (for example, amputation of the leg above the knee). Workers can also be given benefits for unspecified injuries to scheduled body parts. In this case, a rating for the percentage of impairment is multiplied by the scheduled amputation value of the body part. Finally, there are awards for unspecified injuries to unscheduled body parts (including, notably, backs and necks). In these cases, physicians make use of a set of rules and guidelines issued by the Department of Labor and Industry to assign a "percentage of total bodily impairment" caused by the injury. This percentage is then multiplied by a scheduled total bodily impairment value, which was $118,800 as of July 1994. As Table 1 indicates, during the 1993–1994 period, awards below $6,600 (a little over half of all awards) were paid out in a lump sum, while awards greater than that amount were paid out in monthly installments.

Table 2 reports the percentage of injured workers receiving permanent disability awards in various age categories in Washington, Wisconsin, and California. The figures in the cells reflect the ratio of

**Table 2  Share of Workers' Compensation Cases with PPD Benefits by Age Group (%)**

|  | Age group | | | |
|---|---|---|---|---|
| Sample | Under 35 | 35–54 | Over 55 | Overall |
| Wisconsin[a] | 14.1 | 21.2 | 27.9 | 18.1 |
| Washington[b] | 17.1 | 27.0 | 39.0 | 23.4 |
| California 1991–96[c] (self-insured) | 37.2 | 47.0 | 49.2 | 44.0 |
| California 1993[d] (insured) | ——— Data unavailable ——— | | | 42.9 |

[a] Wisconsin Division of Workers' Compensation, authors' calculations.
[b] Washington Department of Labor and Industries, authors' calculations.
[c] Random sample of self-insured indemnity claims data collected by RAND.
[d] Workers' Compensation Insurance Ratings Bureau data, authors' calculations.

claims receiving PPD awards to all claims with income benefits, that is, all claims involving compensation for lost time and/or PPD benefits. In Washington, 23.4 percent of claims with income benefits in the period examined involved PPD awards. However, this percentage rises with age and is 39 percent for injured workers 55 years or older.

### Wisconsin

Wisconsin has two kinds of PPD benefits, functional impairment benefits and earnings capacity benefits. Functional impairment benefits are based upon a physician impairment rating. Earning capacity benefits are paid only to workers with nonscheduled injuries (typically head, back, or neck injuries) who do not return to work or who are rehired at no more than 85 percent of their former wage. Typically, workers qualifying for earning capacity benefits have not returned to their former employer. Earning capacity benefits use the same formula per percentage point of permanent disability, but the disability percentages tend to be much larger than for functional impairment benefits. They are determined by reports of "vocational experts" on the effect of the impairment on the worker's wage-earning capacity.

Table 1 displays PPD benefit levels in Wisconsin for 1989–1990 injuries. PPD benefits are subject to a maximum weekly benefit of $125 for injuries occurring in 1989 and $131 for those occurring in 1990. This maximum weekly benefit represents just over one-third of the maximum weekly TTD benefit. Each percent of permanent disability of the body as a whole is allocated 10 weeks' benefits. For 1989 injuries, this implies a maximum benefit payment of $1,250 per percentage point of disability. Generally, benefits are paid monthly, so that monthly maximum PPD benefits for 1989–1990 injuries were about $500. Only 18.1 percent of workers with lost-time workers' compensation cases received PPD benefits in Wisconsin in 1989–1990 (Table 2).

### California

California's method for setting permanent disability benefits is distinctive and perhaps the most complex of the three states. All disabilities are described and ranked in a rating system that is unique to California. This rating system includes medical descriptions of impairments as well as work restrictions (such as different ratings for "no heavy lifting" and "no very heavy lifting"). It also includes compensation for "subjectives" such as chronic pain, even in the absence of medical evidence to support it.

As a result of this relatively permissive description of permanent disability, California has a considerably larger fraction of claims with permanent disability. As seen in Table 2, more than 40 percent of individuals receiving income benefit payments also receive permanent disability benefits. As in Wisconsin and Washington, the fraction with permanent disabilities increases with age, so that for workers over 55, almost half receive permanent disability benefits.[14]

California is also unique in the extent to which benefits are adjusted to account for the individual circumstances of the injured worker. On the assumption that the same injury will lead to different losses depending upon the occupation of the injured worker, California's disability rating system assigns different values for the same injury in different occupations. For instance, an injury that affects speech will lead to higher benefits for a radio announcer than for a bricklayer; however, an injury that affects the shoulder will lead to a higher benefit for the bricklayer. Finally, on the assumption that recovery is harder with age, higher benefits are paid for older workers.

Table 1 shows that the maximum benefit levels for temporary and permanent disabilities in California are similar to those in Wisconsin (and difficult to compare with Washington's). The formula for weeks is very complex, with the number of weeks for each additional disability rating point increasing with the disability rating. Using the actual distribution of PPD awards, the table shows the number of weeks of PPD benefits by quartile of award for Wisconsin and California. In general, California has longer periods of PPD than Wisconsin.

## EARNINGS LOSS AND REPLACEMENT RATE
## ESTIMATES BY STATE

In Table 3, we report the losses for all three states, together with the total income benefits paid, the preinjury average quarterly earnings, and the pretax replacement rate. Total income benefits paid includes temporary total disability and permanent partial disability benefits in all three states. In addition, in California and Wisconsin, injured workers are allowed to accept a cash settlement for the future value of the medical care in exchange for releasing the insurer or employer for any liability for future medica expensesl. This is not allowed in Washington. Finally, all three states pay a vocational rehabilitation (VR) maintenance allowance, which is paid while the worker is unable to work due to participation in VR.[15]   Losses are reported in each state for 3.5 years and 10 years after injury. In all three states, the estimates at 3.5 years are based on observed postinjury earnings. Estimates at 10 years are based on projecting the losses an additional 6.5 years, discounted and based on the loss estimated for the final year observed.

Table 3 shows that losses in Washington and Wisconsin are very similar; losses in California appear to be considerably higher. California income benefits paid are also considerably higher than those in Washington and Wisconsin, but not high enough to cover the differences in losses.[16] This is shown in the far right column of Table 3, which reports the pretax replacement rate at 10 years among states. In Washington and Wisconsin, the replacement rate is over 45 percent, while in California, the replacement rate is below 40 percent.[17]

**Table 3  Average Losses by Years from Injury and Pretax Replacement Rate, PPD Cases**[a]

| Sample | Preinjury quarterly earnings ($) | Total income benefits ($) | Losses by years from injury ($) | | Replacement rate of 10-yr. losses |
|---|---|---|---|---|---|
| | | | 3.5 | 10[b] | |
| California | 5,284 | 21,229 | 26,383 | 56,340 | 0.377 |
| Wisconsin | 5,868 | 14,196 | 17,602 | 30,746 | 0.462 |
| Washington | 5,601 | 14,975 | 15,358 | 32,427 | 0.462 |

[a] Dollar values in 1984 dollars.
[b] Projected.

Although useful for comparing among states, the after-tax replacement rate might be preferred as a measure of adequacy because workers' compensation benefits are tax-free.  In after-tax dollars, the earnings loss would be 20–30 percent lower, and therefore the replacement rate would be higher.  However, two other sources of bias are in the opposite direction.  First, the choice of 10 years for the replacement rate is arbitrary.  In work in progress by the authors using California data, losses are found to continue at much the same annual level even with seven years of observed postinjury earnings.  Since virtually all injured workers have already received all workers' compensation benefits by five years, but losses may continue for many years after that, the replacement rate for longer periods would be lower.  Also, fringe benefits are a significant source of compensation.[18]  Some fringe benefits are tied to earnings, and others may be lost if the disabled worker cannot return to the preinjury job.[19]

Table 4 shows losses over the observed period of 3.5 years and losses projected to both 6.5 years and 10 years for three age groups.  Estimates are reported only for Washington and Wisconsin, because data limitations prevent the calculation of these estimates for California.  The table shows that, in both states, losses increase with age.  In

**Table 4  Losses by Age Group and State, PPD Cases (1994 $)**

| Sample | Under 35 | 35–54 | Over 55 |
| --- | --- | --- | --- |
| Wisconsin | | | |
| Preinjury quarterly earnings | 4,917 | 6,625 | 6,276 |
| Losses (3.5 yr.) | 13,832 | 19,038 | 26,287 |
| Losses (projected 6.5 yr.) | 18,159 | 23,842 | 45,880 |
| Losses (projected 10 yr.) | 24,317 | 30,678 | 56,271 |
| Income benefits received | 12,475 | 15,477 | 15,990 |
| Washington | | | |
| Preinjury quarterly earnings | 4,798 | 6,687 | 7,556 |
| Losses (3.5 yr.) | 14,782 | 15,190 | 17,691 |
| Losses (projected 6.5 yr.) | 22,265 | 22,825 | 30,295 |
| Losses (projected 10 yr.) | 30,383 | 31,110 | 43,969 |
| Income benefits received | 14,790 | 15,650 | 12,428 |

Wisconsin, injured workers under 35 experience losses of $13,832 over the 3.5 years following injury, while workers over 55 experience losses almost twice as large. In Washington, the increase in lost earnings with age is less dramatic, with workers under 35 losing $14,782 over the 3.5 years following injury, and injured workers 55 and over losing an estimated $17,691.

Because earnings increase with age, and higher-paid workers will lose more for the same amount of lost work time, when comparing among age groups it is useful to normalize the lost earnings by preinjury earnings. Dividing the loss by the preinjury quarterly earnings provides a measure of lost earnings in terms of quarters of lost earnings at the preinjury earnings level. Using this measure, the age pattern of losses for injured workers in Wisconsin is different than in Washington. In Wisconsin, workers over 55 lose the equivalent of almost one year of preinjury earnings during the 3.5 years after injury, compared with less than nine months (three quarters) for each of the other two age groups. This suggests that older disabled workers in Wisconsin experience more time out of work following the injury than younger disabled workers. In contrast, the youngest disabled workers in Washington experience the largest earnings losses relative to the preinjury earnings. Injured workers in Washington under 35 experience over nine months (three quarters) of lost preinjury earnings; by comparison, workers over 55 experience less than seven months of losses.

Projecting losses to 10 years after injury produces results for Wisconsin that are qualitatively similar to the losses for 3.5 years: older disabled workers experience considerably larger losses measured absolutely or in months of lost earnings. At 10 years postinjury, months of lost earnings in Washington become similar among age groups. In both states, replacement of lost earnings during the first 10 years after the injury is considerably lower for workers over 55. In Figure 1, the replacement rate of 10-year losses by age group is shown for Washington and Wisconsin. For the two age groups below 55, the replacement rate is approximately one-half. For the injured workers aged 55 and over, the replacement rate in both states is 28 percent.[20]

Our 10-year projections may provide an overstatement of losses for workers over 55, since by age 65, it is likely they will have retired even if they had not been injured and therefore would have received no further earnings losses.[21] For this reason, we also report 6.5-year pro-

**Figure 1  Projected 10-Year Earnings Replacement Rate by Age:
Washington and Wisconsin PPD Cases**

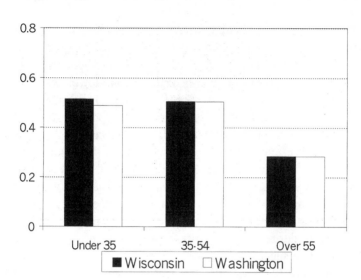

jections for losses (3.5 observed years and 3 projected years at the last quarter's average loss), which presumably are less likely to be biased in this manner. The 6.5 year projected replacement rate of 0.41 for Washington and 0.35 for Wisconsin is lower than even the 10-year projected replacement rate for the younger age groups.

The results in Figure 1 and Table 4 suggest that the adequacy of replacement rates is lowest for the oldest injured workers. It should be noted, though, that the 10-year replacement rate provides a limited window during which to observe losses. It is possible that losses beyond the observed period for workers in the oldest age category (over 55) will be considerably lower or nonexistent because many would have retired even had they not been injured. Younger workers may lose less during the first few years but over their lifetime may lose more.[22]

Table 5 reports on how well PPD benefits are tailored to lost earnings. As noted earlier, disability ratings are used in all three states to predict which workers have greater disability so that higher benefits can be targeted to the most serious cases. If this system were success-ful, we would expect benefits would increase at least in proportion to losses. To examine this, the table divides the distribution of income benefits into quintiles and calculates the average losses within each quintile. We would expect that the losses would increase with the income benefit quintile. In California, the lowest benefit quintile had losses that are five-sixths the losses of the second lowest quintile; how-ever, benefits in the first quintile are 30 percent of those of the second quintile. An already low replacement rate of 19 percent for the second quintile is far lower than that for the first (7 percent). The results for Washington are even more dramatic. While the highest quintile receives benefits five times larger than those of the lowest quintile, losses are only 25 percent higher. Losses in the second and fourth quintiles are lower than in the first and third, respectively. In contrast, losses in Wisconsin increase monotonically with income benefits, lead-ing to very similar replacement rates in all but the highest quintile.[24]

The relative success in equitably distributing benefits in Wisconsin may be driven by Wisconsin's two-tier system, which pays earnings capacity benefits only to workers who either do not return to work or who return at a substantially lower wage. Workers receiving earnings capacity benefits will almost always have higher losses. Washington's relative inability to target benefits to the more serious cases may be driven by the limitations of the impairment-based system used to set benefits. It is possible that information on the type of injury alone does not capture as much variation in the postinjury outcomes as economic factors such as the ability to return to work (the payment of earnings capacity benefits in Wisconsin) or the personal characteristics of the injured (the occupational and age adjustments to disability ratings used in California).

Several recent papers have noted that, particularly in permanent disability cases, absence from work following the initial return to work is common among workers with occupational injuries (Biddle 1998; Butler, Johnson, and Baldwin 1995; Galizzi and Boden 1996; Reville 1999). For this reason, we depart from the approach often adopted in the workers' compensation literature of examining duration to first return to work, and instead we examine differences over the years after the injury between the fraction of injured workers and controls without reported earnings. This allows both the injured workers and the con-

**Table 5 The Relationship of Losses and Total Income Benefits, by PPD Benefit Percentile**

| Sample | | Permanent disability benefit percentile | | | | | |
|---|---|---|---|---|---|---|---|
| | | 0–20 | 21–40 | 41–60 | 61–80 | 81–100 |
| California 1993 injuries | Losses at 3.5 yr. ($) | 14,654 | 17,818 | 26,319 | 37,043 | 69,937 |
| | Losses projected 10 yr. ($) | 24,120 | 29,948 | 43,107 | 55,754 | 114,226 |
| | Income benefits received[a] ($) | 1,695 | 5,689 | 12,391 | 24,158 | 61,621 |
| | 10-yr. replacement rate (%) | 7 | 18.9 | 28.7 | 44.1 | 53.9 |
| Washington 1993–94 injuries | Losses at 3.5 yr. ($) | 13,493 | 13,499 | 16,199 | 5,915 | 17,679 |
| | Losses projected 10 yr. ($) | 30,512 | 28,834 | 34,555 | 32,485 | 35,775 |
| | Income benefits received[a] ($) | 4,395 | 8,859 | 14,095 | 18,086 | 29,433 |
| | 10-yr. replacement rate (%) | 14.4 | 30.8 | 40.8 | 55.7 | 82.3 |
| Wisconsin 1989–90 injuries | Losses at 3.5 yr. ($) | 6,078 | 9,209 | 14,616 | 18,976 | 37,595 |
| | Losses projected 10 yr. ($) | 8,255 | 13,816 | 20,957 | 32,036 | 65,713 |
| | Income benefits received[a] ($) | 3,299 | 6,259 | 9,912 | 14,703 | 38,425 |
| | 10-yr. replacement rate (%) | 40.0 | 45.3 | 47.3 | 45.9 | 58.5 |

[a] Temporary plus permanent disability benefits.

trols to move in and out of the labor force, but if the fraction of injured workers out of the labor force exceeds the fraction of controls, then we assume this is injury-related.[24] This estimate of injury-related non-employment is reported in Table 6 for 3, 5, 10, and (where available) 20 quarters after injury.

Table 6 shows that in all three states, injury-related non-employment continues to be significant even 10 quarters following injury. It is clear that California's considerably higher earnings losses are associated with much higher rates of injury-related non-employment. Both the 1992 and 1993 injured workers have injury-related non-employment exceeding 15 percent for the first 2 1/2 years, though similar rates are never observed in Washington or Wisconsin, not even during the first quarter after injury. As shown in Reville and Schoeni (1999), injury-related non-employment is higher in recessions, and the difference between the states may be in part driven by the severity of the recession experienced in California in the early 1990s. There may be other reasons for the difference, including differences in litigation rates among the states and differences in the characteristics of jobs, workers, and industries. We plan to explore these differences in future studies.

Table 7 shows non-employment for Washington and Wisconsin by age group. In both Washington and Wisconsin, compared with nondisabled workers, workers over 55 with permanently disabling injuries are increasingly likely to be out of work as time from the injury increases. This suggests that a disabling workplace injury (as with the onset of other health conditions) may lead older workers to choose to retire earlier than they would have otherwise.

**Table 6  Injury-Related Non-Employment Rate by Quarters from Injury (%)**

| Sample | Quarters | | | |
|---|---|---|---|---|
| | 3 | 5 | 10 | 20 |
| California 1993 injuries | 25 | 23 | 17 | 9 |
| Washington 1993–94 injuries | 12 | 11 | 9 | ND[a] |
| Wisconsin 1989–90 injuries | 12 | 12 | 12 | ND |

[a] ND = no data available.

**Table 7  Injury-Related Non-Employment Rates by Quarters from Injury and by Age Group, PPD Cases in Wisconsin and Washington (%)**

| Sample | Quarters | | |
|---|---|---|---|
| | 3 | 5 | 10 |
| Wisconsin | | | |
| Age <35 | 11 | 10 | 9 |
| Age 35–54 | 8 | 11 | 12 |
| Age 55+ | 12 | 17 | 27 |
| Washington | | | |
| Age <35 | 13 | 11 | 7 |
| Age 35–54 | 12 | 12 | 10 |
| Age 55+ | 13 | 15 | 18 |

## CONCLUSION

This paper examines the losses experienced by workers with permanent disabilities in California, Washington and Wisconsin and compares the adequacy of compensation received from those states' workers' compensation systems. We find evidence of substantial losses from permanently disabling injuries in the three states. The state programs differ substantially in the proportion of workers' compensation cases receiving permanent disability benefits and in the average losses sustained by these injured workers, reflecting both differences in the laws and practices in those states. In general, California stands out: a higher proportion of injured workers received permanent disability benefits in California, experiencing higher average losses and receiving higher average benefits (but replacing a lower fraction of lost earnings). Wisconsin's system appears to lead to better targeting of benefits to losses, while Washington's impairment-based PPD schedule leads to losses unrelated to benefits paid.

It is possible that some of the differences among the states are driven by differences in industry mix, demographics, and economic conditions. At this point, we also cannot rule out the possibility that the differences are driven, at least in part, by differences in methods used. However, our preliminary research (which is still in progress) on disabling injuries in Florida, a state with industry mix and demographics that are similar to those of California, has found losses that are at least as close to those in California as to Wisconsin's or Washington's. This research has used the same methods we have used in Wisconsin, which suggests that the methods do not drive the observed differences. In our ongoing research, we are estimating losses with similar control groups and will examine how measured interstate differences (such as industry mix) affect the disparities in the losses we have measured.

Besides differences in earnings losses, California also pays PPD benefits to more than twice the proportion of workers with lost-time injuries than do the other two states (see Table 2). This does not necessarily imply that more workers in California suffer long-term losses; as noted earlier, California has a relatively more permissive definition of permanent disability than the other states, with greater reliance on subjective complaints (such as pain) and on work restrictions. However, Biddle (1998) and Boden and Galizzi (1999) both found that individuals with long-term temporary disability benefits (more than four weeks) but lacking permanent disability benefits have losses that are, on average, almost as large as those in PPD cases and that these losses continued at least to the end of the period they observed.[25] The long-term TTD group is larger in these states than the group receiving permanent disability benefits. Since they do not receive PPD benefits but have similar losses, these workers also had the lowest replacement rates. Within this group, there are certain to be a significant number of people who would have qualified for PPD benefits had they been injured in California. Accounting for this might reduce the differences in replacement rates among states, even if it does not reduce the differences in earnings losses.

Our data indicate that workplace injuries and illnesses are important sources of disability throughout the working life, but that they are particularly so for older workers. When older workers are injured, they appear to suffer more permanently disabling injuries, and those with permanent disabilities experience more injury-related non-employment. Current evidence on the relationship of age and losses is ambiguous. Still, older workers in the states we have studied appear to recover a smaller proportion of their losses from workers' compensation than do other injured workers, at least over the first few years after injury. This raises concerns about the extent to which the uncompensated burden of work-related disabilities of older workers falls on the workers and their families or is absorbed by other public and private insurance systems.

The mechanisms behind the age-related differences in employment and losses are unclear. We do not know the extent to which they are simply caused by age-related physiological effects like delayed and incomplete recovery, nor do we yet understand the interaction between retirement decisions and the onset of work-related disabilities. Health and disability has been shown to be a primary reason for retirement (Anderson and Burkhauser 1985; Blau, Gilleskie, and Slusher 1997; Bound 1991; Sherman 1985; Stern 1988), but the extent to which health and disability is driven by occupational factors is unknown. Finally, we have questions about how the nature of employer accommodations may differentially affect older and younger workers. Studies have shown that when the employers provide accommodations for disabled workers and rehire injured workers, time lost from work is reduced substantially and the employment trajectory is improved (Burkhauser, Butler, and Kim 1995; Galizzi and Boden 1996).

The analysis of disability from workplace injuries is likely to prove useful not only in its own right, but also in helping us to understand more about the labor-market impacts of nonworkplace health shocks on older workers. In particular, occupational injuries provide unusually good availability of administrative data and potential access to more detailed data about the behavior of both the supply and demand sides of the labor market for disabled workers.

## Notes

The authors gratefully acknowledge the support of the National Institute for Occupational Safety and Health, and the State of California Commission on Health and Safety and Workers' Compensation.

1. A considerable literature in economics exists on the incentive effects of temporary disability benefits. See, for instance, Moore and Viscusi (1990), Krueger (1990), and Meyer, Viscusi, and Durbin (1995).
2. For a discussion of some theoretical issues in the interpretation of earnings losses as a measure of welfare of injured workers, see Reville, Bhattacharya, and Sager (1999).

3. Earnings losses have also been estimated using similar methods in the literature on the impact of downsizing. See, for instance, Jacobson, LaLonde, and Sullivan (1993) and Schoeni and Dardia (1996).

4. Workers were categorized into severity groups based on number of days missed and whether PPD benefits were received, and workers in different groups were allowed to have separate preinjury trends of earnings. The specification allowed the earnings of workers in the comparison group to follow a linear trend in the postinjury period as well, while for each of the injured worker groups, dummy variables for the quarter of injury and the five subsequent quarters allowed earnings to follow a flexible, nonmonotonic path following the injury. After this six-quarter period, a separate linear earnings trend was specified for each injured worker group. Variables were also included to control for the impact of any subsequent injuries on earnings. The Washington estimates were based on a fixed-effects specification, while the Wisconsin estimates used a first-differences approach. The results showed little sensitivity to the specification used.

5. Boden and Galizzi (1999) used a 3 percent rate, but the estimates presented below use a 2.3 percent rate.

6. The use of a fixed-effect regression technique controls for any persistent preinjury differences in the level of earnings between injured workers and the workers in the comparison group. Even before controlling, however, these differences amount to less than 5 percent of quarterly earnings.

7. In each of the three states, workers' compensation claims data are linked to longitudinal quarterly earnings data collected by the state for administration of the unemployment insurance (UI) program. The earnings data are obtained for both the injured workers and the comparison workers. The UI data reports all within-state, before-tax earnings at UI-covered employers (approximately 95 percent of employment in each of the states). If no earnings data are reported for a particular quarter for either injured workers or controls, we assume that zero earnings are received. Earnings data for the self-insured and for workers who move out of state will be missing. This will not bias estimates unless disabled workers are systematically more or less likely to receive these types of earnings.

8. See also Peterson, Reville, Stern, and Barth (1997).

9. For a general discussion of matching in econometrics, see Heckman, Ichimura, and Todd (1997).

10. This test is not directly comparable to the test in Washington and Wisconsin. The $28 difference in California is in levels, while the $17 and $8 differences for the other states reported above were in changes (or growth).

11. Two-thirds of employees in California work at insured firms (firms that purchase insurance). The remaining one-third are employed at self-insured firms.

12. States vary in the statutory justification for permanent disability benefits. Many states, such as California, justify it as compensation for loss of future earnings capacity. Construction of an ordinal scale to rank injuries and set compensation is equally complex with the justifications used in other states, such as compensation for "impairment."

13. The most commonly used rating system is the American Medical Association's *Guides to the Evaluation of Permanent Impairment* (1993).

14. Table 2 reports the fraction with PPD by age using a new sample of self-insured claims recently collected by RAND. Data on age for workers with temporary disability benefits are not available for the insured firms examined in this paper.

15. In addition, workers' legal and medical-legal expenses have not been subtracted from the indemnity paid to the worker, even though they are usually directly paid to attorneys or evaluating doctors.

16. In Reville (1999), estimates of the replacement rate use simulated benefits paid out over time according to the schedule using the information from the WCIRB data on actual disability ratings and various benefits paid. This was intended to insure that the time window for losses and benefits coincide and to eliminate the impact of the settlement of medical costs in the replacement rate. This led to lower total income benefit payments (reflecting the fact that five years of losses were reported and therefore the benefits represented five years of benefits) and therefore lower replacement rates. This approach is not adopted here for consistency with the data available from other states.

17. Berkowitz and Burton (1987), using data from claims in 1968, also found that replacement rates were considerably higher in Wisconsin than in California.

18. According to U.S. Department of Labor (1998), nonwage benefits account for approximately 38 percent of wage and salary income.

19. We interpret the replacement rates as the fraction of losses replaced by workers' compensation benefits. Another interesting estimate would be the fraction of losses replaced by all government benefits. While most of the injured workers are not disabled enough to receive Social Security disability benefits, we suspect that they are more likely to receive them than their controls, and therefore replacement rates counting all benefits would be higher. However, we do not have data on Social Security disability benefits for these workers.

20. This, too, may be somewhat exaggerated by the projection method for losses, which does not account for the decline in losses associated with retirement.

21. The regression specification includes a fourth-order polynomial in age, and therefore we expect that we have accounted for age during the observed period flexibly enough to correctly estimate losses even given the decline in labor force participation after age 65.

22. Benefits for PPD in state workers' compensation systems differentially reflect the two opposing effects of age on lost earnings. As noted earlier, in California, higher benefits are paid to older workers to compensate them for their diminished ability to recover from injury. In contrast, in Colorado, lower benefits are paid to older workers (Barth and Niss 1999), presumably because they are closer to retirement and will not experience lost earnings over as many years.

23. In all states, the replacement rate results for the highest quintile may be exaggerated relative to the lower quintiles by the use of a 10-year projection period. This group is likely to have large and long-term losses.

24. As with earnings, in all three states we found no evidence of significant differences in labor force participation of injured workers and controls prior to injury.

25. Some people who have not received PPD benefits may nevertheless have permanent impairments that cause long-term earnings losses. This may reflect a limitation in the disability rating mechanism used by the state. Alternatively, long-term losses may occur because of labor-market effects that persist after recovery from injury. For example, workers who stay off work several months may lose their preinjury jobs and their investments in skill and seniority at those jobs. Earnings and employment after return could be affected, even if they fully recover from the effects of the injury. Finally, some of the long-term losses may be attributable to employers' unwillingness to hire people with the stigma of past workers' compensation injuries and illnesses. Employers may believe that long spells of work absence mark someone as unreliable or otherwise unacceptable for employment, thus limiting employment opportunities and reducing future earnings for this group.

# References

American Medical Association. 1993. *Guides to the Evaluation of Permanent Impairment.* Fourth ed. Chicago, Illinois: American Medical Association.

Anderson, K.H., and R.V. Burkhauser. 1985. "The Retirement-Health Nexus: A New Measure of an Old Puzzle." *Journal of Human Resources* 20: 315–330.

Barth, Peter S., and Michael Niss. 1999. *Permanent Partial Disability Benefits: Interstate Differences.* Cambridge, Massachusetts: Workers' Compensation Research Institute.

Berkowitz M., and J.F. Burton, Jr. 1987. *Permanent Disability Benefits in Workers' Compensation.* W.E. Upjohn Institute for Employment Research, Kalamazoo, Michigan.

Biddle, Jeff. 1998. *Estimation and Analysis of Long Term Wage Losses and Wage Replacement Rates of Washington State Workers' Compensation Claimants.* Photocopy, Performance Audit of the Washington State Workers' Compensation System.

Blau, D.M., D.B. Gilleskie, and C. Slusher. 1997. "The Effect of Health on Employment Transitions of Older Men." Working paper, University of North Carolina.

Boden, Leslie I., and Monica Galizzi. 1999. "Economic Consequences of Workplace Injuries and Illnesses: Lost Earnings and Benefit Adequacy." *American Journal of Industrial Medicine* 36(5): 487–503.

Bound, J. 1991. "Self-Reported versus Objective Measures of Health in Retirement Models." *Journal of Human Resources* 26(1): 106–38.

Burkhauser, R.V., J.S. Butler, and Y.W. Kim. 1995. "The Importance of Employer Accommodation on the Job Duration of Workers with Disabilities: A Hazard Model Approach." *Labour Economics* 2(2): 109–130.

Butler, R.J., W.G. Johnson, and M.L. Baldwin. 1995. "Managing Work Disability: Why First Return to Work Is Not a Measure of Success." *Industrial and Labor Relations Review* 48: 452–469.

Chirikos, T.N., and G. Nestel. 1989. "Occupation, Impaired Health, and the Functional Capacity of Men to Continue Working." *Research on Aging* 11(2): 174–205.

Dehejia, R.H., and S. Wahba. 1996. "Causal Effects in Non-Experimental Studies: Re-Evaluating the Evaluation of Training Programs." Working paper, Harvard University.

Galizzi, Monica, and Leslie I. Boden. 1996. *What Are the Most Important Factors Shaping Return to Work? Evidence from Wisconsin.* Cambridge, Massachusetts: Workers Compensation Research Institute.

Heckman, James J., and V. Joseph Hotz. 1989. "Choosing among Alternative Nonexperimental Methods for Estimating the Impact of Social Programs: The Case of Manpower Training." *Journal of the American Statistical Association* 84(408): 862–874.

Heckman, James J., Hidehiko Ichimura, and Petra Todd. 1997. "Matching as an Econometric Estimator." Working paper no. 315, Department of Economics, University of Pittsburgh.

Holland, Paul W. 1986. "Statistics and Causal Inference." *Journal of the American Statistical Association* 81(396): 945–960.

Jacobson, Louis S., Robert J. LaLonde, and Daniel G. Sullivan. 1993. "Earnings Losses of Displaced Workers." *The American Economic Review* 83: 685–709.

Johnson, William G., Paul R. Cullinan, and William P. Curington. 1978. *The Adequacy of Workers' Compensation Benefits.* Research Report of the Interdepartmental Workers' Compensation Task Force 6: 95–121.

Krueger, Alan B. 1990. "Workers' Compensation Insurance and the Duration of Workplace Injuries." Working paper 3253, National Bureau of Economic Research, Cambridge, Massachusetts.

LaLonde, Robert. 1986. "Evaluating the Econometric Evaluations of Training Programs." *American Economic Review* 76: 604–620.

Meyer, B.D., W. Viscusi, and D.L. Durbin. 1995. "Workers' Compensation and Injury Duration: Evidence from a Natural Experiment." *American Economic Review* 85(3): 322–340.

Mitchell, Olivia S. 1988. "The Relation of Age to Workplace Injuries." *Monthly Labor Review* 111(7): 8–13.

Moore, M.J., and W.K. Viscusi. 1990. *Compensation Mechanisms for Job Risks: Wages, Workers' Compensation and Product Liability.* Princeton: Princeton University Press.

Peterson, Mark A., Robert T. Reville, Rachel Kaganoff Stern, and Peter Barth. 1997. *Compensating Permanent Workplace Injuries: A Study of California's System.* RAND Corp., MR-920, Santa Monica, California.

Reville, Robert T. 1999. "The Impact of a Permanently Disabling Workplace Injury on Labor Force Participation and Earnings." In *The Creation and Analysis of Linked Employer-Employee Data, Contributions to Economic Analysis,* Julia Lane, ed. Amsterdam: Elsevier Science, North-Holland.

Reville, Robert T., Jay Bhattacharya, and Lauren Sager. 1999. "Measuring the Economic Consequences of Workplace Injuries." Photocopy, RAND Corp., Santa Monica, California.

Reville, Robert T., and Robert Schoeni. 1999. "Local Economic Conditions and the Losses from Disabling Workplace Injuries." Photocopy, RAND Corp., Santa Monica, California.

Schoeni, R.F., and M. Dardia. 1996. "Wage Losses of Displaced Workers in the 1990s." Working paper series 96-14, Labor and Population Program, RAND Corp., Santa Monica, California.

Sherman, S.R. 1985. "Reported Reasons Retired Workers Left Their Last Job: Findings from the New Beneficiary Study." *Social Security Bulletin* 48: 22–30.

Stern, S. 1988. "Measuring the Effect of Disability on Labor Force Participation." *Journal of Human Resources* 25(3): 361–395.

U.S. Department of Labor. 1998. *Employer Costs for Employee Compensation, 1986–1998.* Bureau of Labor Statistics Bulletin 2508. Available on-line (as of June 2000) at http://www.bls.gov/special.requests/ocwc/oclt/ect/ecbl0011.pdf.

# How Working-Age People with Disabilities Fared over the 1990s Business Cycle

Richard V. Burkhauser
*Cornell University*

Mary C. Daly
*Federal Reserve Bank of San Francisco*

Andrew J. Houtenville
*Cornell University*

*I am pleased to report that the American economy today is healthy and strong. Our Nation is enjoying the longest peacetime economic expansion in its history, with almost 18 million new jobs since 1993, wages rising at twice the rate of inflation, the highest home ownership ever, the smallest welfare rolls in 30 years, and unemployment and inflation at their lowest levels in three decades.*

*This expansion, unlike recent previous ones, is both wide and deep. All income groups, from the richest to the poorest, have seen their income rise since 1993. The typical family income is up more than $3,500, adjusted for inflation. African-American and Hispanic households, who were left behind during the last expansion, have also seen substantial increase in income.*

—President William Jefferson Clinton
*Economic Report of the President* (1999)

As President Clinton's remarks indicate, the 1990s were an economically enriching period for the vast majority of American families. Robust economic growth has produced the lowest unemployment and inflation rates in 30 years and lifted living standards across the income distribution. Importantly, the economic recovery of the 1990s reached traditionally economically vulnerable groups including African Americans, Hispanics, those with less than a high-school education, and single mothers with children, often lifting their income to levels beyond previous business cycle peaks (U.S. Census Bureau 1999).

While President Clinton and Americans generally have every reason to be pleased with the current economic expansion, it is important to put this good news into perspective by understanding which, if any, groups have been systematically left behind. One group that frequently is overlooked in such discussions is people with disabilities, even though they constitute a group more likely to be sensitive to economic fluctuations than the general population. In this chapter, we examine how people with disabilities fared over the 1990s business cycle.

## MEASURING ECONOMIC WELL-BEING OVER THE BUSINESS CYCLE

Cross-sectional comparisons of the economic well-being of Americans over time are sensitive to the years over which the comparisons are made. Figures 1a and 1b use two general economic indicators of the business cycle used in the *Economic Report of the President* (1999)—median real family income and civilian unemployment rates—to demonstrate this point. (The actual values are reported in Appendix Table A1.) As can be seen in these figures, business-cycle peaks in 1973, 1979, and 1989 were followed by business cycle troughs in 1975, 1982, and 1992. While an upward-sloping line can be drawn across median real family income points in either the peak or the trough years over this period, this growth was not accomplished smoothly. There were periods of rising median income and falling unemployment (1975–1979 and 1982–1989) as well as periods of economic decline (1973–1975, 1979–1982, and 1989–1992). Under these circumstances, a judicious choice of starting and stopping years could yield upward, downward, or constant measures of economic well-being.

President Clinton's opening paragraph in the 1999 *Economic Report of the President* focused on the growth years of the 1990s business cycle—1993 through 1997—and found that every American was made better off during the period. However, to capture how Americans fared in the 1990s, it is more appropriate to make comparisons over the

**Figure 1a  Median Family Real Income, 1970–1998**

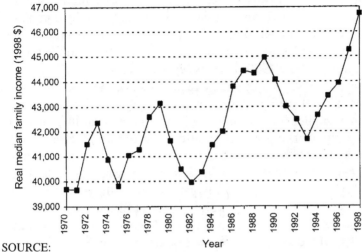

SOURCE:
*Economic Report of the President*, 1994 (Table B-29) and 1999
(Table B33).

**Figure 1b  Civilian Unemployment Rate, 1970–1998**

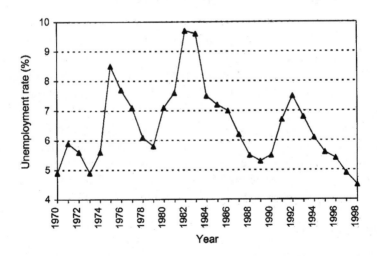

SOURCE: *Economic Report of the President*, 1994 (Table B38) and 1999 (Table B35),
and *Current Population Report* P60-206.

entire business cycle, by comparing peak-to-peak or trough-to-trough years. Consequently, we will examine how people with and without disabilities have fared during the most recent expansion by comparing changes in economic well-being between 1989, the peak of the last business cycle, and 1998, the most recent year of data and the highest year in our data of the 1990s business cycle.[1]

We find that while economic expansion since 1992 has improved the economic well-being of most working-age people, the gains have been much smaller for working-age people with disabilities than for the rest of the working-age population. Furthermore, although the gains through 1998 have returned the average person with a disability to his or her level of economic well-being in the peak year of the 1980s business cycle, the incomes of a large fraction of the population with disabilities in 1998 remained well below that of their 1989 counterparts. Finally, we find that despite a robust economic expansion, men and women with disabilities became less involved in the labor market and more dependent on public transfers during the 1990s.

## DATA SOURCES AND MEASUREMENT ISSUES

We compare the employment, labor earnings, and economic well-being of the noninstitutionalized population with and without disabilities over an 11-year period (1987–1998) using data from the March Current Population Survey (CPS). The CPS is a monthly survey of a nationally representative sample of U.S. households. The annual March Demographic Supplement contains detailed questions about household composition, employment, and sources of income, making it a valuable source of time-series data on the economic well-being of the noninstitutionalized United States population. The sample sizes in each year are in excess of 55,000 households.

### Defining the Sample

Our examination focuses on the experiences of men and women of ages 25 to 61. This limited age range avoids confusing reductions in work or economic well-being associated with disability, with reductions or declines associated with retirement at older ages, or with initial transitions in and out of the labor force related to job shopping at younger ages. Men and women in the Armed Forces are excluded from our analysis.

## DEFINING THE POPULATION WITH DISABILITIES

The Americans with Disabilities Act of 1990 (ADA) defines disability as a physical or mental impairment that substantially limits one or more major life activities, a record of such an impairment, or being regarded as having such an impairment. This definition of disability is much broader than the widely accepted measure developed by Nagi (1965, 1969, 1991).

The Nagi measure, the dominant one in the social science literature, distinguishes among three states of diminished health. The first state describes the existence of a pathology, the presence of a physical or mental malfunction and/or the interruption of a normal process. The second level, an impairment, combines a pathology with a functional requirement—a physiological, anatomical, or mental loss or abnormality that limits a person's capacity and level of function. The final state, disability, is then defined as an inability or limitation in performing roles and tasks that are socially expected. For men—and, increasingly, for women—of working age, market work is a socially expected role.

What is most controversial about Nagi's definition is the relative importance of pathology and environment in determining how a given pathology results in an impairment that then leads to a disability. Less controversial is the recognition that the definition gives to disability as a dynamic process in which the individual pathology and the socioeconomic environment interact. The Nagi measure of disability is more limited than the ADA measure in that it ignores the broader population with disabilities that has successfully integrated into society, as well as those who are not integrated into employment because of perceptions concerning an impairment that does not limit work activity. For a broader discussion of the definition of disability in the context of the ADA, see Gordon and Groves (2000).

## AN EMPIRICAL ESTIMATE OF THE WORKING-AGE
## POPULATION WITH DISABILITIES

Neither the Nagi or the ADA conceptualizations of disability are fully captured by our data. CPS information on health is self-reported and is couched in terms of work limitations. The problems inherent in these types of data are well documented (see Parsons 1980, 1982; Bazzoli 1985; Bound 1991). Still, researchers have shown these measures to be highly correlated with more objective assessments of health (see Bound 1991; Stern 1989). Moreover, as discussed elsewhere (Burkhauser and Daly 1996), we believe such data are capable of identifying people with serious pathologies.

In the CPS, the population with disabilities is defined by a survey question that asks, "Does anyone in this household have a health problem or disability which prevents them from working or which limits the kind or amount of work they can do? If yes . . . , Who is that? (Anyone else?)" While this single question measure of disability is coarser than a measure based on a more detailed set of self-reported questions like those in the *National Health Interview Survey* or on actual medical examination, we believe it is a reasonable first approximation of the population with disabilities.[2]

Based on this question, we find that the prevalence of self-reported disability increased across almost every age, gender, race, and education group between 1988 and 1999.[3] Appendix Table A2 reports the prevalence of disability in the working-age population (aged 25 through 61) for 1988 through 1999. In addition to an increase in the prevalence of disability, there have been changes in the composition of the population over the decade. Appendix Table A3 reports gender, age, race, and education group distributions within the populations with and without a disability for the year 1988 through 1999. Women, those aged 35 to 54, Blacks, Hispanics, and those with more than a high school education comprised a greater share of the population with disabilities in 1999 than they did in 1989. However, with the exception of women, these same categories have grown among those without disabilities. Therefore, it is unlikely that the changes in relative economic well-being between those with and without disabilities that we report are artifacts of changes in population composition.

## Measuring Economic Well-Being

Although we are primarily concerned with the economic status of individuals, we recognize that most people share resources with other coresident individuals and have access to income that does not flow directly to them (this is particularly important for nonworking spouses). Although most researchers agree that the income-sharing unit should be broader than the individual, there remains the issue of precisely who should be included in it. Some U.S. income distribution scholars have defined the unit as encompassing people related by blood or marriage who coreside, i.e., the CPS family sharing unit definition (see, for example, Karoly and Burtless 1995; Danziger and Gottschalk 1995). Others use the broader, household-based, common residence definition.[4]

In this study, we use the CPS household sharing unit definition. We define household income as the sum of all income received by individuals residing in a single residence.[5] This is pretax, posttransfer income.[6,7] To account for the fact that $500 a week provides a higher standard of living for a single-person household than it does for individuals belonging to larger households, we adjust household income by an equivalence factor. Since there is no universally accepted scale, we assume an elasticity with respect to household size of 0.5.[8] Because we are comparing income across years, we adjust income using the CPI-UXI; all income values are in 1998 dollars. Finally, to eliminate potential measurement error at the bottom of the distribution and top-coding at the top of the distribution, we delete the top and bottom 1 percent of the given earnings or household income distribution in each year.[9] However, when we analyze the percentiles and deciles of the distribution of household income, we delete the top and bottom 5 percent.

## Measuring Labor Force Activity and Wage Earnings

The analysis focuses on the role that employment and labor earnings play in the economic well-being of men and women with disabilities. Individuals who report that they work at least 52 hours annually (at civilian jobs or businesses, including temporary, part-time, or seasonal work) are considered to have been employed in the year.[10]

Annual labor earnings include income from all market sources, including primary and secondary jobs and bonus income. Self-employment income is excluded from the calculation of labor earnings.

**Measuring Government Transfer Receipt**

An important component of income for many individuals with disabilities is government-provided transfers. Throughout this chapter, transfers are classified in two ways: individually based and disability-related (disability benefits), and household-based and of any type or form (public transfers). Disability benefits include income from workers' compensation, the Social Security Disability Insurance Program, veterans' benefits, and Supplemental Security Income. Public transfers include all cash benefits not specifically related to health.

## HOW THOSE WITH AND WITHOUT DISABILITIES FARED IN THE 1990s

As Figure 1 showed, 1989 marked the initial peak and 1992 the trough of the 1990s business cycle. While the final peak of the 1990s business cycle has not yet been reached, the most recent year of CPS income data (1998) is used in Table 1 to compare the economic well-being of working age (aged 25 through 61) men and of women with and without disabilities and to examine how it changed over the period.[11]

Both mean and median household-size-adjusted income for our four groups fell as the economy moved down from its 1989 business peak to the 1992 business cycle trough. Importantly, the households of men and women with disabilities experienced a greater percentage decline. Likewise, six years of recovery (1993–1998) lifted the mean real household-size-adjusted income of all groups. However, for those with disabilities, the recovery did not bring the same economic rewards observed for the population without disabilities.[12] Mean income for men with disabilities rose between 1992 and 1998, but the percentage increase was less than that for men without disabilities—7.0 percent for men with disabilities compared with 14.3 percent for men without

**Table 1  Mean and Median Household-Size-Adjusted Real Income and Household Poverty Rates of Civilians Aged 25–61, by Gender and Disability Status[a]**

| Measure/group[b] | 1989 | 1992 | 1998 | Percentage change[c] | | |
|---|---|---|---|---|---|---|
| | | | | 1989–1992 | 1992–1998 | 1989–1998 |
| Mean household income[d] ($) | | | | | | |
| Men without disabilities | 36,460 | 34,465 | 39,756 | –5.6 | 14.3 | 8.6 |
| Men with disabilities | 21,493 | 20,159 | 21,619 | –6.4 | 7.0 | 0.6 |
| Women without disabilities | 32,973 | 31,723 | 36,526 | –3.9 | 14.1 | 10.2 |
| Women with disabilities | 19,998 | 18,701 | 20,074 | –6.7 | 7.1 | 0.4 |
| Median household income[d] ($) | | | | | | |
| Men without disabilities | 32,142 | 30,476 | 33,840 | –5.3 | 10.5 | 5.1 |
| Men with disabilities | 17,154 | 16,161 | 16,419 | –6.0 | 1.6 | –4.4 |
| Women without disabilities | 29,075 | 28,175 | 30,698 | –3.1 | 8.6 | 5.4 |
| Women with disabilities | 15,256 | 13,755 | 14,658 | –10.3 | 6.4 | –4.0 |
| Household poverty rate[e] (%) | | | | | | |
| Men without disabilities | 5.1 | 6.2 | 5.1 | 20.3 | –19.3 | 0.0 |
| Men with disabilities | 22.1 | 22.9 | 23.2 | 3.7 | 1.4 | 5.1 |
| Women without disabilities | 8.7 | 9.7 | 8.1 | 11.2 | –18.7 | –7.5 |
| Women with disabilities | 28.5 | 30.1 | 28.0 | 5.6 | –7.5 | –1.9 |

SOURCE: Authors' calculations based on the March Current Population Survey, 1990–1999.

(continued)

**Table 1 (continued)**

[a] Those less than age 25 or more than age 61 or in the Armed Force are excluded. In our study, persons are considered to have a disability if they report having a health problem or disability which prevents them from working or limits the kind or amount of work they can do.

[b] Disability status is for the year following the income year. In 1994 there were several changes in the CPS. It moved fully to computer-assisted survey interviews. Sample weights based on the 1980 Census were replaced with sample weights based on the 1990 Census. The Monthly Basic Survey was revised, and three new disability questions were added. It is possible that these changes effected the measurement of the population with disabilities either through changes in the sample weights or in the way respondents answered disability questions.

[c] When calculating percentage change, we use the average of the two years as the base.

[d] All dollar amounts are in 1998 dollars. Income is household size by dividing income by the square root of household size. Negative sources of income were converted to zero. In addition, the bottom and top 1 percent of the household size-adjusted income distribution are excluded from the analysis.

[e] An individual is in poverty if his or her household's income falls below the household's threshold income, which is determined by the Census Bureau and considers household size and composition.

disabilities. Income growth was sufficient to return mean real household-size-adjusted income for men with disabilities to its 1989 high, but just barely, and relative to men without disabilities, the growth in household-size-adjusted income between 1989 and 1998 was small. The circumstances for women with disabilities were similar. The mean real household-size-adjusted income of women with disabilities was greater in 1998 than in 1989, but the percentage gain was less than for men and women without disabilities.

Looking at the median rather than the mean of household-size-adjusted income for our four groups yields a bleaker picture for those with disabilities. In 1998, median real household-size-adjusted income of men and women with disabilities remained substantially below its 1989 peak; in contrast, among men and women without disabilities, median income was more than 5 percent higher than its 1989 peak. Table 1 also contains information on the prevalence of poverty among men and women with and without disabilities. The fluctuation in the poverty rates across these groups provides further evidence of the importance of business cycle effects on economic well-being. The

peak-to-trough movement at the start of the 1990s increased the prevalence of poverty in all groups, but recovery reduced poverty rates back
to or below their 1989 levels for all but men with disabilities. Poverty
among men with disabilities continued to rise over the entire period.

## Accounting for Declines in Economic Well-Being of Working-Age People with Disabilities

In all modern industrial societies, earnings from work is the principal source of income for working-age people. Business cycles have a
powerful effect on household economic well-being because they
greatly impact both employment and labor earnings. Table 2 shows the
sensitivity of the average employment, rate, average hours of work, and
average annual labor earnings over the 1990s business cycle for men
and women, with and without disabilities.[13]  The movement from peak
to trough at the start of the 1990s had its most powerful effect on men,
especially those with disabilities. They experienced lower average
employment, and those men who did work had lower average annual
hours of work and lower average annual earnings.

Recovery returned men without disabilities to near their 1989 peak
in average employment and above their 1989 peak in mean hours
worked and mean and median annual earnings. The story is much less
sanguine for men with disabilities. Not surprisingly, average employment fell among men with disabilities between 1989 and 1992, but surprisingly, it continued to fall between 1992 and 1998. In 1998, the
average employment rate for men with disabilities was 34.4 percent,
well below their trough average employment of 41.6 percent. As a
result, men with disabilities were less integrated into the labor market
in 1998 then they were in 1992, the trough year of the recession. For
those men with disabilities who were employed, average hours of work
and mean annual earnings also declined significantly between 1989
and 1992, but then rose as the economy recovered. However, the
growth in mean earnings and hours was below that experienced by
working men without disabilities.

In general, women fared better than men during the 1990s. Average employment, average hours worked, and mean earnings of women
without disabilities rose between 1989 and 1992 and grew even more
with the economic recovery. The gains for women with disabilities

**Table 2  Employment Rates, Mean Annual Hours, and Mean Real Earnings of Civilians Aged 25–61 Who Worked, by Gender and Disability Status[a]**

| Measure/group[b] | 1989 | 1992 | 1998 | Percentage change[c] 1989– 1992 | 1992– 1998 | 1989– 1998 |
|---|---|---|---|---|---|---|
| Employment rate[d] (%) | | | | | | |
| Men without disabilities | 96.1 | 94.8 | 95.1 | −1.4 | 0.4 | −1.0 |
| Men with disabilities | 44.0 | 41.6 | 34.4 | −5.5 | −19.0 | −24.5 |
| Women without disabilities | 77.1 | 77.6 | 80.8 | 0.7 | 4.0 | 4.7 |
| Women with disabilities | 37.5 | 34.3 | 29.5 | −8.9 | −14.8 | −23.7 |
| Mean annual hours[d] | | | | | | |
| Men without disabilities | 2,165 | 2,121 | 2,214 | −2.1 | 4.3 | 2.3 |
| Men with disabilities | 1,595 | 1,560 | 1,577 | −2.2 | 1.1 | −1.1 |
| Women without disabilities | 1,743 | 1,772 | 1,831 | 1.7 | 3.2 | 4.9 |
| Women with disabilities | 1,275 | 1,295 | 1,312 | 1.6 | 1.3 | 2.9 |
| Mean annual earnings[d] ($) | | | | | | |
| Men without disabilities | 38,557 | 36,352 | 40,993 | −5.9 | 12.0 | 6.1 |
| Men with disabilities | 20,582 | 18,964 | 21,172 | −8.2 | 11.0 | 2.8 |
| Women without disabilities | 21,920 | 22,459 | 24,814 | 2.4 | 10.0 | 12.4 |
| Women with disabilities | 12,491 | 13,165 | 14,232 | 5.3 | 7.8 | 13.0 |

SOURCE: Authors' calculations based on the March Current Population Survey, 1990–1999.

[a] Those less than age 25 or more than age 61 or in the Armed Force are excluded. In our study, persons are considered to have a disability if they report having a health problem or disability which prevents them from working or limits the kind or amount of work they can do.

[b] Disability status for the year following the income year. In 1994 there were several changes in the CPS. It moved fully to computer-assisted survey interviews. Sample weights based on the 1980 Census were replaced with sample weights based on the 1990 Census. The Monthly Basic Survey was revised, and three new disability questions were added. It is possible that these changes effected the measurement of the population with disabilities either through changes in the sample weights or in the way respondents answered disability questions.

[c] When calculating percentage change, we use the average of the two years as the base.

[d] Include only those who work 52 hours or more and have positive earnings. For mean earnings only those with positive earnings are included. All dollar amounts are in 1998 dollars. The bottom and top 1 percent of the earnings distribution are excluded from the analysis.

were less pronounced but still surpassed those for men with disabilities. Like their male counterparts, employment for women with disabilities fell throughout the period, but for women with disabilities who remained employed, average hours and mean labor earnings grew rapidly.

The dramatic drop in employment of men and women with disabilities, even during the strong recovery period following 1992, provides one explanation for the decline in household-size-adjusted income shown in Table 1. Although those with disabilities who continued to work saw their real earnings increase, only about one-third of the population in 1998 was employed.

Table 3 provides a more detailed look at the various sources of household income for our four groups and how they changed over the 1990s business cycle.[14]   Mean real household income is divided into five components—own labor earnings, the labor earnings of other household members, own public disability transfers, all other sources of public transfers, and all other sources of household income. The sum of the means of these five income sources equals mean household income. Own labor earnings and the labor earnings of other household members are quite sensitive to the 1990s business cycle, falling (except

**Table 3  Mean Real Income from Various Household Income Sources for Civilians Aged 25–61, by Gender and Disability Status[a]**

| Measure/grous[b] | ($) | | | Percentage change[c] | | |
|---|---|---|---|---|---|---|
| | 1989 | 1992 | 1998 | 1989–1992 | 1992–1998 | 1989–1998 |
| Own earnings | | | | | | |
| Men without disabilities | 34,128 | 31,569 | 36,613 | −7.8 | 14.8 | 7.0 |
| Men with disabilities | 8,029 | 6,834 | 6,352 | −16.1 | −7.3 | −23.3 |
| Women without disabilities | 16,127 | 16,711 | 19,461 | 3.6 | 15.2 | 18.7 |
| Women with disabilities | 4,250 | 4,151 | 3,942 | −2.4 | −5.2 | −7.5 |
| Earnings of other household members | | | | | | |
| Men without disabilities | 18,097 | 17,533 | 19,884 | −3.2 | 12.6 | 9.4 |
| Men with disabilities | 12,580 | 12,151 | 13,564 | −3.5 | 11.0 | 7.5 |
| Women without disabilities | 30,550 | 28,282 | 32,170 | −7.7 | 12.9 | 5.2 |
| Women with disabilities | 16,291 | 15,365 | 15,119 | −5.9 | −1.6 | −7.5 |
| Own public disability transfers[d] | | | | | | |
| Men without disabilities | 82 | 97 | 98 | 16.6 | 0.8 | 17.3 |
| Men with disabilities | 4,117 | 4,425 | 4,710 | 7.2 | 6.2 | 13.5 |
| Women without disabilities | 172 | 155 | 145 | −11.0 | −6.6 | −17.5 |
| Women with disabilities | 2,261 | 2,628 | 3,551 | 15.0 | 29.9 | 44.4 |

**Table 3 (continued)**

| Measure/group[b] | ($) | | | Percentage change[c] | | |
|---|---|---|---|---|---|---|
| | 1989 | 1992 | 1998 | 1989–1992 | 1992–1998 | 1989–1998 |
| All other public transfers[e] | | | | | | |
| Men without disabilities | 1,214 | 1,601 | 1,298 | 27.5 | –20.9 | 6.7 |
| Men with disabilities | 2,937 | 3,392 | 3,244 | 14.4 | –4.5 | 9.9 |
| Women without disabilities | 1,564 | 1,880 | 1,531 | 18.3 | –20.4 | –2.1 |
| Women with disabilities | 3,150 | 3,487 | 3,167 | 10.2 | –9.6 | 0.6 |
| All other sources of household income[e] | | | | | | |
| Men without disabilities | 8,637 | 7,624 | 9,104 | –12.5 | 17.7 | 5.3 |
| Men with disabilities | 7,948 | 6,533 | 7,337 | –19.5 | 11.6 | –8.0 |
| Women without disabilities | 8,222 | 7,184 | 8,779 | –13.5 | 20.0 | 6.5 |
| Women with disabilities | 6,708 | 5,276 | 6,353 | –23.9 | 18.5 | –5.4 |
| Household income | | | | | | |
| Men without disabilities | 62,158 | 58,424 | 66,998 | –6.2 | 13.7 | 7.5 |
| Men with disabilities | 35,611 | 33,336 | 35,208 | –6.6 | 5.5 | –1.1 |
| Women without disabilities | 56,635 | 54,211 | 62,085 | –4.4 | 13.5 | 9.2 |
| Women with disabilities | 32,659 | 30,907 | 32,132 | –5.5 | 3.9 | –1.6 |

(continued)

## Table 3 (continued)

SOURCE: Authors' calculations based on the March Current Population Survey, 1988–1999.

[a] Those less than age 25 or more than age 61 and people in the Armed Force are excluded. In our study, persons are considered to have a disability if they report having a health problem or disability which prevents them from working or limits the kind or amount of work they can do. All dollar amounts are in 1998 dollars. Negative sources of income were converted to zero. In addition, the bottom and top 1 percent of the household income distribution are excluded from the analysis. These results are not adjusted for household.

[b] Disability status for the year following the income year. In 1994 there were several changes in the CPS. It moved fully to computer-assisted survey interviews. Sample weights based on the 1980 Census were replaced with sample weights based on the 1990 Census. The Monthly Basic Survey was revised, and three new disability questions were added. It is possible that these changes effected the measurement of the population with disabilities either through changes in the sample weights or in the way respondents answered disability questions.

[c] When calculating percentage change, we use the average of the two years as the base.

[d] Public disability transfers include Social Security income, disability-related veteran's payments, worker's compensation, Supplemental Security income, and disability income from other government sources.

[e] Other transfers include the public disability transfers of other household members and other personal or household public transfers (public assistance and welfare, other forms of veteran's payments, unemployment compensation, and government education assistance).

for women without disabilities) during the early peak-to-trough years and rising for all but those with disabilities thereafter. The labor earnings of other household members uniformly fell peak-to-trough and rose thereafter for all but the households of women with disabilities.

Not surprisingly, own public disability transfers are a negligible part of the household income of men and women without disabilities, but they are a sizable part of the household income of men and women with disabilities. Public disability transfers rose in real terms between 1989 and 1998 for both men and women with disabilities and offset, in part, the decline in their own labor earnings. Among men with disabilities, real mean public disability transfers increased by 13.5 percent between 1989 and 1998; for women the increase was even larger, jumping by 44.4 percent during the period. The increase in real public disability transfers over the 1990s came primarily from rapid growth in the value of SSI and SSDI benefits; in contrast, workers' compensation and veterans' benefits fell in real terms over the period.[15]  All other public transfers rose during the peak-to-trough years but fell with recovery.  On net, other public transfers rose for both men with and without disabilities over the 1990s business cycle, while remaining steady or falling for women with and without disabilities.

All other sources of household income fell during the peak-to-trough years and rose thereafter for all groups.  However, over the entire period, these sources fell for men and women with disabilities while growing for those without disabilities.  Total mean household income fell from peak to trough and rose thereafter.  Over the entire 1990s business cycle, total mean household income rose for men and women without disabilities and fell for men and women with disabilities.  Because we do not adjust for changes in household size in Table 3, gains in real mean household income are somewhat smaller here than when we do adjust for household size in Table 1, since household size declined over the period.

Table 4 reinforces the point made in Table 3, namely, that declines in labor earnings may explain much of the differences in the fortunes of those with and without disabilities over the 1990s.  The table shows how the shares of the five sources of household income changed over the period.  Working-age men without disabilities provided 57.0 percent of household income in the business-cycle peak year 1989.  This fell to 55.1 percent in trough year 1992 but rose to 56.7 percent by 1998.  In contrast, the share of household income provided by the labor earnings of men with disabilities fell over the entire period.  Their own public disability transfer income was the main source of increased income for the households of men with disabilities.  Again, increases in the share of income provided by SSI and SSDI contributed to this rise. The share of income provided by SSI nearly doubled between 1989 and 1998, from 19.5 percent to 29.3 percent, while the share provided by SSDI grew, from 46.4 percent to 51.3 percent.[16]

Working-age women without disabilities provided an increasing share of household income over the entire period.  In contrast, the share of own labor earnings in the households of women with disabilities declined over the period, but by less than that of men with disabilities. The largest increase in shares for the households of women with dis-

**Table 4   Share of Various Household Income Sources for Civilians Aged 25–61, by Gender and Disability Status[a]**

| Measure/group[b] | ($) | | | Percentage change[c] | | |
|---|---|---|---|---|---|---|
| | 1989 | 1992 | 1998 | 1989–1992 | 1992–1998 | 1989–1998 |
| Own earnings | | | | | | |
| Men without disabilities | 57.0 | 55.1 | 56.7 | −3.4 | 2.9 | −0.5 |
| Men with disabilities | 19.4 | 16.4 | 14.9 | −16.8 | −9.6 | −26.2 |
| Women without disabilities | 32.1 | 34.1 | 36.3 | 6.0 | 6.2 | 12.3 |
| Women with disabilities | 12.9 | 11.9 | 11.7 | −8.1 | −1.7 | −9.8 |
| Earnings of other household members | | | | | | |
| Men without disabilities | 26.1 | 27.0 | 27.5 | 3.4 | 1.8 | 5.2 |
| Men with disabilities | 26.6 | 27.9 | 27.5 | 4.8 | −1.4 | 3.3 |
| Women without disabilities | 47.0 | 44.9 | 45.2 | −4.6 | 0.7 | −3.9 |
| Women with disabilities | 33.6 | 32.9 | 31.4 | −2.1 | −4.7 | −6.8 |
| Own public disability transfers[d] | | | | | | |
| Men without disabilities | 0.3 | 0.4 | 0.4 | 28.6 | 0.0 | 28.6 |
| Men with disabilities | 19.2 | 21.5 | 25.4 | 11.3 | 16.6 | 27.8 |
| Women without disabilities | 0.8 | 0.8 | 0.7 | 0.0 | −13.3 | −13.3 |
| Women with disabilities | 15.6 | 18.7 | 23.4 | 18.1 | 22.3 | 40.0 |
| All other public transfers[e] | | | | | | |
| Men without disabilities | 3.3 | 4.8 | 3.2 | 37.0 | −40.0 | −3.1 |
| Men with disabilities | 14.5 | 15.9 | 13.7 | 9.2 | −14.9 | −5.7 |

**Table 4 (continued)**

| Measure/group[b] | ($) | | | Percentage change[c] | | |
|---|---|---|---|---|---|---|
| | 1989 | 1992 | 1998 | 1989–1992 | 1992–1998 | 1989–1998 |
| Women without disabilities | 6.1 | 7.3 | 5.0 | 17.9 | −37.4 | −19.8 |
| Women with disabilities | 19.1 | 19.8 | 15.8 | 3.6 | −22.5 | −18.9 |
| All other sources of household income | | | | | | |
| Men without disabilities | 13.3 | 12.7 | 12.2 | −4.6 | −4.0 | −8.6 |
| Men with disabilities | 20.3 | 18.4 | 17.9 | −9.8 | −2.8 | −12.6 |
| Women without disabilities | 14.0 | 12.9 | 12.9 | −8.2 | 0.0 | −8.2 |
| Women with disabilities | 18.7 | 16.7 | 17.3 | −11.3 | 3.5 | −7.8 |

SOURCE: Authors' calculations based on the March Current Population Survey, 1988–1999.

[a] Those less than age 25 or more than age 61 and people in the Armed Force are excluded. In our study, persons are considered to have a disability if they report having a health problem or disability which prevents them from working or limits the kind or amount of work they can do. All dollar amounts are in 1998 dollars. Negative sources of income were converted to zero. In addition, the bottom and top 1 percent of the household income distribution are excluded from the analysis. These results are not adjusted for household.

[b] Disability status for the year following the income year. In 1994 there were several changes in the CPS. It moved fully to computer-assisted survey interviews. Sample weights based on the 1980 Census were replaced with sample weights based on the 1990 Census. The Monthly Basic Survey was revised, and three new disability questions were added. It is possible that these changes effected the measurement of the population with disabilities either through changes in the sample weights or in the way respondents answered disability questions.

[c] When calculating percentage change, we use the average of the two years as the base.

[d] Public disability transfers include Social Security income, disability-related veteran's payments, worker's compensation, Supplemental Security income, and disability income from other government sources.

[e] Other transfers include the public disability transfers of other household members and other personal or household public transfers (public assistance and welfare, other forms of veteran's payments, unemployment compensation, and government education assistance).

abilities over the period was in own disability transfers, as was the case with men with disabilities.

## GAINS IN ECONOMIC WELL-BEING ACROSS THE DISTRIBUTION

The measures of the income distribution discussed above are designed to summarize an entire distribution with one value. Yet few distributions can be completely characterized by one parameter. This is particularly true when attempting to describe outcomes for heterogeneous populations such as the population of people with disabilities. Thus, in the remaining analysis we move away from simple summary measures and examine how income, employment, earnings, and public transfer receipt has affected the entire distribution of those with disabilities.

Table 1 showed that on average men and women with disabilities fared less well then the rest of the population over the 1990s. Figures 2a and 2b allow us to look within these averages. Figure 2a shows the change in real household-size-adjusted income between 1989 and 1998 by percentile for the households of women of working age, with and without disabilities; Figure 2b shows the same for men.[17]  Each line cuts the horizontal axis at the percentile at which real income in 1998 equals real income in 1989, i.e., the "crossover point."[18]  Values above the zero axis mean that persons in that percentile were better off in 1998 than in 1989; values below the zero axis mean that persons in that percentile were worse off in 1998.  Thus, this figure provides a quick summary of winners and losers across the income distribution over peak years in the 1990s business cycle.

By 1998, economic growth had "lifted all boats" among the population of working-age men and women without disabilities, moving them above their 1992 lows and their 1989 business-cycle peak levels. While the gains were not uniform, men and women without disabilities at each percentile had more real household-size-adjusted income in 1998 than they did in 1989. The results for women with disabilities (Figure 2a) were much different, with those at the top and the bottom of the income distribution gaining and those in the middle losing. By

**Figure 2a  Women—Change in Household-Size-Adjusted Real Income, 1989 to 1998, by Percentile**

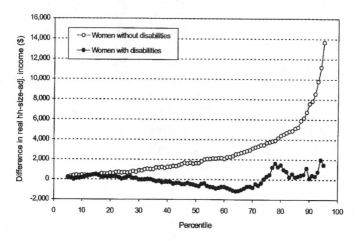

SOURCE: Authors' calculations based on the March Current Population Survey, 1990 and 1999.

**Figure 2b  Men—Change in Household-Size-Adjusted Real Income, 1989 to 1998, by Percentile**

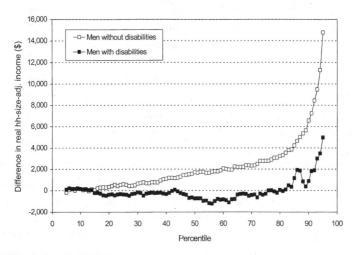

SOURCE: Authors' calculations based on the March Current Population Survey, 1990 and 1999.

1998, the real household-size-adjusted incomes of women with disabilities below the 35th and above the 75th percentiles had surpassed their 1989 peak levels. Yet, women with disabilities in the middle 40 percent of the distribution had lower real household-size-adjusted incomes than their counterparts in 1989.

The results for men with disabilities (Figure 2b) are even gloomier. Those men below the 15th percentile stayed approximately at the same level of real household-size-adjusted income as their counterparts in 1989. Those between the 15th and 75th percentiles had less real household-size-adjusted income in 1998 than did individuals in equivalent percentiles in 1989. Only men in the top 20 percent of the distribution were better off than their 1989 counterparts. Thus, while by 1998 the entire distributions of men and women without disabilities had moved above their 1989 highs, nearly 40 percent of women with disabilities and 80 percent of men with disabilities had been left behind. Most surprisingly, most of those left behind during the 1990s had household-size-adjusted incomes in the middle, rather than at the lower end, of the distribution.

Tables 2, 3, and 4 showed that, on average, men and women with disabilities worked less, earned less, and received more public transfers during the 1990s expansion than they did in 1989, the peak of the 1980s business cycle. In Figures 3, 4, and 5, we look behind these averages and examine how these patterns differed across the distribution of people with disabilities. Figures 3 and 4 show employment rates and receipt of public transfer rates for men and women with disabilities in 1989 and 1998, by deciles of the household-size-adjusted distribution of income.[19] This allows us to examine employment rates for individuals with disabilities who were at equivalent deciles of the income distribution in 1989 and 1998.

Figure 3b shows that employment rates for men with disabilities were lower in 1998 than in 1989 for all but the highest decile of the household-size-adjusted income distribution. Not surprisingly, employment rates in 1989 and 1998 were lowest for those at the lowest deciles of the income distribution. But, consistent with the results in Figure 2b, the largest gaps in employment rates between the two years occurs in the middle deciles of the income distribution. For example, the average employment rate gap in the bottom three deciles was 9.4 percentage points; in contrast, the average gap in the 4th to 7th decile

**Figure 3a  Women with Disabilities—Employment Rates by Decile
of the Household-Size-Adjusted Real Income Distribution,
1989 and 1998**[a]

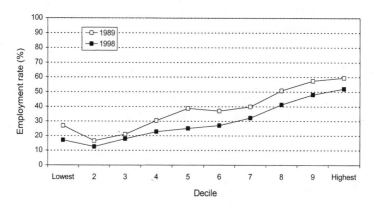

SOURCE: Authors'calculations based on the March Current Population Survey,
1990 and 1999.
[a]Lowest and highest deciles do not include the bottom and top 5 percent
of the distribution.

**Figure 3b  Men with Disabilities—Employment Rates by Decile
of the Household-Size-Adjusted Real Income Distribution,
1989 and 1998**[a]

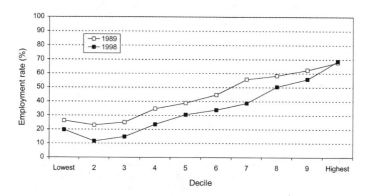

SOURCE: Authors'calculations based on the March Current Population Survey, 1990
and 1999.
[a]Lowest and highest deciles do not include the bottom and top 5 percent
of the distribution.

**Figure 4a  Women with Disabilities—Percentage of Individuals whose Household Receives Public Transfers, by Decile of the Household-Size-Adjusted Real Income Distribution, 1989 and 1998**[a]

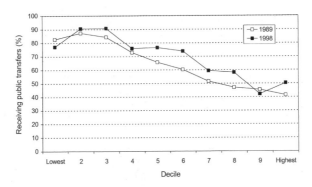

SOURCE: Authors' calculations based on the March Current Population Survey, 1990 and 1999.

[a]Lowest and highest deciles do not include the bottom and top 5 percent of the distribution.

**Figure 4b  Men with Disabilities—Percentage of Individuals whose Household Receives Public Transfers, by Decile of the Household-Size-Adjusted Real Income Distribution, 1989 and 1998**[a]

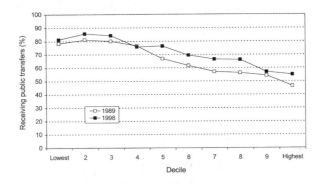

SOURCE: Authors' calculations based on the March Current Population Survey, 1990 and 1999.

[a]Lowest and highest deciles do not include the bottom and top 5 percent of the distribution.

**Figure 5a  Women with Disabilities—Differences in Mean Own Earnings and Household Transfer Income, by Decile of the Household-Size-Adjusted Real Income Distribution, 1989 and 1998[a]**

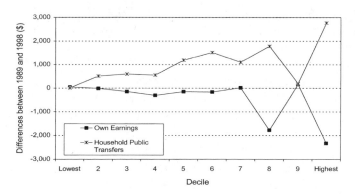

SOURCE: Authors' calculations based on the March Current Population Survey, 1990 and 1999.
[a]Lowest and highest deciles do not include the bottom and top 5 percent of the  distribution.

**Figure 5b  Men with Disabilities—Differences in Mean Own Earnings and Household Transfer Income, by Decile of the Household-Size-Adjusted Real Income Distribution, 1989 and 1998[a]**

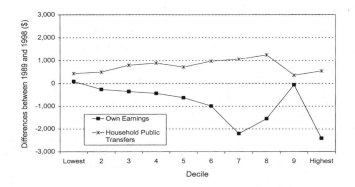

SOURCE: Authors' calculations based on the March Current Population Survey, 1990 and 1999.
[a]Lowest and highest deciles do not include the bottom and top 5 percent of the distribution.

was 11.8 percentage points. The results for women with disabilities (Figure 3a) are similar. In both years, employment rates are highest at higher deciles of the household income distribution. However, as was true for men with disabilities, the largest declines in employment between 1989 and 1998—the biggest gaps—occur in the middle of the income distribution.

Figures 4a and 4b repeat this exercise for public transfer receipt, defined as the percentage of men and women living in a household receiving some type of public benefit.[20]  For both men and women, the percentage of the decile population receiving public transfers rose in all deciles. Again, consistent with the results in Figures 2 and 3, the largest increases in benefit receipt came in the middle of the household-size-adjusted income distribution. Men and women in the bottom three deciles were more likely to receive transfers in each year, but the difference in the proportion receiving benefits by decile evened out substantially during the 1990s.

Figures 3 and 4 showed the proportion of the population of men and women with disabilities employed and receiving benefits in 1989 and 1998. Figure 5 shows how mean labor market earnings and the mean value of public benefits changed between these two years, in terms of the dollar difference in mean own earnings and mean transfer income in 1989 and 1998, by decile of the household-size-adjusted income distribution for men and women with disabilities. The results in Figure 5 illustrate why the household incomes of those in the middle of the distribution (Figure 2) declined between 1989 and 1998. For men (Figure 5b) between the 5th and 7th deciles of the household-size-adjusted income distribution, the dollar decline in own earnings between 1989 and 1998 was larger than the dollar increase in public transfers.[21] For men at most other deciles of the household-size-adjusted income distribution, gains in public transfers were more than sufficient to offset the declines in own earnings and to push the household income of men at these deciles above that of men at equivalent percentiles in 1989.[22] The story is similar for women (Figure 5a). Declines in own earnings in the middle of the income distribution were only partially offset by increases in the value of public benefits, leaving a large fraction of middle-income women with disabilities worse off than their counterparts in 1989.

## CONCLUSIONS

We confirm President Clinton's report that strong economic growth since the recession of 1992 has lifted the economic well-being of most working-age people from the depths at the trough of the 1990s business cycle. However, working-age men and women with disabilities fared less well than those without disabilities. When one looks over the entire 1990s business cycle, the contrast in outcomes between those with and without disabilities is even starker. Men and women without disabilities gained across the entire income distribution between the peak year of the 1980s business cycle, 1989, and the most recent year of data for the current expansion, 1998. In contrast, men and women with disabilities in the middle of the distribution of household income failed to regain the incomes of their counterparts in 1989. While the employment and labor earnings of men and women without disabilities were quite sensitive to the 1990s business cycle (falling in recession and rising with recovery), the employment of men and women with disabilities, surprisingly, fell over the entire 1990 business cycle (although less so in recovery than in recession). This shocking finding explains much of the decline in economic well-being of working-age people with disabilities, despite increases in their disability transfer income. What is responsible for the decline in the labor market attachment of people with disabilities, over both the economic decline of the early 1990s and the longest peacetime economic expansion in our history, is a major policy puzzle that must be solved before the rewards of economic growth are shared by all.

## Notes

This research was funded in part by the United States Department of Education, National Institute on Disability and Rehabilitation Research, cooperative agreement No. 13313980038. It does not necessarily reflect the view of the National Institute on Disability and Rehabilitation Research or the Federal Reserve Bank of San Francisco.

1. Because we have not reached the peak of the 1990s business cycle, our analysis will underestimate the net peak-to-peak gains over that cycle. Nonetheless, our 1989/1992/1998 comparisons describe a relative pattern which is unlikely to be greatly altered as additional years of information become available.

2. It is important to note that self-perception of a disability as captured by this question can be influenced by social context. For instance, reports of a work limitation may change over time, even holding the underlying health condition constant, because access to accommodation may change one's perception of a work limitation over time. See Kirchner (1996) for a fuller discussion of this issue and the uses of the CPS to analyze "access-oriented" policies. See the appendix for a fuller discussion.

3. As we discuss in the appendix, small changes were made to the CPS question on disability in 1994, the year the CPS moved to computer-assisted interviewing. Although we do not examine this in our analysis, both the question change and the move to computer-assisted interviewing may explain the nearly 1 percentage point increase in the prevalence of disability reported in 1994 (Table A2).

4. Atkinson, Rainwater, and Smeeding (1995) and Burkhauser, Crews, and Daly (1997) argued that using the family definition, rather than the less restrictive household-based definition, will produce a bleaker picture of the income distribution because it treats a larger number of individuals as single-person households even when they reside and share the benefits of living with others.

5. In the CPS data, income includes all cash income received from private and public sources. It does not include noncash or in-kind benefits or the imputed income from owner-occupied housing. We convert all negative sources of income to zero.

6. The CPS data do not provide net-of-tax income information. Many income inequality studies do not adjust for taxation (see, for example, Karoly and Burtless 1995; Danziger and Gottschalk 1995), but it would be useful to do so. We have done so elsewhere with other data sets; see, for instance, Burkhauser and Poupore (1997).

7. Specifically, household income is the sum of income from labor earnings, self-employment, farming, alimony, dividends, rent, and interest, as well as income payments from the Social Security system, unemployment and workers' compensation systems, and state and federal public assistance programs.

8. Others who also use an equivalence scale of this approximate value include Karoly and Burtless (1995) and Atkinson, Rainwater, and Smeeding (1995). Equivalence scales contain assumptions about the returns to shared living. Many such scales, even complicated ones, can be approximated well by a single-parameter scale (see Buhmann et al. 1988). An equivalence scale with an elasticity with respect to household size of 1 (the per-capita scale) implies no economies of scale. An elasticity of 0 (i.e., with no size adjustments to household income) implies that an infinite number of individual can live equally well with a given household income as a single person household with that income. See Burkhauser, Smeeding, and Merz (1996) for a discussion of the sensitivity of different equivalence scales in cross-national comparisons. The household size elasticity implicit in the U.S. Bureau of the Census poverty scales is approximately 0.5 (Buhmann et al. 1988). While most poverty studies in the United States use this official scale, it has been severely criticized (see, for example, Citro and Michael 1995).

9.  Deleting the bottom and the top 1 percent of the household-size-adjusted income distribution does not materially affect our results.

10. Annual hours are calculated by multiplying number of weeks worked by average hours worked per week.

11. For a complete time-series (1987–1998) of mean and median household-size-adjusted income for men and women with and without disabilities, see Table A4.

12. Given that we are using cross-sectional data, a natural concern is that we are simply picking up compositional changes in the population of people with disabilities. To test for this possibility we did a simple shift-share analysis, controlling first for changes in age, race, education, and household size and controlling second for these demographic variables and changes in employment rates. The results of this analysis (Table A5) show that if the composition of the population with disabilities was the same in 1998 as it was in 1989, the economic outcomes for those with disabilities would have been worse than those we report. This suggests that the findings we report are not an artifact of demographic shifts, but rather the result of changing economic rewards for the population with disabilities.

13. For a complete time series of employment rates, mean annual hours worked, and mean and median annual earnings for men and women with disabilities, see Tables A6 and A7.

14. For a complete time series of the shares of these various sources of household income, see Table A8.

15. See Table A9 for the complete time series of mean public nondisability and disability transfers, by program.

16. See Table A10 for the complete time series of shares of public nondisability and disability transfers, by program.

17. For each of our four groups, we first estimate real household-size-adjusted income for each percentile of our sample in 1998 and compare it to this same variable for 1989. The difference in their two means is reported in Table 2.

18. For examples using this technique, see Danziger and Gottshalk (1995), Burtless (1996a, 1996b), and Burkhauser, Crews, and Daly (1997).

19. The lowest "decile" only contains those in the 6th through 10th percentiles. The highest "decile" only contains those in the 96th through 100th percentiles.

20. The results for household public transfer receipt are similar to those obtained using own public disability transfer receipt.

21. The real value of other sources of income, such as other household earnings, did not change significantly for any decile of the household-size-adjusted income distribution between 1989 and 1998.

22. An exception to this is men with disabilities in the highest decile of the household-size adjusted income distribution. For these men, large gains in the earnings of other household members offset declines in own earnings.

# References

Atkinson, Anthony, B., Lee Rainwater, and Timothy M. Smeeding. 1995. *Income Distribution in OECD Countries: Evidence from the Luxembourg Income Study (LIS).* Social Policy Studies no. 18. Paris: OECD.

Bazzoli, Gloria J. 1985. "Evidence on the Influence of Health." *Journal of Human Resources* 20(2): 214–234.

Bound, John. 1991. "Self-Reported versus Objective Measures of Health in Retirement Models." *Journal of Human Resources* 26(1): 106–138.

Buhmann, B., Lee Rainwater, Gunther Schmauss, and Timothy M. Smeeding. 1988. "Equivalence Scales, Well-Being, Inequality and Poverty: Sensitivity Estimates across Ten Countries Using the Luxembourg Income Study (LIS) database." *The Review of Income and Wealth* 34(June): 115–142.

Burkhauser, Richard V., and Mary C. Daly. 1996. "Employment and Economic Well-Being Following the Onset of a Disability: The Role for Public Policy." In *Disability, Work, and Cash Benefits*, Jerry Mashaw, Virginia Reno, Richard V. Burkhauser, and Monroe Berkowitz, eds. Kalamazoo, Michigan: W.E. Upjohn Institute for Employment Research, pp. 59–102.

Burkhauser, Richard V., Amy D. Crews, and Mary C. Daly. 1997. "Recounting Winners and Losers in the 1980s: A Critique of Income Distribution Measurement Methodology." *Economics Letters* 54(May): 35–40.

Burkhauser, Richard V., and John G. Poupore. 1997. "A Cross-National Comparison of Permanent Inequality in the United States and Germany." *Review of Economics and Statistics* 79(1): 10–17.

Burkhauser, Richard V., Timothy M. Smeeding, and Joachim Merz. 1996. "Relative Inequality and Poverty in Germany and the United States Using Alternative Equivalency Scales." *The Review of Income and Wealth* 42(4): 381–400.

Burtless, Gary. 1996a. "Widening U.S. Income Inequality and the Growth in World Trade." Paper presented at Mannheim Labor Conference, May.

_____. 1996b. "Trends in the Level and Distribution of U.S. Living Standards, 1973–1993." *Eastern Economic Journal* 22(3): 271–290.

Citro, Connie F., and Robert T. Michael. 1995. *Measuring Poverty: A New Approach.* Washington, D.C.: National Academy Press.

Council of Economic Advisors. 1999. *Economic Report of the President.* Washington, D.C.: U.S. Government Printing Office.

Danziger, Sheldon, and Peter Gottschalk. 1995. *America Unequal.* Cambridge, Massachusetts: Harvard University Press.

Gordon, Kate, and Catherine Groves (eds.). 2000. ADA Symposium Issue: *Berkeley Journal of Employment and Labor Law* 21(1).

Karoly, Lynn A., and Gary Burtless. 1995. "Demographic Change, Rising Earning Inequality, and the Distribution of Personal Well-Being, 1959–1989." *Demography* 32(3): 379–406.

Kirchner, Corinne. 1996, "Looking under the Street Lamp." *Journal of Disability Policy Studies* 7(1): 78–90.

Nagi, Saad. 1965. "Some Conceptual Issues in Disability and Rehabilitation." In *Sociology and Rehabilitation*, M.B. Sussman, ed. Washington, D.C.: American Sociological Association.

_____. 1969. *Disability and Rehabilitation: Legal, Clinical and Self-Concepts of Measurement*. Columbus: Ohio State University Press.

_____. 1991. "Disability Concepts Revisited: Implications to Prevention." In *Disability in America: Toward A National Agenda for Prevention*, A.M. Pope and A.R. Tarlove, eds. Washington, D.C.: National Academy Press.

Parsons, Donald O. 1980. "The Decline in Male Labor Force Participation." *Journal of Political Economy* 88(1): 117–134.

_____. 1982. "The Male Labor Force Participation Decision: Health, Reported Health, and Economic Incentives." *Econometrica* 49: 81–91.

Stern, Steven. 1989. "Measuring the Effect of Disability on Labor Force Participation." *Journal of Human Resources* 24(3): 301–395.

U.S. Census Bureau. 1999. *Money Income in the United States*. Current Population Reports, Consumer Income, P60-206.

# Appendix
# Current Population Survey Data
# and Disability Measurement

## Limitations of Using the CPS to Measure
## the Working-Age Population with Disabilities

Although the Current Population Survey (CPS) has extensive economic information, a number of factors make it less than ideal for examining the population with disabilities. First, the CPS does not survey institutionalized individuals. Second, all information is reported by a single respondent in the household (a "responsible adult"). This person may or may not be the person in this household with a disability and hence may not accurately report information about that person's disability. Third, the CPS has very limited self-reported information on health. Despite these shortcomings, the consistency of the time-series and the coverage of the U.S. population make it a reasonable source of information on the economic fluctuations of the population with disabilities.

## Changes in CPS Disability Question in 1994

In our chapter, persons are considered to have a disability if they report or are reported as having a health problem or disability that prevents them from working or limits the kind or amount of work they can do. From 1988 to 1993, CPS interviews were conducted by individuals without the help of computer-assisted personal or telephone interviewing. Starting in 1994, interviewers were prompted with names and possible inconsistencies by computer software. As part of this change, the questions we use to define disability,

> Does anyone in this household have health problem or disability which prevents them from working or which limits the kind or amount of work they can do? If yes . . . , who is that? (Anyone else?),

were changed to

> (Do you/does anyone in this household) have a health problem or disability which prevent (you/them) from working or which limits the kind or amount of work (you/they) can do? If yes . . . , who is that? (Anyone else?)

In addition, sample weights based on the 1980 census were replaced with sample weights based on the 1990 census. Furthermore, the Monthly Basic Survey was revised and three new disability questions were added. It is possible that these changes affected the measurement of the population with disabilities either through changes in the sample weights or in the way respondents answered disability questions.

**Table A1  Macroeconomic Indicators of the Business Cycle**

| Year | Real median family income (1998 $) | Unemployment rate (%) |
|---|---|---|
| 1970 | 39,694 | 4.9 |
| 1971 | 39,669 | 5.9 |
| 1972 | 41,507 | 5.6 |
| 1973 | 42,360 | 4.9 |
| 1974 | 40,869 | 5.6 |
| 1975 | 39,817 | 8.5 |
| 1976 | 41,046 | 7.7 |
| 1977 | 41,289 | 7.1 |
| 1978 | 42,598 | 6.1 |
| 1979 | 43,143 | 5.8 |
| 1980 | 41,636 | 7.1 |
| 1981 | 40,501 | 7.6 |
| 1982 | 39,952 | 9.7 |
| 1983 | 40,379 | 9.6 |
| 1984 | 41,466 | 7.5 |
| 1985 | 42,014 | 7.2 |
| 1986 | 43,809 | 7.0 |
| 1987 | 44,436 | 6.2 |
| 1988 | 44,353 | 5.5 |
| 1989 | 44,972 | 5.3 |
| 1990 | 44,089 | 5.5 |
| 1991 | 43,009 | 6.7 |
| 1992 | 42,489 | 7.5 |
| 1993 | 41,689 | 6.8 |
| 1994 | 42,654 | 6.1 |
| 1995 | 43,434 | 5.6 |
| 1996 | 43,943 | 5.4 |
| 1997 | 45,260 | 4.9 |
| 1998 | 46,737 | 4.5 |

SOURCE: *Economic Report of the President*, 1994 (Tables B-29 and B38) and 1999 (Tables B33 and B35), adjusted to 1998 dollars using CPI-U, and *Current Population Report*, P60-206, p. 13.

**Table A2  Prevalence of Disability among the Working-Age Civilian Population[a] (%)**

| Groups | 1988 | 1989 | 1990 | 1991 | 1992 | 1993 | 1994[b] | 1995 | 1996 | 1997 | 1998 | 1999 |
|---|---|---|---|---|---|---|---|---|---|---|---|---|
| All | 7.2 | 7.2 | 7.4 | 7.5 | 7.6 | 7.8 | 8.4 | 8.3 | 8.3 | 8.3 | 8.1 | 7.9 |
| Aged | | | | | | | | | | | | |
| 25 through 34 | 4.4 | 3.9 | 4.2 | 4.4 | 4.6 | 4.8 | 5.0 | 4.7 | 4.4 | 4.3 | 3.6 | 3.8 |
| 35 through 44 | 5.9 | 6.2 | 6.0 | 6.3 | 6.4 | 6.5 | 7.0 | 7.3 | 7.2 | 7.1 | 7.0 | 6.7 |
| 45 through 54 | 9.1 | 9.3 | 9.7 | 9.7 | 10.0 | 10.0 | 10.8 | 10.8 | 10.8 | 10.9 | 10.7 | 10.4 |
| 55 through 61 | 15.6 | 16.0 | 16.6 | 15.8 | 15.9 | 15.6 | 17.1 | 16.7 | 16.8 | 16.9 | 16.4 | 16.2 |
| Gender | | | | | | | | | | | | |
| Men | 7.6 | 7.6 | 7.8 | 7.7 | 8.1 | 8.4 | 8.8 | 8.5 | 8.2 | 8.2 | 7.8 | 8.0 |
| Women | 6.7 | 6.8 | 7.0 | 7.2 | 7.2 | 7.2 | 8.0 | 8.2 | 8.4 | 8.3 | 8.3 | 7.9 |
| Race/ethnicity | | | | | | | | | | | | |
| White | 6.7 | 6.8 | 6.9 | 6.9 | 7.2 | 7.4 | 7.8 | 7.7 | 7.6 | 7.8 | 7.6 | 7.4 |
| Black | 11.6 | 11.0 | 11.6 | 11.9 | 11.4 | 10.8 | 13.4 | 13.3 | 13.7 | 13.3 | 12.3 | 12.9 |
| Hispanic[c] | 7.0 | 6.2 | 7.5 | 7.3 | 7.1 | 7.7 | 7.8 | 7.8 | 7.4 | 7.0 | 7.1 | 7.2 |
| Education | | | | | | | | | | | | |
| Less than high school[d] | 16.1 | 16.9 | 17.0 | 16.8 | 18.1 | 18.2 | 20.7 | 19.3 | 19.0 | 18.7 | 18.1 | 17.3 |
| High school | 6.6 | 6.6 | 7.3 | 7.4 | 7.6 | 8.0 | 8.6 | 9.1 | 8.9 | 8.9 | 8.9 | 9.0 |

| More than high school but less than college | 5.7 | 5.5 | 5.1 | 5.6 | 6.0 | 6.5 | 6.7 | 6.8 | 6.9 | 7.2 | 7.0 | 7.1 |
| College or more | 2.6 | 2.6 | 2.8 | 3.0 | 2.7 | 2.6 | 2.7 | 3.0 | 3.2 | 3.2 | 3.1 | 3.1 |

SOURCE: Authors' calculations based on the March Current Population Survey, 1988-1999.

[a] Persons less than age 25 or more than age 61 and people in the Armed Forces are excluded. In our study, persons are considered to have a disability if they report having a health problem or disability which prevents them from working or limits the kind or amount of work they can do.

[b] In 1994 there were several changes in the CPS. It moved fully to computer-assisted survey interviews. Sample weights based on the 1980 Census were replaced with sample weights based on the 1990 Census. The Monthly Basic Survey was revised, and three new disability questions were added. It is possible that these changes effected the measurement of the population with disabilities either through changes in the sample weights or in the way respondents answered disability questions.

[c] Spanish ethnicity superceded race; we recoded Hispanics to be non-White, non-Black, and non-other race.

[d] Beginning in survey year 1992, educational attainment questions in the CPS were changed to reflect credentials and degrees rather than grades (years) complete.

**Table A3 Gender, Age, Race/Ethnicity, and Education Distributions within Populations with and without Disabilities[a] (%)**

| Survey year | Without disabilities | | With disabilities | |
|---|---|---|---|---|
| | Male | Female | Male | Female |
| 1988 | 48.7 | 51.3 | 52.1 | 47.9 |
| 1989 | 48.8 | 51.2 | 51.5 | 48.5 |
| 1990 | 48.6 | 51.4 | 51.8 | 48.2 |
| 1991 | 48.7 | 51.3 | 50.4 | 49.6 |
| 1992 | 48.7 | 51.3 | 51.6 | 48.4 |
| 1993 | 48.7 | 51.3 | 52.8 | 47.2 |
| 1994[b] | 48.8 | 51.2 | 51.5 | 48.5 |
| 1995 | 48.9 | 51.1 | 50.0 | 50.0 |
| 1996 | 49.0 | 51.0 | 48.5 | 51.5 |
| 1997 | 49.1 | 50.9 | 48.8 | 51.2 |
| 1998 | 49.2 | 50.8 | 47.5 | 52.5 |
| 1999 | 48.9 | 51.1 | 49.2 | 50.8 |

**Age**

| | Without disabilities | | | | With disabilities | | | |
|---|---|---|---|---|---|---|---|---|
| | 25–34 | 35–44 | 45–54 | 55–61 | 25–34 | 35–44 | 45–54 | 55–61 |
| 1987 | 37.9 | 30.1 | 20.1 | 11.9 | 22.6 | 24.5 | 24.5 | 28.5 |

| | | | | | | | | |
|---|---|---|---|---|---|---|---|---|
| 1989 | 37.7 | 30.5 | 20.3 | 11.5 | 19.9 | 26.1 | 25.8 | 28.2 |
| 1990 | 36.9 | 31.3 | 20.6 | 11.2 | 20.3 | 24.9 | 27.0 | 27.8 |
| 1991 | 36.1 | 32.0 | 20.6 | 11.3 | 20.6 | 26.6 | 26.5 | 26.3 |
| 1992 | 35.3 | 32.4 | 21.4 | 11.0 | 20.5 | 26.6 | 27.9 | 25.1 |
| 1993 | 34.2 | 32.5 | 22.3 | 11.0 | 20.6 | 26.9 | 28.4 | 24.0 |
| 1994[b] | 33.9 | 33.0 | 22.6 | 10.5 | 19.8 | 27.0 | 29.5 | 23.7 |
| 1995 | 33.2 | 33.1 | 23.3 | 10.4 | 17.9 | 28.8 | 30.4 | 22.9 |
| 1996 | 32.5 | 33.2 | 23.6 | 10.7 | 16.7 | 28.7 | 30.7 | 23.9 |
| 1997 | 31.5 | 33.5 | 24.3 | 10.7 | 15.7 | 28.4 | 31.7 | 24.2 |
| 1998 | 30.6 | 33.5 | 24.8 | 11.1 | 13.2 | 28.8 | 33.0 | 25.0 |
| 1999 | 29.6 | 33.4 | 25.5 | 11.4 | 13.6 | 27.9 | 32.8 | 25.6 |

**Race/ethnicity[c]**

| | Without disabilities | | | | With disabilities | | | |
|---|---|---|---|---|---|---|---|---|
| | White | Black | Hispanic | Other | White | Black | Hispanic | Other |
| 1988 | 78.7 | 10.4 | 7.5 | 3.3 | 72.7 | 17.8 | 7.3 | 2.3 |
| 1989 | 78.2 | 10.6 | 7.7 | 3.4 | 73.8 | 17.0 | 6.6 | 2.6 |
| 1990 | 78.0 | 10.7 | 7.9 | 3.5 | 72.2 | 17.6 | 8.0 | 2.3 |
| 1991 | 77.7 | 10.7 | 8.0 | 3.6 | 71.5 | 17.9 | 7.8 | 2.7 |
| 1992 | 77.2 | 10.8 | 8.2 | 3.8 | 72.6 | 16.8 | 7.6 | 3.0 |

(continued)

**Table A3 (continued)**

### Race/ethnicity[c]

| | Without disabilities | | | | With disabilities | | | |
|---|---|---|---|---|---|---|---|---|
| 1993 | 76.7 | 11.0 | 8.4 | 3.9 | 73.3 | 15.7 | 8.3 | 2.7 |
| 1994[b] | 75.7 | 10.9 | 9.4 | 4.0 | 69.9 | 18.6 | 8.7 | 2.9 |
| 1995 | 75.7 | 11.0 | 9.6 | 3.7 | 69.9 | 18.7 | 9.0 | 2.5 |
| 1996 | 74.7 | 11.0 | 9.8 | 4.4 | 68.4 | 19.3 | 8.7 | 3.7 |
| 1997 | 73.9 | 11.0 | 10.3 | 4.7 | 69.2 | 18.7 | 8.6 | 3.5 |
| 1998 | 73.3 | 11.2 | 10.6 | 4.9 | 69.1 | 17.9 | 9.2 | 3.8 |
| 1999 | 73.2 | 11.2 | 10.7 | 5.0 | 67.6 | 19.2 | 9.7 | 3.6 |

### Education[d]

| | Without disabilities | | | | With disabilities | | | |
|---|---|---|---|---|---|---|---|---|
| | Less than high school | High school | More than H.S., less than college | College or more | Less than high school | High school | More than H.S., less than college | College or more |
| 1988 | 16.0 | 40.6 | 19.3 | 24.1 | 39.8 | 36.9 | 15.1 | 8.3 |
| 1989 | 15.3 | 40.1 | 19.4 | 25.2 | 40.2 | 36.7 | 14.5 | 8.6 |
| 1990 | 14.7 | 39.9 | 20.3 | 25.1 | 37.7 | 39.5 | 13.8 | 9.0 |
| 1991 | 14.4 | 39.8 | 20.7 | 25.2 | 36.0 | 39.2 | 15.3 | 9.5 |
| 1992 | 13.6 | 36.4 | 24.8 | 25.3 | 36.3 | 36.3 | 19.0 | 8.5 |
| 1993 | 12.8 | 35.4 | 25.8 | 25.9 | 33.9 | 36.6 | 21.2 | 8.3 |

| | | | | | | | | |
|---|---|---|---|---|---|---|---|---|
| 1994[b] | 12.4 | 34.3 | 27.1 | 26.3 | 35.3 | 35.2 | 21.4 | 8.1 |
| 1995 | 12.0 | 33.6 | 27.3 | 27.1 | 31.7 | 36.8 | 22.1 | 9.3 |
| 1996 | 12.3 | 33.2 | 27.0 | 27.5 | 31.9 | 36.0 | 22.0 | 10.0 |
| 1997 | 12.1 | 33.3 | 27.0 | 27.7 | 30.7 | 36.0 | 23.3 | 10.1 |
| 1998 | 11.7 | 33.0 | 27.0 | 28.3 | 29.5 | 36.9 | 23.3 | 10.3 |
| 1999 | 11.4 | 32.4 | 26.9 | 29.2 | 27.7 | 37.3 | 23.9 | 11.0 |

SOURCE: Authors' calculations based on the March Current Population Survey, 1988–1999.

[a] Persons less than age 25 or more than age 61 and people in the Armed Forces are excluded. In our study, persons are considered to have a disability if they report having a health problem or disability which prevents them from working or limits the kind or amount of work they can do. Disability status is for the year following the income year.

[b] In 1994 there were several changes in the CPS. It moved fully to computer-assisted survey interviews. Sample weights based on the 1980 Census were replaced with sample weights based on the 1990 Census. The Monthly Basic Survey was revised, and three new disability questions were added. It is possible that these changes effected the measurement of the population with disabilities either through changes in the sample weights or in the way respondents answered disability questions.

[c] Spanish ethnicity superceded race; we recode Hispanics to be non-White, non-Black, and non-other race.

[d] Beginning in survey year 1992, educational attainment questions in the CPS were changed to reflect credentials and degrees rather than grades (years) complete.

**Table A4  Mean and Median Household-Size-Adjusted Real Income of Civilians Aged 25–61, by Gender and Disability Status[a] ($)**

| Income year | Mean | | | | Median | | | |
|---|---|---|---|---|---|---|---|---|
| | Men | | Women | | Men | | Women | |
| | Without disabilities | With disabilities | Without disabilities | With disabilities | Without disabilities | With disabilities | Without disabilities | With disabilities |
| 1987 | 35,266 | 21,473 | 32,305 | 19,459 | 31,210 | 17,219 | 28,706 | 14,862 |
| 1988 | 35,748 | 20,865 | 32,591 | 19,597 | 31,831 | 16,516 | 28,961 | 14,775 |
| 1989 | 36,460 | 21,493 | 32,973 | 19,998 | 32,142 | 17,154 | 29,075 | 15,256 |
| 1990 | 35,258 | 20,010 | 32,261 | 20,190 | 31,159 | 16,182 | 28,397 | 15,288 |
| 1991 | 34,491 | 20,624 | 31,884 | 18,983 | 30,631 | 16,386 | 28,259 | 14,403 |
| 1992 | 34,465 | 20,159 | 31,723 | 18,701 | 30,476 | 16,161 | 28,175 | 13,755 |
| 1993 | 34,383 | 19,386 | 31,712 | 18,190 | 30,310 | 15,155 | 27,908 | 13,480 |
| 1994[b] | 34,965 | 20,005 | 32,281 | 19,349 | 30,760 | 15,139 | 28,377 | 14,958 |
| 1995 | 36,241 | 20,303 | 33,626 | 19,717 | 30,902 | 15,672 | 28,541 | 14,830 |
| 1996 | 36,940 | 20,265 | 34,255 | 19,288 | 31,340 | 15,339 | 29,088 | 14,035 |
| 1997 | 38,124 | 20,828 | 35,457 | 20,307 | 32,035 | 15,835 | 29,958 | 14,633 |
| 1998 | 39,756 | 21,619 | 36,526 | 20,074 | 33,840 | 16,419 | 30,698 | 14,658 |

SOURCE: Authors' calculations are based on the March Current Population Survey, 1988–1999.

[a] Those less than age 25 or more than age 61 or in the Armed Forces are excluded. In our study, persons are considered to have a disability if they report having a health problem or disability which prevents them from working or limits the kind or amount of work they can do. Income is household size by dividing income by the square root of household size. Negative sources of income were converted to zero. In addition, the bottom and top 1 percent of the household size-adjusted income distribution are excluded from the analysis. Disability status is for the year following the income year.

[b] In 1994 there were several changes in the CPS. It moved fully to computer-assisted survey interviews. Sample weights based on the 1980 Census were replaced with sample weights based on the 1990 Census. The Monthly Basic Survey was revised, and three new disability questions were added. It is possible that these changes effected the measurement of the population with disabilities either through changes in the sample weights or in the way respondents answered disability questions.

**Table A5  Mean Household-Size-Adjusted Real Income When Controlling for Changes in Age, Race, Education, Household Size, and Employment for Civilians Aged 25–61, by Gender and Disability Status**[a]

| | ($)[c] | | Percentage |
|---|---|---|---|
| Group[b] | 1989 | 1998 | change[d] |
| No controls (Same as Table 1) | | | |
| Men without disabilities | 36,460 | 39,756 | 8.6 |
| Men with disabilities | 21,493 | 21,619 | 0.6 |
| Women without disabilities | 32,973 | 36,526 | 10.2 |
| Women with disabilities | 19,998 | 20,074 | 0.4 |
| Controlling for changes in age, race, education and household size | | | |
| Men without disabilities | 36,460 | 37,928 | 3.9 |
| Men with disabilities | 21,493 | 20,539 | −4.5 |
| Women without disabilities | 32,973 | 34,042 | 3.2 |
| Women with disabilities | 19,998 | 19,179 | −4.2 |
| Controlling for changes in age, race, education, household size and employment | | | |
| Men without disabilities | 36,460 | 38,077 | 4.3 |
| Men with disabilities | 21,493 | 21,551 | 0.3 |
| Women without disabilities | 32,973 | 33,945 | 2.9 |
| Women with disabilities | 19,998 | 19,800 | −1.0 |

SOURCE: Authors' calculations based on the March Current Population Survey, 1990–1999.

[a] We controlled for changes in population characteristics by imposing the 1989 proportion in each subpopulation when we calculated the 1998 mean. Those less than age 25 or more than age 61 or in the Armed Forces are excluded. In our study, persons are considered to have a disability if they report having a health problem or disability which prevents them from working or limits the kind or amount of work they can do.

## Table A5 (continued)

[b] Disability status is for the year following the income year. In 1994 there were several changes in the CPS. It moved fully to computer-assisted survey interviews. Sample weights based on the 1980 Census were replaced with sample weights based on the 1990 Census. The Monthly Basic Survey was revised, and three new disability questions were added. It is possible that these changes effected the measurement of the population with disabilities either through changes in the sample weights or in the way respondents answered disability questions.

[c] All dollar amounts are in 1998 dollars. Income is household size by dividing income by the square root of household size. Negative sources of income were converted to zero. In addition, the bottom and top 1 percent of the household size-adjusted income distribution are excluded from the analysis.

[d] When calculating percentage change, we use the average of the two years as the base.

Table A6  Employment Rates and Mean Annual Hours of Civilians Aged 25–61 Who Worked, by Gender and Disability Status[a, b]

| Earnings year[b] | Employment rate[c] (%) | | | | Mean annual hours for the employed | | | |
| | Men | | Women | | Men | | Women | |
| | Without disabilities | With disabilities | Without disabilities | With disabilities | Without disabilities | With disabilities | Without disabilities | With disabilities |
|---|---|---|---|---|---|---|---|---|
| 1987 | 94.5 | 42.9 | 75.2 | 33.9 | 2,151 | 1,568 | 1,725 | 1,276 |
| 1988 | 94.5 | 42.9 | 76.6 | 36.2 | 2,163 | 1,559 | 1,735 | 1,299 |
| 1989 | 96.1 | 44.0 | 77.1 | 37.5 | 2,165 | 1,595 | 1,743 | 1,275 |
| 1990 | 95.9 | 42.1 | 77.6 | 34.9 | 2,145 | 1,553 | 1,748 | 1,316 |
| 1991 | 95.4 | 41.5 | 77.8 | 35.1 | 2,113 | 1,548 | 1,759 | 1,303 |
| 1992 | 94.8 | 41.6 | 77.6 | 34.3 | 2,121 | 1,560 | 1,772 | 1,295 |
| 1993 | 94.4 | 37.1 | 78.3 | 33.4 | 2,153 | 1,521 | 1,777 | 1,295 |
| 1994 | 94.8 | 38.0 | 79.1 | 36.0 | 2,177 | 1,552 | 1,775 | 1,274 |
| 1995 | 94.7 | 34.9 | 79.7 | 33.9 | 2,180 | 1,602 | 1,804 | 1,285 |
| 1996 | 94.9 | 38.2 | 80.1 | 33.9 | 2,184 | 1,525 | 1,808 | 1,287 |
| 1997 | 95.2 | 35.5 | 80.7 | 31.9 | 2,193 | 1,477 | 1,815 | 1,277 |
| 1998 | 95.1 | 34.4 | 80.8 | 29.5 | 2,214 | 1,577 | 1,831 | 1,312 |

SOURCE: Authors' calculations based on the March Current Population Survey, 1988–1999.

[a] Those less than age 25 or more than age 61 or in the Armed Forces are excluded. In our study, persons are considered to have a disability if they report having a health problem or disability which prevents them from working or limits the kind or amount of work they can do. Disability status is for the year following the income year.

[b] In 1994 there were several changes in the CPS. It moved fully to computer-assisted survey interviews. Sample weights based on the 1980 Census were replaced with sample weights based on the 1990 Census. The Monthly Basic Survey was revised, and three new disability questions were added. It is possible that these changes effected the measurement of the population with disabilities either through changes in the sample weights or in the way respondents answered disability questions.

[c] Employment is defined as working 52 hours or more annually.

**Table A7  Mean Real Earnings of Civilians Aged 25–61 Who Worked and had Positive Earnings, by Gender and Disability Status[a] (1998 $)**

| Earnings year | Men | | Women | |
|---|---|---|---|---|
| | Without disabilities | With disabilities | Without disabilities | With disabilities |
| 1987 | 38,623 | 22,265 | 21,402 | 11,964 |
| 1988 | 38,853 | 21,383 | 21,640 | 12,873 |
| 1989 | 38,557 | 20,582 | 21,920 | 12,491 |
| 1990 | 37,018 | 20,337 | 21,919 | 13,253 |
| 1991 | 36,065 | 20,462 | 22,019 | 12,582 |
| 1992 | 36,352 | 18,964 | 22,459 | 13,165 |
| 1993 | 36,261 | 18,789 | 22,503 | 13,672 |
| 1994[b] | 36,953 | 20,118 | 22,793 | 12,855 |
| 1995 | 37,958 | 20,699 | 22,974 | 13,180 |
| 1996 | 38,325 | 19,994 | 23,276 | 12,044 |
| 1997 | 39,334 | 19,325 | 23,893 | 13,490 |
| 1998 | 40,993 | 21,172 | 24,814 | 14,232 |

SOURCE: Authors' calculations based on the March Current Population Survey, 1988–1999.

[a] Those less than age 25 or more than age 61 or in the Armed Forces are excluded. In our study, persons are considered to have a disability if they report having a health problem or disability which prevents them from working or limits the kind or amount of work they can do. In addition, the bottom and top 1 percent of the earnings distribution are excluded and only those who work 52 hours or more annually with positive earnings are included in the analysis. Disability status is for the year following the income year.

[b] In 1994 there were several changes in the CPS. It moved fully to computer-assisted survey interviews. Sample weights based on the 1980 Census were replaced with sample weights based on the 1990 Census. The Monthly Basic Survey was revised, and three new disability questions were added. It is possible that these changes effected the measurement of the population with disabilities either through changes in the sample weights or in the way respondents answered disability questions.

**Table A8  Share of Various Household Income Sources for Civilians Aged 25–61, by Gender and Disability Status[a, b]**

| | Men | | | | | | | | | |
|---|---|---|---|---|---|---|---|---|---|---|
| | Without disabilities | | | | | With disabilities | | | | |
| Income year | Own labor earnings | Others' labor earnings | Public disability tranfers[c] | Other public tranfers[d] | All other income | Own labor earnings | Others' labor earnings | Public disability tranfers[c] | Other public tranfers[d] | All other income |
| 1987 | 57.8 | 25.1 | 0.3 | 3.5 | 13.2 | 19.4 | 26.2 | 19.7 | 14.8 | 19.9 |
| 1988 | 58.1 | 25.4 | 0.3 | 3.3 | 12.9 | 18.8 | 26.0 | 20.3 | 15.2 | 19.7 |
| 1989 | 57.0 | 26.1 | 0.3 | 3.3 | 13.3 | 19.4 | 26.6 | 19.2 | 14.5 | 20.3 |
| 1990 | 56.2 | 26.3 | 0.3 | 3.8 | 13.4 | 17.5 | 26.5 | 19.6 | 15.3 | 21.2 |
| 1991 | 55.7 | 26.9 | 0.3 | 4.2 | 12.9 | 17.7 | 27.5 | 20.2 | 15.2 | 19.4 |
| 1992 | 55.1 | 27.0 | 0.4 | 4.8 | 12.7 | 16.4 | 27.9 | 21.5 | 15.9 | 18.4 |
| 1993 | 55.0 | 27.5 | 0.3 | 4.9 | 12.3 | 14.7 | 27.0 | 20.7 | 17.7 | 19.4 |
| 1994 | 56.1 | 27.5 | 0.3 | 4.4 | 11.7 | 16.4 | 26.5 | 22.2 | 16.1 | 18.8 |
| 1995 | 56.9 | 27.5 | 0.4 | 4.3 | 10.8 | 16.1 | 27.1 | 22.9 | 16.0 | 17.7 |
| 1996 | 56.9 | 27.9 | 0.4 | 4.0 | 10.9 | 17.1 | 27.1 | 22.4 | 16.8 | 16.7 |
| 1997 | 56.4 | 27.7 | 0.4 | 3.5 | 12.0 | 14.6 | 27.0 | 26.0 | 15.0 | 17.1 |
| 1998 | 56.7 | 27.5 | 0.4 | 3.2 | 12.2 | 14.9 | 27.5 | 25.4 | 13.7 | 17.9 |

(continued)

**Table A8 (continued)**

## Women

| Income year | Without disabilities | | | | | With disabilities | | | | |
|---|---|---|---|---|---|---|---|---|---|---|
| | Own labor earnings | Others' labor earnings | Public disability tranfers[c] | Other public tranfers[d] | All other income | Own labor earnings | Others' labor earnings | Public disability tranfers[c] | Other public tranfers[d] | All other income |
| 1987 | 31.0 | 47.5 | 0.8 | 6.7 | 14.0 | 11.3 | 35.4 | 15.4 | 19.2 | 18.5 |
| 1988 | 31.8 | 47.2 | 0.7 | 6.6 | 13.8 | 13.2 | 33.1 | 16.4 | 17.9 | 19.3 |
| 1989 | 32.1 | 47.0 | 0.8 | 6.1 | 14.0 | 12.9 | 33.6 | 15.6 | 19.1 | 18.7 |
| 1990 | 32.7 | 46.3 | 0.7 | 6.3 | 14.0 | 12.6 | 34.5 | 17.0 | 18.0 | 17.9 |
| 1991 | 33.3 | 45.6 | 0.7 | 7.0 | 13.4 | 12.7 | 32.7 | 18.0 | 19.2 | 17.3 |
| 1992 | 34.1 | 44.9 | 0.8 | 7.3 | 12.9 | 11.9 | 32.9 | 18.7 | 19.8 | 16.7 |
| 1993 | 34.1 | 44.9 | 0.9 | 7.4 | 12.7 | 12.4 | 31.7 | 19.0 | 19.4 | 17.1 |
| 1994 | 34.5 | 45.6 | 0.9 | 6.7 | 12.3 | 13.0 | 34.0 | 18.1 | 17.6 | 17.1 |
| 1995 | 35.2 | 46.0 | 0.9 | 6.3 | 11.7 | 13.2 | 35.8 | 19.4 | 16.7 | 14.9 |
| 1996 | 35.6 | 45.8 | 0.9 | 6.0 | 11.7 | 12.4 | 35.2 | 20.6 | 17.2 | 14.6 |
| 1997 | 35.9 | 45.2 | 0.7 | 5.6 | 12.6 | 11.7 | 33.2 | 22.0 | 15.6 | 16.9 |
| 1998 | 36.3 | 45.2 | 0.7 | 5.0 | 12.9 | 11.7 | 31.4 | 23.4 | 15.8 | 17.3 |

SOURCE: Authors' calculations based on the March Current Population Survey, 1988–1999.

[a] Those less than age 25 or more than age 61 or in the Armed Forces are excluded. In our study, persons are considered to have a disability if they report having a health problem or disability which prevents them from working or limits the kind or amount of work they can do. Negative sources of income were converted to zero. In addition, the bottom and top 1 percent of the household income distribution are excluded from the analysis.

[b] Disability status is for the year following the income year. Beginning in survey year 1994, computer-assisted interview were used, which slightly modified the question we use to define disability.

[c] Public disability transfers include Social Security income, disability-related veteran's payments, worker's compensation, Supplemental Security income, and disability income from other government sources.

[d] Other transfers include the public disability transfers of other household members and other personal or household public transfers (public assistance and welfare, other forms of veteran's payments, unemployment compensation, and government education assistance).

Table A9  Mean Public Transfer Real Income from Various Sources for Civilians Aged 25–61, by Gender and Disability Status[a] (1998 $)

| Income year | Total public transfers | Public nondisability transfers | Total public disability transfers | From specific public disability transfer programs | | | |
|---|---|---|---|---|---|---|---|
| | | | | SSI | SSDI | Disability veterans' benefits | Workers' compensation |
| Men without disabilities | | | | | | | |
| 1987 | 345 | 254 | 90 | 8 | 50 | 31 | 1 |
| 1988 | 314 | 225 | 90 | 8 | 45 | 31 | 6 |
| 1989 | 301 | 218 | 82 | 8 | 43 | 28 | 3 |
| 1990 | 363 | 273 | 91 | 13 | 44 | 33 | 1 |
| 1991 | 443 | 356 | 88 | 16 | 44 | 27 | 1 |
| 1992 | 531 | 434 | 97 | 15 | 55 | 25 | 2 |
| 1993 | 475 | 387 | 88 | 15 | 45 | 27 | 1 |
| 1994[b] | 409 | 317 | 92 | 19 | 46 | 26 | 1 |
| 1995 | 427 | 319 | 108 | 15 | 62 | 31 | 0 |
| 1996 | 382 | 290 | 92 | 17 | 48 | 27 | 0 |
| 1997 | 321 | 231 | 90 | 15 | 47 | 27 | 1 |
| 1998 | 313 | 215 | 98 | 11 | 53 | 33 | 1 |

Men with
disabilities

| Year | | | | | | | |
|---|---|---|---|---|---|---|---|
| 1987 | 4,520 | 429 | 4092 | 545 | 2,456 | 709 | 382 |
| 1988 | 4,721 | 557 | 4164 | 686 | 2,373 | 745 | 360 |
| 1989 | 4,526 | 414 | 4112 | 663 | 2,392 | 668 | 389 |
| 1990 | 4,353 | 486 | 3866 | 565 | 2,402 | 571 | 328 |
| 1991 | 4,580 | 428 | 4151 | 744 | 2,413 | 644 | 350 |
| 1992 | 4,970 | 545 | 4426 | 776 | 2,603 | 597 | 450 |
| 1993 | 4,445 | 526 | 3919 | 892 | 2,478 | 495 | 54 |
| 1994[b] | 4,515 | 493 | 4022 | 814 | 2,673 | 481 | 54 |
| 1995 | 4,900 | 466 | 4434 | 865 | 2,951 | 567 | 51 |
| 1996 | 4,742 | 375 | 4366 | 977 | 2,903 | 454 | 32 |
| 1997 | 5,323 | 292 | 5030 | 1,016 | 3,375 | 607 | 32 |
| 1998 | 5,167 | 457 | 4710 | 1,136 | 2,930 | 595 | 49 |

(continued)

**Table A9 (continued)**

| Income year | Total public transfers | Public nondisability transfers | Total public disability transfers | From specific public disability transfer programs | | | |
|---|---|---|---|---|---|---|---|
| | | | | SSI | SSDI | Disability veterans' benefits | Workers' compensation |
| Women without disabilities | | | | | | | |
| 1987 | 487 | 323 | 164 | 24 | 137 | 3 | 0 |
| 1988 | 458 | 307 | 151 | 24 | 123 | 3 | 1 |
| 1989 | 485 | 312 | 173 | 23 | 143 | 4 | 3 |
| 1990 | 497 | 342 | 156 | 25 | 125 | 3 | 3 |
| 1991 | 517 | 371 | 146 | 26 | 117 | 2 | 1 |
| 1992 | 554 | 399 | 155 | 34 | 117 | 1 | 3 |
| 1993 | 611 | 421 | 190 | 47 | 139 | 3 | 1 |
| 1994[b] | 585 | 382 | 203 | 37 | 164 | 1 | 1 |
| 1995 | 522 | 340 | 183 | 46 | 133 | 4 | 0 |
| 1996 | 491 | 309 | 182 | 49 | 130 | 2 | 1 |
| 1997 | 425 | 258 | 167 | 38 | 127 | 1 | 1 |
| 1998 | 390 | 244 | 147 | 36 | 108 | 2 | 1 |

Women with
disabilities

| | | | | | | | |
|---|---|---|---|---|---|---|---|
| 1987 | 2,881 | 677 | 2203 | 828 | 1,282 | 10 | 83 |
| 1988 | 2,930 | 645 | 2283 | 740 | 1,314 | 35 | 194 |
| 1989 | 2,854 | 597 | 2257 | 757 | 1,248 | 51 | 201 |
| 1990 | 3,091 | 619 | 2472 | 892 | 1,391 | 48 | 141 |
| 1991 | 3,091 | 623 | 2467 | 870 | 1,431 | 46 | 120 |
| 1992 | 3,317 | 687 | 2631 | 925 | 1,469 | 52 | 185 |
| 1993 | 3,360 | 671 | 2690 | 1,030 | 1,623 | 22 | 15 |
| 1994[b] | 3,275 | 718 | 2556 | 963 | 1,528 | 38 | 27 |
| 1995 | 3,545 | 684 | 2861 | 1,072 | 1,750 | 17 | 22 |
| 1996 | 3,575 | 577 | 2999 | 1,088 | 1,875 | 5 | 31 |
| 1997 | 3,627 | 443 | 3185 | 1,130 | 1,981 | 46 | 28 |
| 1998 | 3,968 | 410 | 3559 | 1,188 | 2,225 | 125 | 21 |

SOURCE: Authors' calculations based on the March Current Population Survey, 1988–1999.

[a] Those less than age 25 or more than age 61 or in the Armed Force are excluded. In our study, persons are considered to have a disability if they report having a health problem or disability which prevents them from working or limits the kind or amount of work they can do. In addition, the bottom and top 1 percent of the household income distribution are excluded from the analysis. These results are not adjusted for household. All dollar values are in 1998 dollars. Disability status is for the year following the income year.

[b] In 1994 there were several changes in the CPS. It moved fully to computer-assisted survey interviews. Sample weights based on the 1980 Census were replaced with sample weights based on the 1990 Census. The Monthly Basic Survey was revised, and three new disability questions were added. It is possible that these changes effected the measurement of the population with disabilities either through changes in the sample weights or in the way respondents answered disability questions.

**Table A10  Shares of Public Transfer Income from Various Sources for Civilians Aged 25–61 Who Receive Public Transfer Payments, by Gender and Disability Status[a] (%)**

| Income year | Total public nondisability transfers | Total public disability transfers | From specific public disability programs | | | |
| | | | SSI | SSDI | Disability veterans' benefits | Workers' compensation |
|---|---|---|---|---|---|---|
| Men without disabilities | | | | | | |
| 1987 | 82.1 | 17.9 | 1.5 | 6.5 | 9.7 | 0.2 |
| 1988 | 81.3 | 18.8 | 1.7 | 6.8 | 9.9 | 0.4 |
| 1989 | 81.9 | 18.0 | 1.6 | 7.2 | 8.8 | 0.4 |
| 1990 | 84.1 | 15.9 | 2.4 | 5.8 | 7.5 | 0.2 |
| 1991 | 86.3 | 13.7 | 2.1 | 4.5 | 6.9 | 0.2 |
| 1992 | 86.5 | 13.5 | 1.9 | 5.5 | 5.8 | 0.3 |
| 1993 | 85.7 | 14.4 | 2.2 | 5.4 | 6.6 | 0.2 |
| 1994[b] | 82.5 | 17.5 | 3.3 | 5.9 | 8.0 | 0.3 |
| 1995 | 82.3 | 17.7 | 2.3 | 7.8 | 7.5 | 0.1 |
| 1996 | 82.3 | 17.8 | 3.5 | 7.7 | 6.6 | 0 |
| 1997 | 80.4 | 19.5 | 3.6 | 7.5 | 8.2 | 0.2 |
| 1998 | 79.5 | 20.4 | 2.6 | 8.2 | 9.3 | 0.3 |
| Men with disabilities | | | | | | |
| 1987 | 17.9 | 82.1 | 15.6 | 47.3 | 13.3 | 5.9 |
| 1988 | 17.9 | 82.1 | 19.6 | 46.8 | 10.1 | 5.6 |
| 1989 | 17.1 | 82.9 | 19.5 | 46.4 | 10.8 | 6.2 |
| 1990 | 19.3 | 80.7 | 17.3 | 48.2 | 9.3 | 5.9 |
| 1991 | 17.2 | 82.8 | 21.5 | 47 | 8.8 | 5.5 |
| 1992 | 17.9 | 82.1 | 21.8 | 46.6 | 7.6 | 6.1 |
| 1993 | 19.0 | 81.0 | 25.5 | 47.5 | 6.9 | 1.1 |
| 1994[b] | 18.3 | 81.7 | 22.8 | 49.6 | 8.0 | 1.3 |
| 1995 | 15.0 | 85.0 | 23.2 | 52.1 | 8.2 | 1.5 |
| 1996 | 14.1 | 86.0 | 25.4 | 53.7 | 6.2 | 0.7 |
| 1997 | 9.1 | 90.9 | 25.2 | 58.8 | 6.6 | 0.3 |
| 1998 | 10.7 | 89.2 | 29.3 | 51.3 | 8.0 | 0.6 |

## Table A10 (continued)

| Income year | Total public nondisability transfers | Total public disability transfers | From specific public disability programs | | | |
|---|---|---|---|---|---|---|
| | | | SSI | SSDI | Disability veterans' benefits | Workers' compensation |
| **Women without disabilities** | | | | | | |
| 1987 | 76.0 | 24.1 | 3.8 | 19.4 | 0.8 | 0.1 |
| 1988 | 76.9 | 23.1 | 4.2 | 18.2 | 0.6 | 0.1 |
| 1989 | 75.7 | 24.4 | 4.0 | 19.1 | 0.5 | 0.8 |
| 1990 | 79.3 | 20.8 | 3.7 | 15.9 | 0.5 | 0.7 |
| 1991 | 82.0 | 18.0 | 3.6 | 13.8 | 0.4 | 0.2 |
| 1992 | 80.6 | 19.2 | 4.4 | 13.9 | 0.3 | 0.6 |
| 1993 | 80.5 | 19.5 | 5.4 | 13.6 | 0.3 | 0.2 |
| 1994[b] | 77.6 | 22.4 | 4.9 | 17.1 | 0.2 | 0.2 |
| 1995 | 76.2 | 23.8 | 6.5 | 16.7 | 0.6 | 0 |
| 1996 | 75.5 | 24.5 | 6.5 | 17.2 | 0.5 | 0.3 |
| 1997 | 76.1 | 23.8 | 6.2 | 17.2 | 0.3 | 0.1 |
| 1998 | 76.8 | 23.2 | 6.5 | 16 | 0.5 | 0.2 |
| **Women with disabilities** | | | | | | |
| 1987 | 31.1 | 68.8 | 27.2 | 38.6 | 0.6 | 2.4 |
| 1988 | 27.9 | 72.3 | 27.4 | 39.3 | 1.2 | 4.4 |
| 1989 | 27.2 | 72.9 | 27.6 | 39.2 | 1.0 | 5.1 |
| 1990 | 29.4 | 70.7 | 28 | 37.9 | 0.9 | 3.9 |
| 1991 | 28.6 | 71.4 | 28.8 | 38.4 | 0.6 | 3.6 |
| 1992 | 27.5 | 72.5 | 28.3 | 38.7 | 0.8 | 4.7 |
| 1993 | 27.0 | 73.0 | 30.6 | 41.6 | 0.3 | 0.5 |
| 1994 | 29.3 | 70.8 | 30.3 | 38.6 | 0.8 | 1.1 |
| 1995 | 24.5 | 75.5 | 31.9 | 42.7 | 0.4 | 0.5 |
| 1996 | 22.5 | 77.6 | 32.7 | 43.6 | 0.3 | 1.0 |
| 1997 | 18.4 | 81.5 | 32.6 | 47.4 | 0.7 | 0.8 |
| 1998 | 15.9 | 84.0 | 34.1 | 48.1 | 1.4 | 0.4 |

SOURCE: Authors' calculations based on the March Current Population Survey, 1988–1999.

(continued)

## Table A10 (continued)

[a] Those less than age 25 or more than age 61 or in the Armed Forces are excluded. In our study, persons are considered to have a disability if they report having a health problem or disability which prevents them from working or limits the kind or amount of work they can do. In addition, the bottom and top 1 percent of the household income distribution are excluded from the analysis. Disability status is for the year following the income year.

[b] In 1994 there were several changes in the CPS. It moved fully to computer assisted survey interviews. Sample weights based on the 1980 Census were replaced with sample weights based on the 1990 Census. The Monthly Basic Survey was revised, and three new disability questions were added. It is possible that these changes effected the measurement of the population with disabilities either through changes in the sample weights or in the way respondents answered disability questions.

# Health, Disability, and the Aging Workforce from the Employer's Perspective

Bruce G. Flynn
*Watson Wyatt Worldwide*

Each year, the Washington Business Group on Health and Watson Wyatt Worldwide survey large employers regarding their disability management practices. This year's survey collected responses from 178 large organizations (greater than 1000 employees) representing all segments of the economy (finance, manufacturing, high technology, etc.). The survey results indicate that employers have seen their disability costs level off or even decrease during the last three years, in large part due to state workers' compensation reform and a competitive insurer marketplace for disability coverage (Figure 1, on p. 352).

However, many attribute a significant portion of the stability of short-term disability (STD)/workers' compensation (WC)/long-term disability (LTD) costs to the emergence of integrated disability management programs that seek to control disability costs through early identification, medical case management, and early return-to-work (RTW) interventions in the workplace. Approximately 43 percent of large employers now report having implemented integrated disability management (DM) programs (up from 26 percent four years ago). Such programs encompass a broad range of activities including safety training, case management, transitional work programs, and supervisory training (Figure 2). The effectiveness of these programs is typically linked to a reduction of disability benefit costs.

The survey further reveals that the most effective disability cost containment outcomes are correlated with implementation of multiple disability management program activities (Figure 3a, b, c). The integration of multiple program elements across occupational and nonoccupational disability programs also resulted in improved disability benefit cost control outcomes (Figure 4).

Despite DM program developments, the strategy of choice for many organizations has been and continues to be to actively assist individuals in obtaining Social Security Disability Income (SSDI) benefits (Hunt et al. 1996). Thus, when private sector employers fail to accommodate individuals and return them to work, the final solution is one of cost-shifting to public disability programs. Although DM and accommodation activities by employers have slowed the departure of individuals with disabilities from the workforce, it appears inevitable that some portion continue to migrate to public sector disability systems (Burkhauser, Butler, and Kim 1995).

Exploring the connection between the impacts of DM programs and their effects on the costs and utilization of public disability benefits is the purpose of a research program undertaken by the Rehabilitation Research and Training Center (RRTC) on Workplace Supports at Virginia Commonwealth University in collaboration with WBGH, Watson Wyatt, and the UnumProvident insurance company. Current studies have documented the migration of workers who develop a work-limiting disability from private to public sources of income replacement, referred to as the Progression of Disability Benefits (PODB). In the next phase of this research, the rate of PODB on an employer-by-employer basis will be compared for employers who have implemented DM programs and those without DM programs. It is expected that employers with active DM programs will "pass through" fewer disabled employees (from STD and WC to LTD, and on to SSDI) than those who do not engage in active disability management.

Still, significant challenges loom as the workforce ages:

- Health care: a shift in the needs of disabled workers from medical care for acute injuries and conditions to care for chronic, ongoing health problems will challenge the health system to respond with effective prevention and disease management services which will maintain employees' ability to be productive at work.

- Functional outcomes: the integration of health and disability management will increasingly focus on improvement of functional outcomes (not simply clinical outcomes). Development of valid and meaningful measures of functional improvement will require collaboration between health and disability researchers, purchasers, insurers, policy experts, and quality/accreditation evaluators.

- Workplace flexibility: accommodation of the restrictions of employees with disabilities requires flexible work policies with respect to work assignments, work design, and work scheduling. Successful disability management efforts with aging workers will hinge on the availability of telecommuting, flexible time, and work redesign options.

Thus, maintenance of a productive workforce as the average age increases will require concerted effort from health care providers, policymakers, insurers, and employers to optimally manage chronic conditions, track and respond to disability trends in the workforce, improve or maintain functional abilities, and retain or return employees with disabilities to work. The following public policy initiatives would support the efforts of employers to attain these goals:

- An integrated, seamless disability benefit system linking income support and return-to-work services regardless of the cause of an individual's disability;

- Confidentiality regulations that protect individual medical information while assuring that employers and insurers have access to the health and disability information needed to improve employee and organizational health and productivity;

- Tax incentives for employers who practice effective disability management; and

- Safety, health, and disability discrimination regulation which promotes workplace flexibility and rewards efforts of innovative employers.

### Figure 1  How Have Costs Changed as a Percentage of Payroll over the Past Three Years?

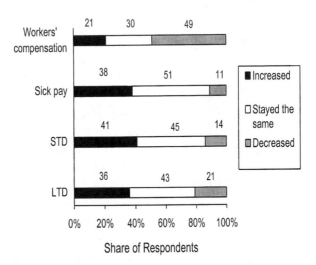

SOURCE: Washington Business Group of Health and Watson Wyatt. *Staying @ Work—Increasing Shareholder Value Through Integrated Disability Management*, 1999, Washington, D.C.

### Figure 2  Popularity of Disability Management Activities

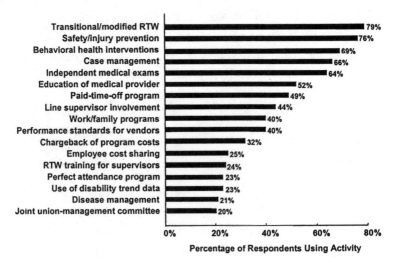

**Figure 3a  Effectiveness of Top Four Disability Management Activities in Decreasing Workers' Compensation Costs**

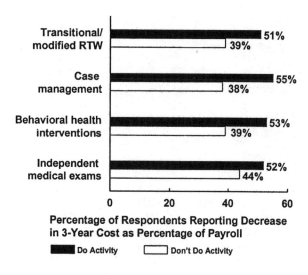

**Figure 3b  Effectiveness of Top Four Disability Management Activities in Decreasing STD Costs**

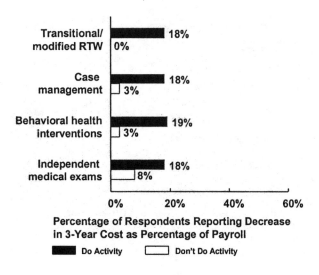

## Figure 3c  Effectiveness of Top Four Disability Management Activities in Decreasing LTD Costs

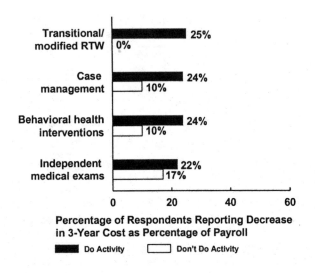

Percentage of Respondents Reporting Decrease in 3-Year Cost as Percentage of Payroll

Do Activity      Don't Do Activity

## Figure 4  Effect of Integrating Multiple Program Elements across Workers' Compensation, LTD and STD

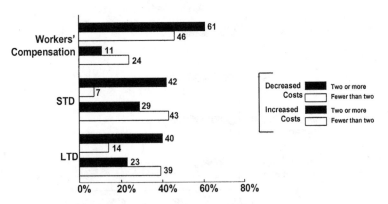

Share of Respondents Reporting Decreases or Increases in Three-Year Cost as Percentage of Payroll

# References

Burkhauser, R.V., J.S. Butler, and Y.M. Kim  1995.  "The Importance of Employer Accommodation on the Job Duration of Workers with Disabilities: A Hazard Model Approach." *Labour Economics* 2(2): 109–130.

Hunt, H.A., R.V. Habeck, P. Owens, and D. Vandergoot.  1996.  "Lessons from the Private Sector." In *Disability, Work and Cash Benefits*, J. Mashaw, V. Reno, R.V. Burkhauser, and M. Berkowitz, eds.  Kalamazoo, Michigan: W.E. Upjohn Institute for Employment Research.

Chronic Illness and Disability;

# Commentary

Vicki Gottlich
*Center for Medicare Advocacy*

(US/

Patricia Nemore
*Center for Medicare Advocacy*

J14
I18

**Ms. Gottlich:**

Since my boss is sitting in the back of the room, I have to say that I also just joined the Center for Medicare Advocacy. With Alfred Chiplin, who is an Academy Member, and Toby Edelman, who also used to be at the National Senior Citizens Law Center, we're establishing the Healthcare Rights Project.

Trish and I have decided that we're the tokens in this conference. We're the token nonresearchers, nonacademics. We're advocates and attorneys, and our comments are going to be based on our clients, who are really the real people whom Michele Singletary talked about.

I'm going to be talking about employer-sponsored insurance and Medicare. Trish is going to be talking about Medicaid. I can talk real fast because I'm from New York.

In terms of employer-sponsored insurance, I wanted to raise three issues that are crucial for people with chronic illness and people with disabilities. They are the voluntariness of the program, the cost of the program, and the lack of recourse available to participants and beneficiaries in employer-sponsored health insurance plans.

We've heard a lot today that the health insurance system is voluntary. You can look at the numbers of people who are covered under employer-sponsored health insurance as a glass half full or a glass half empty. I think of it as a glass half empty. I think that there are a lot of people who work for employers that offer health insurance who are either not covered by their plan or who can't afford to participate in the plan.

But when we talk about voluntariness of the employer-sponsored system, it's more than the voluntary nature of offering a plan. It's the voluntary design of the plan. Some of the benefit plans are really good, as Wally Maher said this morning, and some of the plans are really awful. And I've had clients say to me I'm not going to enroll in this plan because it costs too much and I get nothing out of it. It doesn't help me for the kinds of things that I need.

The other issue with voluntariness is the ability of the employer to change the health plan whenever the employer wants to with very little input from the employee community. We as lawyers are familiar with the case, the *McGann* case and the *Owens* case in which employers decided to terminate coverage for AIDS-related illnesses after beneficiaries filed claims for AIDS-related illnesses.

Employers are also terminating retiree health plans, increasing co-payments and deductibles in retiree health plans as a result of new accounting standards. And if you look at the statistics, the number of people covered by retiree health plans has decreased in the past 10 years. That leads us to cost. We've already heard about the cost of COBRA health care continuation insurance. You need to remember that COBRA offers a special benefit for people who have been found eligible for Social Security disability, and those individuals can purchase an extension of COBRA from months 19 through 29 until they become eligible Medicare. The kicker there is that the premium is 150 percent of the cost, and that's often unaffordable for a lot of people who really need health insurance.

The other issue of cost is the increase in the cost of premiums, deductibles, and co-pay. People who used to be able to afford to purchase or buy into or be covered by their employer plans can no longer be covered by those plans because of the costs.

The third issue that I've done a lot of work on is recourse, and I'm going to give you examples. I cannot tell you the number of clients I have seen who are people with chronic illness, who had been covered under a plan, a health plan with very good benefits, who are suddenly told that they are no longer eligible for those particular benefits or covered for the services that they need. There's not been a change in the health plan. There's not been a change in their health status. There's no cap on the benefit. It's just that there is some twitch by the employer; maybe they'll claim that something that was skilled services is no longer skilled services. That's very frequent.

And the recourse of the individual is to file an appeal. While under ERISA you can take legitimately 360 days to complete the appeals process. There is no expedited review as there is under Medicare managed care or under Medicaid. So for clients who are poor, they can't afford to continue paying for the service out of pocket. Their choice is to forgo the service, to change their lifestyle; I've had individuals who could have been cared for at home and end up going to a nursing home or going on Medicaid. I've seen too many people who should be getting benefits under their employer-sponsored plan switch to Medicaid. It means the employer is off the hook, but we as taxpayers are paying for the benefit.

Medicare does better for people with disabilities. Of the 39 million Medicare beneficiaries, 5 million are younger people who are eligible because they receive Social Security disability benefits. Karen did a good job of explaining why Medicare provides such a good benefit for people with disabilities. It's a stable benefit. Once you're eligible for Medicare, you're eligible Medicare and the population that we're talking about generally does not go off Social Security disability benefits, so they don't lose their access to Medicare. But Medicare also has some problems for people with chronic conditions. The first one is the Medicare coverage package. We hear a lot about the issue of prescription drugs, and I work on that issue as well as a lot of people in this room, but another bigger issue is the lack of coverage for chronic care. There are home health benefits. There are limited long-term care benefits. They are not sufficient. There's going to be a roundtable discussion tomorrow morning. I encourage people to go hear that discussion, because it's really an important issue for people with disabilities.

The other issue is one that the Alzheimer's Association has been working on, which is that routine services that are provided under Medicare are pursuant to local medical review policies, not provided to people with certain disabilities. So the Alzheimer's Association has started to look at several of the local medical review policies and discovered that things like MRIs, routine blood work to determine whether or not you have dementia or maybe have a vitamin deficiency, or some rehabilitative therapies are not available to somebody with a diagnosis of Alzheimer's disease, or dementia, or sometimes multiple sclerosis, or Lou Gehrig's disease—to certain kinds of chronic illnesses.

The problem with the local medical review policies is that they're not made up by HCFA. There is no national review of these policies. And, in fact, if you go through the administrative process and you get to the administrative law judge, the ALJ is not bound by these policies; but they are the first barrier and very few people appeal.

Another issue that affects people with disabilities is the issue of medigap coverage. As most of you know, people who are on traditional Medicare often will buy a medigap policy to supplement their Medicare coverage. The Medicare statute guarantees that medigap policies will be issued to people who become eligible for Medicare, based on age. So if you're 65 and you become eligible for Medicare, there's a window in which you are guaranteed to be issued a medigap policy regardless of your health condition or your health status. There's no such guarantee for people with disabilities. The Department of Health and Human Services tried to get that included in the Balanced Budget Act of 1997. It was not passed. It's a very important issue for people with disabilities. The other thing that is interesting is that in a lot of states there are no medigap policies available for people with disabilities or else the policies that are available are low-rated policies.

I'm going to conclude with one anecdote. When I was in Tennessee, the State Health Insurance Counseling Program told me they'd received a phone call from a man who was on Medicare because of disability. He had previously worked in the State Insurance Office, so he was very familiar with the insurance policies. He tried to get a medigap policy. The only policy that was available to him was very costly and it was rated D. So he said, I as an insurance commissioner am not going to pay a lot of money for a policy that is a worthless policy. It's a very important issue.

### Ms. Nemore:

Last week, Vicki and I attended the Families USA Health Action 2000 conference, which, as you might expect, was a little bit different in tone from this conference, and we heard in the opening plenary the exhortations of Michael Moore, the film maker who produced "Roger and Me" and "The Big One," basically exhorting us to take to the streets with cameras in hand to document the failings of our health care system. And so it's an interesting shift for me to come to your conference and hear the presentations of researchers who I would hope are providing the research base for us to move into public policy stances that are consistent with the name of the National Academy for Social

Insurance. I feel like we haven't heard a lot about the concept of social insurance today, and I hope that that topic will continue to emerge in the remaining hours of the conference today and tomorrow.

Vicki and I are on the panel as presenting a consumer perspective on the issues of health care for people with chronic disabilities; neither Vicki nor I are consumers of Medicare or Medicaid, and I think it's really important for us all to be aware of that. We are advocates for those people, but we are not consumers of those programs. And I suspect if you had consumers of those programs presenting a perspective, they would be a lot less polite than I think this forum warrants us to be.

That said, I would like to remind us of some things about the Medicaid program and what its role is in coverage of people with chronic disabilities, people with disabilities, and generally with the more needy segments of our society.

The Medicaid program is a needs-based program, so in order to get benefits you have to have low income and resources. It is a program based on both categorical and financial eligibility. You have to fit into a category. You have to be a child who needs care or the parent of a child who needs care under the old AFDC segment, or you have to be a person in the SSI segment who is aged, blind, or disabled. Generally, most of Medicaid requires that you fit into one of those two categories, and you have to meet the financial income and resource tests.

A good thing about Medicaid is that it does focus resources on the people most in need and on people with very high medical expenses. Another good thing about Medicaid is that it has a core package of services that are required to be provided by all states. There is also in Medicaid a whole range of services that are not required to be provided by states, that are optional, and I'll get a little bit more into that in a minute. That can be a serious problem for people. It's one of the less salient features of the program in terms of meeting people's whole needs.

It's an entitlement program. If you fit into the categories and you fit the financial eligibility, you are entitled to Medicaid. That makes it different from CHIP; the new CHIP program for children is not an entitlement, and that makes a big difference. There are issues about how we expand public coverage and which direction to go.

A really important aspect of Medicaid that we often hear compared with the private health insurance sector is due process rights under

Medicaid.  The review system in Medicaid is really very good.  It doesn't always work as well as it's supposed to, but what's on paper is a constitutional guarantee of due process, due to the *Goldberg v. Kelly* case from 1969 that says people in brutal need have a constitutional right to due process. and there is a fair hearing process and review process that's really better than what we who have private sector insurance have, and it's really better than Medicare.  So that's a very good aspect of it.  And there is a huge body of case law that fleshes out what people's rights are in Medicaid, which has some very, very strong positive elements of what it means to be entitled to a core package of services.

What does Medicaid do for people with disabilities?  The easiest route in is receipt of SSI disability.  Generally, until our recent move into trying to help people back into the labor force, that meant that you were not working.  So in order to get the SSI coverage, you were a disabled person who was unable to work.

The one category of Medicaid coverage that is an exceptionto the "unable to work" norm is called the qualified severely impaired individual category.  This is for people who were on SSI, were not working, have gone back into the workforce, and but for their earnings they would still be entitled to SSI.  So it allows you to disregard all your earnings and still get Medicaid coverage.  That's required for the states to include in their program.

One of the things that is important to remember about Medicaid is that there are a lot of categories, and that's a significant drawback to the policy.  That is something that makes Medicare as a public program far more attractive.  You get Medicare because you're 65 or you get Medicare because you're disabled, period.  You don't have to fit into one of 27 different categories.

There are a couple of required Medicaid categories of SSI-related people who might be disabled people who are entitled to Medicare.  There are also 16 options that states can choose, and that's where some of the new work incentives pieces from the last couple of years, have come in.  There is a buy-in: states can choose to have a buy-in program for people with incomes up to 250 percent of poverty.  They can choose, out of the work incentive package that was passed in this past session of the Congress, to cover people between the ages of 16 and 65, and the state can set the income and resource levels.  That's a very significant change from normal Medicaid, because even if you fit into the working disabled category where your earnings are disregarded, SSI has resource limitations which are very, very strict, and a lot of people can't meet those. So under this new option, states can expand, eliminate, do what they want with respect to resources. There is another category for states to choose to cover people who have gone back into the workforce and are actually found no longer disabled, but who still have a severe medical condition, and the state can choose to cover those people as well without the income and resource limits.

Again, the problems are that these are state options. States have to choose them in order for them to be of any value to people.

The Medicaid program requires states to cover a core package of services, which includes in-patient, out-patient, lab, x-ray, doctors' visits, and a couple of other important things that aren't necessarily particularly relevant for people with disabilities. The things that are most necessary probably for a lot of people with disabilities are all state options: drugs, prosthetic devices, durable medical equipment, physical therapy, other kinds of rehab, private duty nursing, and personal care.

All states provide drug coverage. Most states provide most of those other services and supplies, but they are state options. A state can choose to pull out of those services without any legal ramifications. It can obviously have serious political ramifications and obviously do terrible harm to people who need the services, but they can opt out of providing those.

There are a number of people with disabilities who get coverage under both Medicare and Medicaid, and they don't intersect necessarily very well. Medicaid actually has better home health provisions, which can be very important and beneficial to people with disabilities.

One of the pieces of the work incentives legislation that was passed this past year was to provide grants for the states to develop an infrastructure to help people going back to work who are disabled. One of the requirements for a state to get that grant is that it makes personal care services available to people in the workforce. This is a tremendously important benefit and could be very valuable to people.

That is a brief overview of what Medicaid offers. Medicaid is so complex, and the access to the program—through the process of applying and showing how much income you have and how many resources you have and providing all that verification—is an enormous barrier to people. We've heard over and over again, "I don't want the government messing in my business." "I don't want to have to show that." That's a huge difference between Medicare and Medicaid. To get Medicare, you just show you're disabled or over 65, and you're entitled to Medicare based on your earnings. And that is one of the most serious drawbacks of the Medicaid program.

Chronic Illness and Disability:

# Commentary

Barbara Wolfe
*University of Wisconsin–Madison*

(US/

These papers address the topic of chronic illness, disability, and related policy issues for an aging workforce. Biddle, Boden, and Reville ask about the adequacy of workers' compensation benefits for those with long-term or permanent disabilities; Burkhauser, Daly, and Houtenville ask how well the disabled have fared in terms of work and income over the last business cycle; Gottlich and Nemore provide a primer on obtaining health care insurance coverage.

What might we like to know about the circumstances that led to these papers? Here are a few pertinent questions.

1) How well do our insurance/protection systems perform for older workers who develop chronic illness or suffer an accident that leads to a disability with long-term consequences? Can we learn something from alternative approaches among the states that can guide us in better designing workers' compensation? How well do our other programs that provide benefits to the long-term disabled perform as a safety net?

2) Overall, how well are the disabled doing, and how has this changed in the last decade? Are the disabled gaining in this booming labor market? How are they doing in terms of earnings? Are they doing as well as other groups; if so, which groups? How hard were they hit in the last recession and what might this suggest for the future when macroeconomic conditions change? How well do transfers do in maintaining the income of persons with disabilities and the families in which they live?

3) Do persons with disabilities have access to comprehensive health insurance? If working, what are their rights to employer-provided coverage? To individual insurance? What role does the public sector play in terms of direct provision, helping gain private coverage? If persons with disabilities were to regain or

363

improve health, what is their access to coverage? Does the "system" inhibit the return to work of disabled individuals? What are the recent changes designed to minimize this negative incentive to return to work?

4) And, finally, we would like to derive a sense of how well the disabled are doing overall—in earnings, income, total compensation, and health insurance coverage. How are they faring compared with how they would have been expected to fare if not disabled? How well are they faring in terms of avoiding poverty?

Addressing these issues is clearly a tall order; however, I am going to use this framework to think about these papers. I discuss them in the order they were presented.

## BIDDLE, BODEN, AND REVILLE

The first paper, by Biddle, Boden, and Reville, analyzes the experience of three states with regard to the replacement of earnings by workers' compensation. It is an interesting presentation of those policies, including the schedule in each of the three states and the philosophy underlying these approaches. Learning about replacement of lost earnings is more difficult in the case of workers' compensation, because there are continuing earnings in most cases, in contrast with the traditional income replacement programs such as Social Security (SSDI). The calculation when individuals have earnings is much more complicated than when they do not.

The authors calculate a unique replacement rate: replacement of earnings that the individual would have expected to receive if not injured. This way of asking the question poses a technical or econometric difficulty: how to know the correct counterfactual, or what the person would have earned if not injured. The authors use different approaches in each state; the biggest difference is between California and the other two states. (It would be preferable if the authors could use a similar approach, but it is not clear whether this is possible given data constraints.)

### The Comparison Groups for the Counterfactual Are Troublesome

Why use individuals who had "some accident"? Is this the appropriate counterfactual? Why use individuals in the same firm, since this leads to very small sample sizes and many firms have very heterogeneous workers? What do they do with individuals who work in smaller firms where there are few similar employees? I'd prefer to see the authors use employees of the same occupation, age, gender, and industry to develop the counterfactuals. This should be feasible among states.

### Methodology

Using fixed effects may overcorrect for factors that directly influence earnings. They want to correct for unobserved factors such as motivation, drive, etc., but they also correct for young children at home (which changes over time) and for on-the-job training, which also changes over time.

### Discount Rate

The rate they use, 2.3 percent, is rather low; they should test for sensitivity.

### Results

Perhaps most interesting is the relative success of a two-tiered system, such as that of Wisconsin, where payments are better targeted on those with the greatest need. Thus, the comparison using quintiles provides insight on the relative success of these alternative workers' compensation programs. This is a system that uses a functional impairment benefit along with an earnings capacity benefit, and the advantage of this, at least as indicated by the results, appears to be that they can target payments to individuals who do not return to work or are rehired at a much lower proportion of their former wage.

The comparison among states also suggests that there is a trade-off between the percentage of awards that provide cash for permanent disability and the replacement rate (which is not surprising). Unfortunately, since the statistical match and dates differ somewhat among states, the paper cannot fully eliminate the role of state differences in comparing the states.

## BURKHAUSER, DALY, AND HOUTENVILLE

I turn next to the paper by Burkhauser, Daly, and Houtenville, who address an interesting question: how well have disabled persons and their families fared in this labor market during an economic boom? They cover two aspects: how persons with disabilities fare in the labor market, and the probability of application to, and the resulting leniency and generosity of, transfers to persons with disabilities.

During a labor market expansion, especially a sustained one, we would expect a decline in unemployment among all groups, including those with disabilities. We expect opportunities to substantially increase for most persons and, given a sustained increase, to improve for those with the poorest labor market opportunities, including the disabled.

We also expect that with welfare reform (TANF) there will be some increase (shift over) of claims for SSDI and SSI. A recent Lewin report (1999) tracks some of this, and we know that there has been a considerable expansion of the earned income tax credit (EITC), designed to make work pay for lower-income workers with children. We don't know a great deal about health coverage of this population, although we do know that insurance coverage is down for adults, especially those with health difficulties (and there may be associated incentives concerning working).

### Approach

The authors use annual CPS data. The key identification issue is who is disabled, which they base on a general question on disability: whether the respondent is limited in ability to work or kind and amount of work. This is a very general question, as the authors recognize. The years covered in the analysis are 1988–1999. This is undoubtedly the best data source, but the disability measure is limited, and there are significant underreporting issues, especially of income from transfers that have increased over time.[1]

The authors first examine the pattern of disability, finding an increase through 1994 and then a decline, as we would expect. One can see in particular a decline in the number of young people with reported disabilities, such that mean age is up over the period. In addition, there appear to be more females with disabilities; and in terms of education, high school graduates show the biggest increase. Overall, the pattern of demographic changes might lead one to expect a decline in earnings and earnings-related transfers. (On average, females earn 75 percent on the dollar.) This would be the case without a change in the macroeconomy, simply focusing on demographic characteristics.

## Minor Issues

Why use a 0.5 equivalence scale? There is at least some increasing agreement that it is preferable to use two- and three-parameter scales for the poverty measure, as they better incorporate economies of scale. I would like to see a sensitivity test using alternative scales.

Studies of income distribution are heavily affected by the different procedures that researchers choose to measure inequality. A major issue is to assess the direction and the extent of the change in inequality when different adjustments for household size and composition are allowed. For example, Coulter, Cowell, and Jenkins (1992) found that when the value of $e$ was increased from zero to 1, inequality first decreases and then increases, forming a U-shape. They explained the theoretical relationship between equivalence scales and inequality: the well-being ($W_i$) of an individual is a function of four different variables: total household income ($H$), household size ($S$), elasticity of scale ($\varepsilon$), and household characteristics ($\eta$):

$$W_i = Y(H_i, S_i, \varepsilon, \eta).$$

An example of a two-parameter scale is that for OECD:

$$W = \frac{H}{1 + 0.7(A-1) + 0.5C}$$

where $A$ are adults and $C$ are children. So, there is an issue with regard to the relatively arbitrary value of an equivalence scale utilized.

There is an issue regarding the sample as well: Why call someone with 1 hour of work per week a member of the labor force? What would happen if they looked only at those who work a minimum of 20 hours per week for at least half of a year? The authors might perform a sensitivity analysis to see how sensitive the results are to this broad definition.

Bigger concerns include the EITC, other noncash forms of compensation, and a change in underreporting. The EITC was greatly expanded over this time period, which is most important for those with low earnings and with children. While it is not clear how important this issue is to this population, it seems clear that omitting the EITC leads to an understatement of income. There is systematic underreporting, but it is not consistent across types of income. Most recently there has been a big shift concerning transfers: a large decline in reporting relative to administrative totals, so underreporting is likely to add to the decline in reported (but not in actual) income. This problem has grown worse in recent years. For example, Douglas Besharov (1999) has stated that

> assertions about declines in Medicaid coverage are often based on analyses of the Census Bureau's Current Population Survey (CPS), the government's primary data source for measuring employment, earnings, poverty, welfare receipt, and a range of other important outcomes. Unfortunately, the survey appears to miss about one-third of AFDC/TANF, food stamp, and Medicaid recipients. Perhaps even more important, this problem has been getting worse in recent years, a deterioration that has important implications for judging the impact of welfare reform.

According to the CPS, between 1993 and 1997 the number of children under 15 enrolled in Medicaid declined by 3.2 million. But reliable administrative data from the Health Care Financing Administration (HCFA) show an increase of 400,000. For the period 1995–1997, HCFA data also show a decline of 700,000 children, but the CPS shows a much larger decline of 1.7 million. These kinds of discrepancies document the importance of underreporting.

Another issue concerns the measurement of income. Is the measure reported the one that the analysts should be interested in, or is it a fuller measure of disposable income and close substitutes? If the latter, then there are two questions: 1) whether and how to value noncash income, such as health insurance and, for those of low income, food stamps; and 2) how to measure disposable income rather than gross income (subtract taxes).

Noncash income to U.S. families has grown substantially in the past 25 years. In the 1980s, over half of government transfer spending for the poor was in the form of noncash benefits, according to the U.S. Bureau of the Census. This growth of benefits to the poor has been paralleled by a growth of nonwage compensation to wage earners, induced in part by tax laws exempting such compensation from income and payroll taxes. By 1990, employer costs for nonwage compensation had grown to over one-quarter (27.6 percent) of total compensation costs, up from 19.4 percent in 1966. By excluding this form of income and its distribution, the story is incomplete.

To conclude, it may well be true that persons with disabilities have not done as well, and this clearly seems to be the case for earnings. The authors might improve this study if they included an imputed value for EITC; conducted a Oaxaca decomposition to see how much is change in characteristics (more women, older); tested for sensitivity to equivalence scale used; and adjusted for underreporting following Census Bureau methodology. Finally, there is a puzzle regarding applications for benefits. A recent Lewin study (1999) found a sharp decline in SSI applications after 1993. While these are not strictly comparable, the big difference is surprising.

The pattern that the authors find, however—the largest declines in employment in middle-income groups, far bigger increases in dollars of SSDI awarded to women, and lower income among women and men in the middle-income group compared to 1989 levels—seems unexpected and surely worthy of further exploration to try to understand why these individuals and their families are not doing as well as we might anticipate.

## GOTTLICH AND NEMORE

The final paper, by Gottlich and Nemore, is a useful guide for any-one interested in learning how to obtain benefits under three different sets of programs (private, Medicaid, or Medicare), taken one at a time. This is very useful to someone who wants to know the options for coverage. For researchers and policymakers, it might be more useful to draw them together to obtain a picture of the probability that older persons with disabilities could obtain private, social security, or public health insurance (Medicaid or Medicare) coverage. And, the authors could usefully add a discussion of the issue of returning to work; that is, if a person has coverage through one system, such as Medicare, and wishes to return to the work force, what are the options and probabilities of private coverage? Finally, it would be very helpful to have some sense of adequacy of coverage; that is, are these folks at high risk of lacking coverage? Of lacking coverage for some required care? Are high deductibles or high required co-pays an issue that needs to be considered? If these are policy problems, it would be a welcome addition if the authors would make suggestions for obtaining and improving coverage.

Other questions could be asked. Is ERISA a problem in terms of persons with disabilities obtaining coverage, or does it help? Are there antidiscrimination laws that might aid this population under ERISA? Is an individual with a specific medical condition who is returning to work more likely to be covered with a firm under ERISA or under state law? (And does the answer differ by state?) Are there likely to be labor market consequences if there is increased regulation on the provision of coverage? There is an issue that links this paper to the others, and here I quote from Daniel Weinberg (1995):

> Of key concern to understanding well-being is the valuation of medical benefits, both the government health programs—Medicare (medical aid to the elderly) and Medicaid (medical aid to the poor)—and employer-provided health insurance. The valuation of medical benefits is particularly difficult, because coverage of high medical expenses for someone who is sick does nothing to improve his or her poverty status (although the benefits clearly make him or her better off). Even if one imputes the value of an equivalent insurance policy to program participants, these benefits

(high in market value due to large medical costs for the fraction who do get sick) cannot be used by the recipients to meet other needs of daily living. However, not having coverage clearly detracts from economic well-being and possibly health itself.

The bottom line of this message is that we need to incorporate the value of coverage (or lack of it) in order to get a more comprehensive view of the well-being of persons with disabilities over time, across characteristics, and in comparison with persons who are not disabled.

## OVERVIEW ISSUES

Is the best way to learn about the success of a program to address the replacement rate? I would like to see more on dollar value of benefits. I would like to have the authors address the role of workers' compensation in reducing or eliminating poverty, an income concept like net income of individual and family. What is presented is earnings loss and replacement of lost earnings, a valid measure of economic well-being, nonetheless.

As in the Burkhauser paper, I would like a full measure of income, including EITC, taxes, and other disability-related transfer programs benefits such as SSDI and SSI, to see what has happened to income and to poverty rates over this time period. How are those worst off among the disabled who receive workers' compensation faring?

To conclude my comments, these three studies bring readers a sense of the economic well-being and access to health care of persons with disabilities. At some level the papers all critique the others: earnings and income as defined in the Burkhauser study does not include the value or even the presence of health insurance, which is clearly very important for this population. Workers' compensation is only one part of income. We would like to know more about its role and interaction with other transfers and with earnings. The studies are also linked in trying to answer an additional question: "Does the potential for high medical expenditures influence future earnings opportunities?"

Ultimately these studies are purely descriptive. They do not ask whether a change in one program, such as health care coverage, would influence such choices as whether or not to work and number of hours, nor whether better labor market opportunities change the generosity of workers' compensation. The studies all add to our knowledge of the situation of persons with disabilities with regard to income and access to health care coverage, but our picture is still incomplete. In the future, we would like to add to the picture painted by Burkhauser, Daly, and Houtenville the presence and value of health care coverage and workers' compensation benefits (though they may be included), to adjust for underreporting of various sources of income, and take account how these change with the state of the economy, with the workers' compensation policy of the state, and state and ERISA laws regarding health insurance coverage.

## Note

1. According to the Census Bureau, ". . . for many different reasons, there is a tendency in household surveys for respondents to underreport their income. From an analysis of independently derived income estimates, it has been determined that income earned from wages or salaries is much better reported than other sources of income and is nearly equal to independent estimates of aggregate earnings" (Coder and Scoon-Rogers 1996).

## References

Besharov, Douglas J. 1999. Testimony before the Subcommittee on Human Resources, House Committee on Ways and Means, Hearing on the Effects of Welfare Reform, May 27.

Coder, John, and Lydia Scoon-Rogers. 1996. "Evaluating the Quality of Income Data Collected in the Annual Supplement to the March Current Population Survey and the Survey of Income and Program Participation." Working paper, U.S. Bureau of the Census, July.

Coulter, F.A.E., F.A. Cowell, and S.P. Jenkins. 1992. "Equivalence Scale Relativities and the Extent of Inequality and Poverty." *The Economic Journal* 102: 1067–1082.

Lewin Group, Inc. 1999. *Policy Evaluation of the Overall Effects of Welfare Reform on SSA Programs.* Washington, D.C.: Lewin Group, April 23.

Weinberg, Daniel H. 1995. *Measuring Poverty: Issues and Approaches.* U.S. Bureau of the Census, Washington, D.C., December 14.

# Session 4
# Is Working Longer and
# Retiring Later Possible?
# Is it Desirable?

# Retirement Trends and Policies to Encourage Work among Older Americans

Gary Burtless
*The Brookings Institution*

Joseph F. Quinn
*Boston College*

The United States and other industrial nations face key challenges associated with a graying population. Depressed birth rates and rising longevity have increased the dependency ratio throughout the industrialized world. Population projections of the Social Security Trustees suggest the U.S. aged-dependency ratio—the ratio of Americans older than 64 to Americans aged 20 to 64—will increase almost 70 percent between 2000 and 2030. The increase will be even larger in some other rich countries. As the U.S. population grows older, the cost of paying for pension and health benefits must rise, boosting tax burdens and impairing the nation's ability to pay for other government obligations. The burden imposed by an aging population would rise more gradually if workers could be persuaded to delay their retirements and continue contributing to the health and pension systems.

In this chapter, we consider long-term trends in retirement, as well as recent trends that signal at least a pause in the historical pattern of earlier withdrawal from the workforce. We also discuss public policies that might reinforce the very recent trend toward greater labor force participation among older workers.

## RETIREMENT TRENDS

At the beginning of the last century, retirement was relatively uncommon but not unknown. Two out of three American men past age 65 were employed, but one-third were not (U.S. Department of Commerce 1975, p. 132).[1] By middle of the twentieth century, retirement

375

was far more common. Fewer than half of men 65 and older held a job in 1950. By 1985, the proportion at work fell still further. Just 16 percent of men over 65 were employed or actively seeking a job; 84 percent were outside the active labor force. The percentage of women past 65 who were employed or looking for work also shrank during the first four decades after World War II, though this was mainly because the average age of women past 65 was rising. The reduction in women's employment was far smaller than among men in part because the percentage of older women who worked outside the home was quite low in the 1940s.

The decline in labor force participation at older ages has not been confined to the United States. It is characteristic of all rich industrialized countries. In most European countries, employment rates among the elderly are now significantly below those in the United States (Quinn and Burkhauser 1994). Along with a shrinking work week and rising paid employment among married women, earlier retirement among men has been a distinctive feature of economic progress in all the developed countries.

### Trends in the United States

The pattern of declining work among older men is clearly evident in Figure 1. Each line in the figure traces the labor force participation rate of older American men, by age, in a different year of the past century.[2] (A person is considered to be a labor force participant if he or she holds a job or is actively seeking work.) The top line shows age-specific participation rates of older men in 1910. Note that there is a clear pattern of labor market withdrawal with advancing age. Even at age 72, however, the male participation rate in 1910 was over 50 percent. Participation rates in 1940, 1970, 1984–1985, and 1998–1999 are displayed in the lower four lines. Each of these lines shows a characteristic pattern of labor market withdrawal as men grow older. The crucial difference between 1910 and later years is that the fall-off in labor force participation begins at an earlier age and proceeds at a faster pace.

The decline in male participation was neither smooth nor uniform over the century. By far the largest proportionate declines in participa-

**Figure 1  Labor Force Participation of Men at Specific Ages, 1910–1999**

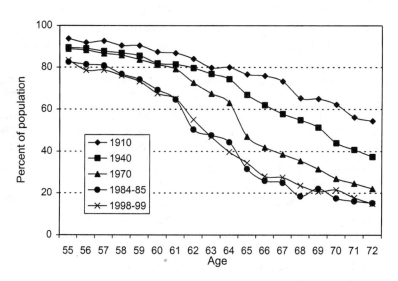

SOURCE: Ransom, Sutch, and Williamson (1991); Munnell (1977); and authors' tabulations of March Current Population Survey files for 1984–85 and 1998–99

tion occurred among men past the age of 65. In 1998–1999, for example, the participation rate among 72-year-olds was only one-quarter of the equivalent rate in 1910. The fall-off in participation was smaller at younger ages. In general, large declines in participation occurred in the early and middle parts of the century for the oldest age groups; major declines occurred after 1960 among younger men. The largest percentage declines among men older than 70 occurred between 1910 and 1940. The fastest declines among 65- to 69-year-olds took place between 1940 and 1970. The biggest declines among men under 65 did not occur until after 1960, after the earliest age of eligibility for Social Security benefits was reduced to 62. A striking feature of Figure 1 is that there has been no decline in older men's participation rates since the mid 1980s. After a long period of decline, the participation rates of older men stabilized or even increased slightly after 1985.

The story for older American women is different. Older women's participation rates in the post–World War II era have reflected two partially offsetting phenomena: the early retirement trend of older workers in general and the increasing labor force participation of married women. As a result of the latter, the participation rates of older women did not exhibit the dramatic postwar declines seen among men. Instead, as shown in lower panel of Table 1, age-specific labor force participation rates generally increased among women. Between 1950 and 1998–1999, the female participation rate rose 39 percentage points at age 55, 26 points at age 60, 8 points at age 65, and 7 points at age 70.

What is similar to the male experience is the shift in trends after 1985. As with men, there is a noticeable break from the earlier trend in older women's labor force participation. Between 1970 and 1985, older women's labor force participation rate barely increased at all, and it even declined among people past age 62. In contrast, female participation rates surged in the 15 years after 1985. Figure 2 shows the annual percentage-point change in participation at selected ages in the

**Table 1  Labor Force Participation Rates at Selected Ages by Sex, 1940–1999 (% of population)**

| Year | Age 55 | 60 | 62 | 65 | 70 |
|------|--------|----|----|----|----|
| Men |  |  |  |  |  |
| 1940 | 90 | 82 | 80 | 67 | 44 |
| 1950 | 88 | 82 | 80 | 68 | 45 |
| 1960 | 90 | 83 | 79 | 54 | 33 |
| 1970 | 89 | 81 | 73 | 47 | 27 |
| 1984–85 | 83 | 69 | 50 | 32 | 17 |
| 1998–99 | 83 | 68 | 55 | 34 | 21 |
| Women |  |  |  |  |  |
| 1940 | 20 | 17 | 15 | 12 | 6 |
| 1950 | 28 | 23 | 21 | 16 | 8 |
| 1960 | 43 | 35 | 29 | 20 | 12 |
| 1970 | 50 | 43 | 36 | 22 | 11 |
| 1984–85 | 52 | 44 | 32 | 17 | 10 |
| 1998–99 | 67 | 49 | 43 | 24 | 15 |

SOURCE: Munnell (1977), p. 70, and authors' tabulations of March Current Population Survey files for 1984, 1985, 1988, and 1999.

**Figure 2 Annual Change in Labor Force Participation Rate at Selected Ages, 1970–1985 and 1985–1999**

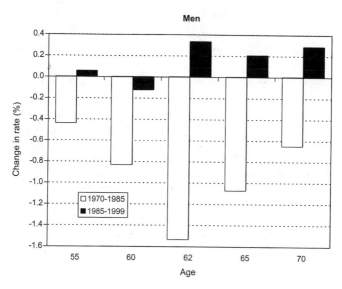

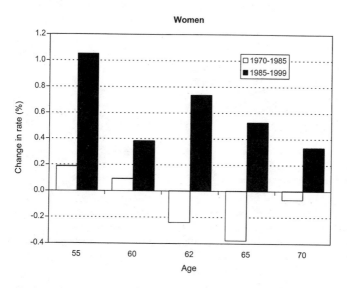

SOURCE: Authors' tabulations based on Munnell (1977), p. 70, and March Current Population Survey files for 1984, 1985, 1998, and 1999.

two different periods. The top panel shows trends in the participation rate of older men, and the lower panel shows trends at the same five ages for women. At age 62, the male participation rate fell 1.5 percentage points a year from 1970 to 1985. The rate among 62-year-old women declined 0.2 points a year over the same period. Between 1985 and 1999, the male participation rate at age 62 rose 0.3 percentage points per year; the female rate increased 0.7 points per year. At each age, the rate of increase in participation rates accelerated, the rate of decline in participation rates shrank, or a decline in participation rates was reversed. The similarity of the break points in the male and female time series is striking (Quinn 1999b). Women's participation rates at older ages have risen strongly over the past 15 years, while among older men, the long-term decline in participation rates has ended and may even have reversed.

Historical information about participation rates can be used to trace out the long-term trend in retirement. Figure 3 shows the trend in the "average" male retirement age if we define that age as the youngest

**Figure 3  Average Retirement Age of American Men, 1910–1999**

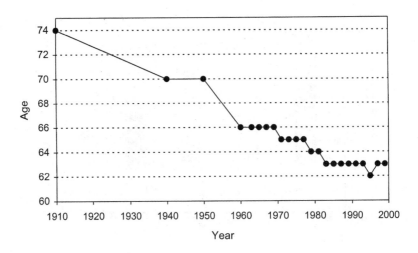

SOURCE: Authors' tabulations of data in Ransom, Sutch, and Williamson (1991) and Munnell (1977) and in March Current Population Survey files for 1963–1999.

age at which fewer than half the men in the age group remain in the workforce. Under this definition, the average male retirement age fell from 74 years in 1910 to 63 years in 1998–1999, a drop of about 1.2 years per decade. The tabulations in Figure 3 also indicate, however, that the trend toward earlier male retirement has recently slowed and may even have ceased.

The decline in the average retirement age has occurred in an environment of rising life expectancy among older Americans, especially in the period since 1940. Falling mortality rates among the elderly added almost four years to the expected life span of a 65-year-old man and more than 5.5 years to the life expectancy of a 65-year-old woman after 1940. Since expected male life spans increased about 0.8 years per decade during a period in which the retirement age dropped 1.2 years per decade, the amount of the male life span devoted to retirement climbed about 2 years per decade, adding almost 12 years to the amount of time men spend in retirement. Retirement now represents a substantial fraction of a typical worker's life. For many workers, retirement will last longer than the period from birth until full-time entry into the job market.

## Trends in Other Rich Countries

The long-term trend toward earlier retirement in the United States has been matched—and usually surpassed—by equivalent trends in other rich countries. In a recent survey of the determinants of retirement in rich countries, OECD economists produced estimates of the average retirement age in 24 high-income nations (Blöndal and Scarpetta 1998). They estimated the average age at which men and women withdrew from the active workforce for selected years between 1950 and 1995. Their estimates show that the average retirement age has declined in nearly all of the countries since 1950. In 1950, the average retirement age for men was 65 or higher in almost all the 24 countries. By 1995, the male retirement age had fallen everywhere except Iceland. In most countries, the drop in the average retirement age was at least three years. In a quarter of the countries, an average male now leaves the workforce before attaining age 60. The drop in the average retirement age of women has been even faster.

As one of the richest OECD countries, the United States might be expected to have one of the lowest retirement ages. Instead, it has one of the highest. In 1950, its average retirement age placed the United States in the middle of the 24 countries surveyed by the OECD. By 1995, it had one of the oldest retirement ages. Only four out of the 24 countries had a higher male retirement age (Iceland, Japan, Norway, and Switzerland) and only five had a higher female retirement age (Iceland, Japan, Norway, Sweden, and Turkey). Figure 4 shows the 1960–1995 trend in average retirement ages in the seven largest OECD economies, separately for men and women. In all seven countries, women retire at a younger age than men. (The male/female gap in retirement ages averaged 2.5 years in 1995.) In all seven countries, the average retirement age of both men and women has fallen over time; but, the decline has been smaller in the United States, and especially in Japan, than in the other five countries.

Some of the recent divergence in retirement trends is due to differences in the state of the overall job market. The United States and Japan maintained much lower unemployment rates than the other five countries through most of the 1990s. The tighter labor markets in those two countries probably encouraged older workers to remain employed longer than they would have if the unemployment rate approached European levels. It is also likely, however, that cross-country differences in old-age and disability pensions, unemployment benefits, and health insurance coverage played important roles in keeping older American and Japanese workers in the labor force (Gruber and Wise 1999).

The retirement-age trends displayed in Figure 4 obviously have different implications for a nation depending on whether its working-age population is growing or shrinking. The extra burden implied by an earlier retirement age is easier to bear if the working-age population is expanding rapidly, either as a result of natural population increase or immigration. In this respect, Canada and the United States enjoy a significant advantage over the other five countries. High immigration and moderate fertility rates ensure substantial labor force growth in North America over the next few decades, even if U.S. and Canadian retirement ages should continue to fall. Germany, Italy, and Japan face much less favorable prospects; fertility in all three countries is extremely low, and immigration into Japan is negligible. The three

**Figure 4  Estimates of the Average Age of Transition out of Active
Workforce in the G-7 Countries, 1960–1995**

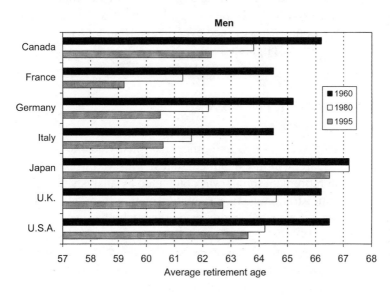

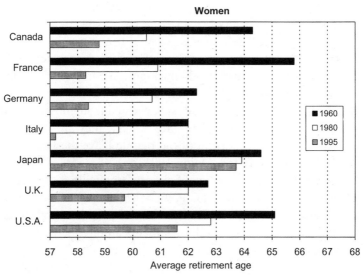

SOURCE: Blöndal and Scarpetta (1998).

countries face a future in which their active working populations will decline, even if the average retirement age remains unchanged (Bosworth and Burtless 1998). If the average age at retirement continues to decline, these countries will face even heavier burdens in supporting their growing elderly populations.

## EXPLAINING THE TRENDS

Research by economists and others has shed valuable light on the evolution of retirement in the United States. Most of the early research on American retirement trends was conducted by analysts in the Social Security Administration using survey information from retired workers receiving Social Security benefits or workers who had recently retired (Quinn et al. 1990, pp. 43–53; Quinn 1991, pp. 119–123). In the earliest surveys of new retirees, an overwhelming majority of male respondents said they retired because they were laid off by their last employer or were in such poor health that further work was unappealing or impossible. In the 1940s and early 1950s, fewer than 5 percent of new retirees reported leaving work because of a wish to retire or enjoy more leisure; about 90 percent left because of poor health or a layoff. These explanations for retirement dominated survey responses and the research literature from the 1940s through the early 1970s. Only a very small percentage of retired men reported leaving work because they wanted to retire. An early analyst suggested that "most old people work as long as they can and retire only because they are forced to do so . . . [O]nly a small proportion of old people leave the labor market for good unless they have to" (Quinn 1991, p. 120).

In recent surveys of new Social Security beneficiaries, a larger percentage of pensioners reports leaving work because of a desire to enjoy additional leisure or to retire. By the early 1980s, the desire to leave work explained nearly half of all retirements among men 65 or older, while poor health accounted for only a little over 20 percent and involuntary layoff about 15 percent of retirements. The proportion of workers who say they have retired for purely voluntary reasons is plainly on the increase.

Many people will accept these responses at face value, but there are reasons to be skeptical of the story they tell. From 1940 through the early 1970s, well over a third of respondents explained their entry into retirement as the result of involuntary job loss. While this explanation might seem plausible, labor economists recognize that millions of workers lose their jobs each year without choosing to retire. The overwhelming majority of workers who state that job loss was the reason for their retirement lost several jobs earlier in their careers, but on no previous occasion did their layoffs cause them to permanently exit the labor force. When forced into unemployment at younger ages, these same workers looked for another job and eventually found one. It is natural to ask why job loss pushed them into retirement on this one occasion but not on the others.

Even the explanation of "poor health" should be treated with caution. Social Security beneficiaries may account for their retirement with the explanation that bad health left them no alternative, but it seems reasonable to ask whether their decision to retire would have been different if Social Security or other pensions were unavailable. In the early postwar era, some retirees may have explained their employment status in terms of job loss or bad health because the desire for more leisure was not yet considered an acceptable reason to be without a job. As retirement has come to be considered a normal and even desirable part of life, workers may feel less reason to describe their joblessness as involuntary.

## Wealth, Health, and the Physical Demands of Work

However we interpret the survey responses of people who collect pensions, it should be plain the long-term trend toward earlier male retirement has had an important voluntary component. The trend in survey responses suggests this is true, and a growing body of research evidence also supports the conclusion. The simplest and probably most powerful explanation for earlier retirement is rising wealth. The United States and other industrialized countries have grown richer over time. Real per capita GDP in the United States has more than doubled since 1960, increasing about 2 percent a year. Some of this increased wealth has been used to purchase more leisure. Americans stay in school longer than they once did, enter the workforce later, work fewer hours per year, and leave the labor force earlier.

For many of today's retired workers, the increases in wealth flowing from greater national prosperity have been augmented by windfall gains from two sources: higher prices for the houses they own and generous benefits from Social Security and Medicare. Because the Social Security system has historically been very generous, most generations retiring up to the present have received larger pensions than their contributions alone could have paid for if the contributions had been invested in safe assets. Workers who retired under Social Security before the mid 1980s received pensions well in excess of the benefits they would have received if Social Security offered normal returns on their contributions (Leimer 1994; Geanakopolos, Mitchell, and Zeldes 1998). Retired Americans continue to receive Medicare benefits that are vastly larger than those that could be financed solely out of their contributions and the interest earnings on those contributions. This fact is well known to students of social insurance, who recognize that most early contributors to a pay-as-you-go retirement system obtain exceptional returns on their contributions. The exceptional returns on Social Security and Medicare taxes, like those on owner-occupied homes, have increased the amount of consumption that older Americans can afford. One way workers have used these windfall gains is to retire at a younger age.

While some researchers have attributed most of the postwar decline in male labor force participation to the introduction and liberalization of Social Security, most specialists think the impact on retirement has been considerably smaller. Because of the long-term rise in productivity, workers are much wealthier today than they were at the beginning of the twentieth century. This would have led workers to retire earlier than previous generations, even in the absence of Social Security and Medicare. Social Security, Medicare, and employer-sponsored retirement plans were established and expanded in part to help workers achieve the goal of living comfortably without work in old age. If these programs had not be developed, it is likely that workers and employers would have found other ways to achieve the same goal.

Of all the explanations advanced for earlier retirement, two of the least persuasive are declining health and the changing physical requirements of work. While nearly all good retirement studies find that health plays an important role in the timing of retirement, there is no convincing evidence that the health of 60-year-olds or 65-year-olds was declining over the period in which older Americans' labor force participation rates were falling. Declining mortality rates as well as recent evidence about the trend in the physical disabilities of the aged suggest instead that the health of Americans is improving, at least in early old age. Moreover, analyses of the growth of different kinds of occupations and in their physical requirements imply that the physical demands of work are now easier to meet than they were in the past. A much smaller proportion of jobs requires strenuous physical effort; and a larger percentage requires only moderate or light physical exertion (Manton and Stollard 1994; Baily 1987). Of course, within every generation there will be workers who are in poor health and who work in physically demanding jobs. These workers will be among the first to retire. But it seems unlikely that general health deterioration or widespread increases in the physical demands of employment can explain the general tendency for recent generations to retire earlier than workers in the past.

**Financial Incentives**

Besides increasing most current retirees' lifetime wealth, the Social Security system also affects the financial attractiveness of remaining at work. Most workers can choose to collect Social Security starting at age 62, and many do. The effect of Social Security on retirement behavior before age 62 depends on the Social Security tax and on the benefit formula that links eventual monthly pensions to a worker's past covered earnings. Employers and workers pay a combined tax equal to 12.4 percent of wages into the system. The tax thus reduces workers' wages by about 12 percent in comparison with the wages they would earn if the program did not exist. On the other hand, contributions allow a worker to earn credits toward a Social Security pension. The pension entitlement goes up as the worker's covered lifetime wages increase. Whether the increase in the pension entitlement is large enough to compensate a worker for his extra contributions is an empirical question. Low-wage workers typically receive favorable treatment under the Social Security benefit formula, so they often receive a generous return on their extra contributions. High-wage workers usually receive lower returns. For any worker who is less than 62 years old, Social Security affects the marginal return from working by reducing net current pay by about 12 percent and increasing the present value of future Social Security pensions. Whether this increases or reduces the willingness of a worker to continue working depends on the exact amount of the future pension increase (which depends on the worker's expected longevity) and on the worker's feelings about the relative value of current versus future income and the attractiveness of immediate retirement.

Starting at age 62, Social Security has a different kind of effect on the retirement decision. When a worker delays receipt of retirement benefits by working another year after the earliest age of eligibility, two things happen, one good and one bad. The bad news is that the worker passes up the chance to collect a Social Security check. The good news is that future retirement benefits will be higher because average lifetime earnings are recalculated and because the monthly pension check is increased for every month of delay in asking for benefits. If a worker is entitled to a $500-per-month pension, for example, she sacrifices $500 in retirement income every month she postpones retirement past age 62. If her regular monthly pay is $10,000, this represents a small sacrifice. But if her usual pay is $1,000, the sacrifice amounts to half her wage. Between the ages of 62 and 64, the Social Security formula offers average workers a fair compensation for giving up a year's benefits. Monthly benefits are adjusted upwards about 8 percent for each year's delay in claiming them. For workers with average life expectancy and a moderate rate of time preference, this adjustment is just large enough so that the sacrifice of a year's benefits is compensated by eligibility for a higher pension in the future. After age 65, however, the benefit formula has historically been less generous toward delayed retirement. Postponement of retirement after that age was not fairly compensated by increases in the monthly pension. For most workers this is true even taking account of the fact that the basic pension calculation gives them extra credit for their most recent wages.[3] In essence, the Social Security formula forces workers who delay retirement after 65 to accept a cut in the lifetime value of their Social Security payments. This is a clear inducement to retire no later than age 65.

It is worth noting that almost no workers are "average." A benefit calculation rule that is age-neutral or actuarially fair on average can still provide strong financial incentives to retire for a worker who has below-average life expectancy. This worker may not expect to live long enough for the future benefit increase to make up for the benefits he gives up by delaying retirement for one more year. Similarly, a worker who applies a high discount rate when evaluating future benefits may not be impressed that the pension adjustment is "fair" for an average worker. For workers who are impatient to consume, an 8-percent hike in benefits starting one year from today may not be enough to compensate for the loss of 12 monthly benefit checks over the next year. Even an actuarially fair pension adjustment might be insufficient to persuade workers who are tired of their jobs to delay retirement.

One reason that many people must retire in order to collect a Social Security check is that the program imposes an earnings test in calculating the annual pension. Workers who are between age 62 and 64 and who earn more than $10,800 a year lose $1 in annual benefits for every $2 in earnings they receive in excess of $10,800. Until recently, workers between 65 and 69 lost $1 in benefits for every $3 in annual earnings in excess of $17,000. (Pensioners age 70 and older did not face an earnings test.) At one time the earnings limits were much lower, discouraging pensioners from work and possibly encouraging them to postpone claiming a pension until they were confident their earnings would remain low.

Many employer-sponsored pension plans are structured similarly to Social Security pensions. Workers who are covered under an old-fashioned defined-benefit plan earn pension credits for as long as they work for the employer that sponsors the plan (sometimes up to a maximum number of years). The longer they work under the plan, the higher their monthly pension. Most defined-benefit plans are structured to encourage workers to remain with the employer for a minimal period (say, 10 years) or until a critical age (say, age 55). Workers who stay for shorter periods may receive very little under the plan. On the other hand, workers who stay in the job too long may see the value of their pension accumulation shrink. This would happen if the plan offered benefits to workers starting at age 55 but then failed to significantly increase the monthly benefit for workers who delayed retirement after age 55. If a 55-year-old worker can collect a monthly pension of

$1,000 when he retires immediately and a monthly check of $1,001 if he delays his retirement one year, he will clearly lose a substantial amount of lifetime benefits—nearly $12,000—for each year he postpones receipt. The worker essentially suffers a pay cut when he reaches age 55, and the cut is equal to the loss in lifetime benefits he suffers by postponing retirement. Such a pay cut might seem illegal under U.S. age discrimination laws, but it is perfectly legal as long as the pay cut is reflected in reduced lifetime pensions rather than reduced money wages. Many employers find this kind of pension formula to be an effective prod in pushing workers into early retirement.

There is one important difference between Social Security and employer-sponsored defined-benefit pensions. Social Security imposes an earnings test on income received from all employment, including self-employment. Employer-sponsored pensions may impose an even tougher earnings test, but the test applies only to earnings received from the sponsoring employer or group of employers. Workers who wish to claim a pension may be forced to leave the job on which they earned the pension, but they are not forced to leave work altogether. Nevertheless, the effects of employer-sponsored pensions on retirement may be similar to those of Social Security, because many older workers find it hard to get attractive job offers after they have retired from their career jobs.

This explanation of the financial incentives in Social Security and employer-sponsored pensions sheds some light on the retirement trends discussed earlier. Social Security is now the main source of cash income of households headed by someone 65 or older. The program provides slightly more than 40 percent of the total cash income received by the aged. Among aged households in the bottom 60 percent of the elderly income distribution, Social Security provides over three-quarters of cash income. Until 1941, Social Security provided no income at all to the aged. Today the program replaces about 42 percent of the final wage earned by a full-career single worker who earns the average wage and claims a pension at age 65. If the worker has a non-working dependent spouse, the benefit replaces 63 percent of the worker's final wage. Benefits are clearly large enough so they can be economically significant in influencing the choice of retirement age.

The distributions of male retirement ages in 1940, 1970, and 1998–1999 are plotted in Figure 5. The chart shows the percentage of men

**Figure 5  Male Retirement Rate by Age, 1940–1999**

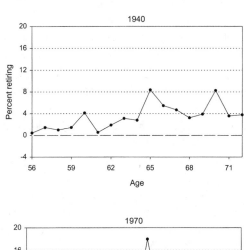

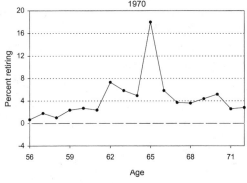

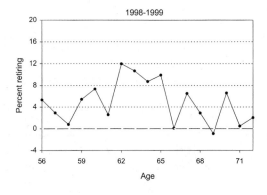

SOURCE: Authors' tabulations of data in Figure 1.

leaving the labor force at each age from 56 to 72, computed as a fraction of the men in the labor force at age 55.[4]    The calculations are based on the data displayed in Figure 1.  Not surprisingly, the retirement-age distributions for 1970, and especially for 1998–1999, are skewed toward the left.  Labor force withdrawal occurred at earlier ages in those years than it did in 1940.  Both the 1970 and 1998–1999 distributions show evidence of clustering in retirement at particular ages.  In 1970, the peak rate of retirement occurred at age 65; by 1998–1999, the peak occurred at age 62.  There are peaks in the distribution of retirements in 1940 at ages 65 and 70, but these are far lower than the peaks in 1970 and 1998–1999, when the timing of retirements was influenced by Social Security.

Our description of the financial incentives in Social Security suggests a simple explanation for the clustering of retirements at ages 62 and 65, at least in years after 1940.  Workers who continued to work beyond age 65 gave up Social Security benefits for which they were not fairly compensated.  This feature of the benefit formula clearly encourages retirement at age 65.  The clustering of retirements at age 62 can be explained using similar logic.  Starting in 1961, age 62 became the earliest age at which men could claim a Social Security pension.  Before 1961, there was no evidence of clustering in retirements at age 62, but by 1970, retirement was more common at 62 than at any other age except 65.  By the mid 1990s, age 62 was by a wide margin the most popular age of retirement.  In principle, the Social Security formula fairly compensates "average" workers if they delay claiming a pension past age 62.  As we have seen, however, a worker with a high rate of time preference or short life expectancy might not regard the compensation as fair.  In that case, we should expect many workers to prefer retiring at age 62 rather than a later age.

Of course, the clustering of retirements at ages 62 and 65 may be due to factors other than Social Security.  It is hard to believe, however, that health or work opportunities decline abruptly at particular ages.  Another explanation is that some workers were affected by mandatory retirement rules.  This explanation may have been valid in 1940 and 1970, when mandatory retirement rules covered up to one-half of American workers, but it is not persuasive today.  Amendments to the Age Discrimination in Employment Act passed in 1986 prohibit employers from dismissing workers solely on account of their age.

The simplest alternative explanation for the clustering of retirement ages is that workers are affected by employer-sponsored pension plans, yet many older workers are not covered by an employer plan. The Current Population Surveys suggest that employer-sponsored pensions do not provide a large percentage of income to older Americans except in more affluent households. But, for those workers who are covered by a private pension plan, the financial incentives in the plan may provide powerful incentives for workers to leave their career jobs at a particular age.

## Health Insurance

Unlike most other industrialized countries, the United States does not provide universal health insurance to its citizens. Instead, most working-age Americans receive health insurance coverage as part of an employer's compensation package. In 1995, 72 percent of American workers between 18 and 64 had health insurance coverage under an employer-based plan, either through their own employer or through the employer of another family member. Some workers obtain insurance through publicly provided Medicaid or privately purchased health plans, but 18 percent of American workers were left uninsured. Some employers offer continuing health insurance to their workers, even after they leave the firm. In 1995, of those full-time employees in medium and large firms who had health insurance on their jobs, 46 percent also had retiree health coverage before age 65, and 41 percent had retiree coverage at ages 65 and older. The percentage of the labor force employed by firms offering such protection is shrinking, and many employers now require their retired workers to pay for more of the cost of the plans (EBRI 1997a).

The nation's peculiar health insurance system provides a complicated set of incentives for retirement. Health insurance is particularly important for workers who are past middle age but not yet eligible for Medicare, because many of them face high risk of incurring heavy medical expenses. Workers with health insurance on the job who would lose it if they retire have an obvious incentive to remain on the job, at least until age 65 when they become eligible for Medicare. Those with postretirement health benefits have less incentive to remain employed, although how much less depends on how the insurance costs after retirement are shared between the employee and employer.

As with Social Security and private pensions, there is considerable evidence that health insurance coverage before and after retirement has an important influence on individual retirement decisions. Gustman and Steinmeier found, for example, that the effects of insurance plans are similar in nature to those of employer-sponsored pension plans (Gustman and Steinmeier 1994). If workers can become eligible for retiree health benefits only after a delay, the availability of the plan tends to delay workers' retirements until they gain eligibility. After eligibility has been achieved, the availability of retiree health benefits encourages earlier retirement than would occur if no benefits were offered. Quinn estimated that men and women in career jobs in 1992 were 8 to 10 percentage points less likely to leave their jobs over the next four years if they would lose health insurance coverage by doing so (Quinn 1999a). Inferring the overall effect of health insurance incentives on retirement patterns is tricky, however. A number of components of employee compensation, including wage rates, pension coverage, health insurance, and retiree health benefits tend to be highly correlated with one another. This makes it difficult to distinguish statistically between the separate effects of each component of compensation. Nonetheless, the rising importance of health insurance coverage to older Americans suggests that the evolution of the public and private health insurance system may have had a sizable impact on retirement patterns.

## The Change in Retirement Trends after 1985

There are two types of explanation for the slowdown or reversal of retirement trends in recent years. One hypothesis is that permanent changes in the environment for retirees have encouraged additional work by older Americans. Under this conjecture, the long-term trend toward earlier retirement is over. Another view is that temporary cyclical factors are responsible for a pause in the historical retirement trend. When these cyclical factors are behind us, the historical trend toward earlier retirement will resume. Although it will be many years before we can be sure of the relative importance of these explanations, it is possible to assess some of the permanent and temporary factors that have influenced recent retirement trends.

The most important cyclical factor affecting retirement is the state of the economy. The American economy is currently growing strongly, and the unemployment rate is near a 30-year low. The second half of the 1980s and the 1990s saw lengthy economic expansions and strong employment growth. There was only one recession after 1985. These factors made it easier for workers to find jobs when they were dismissed and more likely to find the terms and conditions of employment that they desire. In contrast, economic growth was much lower even in the 15 years after 1970. That period saw three recessions, and two of those recessions—in 1974–1975 and 1981–1982—were the worst of the postwar era. Weak labor demand discourages jobless workers from persisting in their job search. Strong demand creates employment options for older workers who want to keep working.

Although we think a strong economy has contributed to the recent rise in older Americans' participation rates, it is probably not a big part of the story. The economy also grew strongly and unemployment reached very low levels in the 1960s, yet older men's labor force participation rates fell in the decade and older women's participation rates changed very little (see Table 1). In earlier work, Quinn estimated the impact of the business cycle on older workers' participation rates and found that changes in the overall unemployment rate account for a relatively small proportion of the change in participation trends since 1985 (Quinn 1999b). Most of the change in participation trends since 1985 is probably due to factors other than the cyclical movement in economy-wide unemployment.

It is easier to point to factors that have permanently changed in a way that encourages later withdrawal from the job market. One important change is that the nation's main pension program, Social Security, is no longer growing more generous. Workers who retired between 1950 and 1980 retired in an environment in which Social Security benefits were rising, both absolutely and in relation to the average earnings of typical American workers. Most workers received pensions that were higher than those they would have obtained if their Social Security contributions had been invested in safe assets. The maturation of the Social Security program meant that fewer workers who retired after 1985 received windfalls from the program. The Social Security amendments of 1977 and 1983 brought an end to a four-decade expansion and liberalization of benefits. In fact, the amendments trimmed retirement benefits modestly in order to keep the program solvent.

Congress has changed Social Security rules and the pension formula to make work late in life more attractive. The amount of income a recipient can earn without losing any Social Security benefits has been increased, and the benefit loss for each dollar earned over the exempt amount was reduced (from 50 to 33 cents) for pensioners between 65 and 69. In 2000, the earnings test was eliminated altogether for workers aged 65 and older. In the 1977 and 1983 Social Security amendments, Congress also increased the reward that workers receive for delaying initial benefit receipt past the normal retirement age (NRA). Instead of penalizing work after the NRA, Social Security is becoming more age-neutral. When this formula change is fully implemented, for workers attaining age 62 after 2004, the adjustment for delayed benefit receipt will be approximately fair for retirements up through age 70. It is nearly so today. There will be no financial penalty for delaying retirement beyond the normal retirement age.

Important changes have also occurred in the private sector. There has been a sharp increase in the relative importance of defined-contribution pension plans and a continuing decline in the importance of defined-benefit plans. Defined-contribution plans are age-neutral by design, and therefore they have none of the age-specific work disincentives that are common in traditional defined-benefit plans. As a growing percentage of workers reaches retirement age under defined-contribution plans, there will be less reason for workers to leave their jobs to avoid a loss in lifetime retirement benefits.

Some changes in the environment for retirees are the result of policy initiatives aimed specifically at encouraging more work at older ages. For example, mandatory retirement has been nearly eliminated in the United States. In the early 1970s, about half of all American workers were covered by mandatory retirement provisions that required them to leave their jobs no later than a particular age, usually age 65. In 1978, the earliest legal age of mandatory retirement was raised from 65 to 70, and in 1986, mandatory retirement provisions were outlawed altogether for the vast majority of workers. The increase and eventual elimination of mandatory retirement ages not only increased the options open to older employees who wanted to remain on their jobs, but also sent an important message to Americans about the appropriate age to retire.

This message was reinforced by a provision of the 1983 Social Security amendments that is gradually raising the normal retirement age in Social Security from 65 to 67. The higher NRA will become fully effective for workers who reach age 62 in 2022. So far as we know, the United States was the first industrial nation to pass a law lifting the retirement age under its main public pension program. Although few workers may be aware of the higher retirement age, many are affected by it already. Workers reaching age 62 in 2000 face a normal retirement age of 65 years and 2 months, which means that they will qualify for age-62 pensions that are 1 percent smaller than age-62 benefits under the traditional NRA. The delay in the eligibility age for unreduced pensions has an effect on benefit levels that is almost identical to across-the-board benefit cuts.

These changes suggest that the future will not look like the past. The relative attractiveness of work and retirement at older ages has been altered in favor of work, though the changes may have produced only modest effects so far. The break in the early retirement trend that occurred in the mid 1980s suggests that changes in the retirement environment are having an impact in the expected direction.


## SHOULD WE ENCOURAGE LATER RETIREMENT?

Even if the trend toward earlier retirement has stopped or reversed, it is natural to ask whether the nation should take additional steps to encourage later retirement. One reason for doing so is concern over public finances. Social Security is the largest item in the federal budget. In 1995, Social Security outlays represented 4.6 percent of GDP and a little less than 22 percent of overall federal spending. After the income tax, the program is the most important source of federal tax revenues. Over the next 10 to 15 years, the financial outlook for Social Security is relatively secure, even under pessimistic assumptions about the state of the economy. When the baby-boom generation reaches retirement age in the second decade of the century, however, benefit payments will begin to climb much faster than tax revenue. Outlays will exceed taxes and will eventually exceed tax revenues plus interest payments earned by the trust funds. Under the intermediate assumptions of the Social Security Trustees, the trust funds will begin to shrink. Unless benefits are trimmed or tax rates increased, the trust funds will eventually fall to zero, making it impossible under current law to make timely benefit payments. The financial condition of the Medicare program is more perilous than that of Social Security. The reserves of the system are smaller, and they will be depleted much sooner than the OASDI trust funds.

Restoring both Medicare and Social Security to long-term solvency will be costly. The federal budgetary cost of achieving solvency would obviously be smaller if workers' eligibility for benefits under the two programs were delayed. In the remainder of this chapter, we focus on options to encourage later retirement under the Social Security program.

The solvency of Social Security, like that of any pension program, depends on four crucial elements: 1) the contribution rate imposed on workers and their employers; 2) the pension fund's rate of return on its investments; 3) the age of eligibility for pensions; and 4) the average monthly pension paid to retirees. The first two elements determine the annual amount of funds flowing into the system, and the last two determine the annual amount flowing out of the system. Each of the four elements must be carefully calibrated to ensure that benefit promises are matched by expected future revenues. If a pension program is exactly solvent and one of the four elements changes, some adjustment in the other three elements may be necessary to restore the solvency of the program. For example, if the rate of return on pension fund investments falls, it will be necessary to increase the contribution rate, delay the age of eligibility for pensions, or lower monthly pensions in order to restore the pension program to solvency.

Improvements in life expectancy increase the funding requirements of a pension plan. If contributors live one additional year in retirement, the plan must find enough extra resources to finance the added benefit payments. To keep the pension system solvent, this requires higher contributions to the program, a higher rate of return on investments, a delay in the retirement age, or a reduction in monthly benefits. It is worth emphasizing that this is true for every type of pension plan, whether public or private. If Social Security had never been established, increases in American life spans over the past half century would have required private pension plans to increase their contribution rates, find investments that yield higher rates of return, delay the age of eligibility for pensions, or reduce monthly pension payments.

A large part of Social Security's long-term funding problem arises because of good news about longevity.[5] Americans now live longer than their parents and grandparents did. Their children and grandchildren can be expected to live longer than we do. The improvements in longevity mean that living Americans will survive much longer past age 65 than was true when Social Security was established in the Great Depression. The longevity increases provide the equivalent of a benefit increase to Social Security recipients. The benefit increase must be paid for if the system is to remain solvent.

## Political Unpopularity

While it might seem logical to raise the retirement age in Social Security to reflect improvements in longevity, that logic has so far escaped the general public. American voters and workers routinely reject the idea of a higher retirement age when it is suggested as a solution to Social Security's problems. Lawrence Jacobs and Robert Shapiro recently summarized the findings of 18 polls that asked Americans about their attitudes toward an increase in the retirement age (Jacobs and Shapiro 1998, pp. 381–384). The polls were conducted over a 20-year period ending in 1997, and each poll was administered to at least 750 respondents. With rare exceptions, solid majorities of respondents reject any proposed hike in the retirement age. The size of the majority opposing a higher retirement age was higher in the 1990s than it was in the 1980s. Political leaders apparently take their cue from the polling numbers. Nearly all of the presidential candidates in both political parties have expressed strong opposition to the idea of a higher Social Security retirement age.[6]

Americans' hostility to a higher retirement age does not provide much guidance to policymakers, however. Solid majorities also oppose other basic steps that would solve Social Security's long-term funding problem. Most poll respondents are against higher payroll taxes, lower monthly benefits, and investment of Social Security reserves in stocks, where they would earn a higher return (Jacobs and

Shapiro 1998; EBRI 1997c, p. 11). Many workers may oppose a higher retirement age in Social Security because they intend, or at least hope, to retire several years before attaining the early eligibility age for Social Security benefits. When asked in an EBRI poll when they hope to start retirement, one-third of active workers answered "age 55 or younger." When asked when they actually expect to retire, however, only 15 percent thought their retirements would occur before age 56 (EBRI 1997b, Chart 1). If the Social Security retirement age were increased, early retirement would become a less affordable dream.

**Other Options**

There is no compelling reason to raise either the Social Security retirement age or the average retirement age, of course. If Americans' incomes continue to grow 1 or 2 percent a year, some fraction of the increase can be used to finance comfortable incomes during longer spells of retirement. This means, however, that more of the income earned by active workers must be set aside to pay for longer retirements. This could take the form of higher payroll or income taxes to pay for Social Security benefits to the currently retired or higher personal saving to make up for the loss of monthly Social Security benefits if Social Security pensions are trimmed to preserve solvency. There is some evidence that workers understand this trade-off. When forced to choose between the option of making larger contributions to pay for retirement or accepting smaller pensions after they retire, most workers opt to make larger contributions. By a 2-to-1 majority, workers favor higher payroll taxes over reduced Social Security pensions (EBRI 1997b, Chart 6). This suggests a simple conclusion: Americans would rather set aside more of their wages for retirement than postpone their retirement.

Workers can offset the effect of higher retirement contributions by working longer hours during their prime working years. There is some evidence this is occurring. American work patterns have changed slowly but significantly over the past generation. Since the 1960s, three major trends have affected adults' use of time. Women have joined the paid workforce in record numbers; men have retired from their jobs at younger ages; and both men and women have devoted more years to formal schooling. The effects of these trends on average work effort can be seen in Figure 6, which shows changes in weekly hours of paid work between 1968 and 1998. The weekly average is calculated as the total hours of work during the survey week divided by the total number of men and women in the indicated age group. People who do not work are included in these estimates. (The estimates would show higher average hours if they reflected the work effort only of people who held jobs.)

In spite of the trend toward earlier male retirement since 1968, the figure shows a sizable jump in the total amount of time that Americans spend at work. The increase in hours was driven almost entirely by the surge in women's employment. The CPS interviews show only a small change in average weekly hours among men and women who actually hold a job. Averaging across all ages, women worked 49 percent more hours in March 1998 than they did in March 1968 (20.3 hours a week in 1968 versus 13.6 hours in 1968). The rise was due to a 45 percent jump in the fraction of women holding jobs. Partly offsetting the rise in women's employment was the dip in men's paid work. Most of the

**Figure 6  Average Hours of Work by Age Group in the U.S. Population, 1968 and 1998**

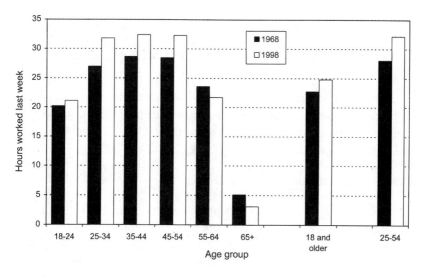

SOURCE: Authors' tabulations of March 1968 and March 1998 Current Population Survey files.

drop occurred as a result of decreasing employment among men past age 54. Across all age groups, the male employment rate fell 6 percentage points (or 8 percent) between 1968 and 1998, but it fell 15 percentage points among men between 55 and 64 and 9 points among men past 64.

The combined effects of the shifts in male and female work patterns are displayed Figure 6. Averaging the trends of both men and women, we see that hours spent on the job increased for people 18 to 54 years old and declined for people past age 54. Older Americans clearly enjoyed more free time in 1998 than did their counterparts in 1968, mainly because of earlier male retirement. For adults between 25 and 54, however, the estimates imply that paid employment consumes a much bigger percentage of available time. The employment rate of people in their prime working years jumped 11 percentage points (almost 17 percent) between March 1968 and March 1998, boosting the average amount of time spent in jobs from 28 hours to 32 hours a week. This increase is equivalent to five extra 40-hour work weeks a year for adults between 25 and 54. In short, Americans are working longer hours between 25 and 54. The increase in hours should help them pay for shorter hours and longer retirements when they are older than 55.

## HOW COULD WE ENCOURAGE LATER RETIREMENT?

Assuming that it is desirable to do so, how might we encourage American workers to delay their retirements further? In this section we consider some alternatives and discuss their likely impact on future trends in the average retirement age.

### Changing the Incentives in Social Security

Since the eligibility age for pensions is one of the main features of Social Security affecting its solvency, it is sensible to consider adjustments in the eligibility age to help restore the system's financing. One possibility is to accelerate the increase in the normal retirement age already scheduled under present law. Instead of phasing in the increase over 23 years (with a 12-year hiatus between the change from 65 to 66 and the change from 66 to 67), Congress could phase in the NRA change over just 12 years. This would mean that the higher NRA will be fully implemented for workers reaching age 62 in 2011, rather than 2022.

A second possibility is to increase the NRA automatically in line with increases in life expectancy after 65. A majority of members of the 1994–1996 Social Security Advisory Council proposed increasing the NRA as necessary after 2011 to maintain a constant ratio of retirement years to potential years of work. Retirement years is defined as life expectancy at the NRA, and potential years of work as the number of years from age 20 to the NRA. Under the Social Security Trustees' intermediate assumptions, this proposal would push up the NRA to age 70 by about 2080. The Social Security Actuary estimates that the combination of accelerating the NRA increase and then increasing the NRA in line with longevity improvements eliminates nearly one-quarter of Social Security's long-term funding gap.

Lifting the NRA while leaving the early eligibility age (EEA) unchanged produces almost exactly the same effect on retired workers' Social Security benefits as a proportional reduction in the full pension (usually referred to as the "primary insurance amount," or PIA). Even though most people describe an increase in the normal retirement age as a "delay" in the retirement age, it is in fact closer to a reduction in the monthly benefit amount. Workers can still obtain pensions at the same age as before, but their monthly pensions are smaller, no matter what age they choose.

There are some important non-economic differences between raising the NRA and cutting the full Social Security pension, however. First, increasing the NRA signals to workers that the same monthly benefit can be obtained by postponing retirement, which may encourage some workers to delay retirement rather than accept a lower pension. Sponsors of employer pension plans might also be induced to modify their plans to encourage delayed pension acceptance if the Social Security NRA were increased. Second, in light of the well-known improvements in life expectancy, American workers might find increases in the retirement age to be more understandable and fairer than equivalent reductions in full pensions. By increasing the retirement age rather than reducing full pensions, Congress conveys the message that the benefit level is appropriate, but the timing is not—workers ought to postpone their retirements.

Congress might increase the early eligibility age (EEA) at the same time and at the same pace as it increases the NRA. An increase in the EEA is fundamentally different from an increase in the NRA. If the EEA is increased above age 62, 62-year-old workers will be prevented from obtaining old-age pensions. Under current law they can collect reduced old-age pensions or they can apply for Disability Insurance (DI) pensions. When the possibility of obtaining old-age pensions is eliminated, some 62-year-olds who otherwise would have received old-age pensions will apply for DI. This will increase Social Security administrative costs, because eligibility is much more expensive to determine in the DI program. It may also impose serious hardship on workers whose DI applications are denied.

These consequences of increasing the early eligibility age make many people reluctant to tamper with it. Many policymakers are more uneasy about a reform that denies benefits completely to an identifiable class of people than they are about one that reduces benefits modestly to a much wider population. It is important to recognize why Social Security has an early eligibility age, however. If workers could apply for benefits as soon as they accumulated enough earnings credits, some low-income workers would be tempted to apply for benefits in their late fifties or even their late forties. At such ages, however, their monthly benefits would be very low, because early pensions are reduced below the full pension in proportion to the number of months between the age a worker claims benefits and the NRA. The low level of the initial pension might not represent a problem for a worker who is 50 or 60 years old and can supplement monthly pensions with modest wages or an employer-sponsored pension. But, it could cause serious hardship when a worker reaches age 68 or 70 and finds she is no longer able to work and the company pension no longer covers the cost of groceries and the monthly rent. The existence of the early entitlement age prevents short-sighted workers from applying for pensions that will be too small to support them throughout a long retirement.

When the NRA eventually reaches 67, workers claiming early pensions at age 62 will receive 70 percent of a full pension, a 30 percent reduction below the full pension rather than the current 20 percent reduction. If the NRA were eventually increased to 70 and the early eligibility age remained unchanged, workers claiming pensions at age 62 would receive monthly benefits as low as 52 percent of a full pension—probably too little to live on for a low-wage worker with few other sources of income.  If the NRA is increased above 67, it seems sensible to increase the early eligibility age as well.  Since Social Security is intended to assure a basic floor of support for retired Americans, it seems perverse to allow full-career workers to claim benefits so early that their monthly benefit will be too low to live on.  This implies that the early eligibility age must eventually be raised above 62 if the NRA rises much above age 67.  In order to implement this reform in a humane way, Congress might consider liberalizing eligibility requirements for Disability Insurance benefits starting at age 62.  People who have worked in physically demanding occupations and are in impaired health could be given access to benefits that permit them to retire with a decent standard of living, even if they do not meet the strict standard for health impairment that is used to evaluate DI applications today.

## Effects of Changing the NRA and EEA on Actual Retirement Ages

It is natural to ask whether increasing the early and normal retirement ages would have much effect on when workers actually retire. Almost all researchers who have examined this question agree that such reforms would tend to increase the average age at retirement, though the effect may not be large.  This conclusion was reached in a great majority of economists' studies conducted in the 1980s and early 1990s.  Most studies found that even large changes in Social Security would cause only small changes in the average retirement age.  Burtless and Moffitt (1985) estimated, for example, that increasing the normal retirement age in Social Security from 65 to 68 would add only a little more than four months to the full-time working careers of men who have no disabilities.[7]

One way to assess the impact of Social Security reforms is to examine differences in retirement patterns among people who face different incentives because the program has been changed in an unanticipated way.  In 1969 and again in 1972, Social Security benefits were increased much faster relative to wages than at any time in the recent past.  By 1973, benefits were 20 percent higher than would have been the case if pensions had grown with wages as they did during the 1950s and 1960s. In 1977, Congress passed amendments to the Social Security Act sharply reducing benefits to workers born in 1917 and later years (the "notch" generation) in comparison with the benefits available to workers born before 1917.

Burtless (1986) studied the first episode, and Krueger and Pischke (1992) examined the second. Both studies reached an identical conclusion: major changes in Social Security generosity produced small initial effects on the retirement behavior and labor force participation of older men. Burtless found, for example, that the 20 percent benefit hike between 1969 and 1973 caused only a two-month reduction in average retirement age of men who were fully covered by the more generous formula. This is equivalent to a reduction in the labor force participation rates of 62-year-old and 65-year-old men of less than 2 percentage points. The effects of the 1977 amendments found by Krueger and Pischke were even smaller.

These findings suggest that an increase in the normal retirement age will probably have only a small effect on the age that male workers withdraw from the workforce. It is harder to predict the effects of an increase in the early retirement age because we do not have good enough historical evidence to evaluate the impact of this kind of change. When the earliest age of eligibility for Social Security retirement benefits was decreased from 65 to 62 (in 1956 for women and in 1961 for men), labor force participation rates fell significantly and much faster than they had previously. The reversal of this policy would likely have a larger impact than the change in the normal retirement age, especially for low wage workers who have no other sources of retirement income except Social Security. The magnitude of the increased labor force participation would depend, in part, on how employer pensions responded to the change in Social Security rules and the extent to which eligibility criteria for DI benefits were loosened.

## EMPLOYER RESPONSES

Some people wonder how employers would respond to changes in the early and normal retirement ages in Social Security. Would firms with defined-benefit pension plans increase their early retirement incentives to offset the loss of the Social Security incentives or to make their plans more age-neutral? If workers wanted to delay their retirements to become eligible for more generous Social Security pensions, could the economy create enough extra jobs to employ them? Would employers discriminate against older job seekers, making it hard for them to find and keep jobs?

Historical evidence about the job-creating capacity of the U.S. market is reassuring. Over the long run, the U.S. labor market seems capable of absorbing large numbers of extra workers without a significant rise in joblessness. From 1964 through 1989, when the baby-boom generation reached adulthood and entered the job market, the labor force grew by 50.4 million persons, or slightly more than 2 million new entrants a year. Most of this surge was driven by the jump in U.S. fertility between 1946 and 1964, but part was also due to a growing demand for employment by women, who entered the workforce in record numbers. From 1964 to 1989, the number of Americans holding jobs climbed by 47.7 million, or slightly more than 1.9 million workers a year. In other words, about 95 percent of new job seekers in the period were able to find jobs, though the number of people available for work swelled by two-thirds. The unemployment rate rose only slightly, increasing from 5.0 percent to 5.2 percent.

Many people find it surprising that so many extra job seekers can be absorbed by the labor market. They overlook a basic reality of flexible labor markets like those in the United States. In the long run, employers are free to change their product lines and production methods to exploit the availability of a newly abundant type of labor, and they can adjust relative wages in response to the entry and exit of different classes of workers.

In the 1970s, for example, the wages received by younger workers fell in comparison with those earned by older workers, in large measure because younger workers became much more abundant. Faced with a huge increase in the availability of workers who had limited job experience, employers adopted production methods that took advantage of less experienced workers. Restaurant meals were prepared and served by eleventh-grade students and high school dropouts rather than by experienced cooks or waiters. Gardening and domestic cleaning were performed by unskilled and semiskilled employees rather than by homeowners themselves. In the end, 95 percent of new job seekers were successful in finding jobs. Of course, many of the new jobs were not particularly well paid. The huge increase in the abundance of less-experienced workers is one reason that pay in many jobs fell.

If older workers were forced to wait for two or three extra years for full Social Security retirement benefits to begin, many would choose to remain in their career jobs for a few months or years longer than workers presently do. Older workers who lose their jobs would try harder and more persistently to find new jobs. The jobs that many would find would pay lower wages than the jobs they previously held, as is the case for most workers who leave career jobs today. The availability of increased numbers of older workers would almost certainly depress the relative wages of aged job seekers. Yet, low U.S. fertility means the future labor force will grow slowly, placing some pressure on employers to retain older workers and make jobs attractive to older job-seekers.

Although some observers are pessimistic about the willingness of employers to accommodate the special needs of an aged workforce, such pessimism seems misplaced. Employers have created millions of part-time jobs to accommodate the needs of students and mothers who are only available to work short weekly hours. People who work on part-time schedules pay a price for short hours in terms of low weekly earnings and lost fringe benefits, but they accept these jobs nonetheless. Comparable accommodations could be made for the special needs of older workers. Many older workers who want jobs to tide them over between the time their career jobs end and eligibility for full Social Security pensions will be able to find suitable employment.

## Other Policies

As noted above, Social Security rules are moving toward age-neutrality. Employer pension coverage is shifting toward defined-contribution plans, which have none of the age-specific retirement incentives present in traditional defined-benefit plans. Mandatory retirement has been eliminated for the vast majority of American workers, and equal employment opportunity laws forbid employment discrimination based on age. Federal policies have been enlightened in these areas and are partly responsible for the changes in men's and women's retirement patterns over the past 15 years. Are there other policies that would improve the employment prospects of older Americans? Several come to mind:

- Permit workers aged 65 or older to opt out of additional Social Security contributions. If this option were chosen, workers would also forego the increases in future benefits that these earnings would have caused. A variant of the same idea would be to exempt earnings up to some dollar limit from F.I.C.A contributions as well as Social Security benefit recalculation. This would lower employers' cost of hiring older workers, because their payroll tax liabilities would fall, and it would make older workers relatively more attractive to hire and retain. It would also require Congress to find a source of revenue to make up for payroll taxes lost as a result of the reform.

- Allow employers to offer prorated fringe benefits for employees working less than full-time hours, rather than requiring them to provide the same fringe benefits to all employees working more than 1,000 hours per year (as the Employee Retirement Income Security Act, or ERISA, currently mandates). The present law encourages employers to restrict the hours worked by part-time employees to fewer than 1,000 per year. Giving employers more flexibility would allow older employees and employers to work out mutually agreeable fringe benefit packages that might keep more older workers employed.

- Make Medicare the first source of health insurance coverage for workers over age 65. Current law requires that the employer's health plan serve as "first payer" for a worker who has dual insurance coverage. Employers could provide additional insurance coverage if they chose. The reform would lower employers' cost of hiring or retaining older workers. Of course, it would also increase Medicare outlays, which in turn would require lawmakers to find additional sources of revenue for that program.

- Expand the Earned Income Tax Credit to include workers aged 65 and older who have no dependent children. This would provide a federal earnings subsidy to aged low-wage workers who are currently ineligible for the credit, and it could boost the available supply of older workers.

- Repeal the earnings test to eliminate the perception that pensioners who continue to work after age 62 lose Social Security benefits by doing so. It is true that workers do lose benefits during any year in which their earnings exceed the exempt amount. But for the average worker, the actuarial adjustment before age 65 returns all or most of the foregone pensions through higher future benefits. Of course, most workers are not average, and those who anticipate shorter than average life expectancies or who have high discount rates will still find the earnings test a disincentive to work  Even for average workers the existing test can act as a work disincentive.  Most Social Security recipients seem unaware of the benefit adjustment, so the current earnings test discourages them from earning more than the exempt amount.  The repeal of the earnings test would probably increase recipients' earnings modestly, and the long-term budgetary cost would be negligible.

In an economy as strong as the one we have enjoyed over the past five years, none of these reforms may be needed to encourage higher employment among the aged.  But if voters and policymakers want to provide incentives that will delay workers' exit from the labor force or change employers' attitudes toward older job applicants, some or all the reforms could be helpful.


## CONCLUSION

After a long period of decline, the trend toward earlier retirement came to at least a temporary halt in the mid 1980s. The labor force participation rates of American men past age 60 leveled off, and in the past few years they have actually increased slightly. Participation rates among older women have risen significantly since 1985, though this trend may be the result of the historic shift in women's attitudes toward career employment rather than to a change in their retirement behavior per se. Along with workers in Japan and Scandinavia, Americans now leave the paid workforce later than workers anywhere else in the industrialized world.

The question is, do Americans retire at an age that will ultimately prove unaffordable? As life spans increase, the fraction of life spent in retirement will rise unless we delay our exit from paid work. Improved longevity places heavier burdens on active workers if retirees are supported by contributions from current payrolls. Even without any further improvement in longevity, the long-term decline in birth rates has slowed labor force growth and will eventually increase the ratio of retired to active workers. This will place extra pressure on retirement programs like Social Security and Medicare that depend on payroll taxes for most of their funding. To reduce this pressure, the country could adjust the age of eligibility for early and/or normal retirement benefits and take other measures to encourage workers to postpone their exit from the labor market. These steps would directly improve the finances of Social Security and Medicare. They would encourage some workers to delay their departure from career jobs and induce others to find bridge jobs to tide them over until full retirement benefits begin. The United States has already taken several steps in this direction, and these steps have contributed to the recent growth of employment among older Americans.

Although most workers today claim that they expect to keep working after age 65, or after "retirement," most oppose additional changes in the retirement system that would push them to retire at a later age. A majority resists the idea that a higher retirement age is needed to protect Social Security. The United States is a rich country and will become wealthier in the future. It can certainly afford to maintain current retirement patterns if its citizens choose to spend their additional wealth in this way. The important public policy issue is the importance of this goal in comparison with other legitimate uses of the rise in wealth.

Proponents of a higher retirement age often focus on the long-term trend in older people's employment rates without considering what has happened to work effort and productivity among people before they reach the retirement age. They worry about the budget cost of retirement at age 62 without reflecting on the fact that younger workers may be paying for their longer and healthier retirements by working harder and more productively in their preretirement careers. As long as productivity continues to improve, American society and individual workers can choose how they want to allocate the income gains that flow from higher productivity. The evidence of the twentieth century suggests they will use at least part of it to pay for a longer retirement.

## Notes

The authors are Senior Fellow, The Brookings Institution, Washington, D.C. 20036 (G.B.), and Dean, College of Arts and Sciences, Boston College, Gasson Hall 103, Chestnut Hill, MA 02467 (J.F.Q.). Both authors are affiliates of the Center for Retirement Research at Boston College. We gratefully acknowledge the research assistance of Claudia Sahm of Brookings. This paper was prepared for the annual conference of the National Academy of Social Insurance, Washington, D.C., January 26–27, 2000. The views are solely those of the authors and should not be ascribed to Brookings, the Boston College Center for Retirement Research, or NASI

1. Retirement patterns were much more difficult to measure among women because most worked primarily within the home (and without pay) during most of their adult lives.
2. Labor force participation rates for 1910, 1940, and 1970 are based on responses to employment questions in the decennial censuses. See Ransom et al. (1991), especially pages 45–46, and Munnell (1977), page 70. Rates for 1984–85 and 1998–99 are the arithmetic average participation rates on the March Current Population Survey (CPS) files for 1984, 1985, 1998, and 1999. Participation rates measured on the Census differ somewhat from those measured by the CPS, partly because the main goal of the CPS is to obtain reliable labor force statistics. Adjusting the decennial Census statistics to make them strictly comparable to the CPS estimates would have only a slight effect on the patterns displayed in Figure 1, however.
3. Before their 62nd birthdays, workers who contribute to Social Security for an additional year obtain better future pensions because the basic pension formula is based on workers' average lifetime wages. Between ages 62 and 64 workers who contribute to Social Security obtain that benefit enhancement plus an actuarial increase equal to about 8 percent of the basic pension to compensate them for giving up one year's benefit payments.
4. If the labor force participation rate at age 63 is designated $LFPR_{63}$, the retirement rate at age 63 is calculated as $(LFPR_{62} - LFPR_{63}) \div LFPR_{55}$. This calculation ignores the complications involved in computing true cohort distributions and the effects of mortality rates, immigration, and temporary withdrawal from the labor force. It offers a picture of the timing of labor market withdrawal based on the participation choices of men aged 55 through 72 in a particular year.

5. Much of the future funding problem is due to the maturation of the program (most future retirees will reach the retirement age with enough earnings credits to receive a full pension), slow growth in the future working population, and a long-term slowdown in the rate of real wage growth (which has deprived the system of anticipated revenues). Increased longevity explains only part of the system's funding shortfall.

6. In the GOP presidential candidates' debate in Manchester, New Hampshire, on December 5, 1999, Steve Forbes, Senator John McCain, and Governor George W. Bush all expressed views on increasing the retirement age. Forbes described the idea as a "betrayal": "that's not fair to the people. They were made a promise and it should be kept." McCain said that a retirement age increase was unnecessary. Governor Bush flatly ruled out the possibility he would ask for a retirement-age increase for people already near retirement, and he expressed "hope" such a step would not be needed for younger workers. The Democratic presidential candidates have been equally vehement in their opposition. When asked by Tim Russell whether he supported or opposed hiking the retirement age, Vice President Gore responded "Tim, I strongly oppose raising the retirement age." When Gore posed the same question to Bill Bradley, Bradley responded "We said no. We said no. . . . OK?" (*Meet the Press*, December 19, 1999).

7. Other economists' predictions are discussed in Joseph Quinn et al. (1990).

# References

Baily, Martin N. 1987. "Aging and the Ability to Work: Policy Issues and Recent Trends." In *Work, Health, and Income among the Elderly*, Gary Burtless, ed. Washington, D.C.: Brookings, pp. 59–96.

Blöndal, Sveinbjorn, and Stefano Scarpetta. 1998. "The Retirement Decision in OECD Countries." Economics Department working paper no. 202, Organization of Economic Co-operation and Development, Paris.

Bosworth, Barry P., and Gary Burtless, eds. 1998. *Aging Societies: The Global Dimension*. Washington, D.C.: The Brookings Institution.

Burtless, Gary. 1986. "Social Security, Unanticipated Benefit Increases, and the Timing of Retirement." *Review of Economic Studies* 53(5): 781–805.

Burtless, Gary, and Robert A. Moffitt. 1985. "The Joint Choice of Retirement Age and Postretirement Hours of Work." *Journal of Labor Economics* 3(2): 209–236.

EBRI. 1997a. *EBRI Databook on Employee Benefits*. Fourth ed. Washington, D.C.: Employee Benefit Research Institute.

_____. 1997b. *The 1997 Retirement Confidence Survey: Summary of Findings*. Washington, D.C.: Employee Benefit Research Institute.

————. 1997c. *The Reality of Retirement Today: Lessons in Planning for Tomorrow.* Policy Brief no. 181, Employee Benefit Research Institute, Washington, D.C.

Geanakopolos, John, Olivia Mitchell, and Steve Zeldes. 1998. "Would a Privatized Social Security System Really Pay a Higher Rate of Return?" In *Framing the Social Security Debate: Values, Politics, and Economics*, R. Douglas Arnold, Michael J. Graetz, and Alicia H. Munnell, eds. Washington, D.C.: National Academy of Social Insurance, pp. 137–156

Gustman, Alan L., and Thomas L. Steinmeier. 1994. "Employer-Provided Health Insurance and Retirement Behavior." *Industrial and Labor Relations Review* 48(1): 124–140.

Gruber, Jonathan, and David A. Wise. 1999. "Introduction and Summary." In *Social Security and Retirement around the World*, Jonathan Gruber and David A. Wise, eds. Chicago: University of Chicago Press.

Jacobs, Lawrence R., and Robert Y. Shapiro. 1998. "Myths and Misunderstandings about Public Opinion toward Social Security." In *Framing the Social Security Debate: Values, Politics, and Economics*, R. Douglas Arnold, Michael J. Graetz, and Alicia H. Munnell, eds. Washington, D.C.: National Academy of Social Insurance, pp. 355–388.

Krueger, Alan, and Jörn-Steffen Pischke. 1992. "The Effect of Social Security on Labor Supply: A Cohort Analysis of the Notch Generation." *Journal of Labor Economics* 10(4): 412–437.

Leimer, Dean. 1994. "Cohort Specific Measures of Lifetime Net Social Security Transfers." ORS working paper no. 59, Office of Research and Statistics, Social Security Administration, Washington, D.C., February.

Manton, Kenneth G., and Eric Stollard. 1994. "Medical Demography: Interaction of Disability Dynamics and Mortality." In *Demography of Aging*, Linda G. Martin, and Samuel H. Preston, eds. Washington, D.C.: National Academy Press, pp. 217–279

Munnell, Alicia H. 1977. *The Future of Social Security.* Washington, D.C.: Brookings.

Quinn, Joseph F. 1991. "The Nature of Retirement: Survey and Econometric Evidence." In *Retirement and Public Policy*, Alicia H. Munnell, ed. Dubuque, Iowa: Kendall/Hunt, pp. 119–223.

————. 1999a. *Retirement Patterns and Bridge Jobs in the 1990s.* EBRI Issue Brief no. 206, Employee Benefit Research Institute, Washington, D.C., February.

————. 1999b. *Has the Early Retirement Trend Reversed?* Chestnut Hill, Massachusetts: Retirement Research Consortium and Boston College.

Quinn, Joseph F., and Richard V. Burkhauser. 1994. "Retirement and Labor Force Behavior of the Elderly." In *Demography of Aging*, Linda G. Martin, and Samuel H. Preston, eds. Washington, D.C.: National Academy Press, pp. 56–61.

Quinn, Joseph F., Richard V. Burkhauser, and Daniel A. Myers. 1990. *Passing the Torch: The Influence of Economic Incentives on Work and Retirement.* Kalamazoo, Michigan: W.E. Upjohn Institute for Employment Research.

Ransom, Roger L., Richard Sutch, and Samuel H. Williamson. 1991. "Retirement: Past and Present." In *Retirement and Public Policy,* Alicia H. Munnell, ed. Dubuque, Iowa: Kendall/Hunt, pp. 23–50.

U.S. Department of Commerce, Bureau of the Census. 1975. *Historical Statistics of the United States: Colonial Times to 1970.* Washington D.C.: U.S. Government Printing Office.

# Employer Perspective on Retirement Trends and Policies to Encourage Work among Older Americans

Anna M. Rappaport
*William M. Mercer, Inc.*

As a response to the chapter by Gary Burtless and Joseph F. Quinn, I here consider the environment for employers and how they are responding to the challenges of an aging society.

## EMPLOYERS, POLICY, AND OLDER-WORKER ISSUES

The Burtless and Quinn paper focuses on older workers. When employers focus on human resource issues, they generally do not focus on a particular demographic subset of employees, but rather on the business and on the people needed to get the work done. However, when worker shortages occur, employers seek out any method they can to fill in the gaps.

Burtless and Quinn focus on the impact of Social Security and Medicare benefits, as well as that of pensions and retiree health, on workers' decisions to retire. They also note that employment discrimination is banned, but they do not explore the many requirements of age discrimination legislation. They then provide a list of ideas for policy changes that might encourage later retirement. They approach these ideas from a policy and individual perspective, rather than an employer perspective.

I contend that employers need to be careful if they provide special programs or focus on particular demographic groups. The United States protects older workers through age discrimination legislation. (Other groups are protected as well by different legislation, but the requirements differ.) Age discrimination requirements are complex and apply to many aspects of employment. These requirements must be considered in structuring human resource programs, whether the programs target older workers or not. Employers, in considering new programs, must first focus on business need, but in addition they should focus both on compliance and on avoiding litigation. Involuntary terminations of employment and real or perceived unequal treatment can lead to costly litigation, whether the employer's action was justified or not. That is why employers should exercise care throughout the entire employment process. Whether these requirements deter employers from implementing otherwise desirable programs is unknown. It would be helpful to have research on the implications of this legislation to better understand how it impacts human resource programs and policies and whether it has served as a deterrent to innovation.

Some benefit plan requirements definitely serve as a deterrent to programs that would facilitate older worker employment and phased retirement. It would be desirable to offer programs that allow for partial payment of pensions and continued work. However, such programs are not feasible under current U.S. law. Programs may not allow payment of pensions during periods of continued work prior to normal retirement age, usually age 65. Plans may provide for payment of pensions during periods of continued work after normal retirement age, but this practice is rare. The author located anecdotal information about a retailer and a financial institution who allow continued payments to part-time workers after retirement. The number of retirees electing to work is substantial. There is no provision for plans to make partial payments during periods of reduced work. A desirable next step would be a review of pension legislation to seek out changes needed to accommodate phased retirement. Congress has given a strong signal that it supports the notion of phased retirement in its unanimous vote to repeal the Social Security earnings test. It needs to support that decision with appropriate changes in private pension regulation.

## DEFINITION OF RETIREMENT

Burtless and Quinn define retirement based on exit from the labor force. They define the average age at retirement as the point when half of men have left the labor force. This definition works well from a social perspective, but not from an employer perspective.

From an employer's perspective, the common definition of a retiree is one who has retired from that organization, and what is important is whether benefits are being paid, not whether the individual has found other work. Other work, in the form of bridge jobs, is common. Retirement often takes place in steps, with multiple retirements before a person leaves the labor force. This phenomenon is not new. Traditionally, it was common in the military and certain types of public service (such as police and fire) to retire early, get a benefit, and then go on to further employment, maybe several times.

Today, most gradual or phased retirement uses one or more bridge jobs at an organization other than that of the long-term employer. A key question is whether more employers will develop programs to encourage long-term employees to phase down within their own organizations rather than accepting a bridge job elsewhere.

We need to give further consideration to the definition of retirement. It has been suggested that we should seek a new set of terms to describe different life stages. I do not seek new terms, but rather a different idea. If phasing down through a series of bridge jobs is commonplace, then the idea of retirement as a one-time event does not work any more. We might think of retirement in terms of a financial situation: focus on a period of building assets and a period of using assets to replace or supplement current earnings. The point of retirement is the crossover point. Of course, labor force participation rates would not help us measure retirement on that basis.

## COST/BENEFIT OF USING OLDER WORKERS

Equity markets demand better performance from companies, and employers, in turn, put greater demands on employees. This raises the question, are there advantages in having a workforce with one set of demographics versus another?

I am not aware of any definitive research on this topic. The value and cost of using older workers likely offers both advantages and disadvantages. Older workers have more experience, which can lead to better judgment. This experience is extremely valuable for some types of jobs, particularly those with a long learning curve and a lot of need for human capital, particularly firm-specific human capital. Customers also value long-term relationships and generally do not like to see the people they are doing business with change frequently. In many cases, employers lose valuable history when a long-term employee leaves an assignment. On the other hand, with changes in organizations and technology, current education and training gain importance. If skills are not maintained, the value of long-term experience is largely lost. In addition, some experienced people focus on the past and resist change. The ideal is to have to a balance of experience, current training, and willingness to embrace change.

In recent interviews, top managers at a major financial institution made these comments:

- Some jobs have high firm-specific human capital, whereas others have low firm-specific human capital but a lot of technical knowledge. Employees in the latter jobs move between jobs easily, and long service does not add much value. An example of the first group is the account manager for a major account, and a foreign securities trader is an example of the second.

- Burnout can be a factor, particularly for high-stress jobs. At the point of burnout, it is important for both the employer and employee that the employee make a change and move on, either within the organization or outside of it.

- Customers and the organization both value continuity of service; however, that does not mean people will stay until traditional retirement age.

- Technology will replace many jobs, particularly in the back office. Some of these employees can be retrained and placed in other jobs, but it will not work out for others.

The bottom line is that human resources policies should support long service but not lock people into jobs that they no longer want. I also encountered parallel issues in a specialized manufacturing environment. The engineering and technical staff, as well as the account representatives, have a lot of knowledge that is important to the firm.

Yet for many jobs, the training period is short, and experience adds little value after an initial period, whether that is one day, one month, or one year.

Also, significant cost issues must be reviewed for both pay and benefits. In traditional seniority-based pay systems, longer-term employees got paid more, and older employees with longer service were likely to be among the higher paid. Where the value contributed by a longer-service person is not commensurate with the higher pay, the organization can save money by replacing higher-paid, longer-service employees with lower-paid, shorter-service employees. Employers today address this issue by using different types of compensation programs that are much less linked to seniority.

Employee benefits in the United States may comprise 30–40 percent of cash compensation. Older workers may have higher benefit costs depending on the structure of the programs. Some general comments on benefit costs follow.

- Traditional defined-benefit plans (based on final average pay) cost more for both longer-service and older employees. For large employers in the private sector, the average value of a traditional pension plan is 3–5 percent of pay. Pension benefits and costs in public employment tend to be much higher.

- Defined-contribution plans, unless they have formulas linked to age or service, have the same cost regardless of age or service. Employer contributions to defined-contribution plans range from no contribution to 15 percent of pay.

- Medical care for individuals generally costs more with increasing age (except for maternity benefits, which have a high cost for younger employees). Per employee costs are also influenced by number of covered dependents. The average number of dependent children is likely to increase by age and then decline. How the cost of a health benefit plan varies by employee age depends on the structure of the plan, the numbers of covered dependents, and the plan's cost-sharing provisions. Employer spending per active employee averaged $4,097 in 1999 according to the 1999 Mercer Foster Higgins National Survey of Employer Sponsored Health Plans. Spending per active employee includes the cost of coverage for the employee and covered dependents.

- Vacation time often increases with length of service, so it costs more for longer-service employees.
- Life insurance and disability benefits become more expensive with increasing age.
- Many factors affect absences, and no generalization can be made about patterns of absence and age.

The bottom line is that experienced employees bring greater value to some jobs and that older employees do cost more in many benefit programs. Whether the net impact of these factors is an advantage or disadvantage in employing more longer-service employees depends on the situation.

Companies who offer continued health care to retirees have an added cost for this benefit. As indicated by Burtless and Quinn, the availability of retiree health benefits is an important factor in individual retirement decisions; a lack of retiree health benefits prior to Medicare eligibility is a barrier to retirement. Benefit costs can be a major factor in competition. For example, in the auto industry, the major traditional car companies had mature workforces and provided substantial benefits to retirees. They were competing against start-ups who were either foreign companies manufacturing in the United States or joint ventures and overseas companies. The companies with mature workforces had a substantial cost disadvantage, partly due to benefit costs. These companies had to downsize and ultimately restructure to remain competitive.

## ENVIRONMENT FOR EMPLOYER RETIREMENT PROGRAMS

In the year 2000, the environment provides a backdrop for the employer response to employee benefit issues. Some of the key factors that affect private businesses are as follows.

- Employers are facing shortages of skilled workers for certain jobs. The recruitment and retention of employees has become a high-priority issue for many businesses. This issue creates a good situation for focusing on creating better opportunities for older workers. However, Burtless and Quinn indicate that economic conditions are not a major factor in determining older worker labor force participation rates.

- Business is becoming more global. Many global businesses are working to create common cultures.

- Mergers and acquisitions have become commonplace. Some of the deals are large, and they often cut across countries. Often, the aftermath of the deal is to sell lines of businesses that do not fit the large organization, which results in one large organization and several smaller ones. Many mergers result in the dislocation of a substantial number of employees. Nearly all require revisiting the appropriate retirement programs in the new organization. To integrate organizations, it is usually necessary to provide a common pension program for future periods. In some of these situations, employers offer new benefit packages after the merger. It is common to use early retirement window programs to help implement postmerger changes and workforce adjustments.

- The common trend is to have employees assume more responsibility for their own retirements, including stressing the importance of employee saving, and employers are offering more opportunities for employees to save. However, Americans save relatively little; this strategy is therefore likely to disappoint many people.

- U.S. equity markets have performed with uneven results. While some organizations have seen huge increases in the value of their stocks, others have not. Markets demand strong performance, which drives the fine-tuning of organizational structure. Key employees commonly receive stock options, and many employees get stock purchase opportunities. In many organizations, company stock is an important source of employee wealth that will facilitate retirement.

- The compensation systems of emerging e-commerce businesses have focused much more attention on stock options and ownership opportunities. These businesses, particularly start-ups, can have a large part of their compensation package based on stock.

Traditional businesses as well as new start-ups are feeling the impact of this competition.

- Technology and electronic business are changing the way business is being done. Employees are faced with constant and, at times, overwhelming change. Only some workers adapt well to change. Dealing with employees who do not adapt well can be awkward.

- Employers use a variety of employment systems. These systems include full-time, part-time, contract work, use of temporary employees, and increased use of individuals working as consultants and doing projects on a consulting basis. Some of the most attractive opportunities for using older workers may be outside of full-time employment.

- There is a widespread belief that employment patterns are changing and that employees will change jobs more frequently in the future. Trend data on length of service with current employer by age group show a long-term trend of modest reductions in male length of service and increases in female length of service. The biggest reductions are for males at and just before early retirement age. Male and female tenure patterns are becoming more similar. The data show modest change and do not match the perceptions of radical change.

- Companies are taking employee performance more seriously and working diligently to measure it. In addition, there is much less tolerance to retain a marginal performer. The demands of the competitive environment and equity markets push companies to improve productivity.

- Regulatory and legislative requirements have increased greatly over the last 25 years, and employment-related litigation can be costly. Employers need legal advice when developing virtually all employment policies and practices.

# PRIORITIES FOR HUMAN RESOURCES MANAGEMENT

During 1999, William M. Mercer, Incorporated, surveyed large employers in the United States, the United Kingdom, and continental Europe to better understand their priorities and the factors driving retirement strategies. Table 1 shows the priorities of the multinational respondents to this survey.

Controlling cost levels and attracting new talent were the most important workforce issues faced by respondents, with more than 9 in 10 rating each as critical or major. The biggest difference between U.S.-headquartered companies and companies headquartered in the United Kingdom or continental Europe was that 28 percent of U.S. respondents cited retaining employees longer as a critical issue, compared with only 5 percent of U.K./Europe respondents.

**Table 1  Major Workforce Issues of Multinational Employers in 1999 (%)**

| Workforce issue | Critical issue | Major issue | Minor issue | Not an issue |
|---|---|---|---|---|
| Attracting new talent | 46 | 46 | 8 | 0 |
| Controlling the level of costs | 45 | 48 | 7 | 0 |
| Controlling the variability of costs | 24 | 54 | 21 | 1 |
| Retaining employees longer | 19 | 41 | 32 | 8 |
| Aligning benefit programs with corporate goals | 18 | 54 | 25 | 3 |
| Achieving/maintaining competitive benefit levels | 17 | 65 | 17 | 1 |
| Having consistent benefits across the organization | 9 | 48 | 34 | 9 |
| Having employees invest in company stock | 5 | 18 | 32 | 45 |
| Giving employees benefit choices | 4 | 38 | 49 | 9 |
| Reducing average years of service | 0 | 7 | 37 | 56 |

The Mercer results include responses from 230 organizations with international operations; 63 percent are headquartered in the United States, 12 percent in the United Kingdom, 23 percent in continental Europe, and 2 percent in Australasia. The respondents' international operations range from one location outside the headquarters country to almost 200, averaging 23. U.K./Europe-based companies averaged 30 countries of operation, compared with 17 for U.S.-based respondents. Forty-four percent of respondents have at least 10,000 employees worldwide. These results point to employers trying to retain workers longer, but doing it in a way that controls costs. I view the use of alternative employment arrangements as particularly promising in that regard.

## RETIREMENT PLAN STRUCTURES AND TRENDS

In the United States, we can define differences in retirement plan trends by size and type of employer. Larger private-sector employers, those with at least 1000 employees, often include in their retirement packages a combination of a base plan (which is paid for totally by the employer) and a savings plan (usually a 401(k) plan). The savings plan generally provides for employee contributions and often an employer match, typically 50 percent of the amount paid by the employee up to 6 percent of pay. The base plan may be a traditional final average pay plan, a hybrid plan (like a cash balance plan), or a defined-contribution plan. Traditional plans are still most common, but hybrids are growing in popularity. Many employers also offer employees and dependents continued health care on a cost-shared basis. Nearly all provide a combination of tax-qualified plans and supplemental plans; the supplemental plans are used to make up amounts that cannot be paid in a tax-qualified plan.

In addition, these employers may offer other programs that help the employee build assets for retirement and help the employee own company stock. Medium-sized employers are more likely to use a single plan, most often a defined-contribution (DC) plan, which includes an opportunity for employees to save. Such plans are usually managed through a single outsourced vendor such as a major mutual fund company. Medium-sized employers are unlikely to offer retiree health benefits. Most small employers, those with under 50 employees, do not offer any retirement benefits. Those that do offer retirement benefits are most likely to offer only a defined-contribution plan.

The use of defined-contribution plans has grown in the United States, with these plans part of a combined program in larger organizations and the sole program in medium and smaller organizations. Many countries experience parallel trends. A recent study "Defined Contribution Retirement Plans around the World: A Guide for Employers", published by William M. Mercer, Incorporated, shows the growth in popularity of defined contribution plans and the truly global nature of this trend. Table 2 shows the percentage of companies having plans today and projected to have them in 2003 for selected countries.

## WHAT CAN EMPLOYERS DO?

Many employers are concerned about retention, but relatively few have focused on delaying retirement beyond normal retirement age as a

**Table 2  Employers Sponsoring Defined-Contribution Retirement Plans, Selected Countries (%)**

| Country | 1998 | 2003 (projected) |
|---|---|---|
| Australia | 80 | 90 |
| Hong Kong | 75 | 85 |
| Indonesia | 30 | 45 |
| Japan | 0 | 10 |
| Belgium | 45 | 60 |
| France | 40 | 50 |
| Germany | 10 | 12 |
| United Kingdom | 25 | 35 |
| Canada | 80 | 80 |
| United States | 60 | 70 |
| Mexico | 4 | 25 |

method of increasing retention. However, many of those employers who had large "cliffs" in their retirement plans have focused on this issue. A *cliff* is a liberal early retirement benefit, so an employee who qualifies for this benefit gets a subsidized benefit. For example, the benefit might be available at age 55 with 30 years of service. Such benefits encourage people to stay until the point of the cliff and then do little to encourage staying after that point. They artificially bunch retirements. Many of the employers who had cliffs have redesigned plans to eliminate them for future employees. A variety of transition plans are used to phase-out such provisions. Benefits already earned are protected by law, but benefits to be earned in the future are not. Plans generally reserve the right to the plan sponsor to change benefits to be earned in the future. When plans are changed, most larger organizations offer transition benefits greater than what is legally required to protect employees near retirement, because they often will have made plans based on expected benefits. Eliminating cliffs smooths out retirements by removing or reducing incentives to retire at a particular point in time.

For those employers who want to encourage longer work, a variety of strategies is available. The most important strategy is creative work options. Some older workers would prefer to continue working, but with a different schedule and pace than full-time workers. This option particularly applies to professional and technical people, who have faced increasing demands and schedules for a number of years. Innovative work options are an important first step. Pension design needs to be considered together with innovative work options ensure benefits make sense in light of the work options. As indicated by Burtless and Quinn, defined-contribution plans are age neutral with regard to encouraging retirement. The same is true for cash balance plans. However, neither type of plan automatically goes to the next step and supports phased retirement. Optimal support of phased retirement requires legal changes.

Some of the work options used today involve temporary and consulting work. Under such arrangements, generally no provision is made for benefits and no implication of continued employment beyond the immediate project or assignment. The individual can, however, be hired for further assignments. Many organizations prefer such arrangements, which involve no long-term commitment and less legal risk, although they may require higher out-of-pocket spending for the specific assignment. Some organizations use retiree pools as a method of enabling their retirees to secure temporary work in the company. Another important issue is to establish a culture that values experience as well as provides training to maintain skills and stay up to date.

To be successful with a program to encourage older workers to stay longer, an organization needs to have a strong performance management system fairly applied to all employees. This system is necessary so poor performance can be dealt with fairly. When an organization fails to manage performance effectively, it can sometimes look to retirement as a substitute for managing performance.

Medical benefits are also important. Many people seeking bridge jobs need medical coverage. Offering some medical coverage to part-timers would be a way to attract this group. Cafeteria benefits are also a good idea as employees can tailor their benefits to personal needs.

## NEXT STEPS

The ideas for further work and exploration include the following:

- Research the impact of age discrimination legislation on programs to encourage later work.
- Identify policy changes needed to accommodate phased retirement programs that would permit partial payment of benefits together with continued work.
- Investigate alternative definitions of retirement and the implications of using them.

Burtless and Quinn have also suggested several ideas for further policy incentives. It would be helpful to expose these ideas to various stakeholders to get their reactions.

# Living Longer, but Able to Work?

Glenn Pransky
*Liberty Mutual Center for Disability Research*
and
*University of Massachusetts Medical School*

There is ample evidence that retirement is much more common and is occurring at younger ages than at any previous time in U.S. history. Despite earlier suggestions that this trend is caused by declines in the average health of older working populations (Verbrugge 1984), more recent data has effectively rebutted this assumption by demonstrating a significant wealth effect (Ycas 1987; Shephard 1995). Social welfare policy now seeks to postpone publicly financed retirement. Whether this will succeed or not depends on the ability of those who would retire on Social Security—but are now expected to work longer—to sustain continued and substantial employment. In part, this will be a function of their health status and functional capacity, manifest as the capacity to work in those jobs that will be available to them.

The work status of an individual at any point in time is a function of retirement choices, functional capacity, and the requirements of employment. Involvement in the workforce can be viewed on a continuum from regular, full-time employment to informal, part-time or occasional work. Salary, benefits, and other dimensions of work may vary independently of the level of involvement. Retirement choices reflect an individual's economic resources (including wage replacement benefit adequacy and availability), preferences, employment alternatives, and outlook, as well as societal norms.

The ability to work is also an important influence on the retirement decision. This is best understood in relation to the demands of a particular job and is determined by prior skills and training, the effects of normal aging processes, and the presence of chronic diseases. Job demands include cognitive, interpersonal, and physical requirements; they may be expressed as typical or minimal requirements and may be moderated by accommodations. In order to appropriately assess the effect of aging and health on capacity to work, the contribution of all of these factors must be considered.

## LONGEVITY AND HEALTH

There is no doubt that Americans are living longer (Table 1). Much of the reduction in mortality over the past decade is attributed to improvements in the diagnosis, treatment, and prevention of cardiovascular and other chronic diseases, as well as to lifestyle modifications such as improvements in diet, exercise, and rates of cigarette smoking.

Has success in mortality reduction resulted in an aging population with more morbidity, less ability to function, and thus less average work capacity at a given age? Or, have gains in morbidity paralleled gains in mortality, so that there is a prolongation of disease-free and highly functional years of life? A definitive answer would require repeated, objective measures of illness and function for large successive cohorts of Americans near retirement age—information that is not now available. Most attempts to address these questions have relied upon data from large, national, cross-sectional self-report surveys (Current Population Survey, the National Health Interview Survey [NHIS], and the Health and Retirement Study), or smaller longitudinal datasets from specific studies, such as the University of Pennsylvania graduates study.

The NHIS has been conducted as a stratified, cross-sectional survey of thousands of Americans each year since 1957. Detailed questionnaires ask about health, functional limitations, medical care, and socioeconomic status. Table 2 shows the dramatic age-related increase in men in the prevalence of selected self-reported chronic diseases and

**Table 1  Life Expectancy in the United States at Birth and at Age 65, by Sex (yr.)**

| Year | At birth | | At age 65 | |
|---|---|---|---|---|
| | Males | Females | Males | Females |
| 1900 | 46 | 48 | 12 | 12 |
| 1950 | 66 | 71 | 13 | 15 |
| 1970 | 67 | 75 | 13 | 17 |
| 1995 | 73 | 79 | 16 | 19 |

SOURCE: http://www.cdc.gov/nchs/about/otheract/aging/trendsoverview.htm (Accessed May 2000); Kramarow et al. 1999.

**Table 2  National Health Interview Study, Disease/Condition Prevalence by Age (per 1000 Males)**

|  | NHIS, 1981 | | NHIS, 1996 | |
| --- | --- | --- | --- | --- |
| Disease or condition | Age 45–64 | 65–74 | 45–64 | 65–74 |
| Hypertension | 203 | 315 | 233 | 352 |
| Diabetes | 56 | 29 | 62 | 131 |
| Respiratory | 13 | 42 | 11 | 59 |
| Heart disease | 132 | 266 | 143 | 362 |
| Less than good health |  |  | 163 | 270 |
| Limited in major activity | 195 | 450 | 165 | 251 |
| Limited in any activity | 230 | 490 | 220 | 334 |

SOURCE: Adams, Hendershot, and Marano 1999.

limitations in ability to perform one's major life activity. Major life activity is defined as working or keeping house in those age 45–64. The reported prevalence of several chronic conditions increased significantly from 1981 to 1996. This likely represents a real change, but may be due to reporting biases as a result of better and earlier disease detection (Verburgge 1984, 1989). Despite these increases, the impact of these conditions on function appears to be significantly less in 1996 than in 1981, especially in the elderly. This is consistent with greater prevalence yet lower functional impact of these conditions. Data from a smaller but more detailed Finnish longitudinal study of municipal workers further supports this premise (Tuomi 1997). Only 11 percent of workers with chronic illness said that their health was good in 1981, but the number was 42 percent in 1992. Similar findings also appear in the Health and Retirement Study (Crimmins et al. 1995), where the age-related increase in prevalence of chronic diseases was higher than the age-related increase in disability incidence.

Tables 3 and 4 demonstrate trends in self-reported work disability by age, emphasizing that those who have some functional limitations are much less likely to be working as they age. These responses are somewhat biased by current employment and retirement status. Personal beliefs also influence responses; for example, surveys of those with cardiac conditions have demonstrated self-reported work limita-

**Table 3  Persons with Work Disability by Age, 1998 (% of population)**

| Age group | With work disability | With work disability, not severe | With work disability, severe |
|---|---|---|---|
| 16–24 | 4.1 | 1.5 | 2.7 |
| 25–34 | 5.5 | 2.0 | 3.5 |
| 35–44 | 9.1 | 3.0 | 6.1 |
| 45–54 | 13.2 | 4.6 | 8.6 |
| 55–64 | 23.1 | 7.7 | 15.4 |
| 65–69 | 23.0 | 14.9 | 8.1 |
| 70–74 | 26.4 | 18.5 | 7.9 |

**Table 4  Persons with and without Work Disability Who are Employed or Employable, by Age and Sex, 1998 (percent of group who are employed or employable)**

| | Males | | Females | |
|---|---|---|---|---|
| Age group | With work disability | Without work disability | With work disability | Without work disability |
| 16–24 | 30.9 | 67.5 | 43.8 | 63.2 |
| 25–34 | 41.8 | 96.1 | 36.3 | 79.4 |
| 35–44 | 35.8 | 97.1 | 35.4 | 81.8 |
| 45–54 | 37.5 | 97.3 | 28.9 | 83.5 |
| 55–64 | 21.6 | 81.4 | 15.7 | 63.5 |
| 65–69 | 10.5 | 31.4 | 7.4 | 22.6 |
| 70–74 | 9.5 | 18.6 | 3.3 | 11.6 |

SOURCE: U.S. Census Bureau 2000.

tions that are inconsistent with objective evidence of normal function and disease status (Fitzgerald 1993).

Thus, it is reasonable to conclude that an increased risk of chronic disease and associated functional limitation is an expected consequence of surviving into old age. Although the rates of illness and functional limitations increase with age, in some cases in a nonlinear fashion, there is no evidence of a specific age threshold where dramatic and consistent effects occur (Garg 1991). Although this observation could be a consequence of limitations in available data, the consistency of findings across studies lends credence to this conclusion.

One consistent finding is a major concern in relation to Social Security postponement. Low-income persons are most likely to be entirely dependent on Social Security for retirement. In the NHIS data, the rates and severity of illness and disability are inversely related to income. The American Changing Lives survey (House 1994) also documented a dramatic difference in significant functional limitations in low-income persons versus higher-income persons in every decade of age after 45 years old. A recent longitudinal study of university alumni found that healthy lifestyles were correlated with more disability-free years of life (Vita 1998); however, there is a strong inverse correlation between negative health risk behaviors and income. Thus, survey results and economic projections that are not stratified by income may not be helpful in answering questions about Social Security postponement.

## AGING AND WORK CAPACITY

The effects of the normal aging process may be a much more common potential limitation to extending regular employment for most workers than are specific diseases. Many studies have documented age-related decrements in sensory, cardiovascular, motor, and cognitive function, and decreases in long-term memory, reaction time, learning ability, isometric strength, and job performance (Garg 1991; Robertson and Tracy 1998; de Zwart, 1995). Average changes over a 40-year working lifespan were frequently on the order of 5–15 percent. However, those studies that employed a longitudinal design have often found that the most consistent age-related change is increased variance, greater than the mean change for most measures (de Zwart, Frings-Dresen, and VanDijk 1995; Robertson and Tracy 1998). Thus, it appears that there is more variation in physical and cognitive abilities among older people than among the young. This would also argue against a standard cut-off age for retirement. In a classic review of studies of age-related changes in job performance, Doering (1983) concluded that the results were mixed and inconclusive, although older workers did appear to consistently have difficulties in those rare jobs that required maximal levels of physical exertion.

Work capacity is significant only in relation to the demands of a specific job. Studies of persons with severe disabilities who are highly motivated to seek and maintain employment demonstrate that "objective" measures of ability to engage in gainful employment are poor predictors of actual employability. Many older workers with impairments gradually transition out of physically demanding jobs as they age. Thus, to understand the effects of health on work, job demands and accommodations, job selection, and motivation must all be considered (WHO 1993). Studies of older workers suggest that specific workplace design, training, organization, and accommodation approaches will increase employability (Shephard 1995).

As the economy evolves, the range of jobs available to older workers will change (Table 5), presenting both opportunities and challenges. As work shifts to less physically demanding jobs, many functional limitations will become less important. However, increased cognitive demands, new technologies, and requirements for longer work hours

**Table 5  Projected Job Growth for the Top Ten Occupations, 1998–2008**

| Occupation | Employment in 1998 (thousands) | Change by 2008 | |
|---|---|---|---|
| | | Thousands | % |
| Systems analysts | 617 | 577 | 94 |
| Retail salespersons | 4,056 | 563 | 14 |
| Cashiers | 3,198 | 556 | 17 |
| General managers and top executives | 3,362 | 551 | 16 |
| Truck drivers, light and heavy | 2,970 | 493 | 17 |
| Office clerks, general | 3,021 | 463 | 15 |
| Registered nurses | 2,079 | 451 | 22 |
| Computer support specialists | 429 | 439 | 102 |
| Personal care and home health aides | 746 | 433 | 58 |
| Teacher assistants | 1,192 | 375 | 31 |

SOURCE: Bureau of Labor Statistics 2000.

may present more challenges for older than for younger workers. Innovative training, work organization, and accommodation strategies will be required in order to engage and retain them in these jobs (Sterns and Doverspike 1988).

## CONCLUSION

Although an impressive body of literature is available on health, aging, and work, few conclusions are broadly generalizable. Recent findings of improvement in the average work capacity of older workers does not necessarily lead to a positive conclusion about the feasibility of continued work for those who will depend upon Social Security. Further research is needed to define and evaluate these issues for those who will primarily depend upon this source of income in their later years.

## References

Adams, P.F., G.E. Hendershot, and M.A. Marano. 1999. *Current Estimates from the National Health Interview Survey, 1996.* Vital and Health Statistics Series 10, no. 200, National Center for Health Statistics, DHHS publication no. 99-1528.

Bureau of Labor Statistics. 2000. *Occupational Outlook Handbook.* Bulletin 2520, U.S. Department of Labor.

Crimmins, E.M., M.D. Hayward, L.A. Wray, and R. Lu. 1995. "Prevalence and Incidence of Health Problems in the First 2 Waves of the Health and Retirement Study." Paper presented at the Health and Retirement Survey Workshop, Ann Arbor, Michigan, 1996.

de Zwart, Bart C.H., Monique H.W. Frings-Dresen, and Frank J.H. van Dijk. 1995. "Physical Workload and the Ageing Worker: A Review of the Literature." *International Archives of Occupational and Environmental Health* 68: 1–12.

Doering, M., S. Rhodes, and M. Schuster. 1983. *The Aging Worker: Research and Recommendations.* Beverly Hills, California: Sage Publications.

Fitzgerald, T.E., H. Tennen, G. Affleck, and G.S. Pransky. 1993. "The Relative Importance of Dispositional Optimism and Control Appraisals in Quality of Life after Coronary Artery Bypass Surgery." *Journal of Behavioral Medicine* 16: 25–43.

Garg, A. "Ergonomics and the Older Worker." 1991. *Experiments in Aging Research* 17: 143–155.

House, J.A., J.M. Lepkowski, A.M. Kinney, R.P. Mero, R.C. Kessler, and A.R. Herzog. 1994. "The Social Stratification of Aging and Health." *Journal of Health and Social Behavior* 35: 213–234.

Kramarow, E., H. Lentzner, R. Rooks, J. Weeks, and S. Saydah. 1999. *Health and Aging Chartbook. Health, United States, 1999.* Hyattsville, Maryland: National Center for Health Statistics.

Robertson, A., and C.S. Tracy. 1998. "Health and Productivity of Older Workers." *Scandinavian Journal of Work, Environment, and Health* 24: 85–97.

Shepherd, R.J. 1995. "A Personal Perspective on Aging and Productivity, with Particular Reference to Physically Demanding Work." *Ergonomics* 38: 617–636.

Sterns H., and D. Doverspike. 1988. "Training and Developing the Older Worker: Implications for Human Resource Development." In *Fourteen Steps in Managing an Aging Work Force*, H. Davis, ed. Lexington, Massachusetts: Lexington Books.

Tuomi, K.J. Ilmarinen, J. Seitsamo, P. Huuhtanen, R. Martikainen, C.H. Nygard, and M. Klockars. 1997. "Summary of the Finnish Research Project (1981–1992) to Promote the Health and Work Ability of Aging Workers." *Scandinavian Journal of Work, Environment, and Health* 23(Supp 1): 66–77.

U.S. Census Bureau. 2000. *Current Population Survey Disability: Selected Characteristics of Persons 16 to 74, 1998.* Washington, D.C.: U.S. Government Printing Office.

Verbrugge, L.M. 1989. "Recent, Present, and Future Health of American Adults." *Annual Review of Public Health* 10: 333–361.

Verbrugge, Lois M. 1984. "Longer Life but Worsening Health? Trends in Health and Mortality of Middle-Aged and Older Persons." *Milbank Memorial Fund Quarterly—Health & Society* 62(3): 475–519.

Vita, A.J., R.B. Terry, H.B. Hubert, and J.F. Fried. 1998. "Aging, Health Risks, and Cumulative Disability." *New England Journal of Medicine* 338: 1035–1041.

World Health Organization. 1993. *Aging and Work Capacity.* WHO Technical Report Series 835, Geneva, Switzerland, 49 pp.

Ycas, S. 1987. "Recent Trends in Health near the Age of Retirement: New Findings from the Health Interview Survey." *Social Security Bulletin* 50: 5–45.

# Commentary

Teresa Ghilarducci

*University of Notre Dame*

Who can argue that older people staying active, engaged, and productively working is a bad thing? Brookings Institution's Gary Burtless and Boston College economist Joseph Quinn want older people to work more. They show that the institutional rules of Social Security, social norms, economic prosperity, and employer pension and health plans affect retirement behavior, and they offer changes in tax laws and pension rules that would "incent" more older people to work. Yet, there is considerable disagreement over how much choice people should have between working or not after a certain age.

There is a lot right about Burtless and Quinn's study. It is a compilation of these experts' empirical findings on retirement and work and the detailed interactions of the Social Security's complex delayed requirement credits and earnings test. They sweep over a century of behavior lucidly in order to build the case for specific and easy-to-understand changes in the Social Security system and tax laws. There are, however, serious weaknesses that ultimately make their case for raising the retirement age in Social Security—their major policy prescription—fail. The paper ignores the important differences between the longevity of whites and blacks, the employability of older women compared with that of men, and the relative importance of Social Security benefits for married couples versus single women. Their proposals benefit employers as a group and the highest-earning professionals. The benefits of increasing the retirement age (thus cutting benefits) are not tremendous; Quinn and Burtless admit that increasing longevity is not the major reason for the Social Security system's projected shortfall (their note 18). Moreover, the benefits of maintaining the system are large. Workers will pay higher taxes to keep the retirement age from increasing.

Joseph Quinn and Gary Burtless describe how older people in the United States have connected themselves to their work over the last century. Men are retiring at younger ages except during the last decade. Women are increasing their paid work at all ages. Allowing a paragraph's worth of celebration of the working class's achieving some leisure at the end of their working lives due to increasing wealth, the paper's main focus is to structure policies so that the elderly workers work longer.

The protagonist in the paper is the "U.S. taxpayer" and the burden on this central player is the "burden imposed by an aging population," which could be lessened if workers "could be persuaded to delay their retirements and continue contributing to the health and pension systems." If people are to be persuaded to work longer, then the paper rightly identifies reasons about why people—and by that they mean mostly men—have been persuaded to retire earlier (except in the most recent decade). One theory is that workers have poor health; a second is that older workers face labor market discrimination; and a third is that workers want to retire and can increasingly afford it.

The authors reject the first theory by asserting the physical jobs requiring youngish bodies are on the decline, and that, on average, people live longer. Let us look closely at this bit of received wisdom: first, at the cost of this longevity and, second, at the extent and distribution of it. Figure 1 shows that increased longevity and work ability of the elderly is overblown. The top line shows that life expectancy for a 65-year-old male has increased only a few years since 1950—age 78 to age 81—an increase, but not a dramatic one. What is dramatic, as Burtless and Quinn also emphasize, is that male labor force participation rates are falling. This is a clear demonstration of how workers have chosen to spend the increases in the nation's productive capacity. The "gap" between work and death also represents a long hard fight for victory—that workers pay for—from employers and the state.

Averages hide crucial differences. Unlike whites, African-American males are not enjoying significant increases in longevity. Since five years ago, white males at age 65 live 2.6 percent longer—almost two years—while an African-American male's expectation went up seven months. Even worse is that the lower expected longevity of an African-American male entering the work force at age 20 in 1994 means that on average he'll retire for less than two months at full benefits. Robert Ball warns us that the Social Security system cannot right work and social injustices, but raising the normal retirement age has profound differential effects by race (Table 1).

**Figure 1  Workers Won Retirement: The Gap between Death and Work, 1950–1994**

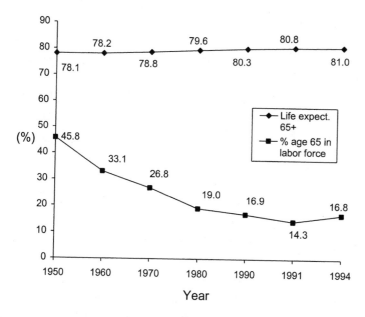

SOURCE: Steurele and Bakija (1994).

In addition to the variation in longevity among groups, it seems that the desire to work past 65 is concentrated in a few select groups. Only 4 percent of the elderly in the lowest income quintile have earnings, whereas almost 40 percent in the top have earnings (EBRI 1995). This corroborates other evidence that higher-income professionals are most likely to voluntarily work past normal retirement age (Bovbjerg 1998).

Quinn and Burtless acknowledge, and I agree, that people with jobs requiring stamina and brawn should get early retirement through the disability insurance system; this is an administrative change and helps those too old to work but not entirely disabled to retire. This proposal increases costs.

The authors argue that retirement became more acceptable as it became more affordable, and that social norms alone affect behavior

**Table 1  Longevity by Race and Sex, 1979–1980 and 1995**

| Race/sex | in 1979–1980 (yr.) | in 1994 (yr.) | Increase in longevity in 15 years (%) |
|---|---|---|---|
| Expected age at death for those at age 20 | | | |
| White male | 72.5 | 74.4 | 2.6 |
| White female | 79.4 | 80.4 | 1.3 |
| Black male | 66.4 | 67.1 | 1.1 |
| Black female | 74.9 | 75.5 | 0.8 |
| Expected age at death for those at age 65 | | | |
| White male | 79.3 | 80.6 | 1.6 |
| White female | 83.6 | 84.1 | 0.6 |
| Black male | 78.3 | 78.6 | 0.4 |
| Black female | 82.1 | 82.2 | 0.1 |

SOURCE: U.S. Department of Commerce 1997.

(controlling for all the other factors). In support of the social approbation hypothesis, they suggest that that ADEA of 1978 that gradually eliminated most mandatory retirement ages may have encouraged the recent increases in work among the elderly by reducing age discrimination and sending a signal to older Americans that work was socially acceptable.

The fact that the social signal affects some groups—like white, upper-income professionals—more than others is not a factor in their analysis. Most workers do not want to retire later and they are willing to pay for it. Most importantly, "encouraging" working more by lowering pensions has high costs paid by some and benefits reaped by others.

To this point, I am reminded of a conversation I overheard in 1997 between the former President of the Bricklayers and Allied Craftworkers Union, John Joyce, and Estelle James, lead author of the World Bank's 1994 pension study, which had a theme similar to that of Burtless and Quinn. She complained about his remarks given in a speech as misinterpreting the World Bank's support for advance funding and partially privatizing the world's pay-as-you-go retirement systems. Our argument is complicated, she protested. Such policies would protect the old and promote economic growth.

He turned, facing her directly and said, "Don't you want workers to work longer?"

"Yes," she said, "That's part of it."

The union president replied, "Then you are taking something away and giving nothing back."

I recall the conversation to make meaningful two observations that Burtless and Quinn acknowledge in their otherwise unambiguous call for older retirement ages. First, they argue that it may desirable to raise the retirement age but U.S. workers don't want to work longer. (They show us that older Americans work longer than most workers in OECD nations.) Eighteen polls over a 20-year period ending in 1997 showed that Americans oppose raising the retirement age. Burtless and Quinn imply that people may be responding to the survey this way because they want to retire even earlier, before age 55. However, Burtless and Quinn concede that workers may understand the cost of what they want; they cite a recent EBRI poll that showed that, by a 2:1 majority, "workers favor higher payroll taxes over reduced Social Security pensions."

Indeed, when given a chance, Americans are willing to pay for what they want. Union demands reflect the preferences of the average worker rather than the marginal or last worker hired in nonunion settings (Freeman 1981). The preferences of union and nonunion workers between pensions and wages are startling. According the Employment Cost Index in the 10-year period between 1980 and 1990, union workers had negative real wage increases but positive two-digit increases in pension contributions. Nonunion workers had the opposite experience: real wages increased by a bit, but pension costs plummeted. There are many factors—age of the workforce and industries—that can explain a huge difference in compensation patterns, but the simplest is consistent with other evidence. When asked, as they are when they vote for a collectively bargained contract, workers are ready to pay for their end of career leisure with reduced wages (Ghilarducci 1997). In other ways, U.S. workers have also demonstrated they will pay to retire. Payroll taxes increased by 16 percent in 1983 when Congress endorsed many of the recommendations of the Greenspan Commission.

Quinn and Burtless also acknowledge that households are also paying for retirement by increasing hours of work when they are younger. The average hours of work by the U.S. population has increased significantly since 1968. Workers between 25–54, on average, work 14 percent more hours than they did 30 years ago, because more women took jobs.

Quinn and Burtless have six proposals.

1) Raise the age at which full Social Security benefits can be received to age 67 (or an age that is increased according to increases in average longevity). This lowers benefits.

2) Exempt older workers from payroll taxes. This, of course, strains the Social Security program.

3) Make employers prorate fringe benefits for part time workers so that firms will more likely hire older workers for more than 35 hours if the cost of hiring them for less increases. This will raise the cost to employers.

4) Make Medicare the first insurance payer. This will raise Medicare costs but might reduce the employers' costs for older workers.

5) Raise the EITC for older workers. This is paid for by general revenue.

6) Repeal the earnings test so that workers receive full Social Security benefits regardless of earnings. This helps those earning over $17,000 per year.

Who wins and who loses?

- Employers win in three ways from Burtless and Quinn's proposals. First, there are significant wage subsidies for employers hiring older workers inherent in expanding the EITC, repealing the earnings test, making Medicare the first payer, and lowering payroll taxes. These reduce wage costs. Second, increasing the supply of workers reduces the bargaining power of all workers and puts downward pressure on wages. Third, higher-income workers would pay for an expanded EITC through general revenues generated by the progressive federal tax system. Proposal three, however, requiring employers to partly pay for the fringe benefits of part time workers, may increase costs if employers don't switch part-time workers to temporary status.

- Higher-income older workers win. Workers who would have worked longer anyway—white-collar professionals—are rewarded by getting a larger delayed retirement credit and by the elimination of the earnings test. Higher-income workers also benefit more than lower-income workers do because they are unlikely to retire at the earlier ages and take the lower pension.

- Middle-class workers lose. Instead of raising the retirement age, the Social Security system can raise payroll taxes. Lower-income workers—those in the first two quintiles—are almost fully subsidized by the EITC. So middle-income workers would have to pay the bulk of this increased cost if the earnings cap is not expanded. However, since these workers are more likely to retire at age 65 or earlier, then they pay for their retirement and "get something back" from their taxes.

- Blue-collar workers, workers in stressful jobs, and jobs sensitive to the business cycle will lose when the normal retirement age increases because they are much more likely to leave at the earlier ages and accept a lower pension.

- Older women lose. Women who do not work longer, and consequently receive a lower pension, will have lower earnings. This group is already at greater risk of poverty; the poverty rate for older single women is 22 percent, compared with 4 percent for older couples (who are more likely to get income from earnings). The wage gap between older men and women is also higher, suggesting that work opportunities for older women are more limited than for older men.

- Workers of all ages lose. If older workers have to work two to three years longer to get full benefits, then the increased supply of older workers searching for jobs depresses bargaining power and wages.

The gap between death and retirement shows a potential labor force ready to work if other sources of income—like Social Security and pensions—are made less certain and generous. In the year 2000, approximately 4.2 million Americans over the age of 65 are expected to be in the labor force. If the labor force participation rates rise to the 1950s level because of smaller Social Security benefits, the number jobs created would have to triple or unemployment will soar, which in turn will suppress wages. Burtless and Quinn assure us that the "job-creating capacity" of the American economy will accommodate this increase supply of workers. They credit the "flexible" U.S. labor market's ability to absorb workers. They acknowledge that "if older workers were forced to wait for two or three extra years for full Social Security retirement benefits to begin," many would work longer in their jobs or spend more time looking for work. This would "certainly depress the wages of aged job seekers."

British Philosopher Bertrand Russell helps us step back from the costs and benefits of reducing pensions and encouraging older people to work by commenting on the urge behind the urge. He writes in the 1935 essay *In Praise of Idleness* (p. 17),

> The idea that the poor should have leisure has always been shocking to the rich . . . When I was a child, shortly after urban working men had acquired the vote a number of public holidays were established. I remember hearing an old Duchess say, "What do the poor want with holidays? They ought to work.

In sum, this paper does not make the case for increasing the retirement age; the current projected numbers of retirees can be paid for through a modest increase in the payroll tax, which by all evidence seems to be acceptable to the American public. Moreover, the cost incidence of raising the retirement age would benefit high-income professional workers and employers at the expense of middle-income and women workers. Given the persistent problem of growing income inequality, any proposal that increases the gap between the top and bottom is unadvisable.

# References

Bovbjerg, Barbara. 1998. Statement before the Senate Committee On Aging, July 16, as Associate Director Income Security Issues, Health, Education, and Human Services Division.

EBRI. 1995. *EBRI Databook on Employee Benefits, Third Edition.* Washington, D.C.: Employee Benefits Research Institute.

Freeman, Richard B. 1981. "The Effect of Unionism on Fringe Benefits." *Industrial and Labor Relations Review* 34(July): 489–509.

Ghilarducci, Teresa. 1997. "Defusing the Retirement Time Bomb: Encouraging Pension Saving." U.S. House Representatives, Committee on Education and the Workforce, Subcommittee on Employer–Employee Relations, February 12. Federal Document Clearing House, http://web.lexis-nexis.com/congcomp/document. (Search congressional universe.)

Russell, Betrand. 1935. *In Praise Of Idleness.* London: George Allen & Unwin Ltd.

Steurele, Eugene, and Jon Bakija. 1995. *Retooling Social Security for the 20th Century.* Washington D.C.: The Urban Institute.

U.S. Department of Commerce. 1997. *Statistical Abstract of the United States, 1997.* Washington, D.C.: U.S. Government Printing Office, Table 118, p. 88.

# Session 5
# Filling Gaps in Health Coverage
## Sharing Responsibility and Costs

# Policy Options for Filling Gaps in the Health Insurance Coverage of Older Workers and Early Retirees

Len M. Nichols
*The Urban Institute*

This chapter offers answers to two questions concerning the health insurance of Americans between the ages of 55 and 64: 1) who has the greatest need for health insurance policy intervention? and 2) which types of policies are likely to be most effective for these subgroups? The chapter draws upon recent literature and other chapters of this book. I present a brief analysis of a broad range of policy options, as well as some quantitative simulation exercises which highlight key features of alternative targeted coverage strategies. While care was taken to make the estimates realistic, all simulations are at best illustrative of certain principles and should not be interpreted as definitive estimates of the cost or coverage impacts of particular proposals. Finally, I use the lessons from the examples to explore a relatively new way of thinking about financing subsidies for the purchase of health insurance. This view may have particular relevance for the age 55–64 cohort as it grows in the coming decades.

## WHO HAS THE GREATEST NEED FOR HEALTH INSURANCE POLICY INTERVENTION?

Recent policy discussions of coverage expansion options often focus on children or their parents, partly because members of the age 55–64 cohort are among the non-elderly most likely to have health insurance in the United States (Campbell 1999; Swartz and Stevenson 2001). Swartz and Stevenson report that only 15 percent of this group lacked health insurance in 1998, compared with 30 percent of 18- to 24-year-olds and 24 percent of 25- to 34-year-olds. Only the prime age working population, 45–54, had a lower incidence of being uninsured (13.6 percent).

However, a compelling case can be made that the consequences of being without health insurance are potentially much more damaging to this oldest pre-Medicare cohort than to other non-elderly citizens, for two reasons. First, the financial risk of no coverage is greater.

Table 1, constructed with 1987 National Medical Expenditure Survey (NMES) data, makes the point about higher financial risk. It reports ratios of per capita spending amounts for all adults, not just workers, by age and health status category. It shows that a 55- to 64-year-old man in good health (self-reporting excellent or good) should expect to spend 2.5 times as much as a young man (21–29) in equally good health. But the age-cost gradient is steeper for men in bad health (fair or poor), at 4.2. For women, the direction is the same, but the severity of the effect is less, largely because maternity costs are associated with younger women. Interestingly, the pure health status gradient is identical across genders at 2.7. Thus, the near-elderly in bad health can expect to spend 2.7 times as much as their cohort counterparts in good health.

Table 2 shows the percentage of each age cohort, by gender, that reported fair or poor health status in the 1987 NMES. These data show that the incidence of bad health increases dramatically with age. So, while they are relatively well covered as a group, 55- to 64-year-olds are indeed more likely to be financially vulnerable to the absence of health insurance coverage than other non-elderly Americans; they can expect to spend more if uninsured for both age and declining health status reasons.

**Table 1  Per-Capita Spending Ratios by Gender, Age, and Health Status**

|  | Males | | Females | |
|---|---|---|---|---|
|  | Good health[a] | Bad health | Good health | Bad health |
| Ages 55–64 / 21–29 | 2.5 | 4.2 | 1.3 | 1.9 |
| Age 55–64, bad/good health | — | 2.7 | — | 2.7 |

SOURCE: Author's calculations using 1987 NMES data.
[a] Good health = excellent or good; bad health = fair or poor.

**Table 2  Share of Each Age Group in Fair or Poor Health Status (%)**

| Age | Men | Women |
|-----|-----|-------|
| 21–29 | 8.8 | 12.0 |
| 30–54 | 14.8 | 18.1 |
| 55–64 | 34.1 | 35.6 |

SOURCE: Author's tabulations using 1987 NMES.

Second, potentially greater vulnerability from having no health insurance is greater health risk. Many studies have found that the uninsured enjoy less access to care and that both their health status and mortality risk are worse than is the case for the insured (Franks, Clancy, and Gold 1993, Franks et al. 1993). None as yet (to my knowledge) have found an age-related dimension to worsened outcomes or greater health risk from being uninsured, but this is surely a testable hypothesis. If it turns out to be true, this would strengthen the case for why the 55- to 64-year-old cohort should be a policy priority. If the hypothesis is false, then the case for helping 55- to 64-year-olds is mostly financial (there would still be access differentials relative to need, since their average need is greater than younger cohorts).

Having established that the age 55–64 cohort deserves policy attention, who within the cohort is the most deserving? The usual and correct answers are the low income and those with low (fair or poor) health status. These two groups always fare less well in the U.S. system of voluntary insurance markets, because comprehensive health insurance is now very expensive relative to low incomes and because insurers protect themselves against adverse selection by imposing limits, restrictions, and outright refusals to insure at any price for some preexisting conditions (Chollet and Kirk 1998; GAO 1998). Among the 55–64 cohort, those living in family units with income less than 200 percent of poverty (hereafter, low-income family units) comprise half the uninsured in the cohort, and those with fair or poor status regardless of income comprise 26 percent of the uninsured in the age group. Seventeen percent of the uninsured in this cohort are both low-income and in bad health.

It is important to remember, as Swartz and Stevenson (2001) and Pollitz (2001) report, that public insurance programs play a vital role for the sickest in this age group, covering about 10 percent of all 55- to 64-year-olds but over half of those who report not working because they are ill or disabled. Given the size of the uninsured population who report fair or poor health status to survey researchers, the public programs are clearly not able to cover all those who need coverage and can't afford to buy it on their own. Still, without Medicare and Medicaid's disabled and medically needy programs, the coverage problem of this age group would be much worse. Also note that because Medicaid and Medicare cover the most disabled of the cohort, the risk of adverse selection from expanding voluntary coverage options for this age group is somewhat reduced.

Swartz and Stevenson report that some subgroups are particularly likely to be uninsured. The unmarried, especially women, and those who had lost a spouse to death or changing circumstance (separated and divorced) of both genders were more likely to be uninsured. Never-married women are particularly vulnerable. Women in general are more likely to rely on nongroup insurance (Swartz and Stevenson 2001), which is less stable in an underwriting environment (which prevails in most of the United States) than is group or public insurance. Thus, the most in need of policy intervention are the low-income and the less-healthy, especially women.

**Predictable Future Strains**

This picture is bleak enough for those who are other than healthy, married, high-income workers, but two trends make it imperative that policymakers begin to consider coverage expansion options for this population in a serious way: the size of the aging baby-boomer cohort and the decline of employer-sponsored retiree health insurance. In 1998, there were 22.9 million people between the ages of 55 and 64; by 2008, there will be 35.2 million. So whatever unique problems they have in getting and keeping health insurance coverage, these problems are going to increase in aggregate magnitude by roughly half in the coming decade.

In addition, a major pillar of coverage for 55- to 64-year-olds, employer-sponsored retirement health insurance (RHI), is eroding.

Partly due to an accounting rule change that created strong incentives to drop RHI and immediately improve a company's balance sheet and stock price, and partly due to the changing labor market in which RHI is perceived as less crucial to attract good workers in an increasingly mobile global economy, there is a clear tendency on the part of employers to reduce the generosity of postretirement health insurance offerings (GAO 1998; McArdle et al. 1999). Between 1985 and 1993, the fraction of workers with access to employer-sponsored retirement health insurance declined from about 75 percent to about 50 percent (U.S. Department of Labor 1995). Perhaps most ominously, even large firms are both dropping RHI and charging early retirees higher and higher premiums for such coverage (McArdle et al. 1999; Loprest and Zedlewski 1998). Employer surveys indicate that fewer workers are likely to have access to RHI in the future (McArdle et al. 1999).

Of course, the other side of the coin is that the absence of good early retirement health insurance options probably keeps workers in the labor force longer (Johnson, Davidoff, and Perese 2000; Karoly and Rogowski 1998; Gruber and Madrian 1995). If public policy were to make generous subsidies widely available, rates of declines in labor force participation by older workers could regain their 1970s momentum (Blau and Gilleskie 1997). Of course, some retirements are involuntary and health-related, even though the person might not be disabled enough to qualify for Medicare or Medicaid. Striking a balance here is clearly important, and thus any new subsidy proposal must be mindful of likely labor force (and payroll tax base) effects. These effects have been established qualitatively, but no consensus has been reached on the magnitude of likely responses to subsidies of varying degrees. This is an important and active area of research.[1]

## WHICH TYPES OF POLICIES ARE LIKELY TO BE MOST EFFECTIVE FOR THE NEEDIEST SUBGROUPS, THE LOW-INCOME AND THOSE WITH HEALTH PROBLEMS?

There are two key dimensions to coverage expansion policies for the near-elderly: the subsidy mechanism and the range of market opportunities for insurance or health services on which the beneficiary may spend the subsidy. The interactions of these dimensions is crucial in determining the ultimate effect of any policy initiative, and thus they really should be considered in tandem. To that end, I present Table 3, which should be thought of as a 4 × 3 matrix, each cell of which is a potential type of coverage expansion policy. This table tries to help the reader see that both dimensions are key to understanding the full set of implications about each policy alternative.

In this section, I briefly discuss some pros and cons of each approach.

## COBRA Extensions

What I mean by mandates are laws forcing employers to make COBRA coverage available to workers for longer periods of time after they leave the firm. Under current law, if an employer offers insurance to active workers, then workers who sever employment (in firms with more than 20 workers) for any reason must be offered the option of continuing to enroll in the employer's plan—in exchange for paying 102 percent of the total premium—for as long as 18 months (and longer under certain circumstances). COBRA provides bridge coverage to Medicare for many individuals who retire before age 65 (Loprest and Zedlewski 1998). The idea behind extending COBRA is

**Table 3  Policy Options for Filling Health Insurance Coverage Gaps for 55- to 64-Year-Olds**

| Subsidy mechanism | Current nongroup market | Reformed nongroup market[a] | Existing risk pools[b] or New Group Purchasing Authority |
|---|---|---|---|
| Employer mandates (COBRA extensions) | NA[c] | NA | √ |
| Existing public program expansions | NA | NA | √ |
| Tax credits | √ | √ | √ |
| Direct subsidies | √ | √ | √ |

[a] Guaranteed issue, premium restrictions, etc.
[b] Purchasing co-ops, FEHBP, Medicaid, Medicare, state high-risk or HIPAA pools.
[c] NA = not applicable.

to permit access to the group market longer, maybe 36 months or until the age of Medicare eligibility is reached (this is sometimes offered as a complement to proposals to raise the age of Medicare eligibility to 67). The virtue of extending COBRA is that access to a shared-risk pool (the employer group) would be enhanced at low (nominally zero) cost to the federal government.

The downsides to COBRA extensions are 1) it does nothing for nonworkers save dependents of recent retirees; 2) while lower than most nongroup premiums, 102 percent of the employer premium is still more than many early retirees can afford to pay; and most seriously, 3) it constitutes an implicit tax on existing workers and firms, since wages will (on average) be lowered to pay for the higher premiums required to cover the cost of retirees. There would also be a second-order reduction in federal tax revenues, since wages are taxed and employer-provided health insurance premium payments are not. Thus, COBRA extensions are not "free" and, on the whole, do not seem to be a particularly effective way of  extending coverage to those in this cohort who need it most. Recall, many of those most in need for early retiree health insurance worked for firms that did not offer employer-sponsored insurance to active workers. Having access to COBRA is fairly highly correlated with income in the first place (Loprest and Zedlewski 1998).

### Public Program Expansions

An administratively straightforward way to expand coverage for those most in need would be to change eligibility for Medicaid or Medicare or both. These programs already serve the very sick and disabled (see Pollitz [2001] for a brief overview of each), and Medicaid also covers many low-income individuals, though typically much younger than this cohort. This approach, like the COBRA extension, would permit coverage expansion to avoid the complexities and inefficiencies of the private nongroup insurance market. These complexities can be severe, as we discuss presently.

The downsides to public program expansion are partly technical but mostly political. The technical problem is in "slightly" increasing the range of conditions or functional diagnoses that are considered "disabled" enough to merit inclusion in either Medicare or Medicaid.

There is concern and some evidence that medical judgments are inconsistent and elastic, leading to an "endogenous" assignment of disability that could expand public program rolls well beyond the intent of the law and agreed upon medical need (Kubik 1996).

The larger objections to public program eligibility expansions are political. The obvious point is the considerable resistance in the Congress to expanding any entitlement program, especially our entitlement insurance programs. In addition, if Medicaid—the joint state and federal program—is the preferred vehicle (and in general it has been the program expanded to accept broader definitions of disability in recent years), then truly effective expansion requires states to share the new federal goals, for they will be asked to spend their own money on this. The variance in state coverage and enrollment of different types of Medicaid eligibles suggests that this "goal sharing" should not be taken for granted.

## Tax Credits

In contrast to public program eligibility expansion, there is currently something of a groundswell of bipartisan political support for tax credits that could be used for the purchase of health insurance. Briefly put, many are attracted to the principle of tax credits, even if there is no agreement yet on key details. This movement seems to be propelled by a confluence of forces in support of one or more of the following: 1) tax equity (why subsidize employer premiums but not the self-employed or nonworkers?); 2) individual choice (partly philosophical and partly a more subtle form of the current backlash against managed care, led by those who have a strong stake in the fee-for-service system and blame employers for foisting managed care on workers); 3) target efficiency (which tax credits can be designed to be); and 4) tax cuts (as tax credits can be described for political purposes). Two recent papers have analyzed tax credits of various forms (Gruber and Levitt 2000; Pauly and Herring 1999b) for the general non-elderly population.

The major downside of tax credits is that they must be administered within the income tax system. This makes it difficult to reach those who have no federal tax liability and do not file tax returns (approximately 45 percent of the uninsured in all age brackets [Gruber and Levitt 2000]). The tax system is a cumbersome avenue for any eligible person of a means-tested program. (The opposition of Treasury professionals to administering subsidies through the tax system is legendary inside the Beltway). Thus, using the tax system to administer a subsidy is likely to result in lower enrollment than would subsidies of equal size that could be obtained with less applicant and administrative burden. Second (and related), for tax credits to work well for the target low-income population, they must be both refundable (for those with zero or low tax liabilities) and available when premiums must be paid, i.e., up front, not in April of the following year. The low-income population cannot finance health insurance with an interest-free loan, otherwise they wouldn't need a subsidy in the first place. Refundability and prepayment raise serious year-end reconciliation complexities and potential reductions in target efficiency. Finally, as Pauly and Herring show and others have long stated (Blumberg 1999), tax credits must be fairly large to do any good at all for the low-income population. This is not a critique of tax credits per se, but rather a statement that they may work better for lower middle-income people than for the truly low-income population.

**Direct Subsidies**

Direct subsidies (a new program, not an extension of Medicare or Medicaid) could be designed to have the technical advantages of tax credits (target efficiency, horizontal equity) without the administrative disadvantages of using the tax system for a means-tested subsidy program. This is not to say that the administrative difficulties of setting up a new subsidy program are trivial. But the motivating idea of a "new and different" subsidy program would be to provide direct purchasing power (and, perhaps, health plan purchasing expertise; more on this later in the discussion of market opportunities) without the regulations and complex vendor-relations histories of Medicare and Medicaid.

One downside of a new direct subsidy program is shared with tax credits, and that is that the subsidies must be large to engender much new coverage. The resulting public price tag contributes to direct subsidies' major political problem, the absence of a widely shared new political vision for a new expansive health insurance entitlement.

## Using the Current Nongroup Market

The nongroup health insurance market is functional in all 50 states and works better than its reputation in some health policy circles, at least according to a new book by Mark Pauly and Brad Herring (1999a). They make one overarching and controversial empirical claim: risks are pooled to nearly equal (and imperfect) degrees by large-group, small-group, and nongroup insurers. They conclude that there is no systematic empirical evidence of aggressive risk rating by nongroup insurers.

Even if one accepts Pauly and Herring's new empirical claims (and I suspect they will remain controversial for at least a while yet), their fundamental deduction is that the primary differences between insurance markets stem from their inherently different administrative loading costs. Group insurance can exploit economies of scale and thus costs less than nongroup insurance can. Thus, high administrative costs are a major downside of the current nongroup market.

Other reports about the actual workings of the nongroup market are not so sanguine on the relative absence of aggressive risk rating (Chollet and Kirk 1998; GAO 1997; Hall 2000). Also, recall that risk rating, as well as age rating (which is ubiquitous and quite reasonable given the expenditure facts presented in Table 1), means that people in our cohort will pay higher equilibrium premiums under the current nongroup market's relative *laissez faire* regulation, even if they can on average find policies to buy as Pauly's empirical results suggest. So, paying more for a given set of benefits plus paying a higher administrative load is the reality for 55- to 64-year-olds in the unreformed nongroup market.

## Reforming the Nongroup Market

Almost all discussions of the actual behavior of nongroup insurers (Hall 1999; Chollet and Kirk 1998), as opposed to the empirical results of Pauly and Herring, invariably lead to calls for some kind of reforms (Swartz and Garnick 2000; Chollet and Kirk 2000; Hall 2000). The basic idea is that guaranteed issue and restrictions on premium variances would guarantee access at affordable prices for most people trying to purchase coverage in the nongroup market. A reformed nongroup market could indeed look a great deal friendlier to the garden variety 55- to 64-year-old than it does in most states today (Pollitz 2001; BCBSA 1999).

However, reforms that increase access for older and sicker would-be purchasers raise average premiums and are quite likely to raise by a substantial amount the premiums of most of those who were purchasing in the prereform environment (Nichols 2000). Empirical evidence on the effect of nongroup reforms is scant if not rare, but the studies that have been done uniformly find that nongroup reforms do indeed reduce net insurance coverage overall (Marsteller et al. 1998; Zuckerman and Rajan 1999; Sloan and Conover 1998). Thus, while reforms would undoubtedly help some (perhaps especially those 55–64 with the greatest health needs), these reforms would also likely cause others to pay more and might cause them to go without coverage altogether.

Perhaps those who would obtain or would retain coverage in a reformed nongroup insurance environment have worse health status than those who voluntarily drop coverage because of premium increases. This is an important area of future research which is not well known at the moment. There are also case studies of how reforms have been implemented with relatively little obvious downsides (Swartz and Garnick 2000; Hall 2000; Nichols 2000). But these successful implementation strategies require a degree of political will (e.g., requiring group insurers to offer products in the nongroup market) that is not present in most states and does not appear to be present in Congress either.

## Buying into Existing Risk Pools

If an unreformed nongroup market is unpalatable to most observers and a reformed nongroup market is fraught with tradeoffs for the unsubsidized to bear, then allowing 55- to 64-year-olds to take their tax credit or direct subsidy into a group setting to purchase health insurance makes a tremendous amount of sense. Large pools exist and could be expanded at much lower administrative costs than either type of nongroup market could offer. Furthermore, they provide natural and existing risk-pooling mechanisms. Among the more attractive options are statewide purchasing cooperatives for employees of small businesses (CHIP in California), the Federal Employees Health Benefit

Plan (FEHBP), or state employee plans (e.g., CALPERS in California). In addition, administrative and marketing efficiencies would result if new subsidies of whatever form were allowed to be used to buy into Medicare or Medicaid. Finally, state high-risk pools or the mechanisms created by states to comply with HIPAA "federal eligibles" could also be opened up to the new beneficiaries at relatively low administrative costs.

The downside of using existing pools is that existing members might not be willing to be rated collectively with the new enrollees, especially if they turned out to be higher than average risks, even controlling for age. Conversely, the new enrollees might not like being charged actuarially fair premiums with high-risk pool members, if that were the mechanism of choice. But once the decision is made to rate the populations separately, some of the administrative efficiencies of group purchase would be lost.

Allowing the newly subsidized 55- to 64-year-olds to buy into public programs would not raise cost issues, because these programs are and would remain free to currently qualified beneficiaries. However, if the new enrollees got substantially different benefit packages—for example, if they got prescription drug coverage through a Medicare + Choice HMO—there might be stronger equity-based opposition raised by current beneficiaries. Further, deciding what price to charge the "buying" enrollees is no simple matter for a public program, for here the relative risk-rating heterogeneity and controversies seep back into the calculation.

### Organizing New Risk Pools and Purchasing Authorities

Alternatively, with a new federal health insurance subsidy program targeted directly at 55- to 64-year-olds, the government could set up a whole new purchasing agency, modeled after the best private or public health plan purchasing agencies, that would organize enrollment and health plan options for the new beneficiaries. This entity could write RFPs and negotiate with health plans and insurers, while coordinating enrollment, beneficiary plan choice, and financial transactions to maximize administrative efficiencies for all. Eligibility standards would have to be established and enforced, but these functions have to be performed somewhere by someone. Creating a whole new purchasing agent would have the major virtue of allowing the new program to establish its own relations with beneficiaries, vendors, and insurers without the legacies and resentments each might bring from the Medicaid or Medicare programs. It may also be the only quick way to get creative about risk adjusting and competitive bidding, both of which may be particularly helpful for insuring the 55–64 population, as we shall discuss later after presenting some simulation results.

The downside of a new agency is that it would surely cost more to run at the outset than the marginal cost of adding these functions to existing Medicare or Medicaid programs. Plus, it would be vulnerable to the charge of government proliferation, since a new federal entity would be born. These disadvantages would have to be weighed against the potential long-run advantages of freedom from existing programs' rules. The ultimate judgment may hinge upon how much like a private sector "sponsor,"—e.g., the Buyer's Health Care Action Group in Minnesota or the Pacific Business Group on Health in San Francisco— Congress would want this new purchasing agent to be. The more freedom to contract and aggressive use of government bargaining power on behalf of beneficiary choices and welfare are valued, the more likely the optimal choice would be a new entity. However, if the public organization of subsidized beneficiaries' purchase of participating health plans is intended to be as passive as most Medicare and Medicaid health plan purchasing has been to date, i.e., if policymakers think of the program as a provider support device as much as a beneficiary subsidy mechanism, then creating a new entity is not likely to be worth the political and administrative trouble.

## A FEW SPECIFIC POLICY SIMULATIONS

In this section, I present some simulation results of the policy options that seem promising and efficient enough to be feasible in our current political environment of parsimony towards coverage expansions (i.e., they are on a financial scale commensurate with Vice President Gore's proposal to cover parents of Medicaid and CHIP children and Governor Bush's modest tax credit proposal). Table 4 presents some contextual facts and basic assumptions.

**Table 4  Some Basic Facts and Assumptions**

| | |
|---|---|
| Total 55–64 population (millions) | 22.9 |
| Uninsured | 3.4 |
| Nongroup | 2.0 |
| Low income | 6.1 |
| Fair/poor health | 5.4 |
| Low income and bad health | 2.6 |
| Est. standard premium ($) | 2,500 |
| Est. high-risk premium ($) | 6,750 |
| Est. community rate ($) | 3,900 |

SOURCE: 1999 CPS and author's calculations in 1998 dollars.

First, recall that there are approximately 23 million people between 55 and 64 today. About 3.4 million are uninsured, while another 2 million purchase coverage in the nongroup market, and thus their hold on health insurance is more tenuous than those insured through work (past or present) or in public programs. About 6 million people in this cohort have incomes below 200 percent of poverty, and 5.4 million report fair or poor health status. Finally, 2.6 million are estimated to have both low income and bad health status.

The key assumption in all policy analyses of coverage expansions is the premium that must be paid for the desired insurance product, for this parameter simultaneously determines both total program cost and enrollment (conditional on the income distribution) in the likely event that some (maybe all) will be made eligible for a partial subsidy. Without exaggeration, one can state that the reliability, representativeness, and quality of publicly available premium data for the nongroup market range from fair to poor. I consulted studies of the nongroup market (GAO 1998; Chollett and Kirk 1998; Chollett 2000; Kirk 2000; Swartz and Garnick 2000; Hall 2000; Pauly and Herring 1999a), high-risk pools (Communicating for Agriculture 1999), analyses of Medicare buy-in proposals (Loprest and Moon 1999; CBO 1998), and both NMES and MEPS data (the latter supplied by John Eisenberg). The premium assumptions in Table 4 represent a judgmental average of all the above sources, where each source estimate or fact was adjusted to account for the particular nature of the underlying pool.

For example, high-risk pool premiums must be adjusted for the fact that they are set below the actuarial value, but claims and administrative costs are published along with premium receipts, so this is fairly simple. What is not published is the degree to which adverse selection into high-risk pools is likely worse than would result from the kinds of subsidy programs for the persons aged 55–64 who are uninsured (and thus not in a state high-risk pool) today. CBO and others made analogous adjustments from the published estimates of nongroup premiums when predicting who would take a Medicare buy-in option. In addition, MEPS data were provided for workers only, and they are healthier than nonworkers in every age cohort. The NMES per capita spending data are in the public domain, and the data based on them that I presented in Tables 1 and 2 are for all 55- to 64-year-olds. They include nonworkers, obviously, but have the disadvantage of also including publicly insured individuals who are unlikely to switch into the new subsidy program and are most likely to be the sickest of all. Plus, the NMES data are from 1987, and while they can be "aged" using HCFA's national health account growth rates, the delivery system is quite different today, so the age- and health status gradients may have changed (though I suspect not much).[2]

I welcome suggestions for better ways to estimate premiums for these kinds of policies, but I believe these estimates are at least "in the town the ballpark is in," to invoke Bob Reischauer's famous description of health reform estimates, and that will suffice for discussion purposes at least. The important fact to note about them is the gap between the high-risk premium ($6,750) and the standard premium ($2,500). The former are computed for those with fair or poor health status, and the latter for those in excellent or good health. The community rate ($3,900) represents the weighted average of each type of person if all nonpublicly insured 55- to 64-year-olds were to become insured through the hypothetical new subsidy program and the ratio of (fair + poor) ÷ total is the same as in 1987.

Table 5 summarizes and compares the three subsidy policy initiatives I explore in some detail. My objective is to maximize coverage of the target population at minimum cost, so in each case, I assume a direct subsidy (to maximize participation and target efficiency) and that

**Table 5  Subsidy Options Simulated**

Income-based subsidy for 55–64 year olds

    100% for those below poverty

    Sliding scale between 100–200%

    Not available for those in public, with ESI/RHI

    Group purchase mechanism

Health status–based subsidy for 55–64 year olds

    100% for those with fair or poor health

    Not available for those in public, with ESI/RHI

    Group purchase mechanism

Income and health status–based subsidy for 55–64 year olds

    100% for low income with bad health

    Not available for those in public, with ESI/RHI

    Group purchase mechanism

beneficiaries will be allowed to select plans through some kind of group purchasing mechanism, the exact nature of which is not specified. To be conservative, I assume this group purchasing agent is less efficient than either Medicare or large employers, and I therefore assign an administrative load on expected health care costs (which includes eligibility determination costs plus the agency's and the insurer's administrative costs) of 20 percent. Other institutional assumptions are that beneficiaries will be guaranteed issue (i.e., no one can be denied coverage because of health status) and that the newly subsidized population will be rated separately from participants in current markets. In each case, I assume the subsidy is targeted and available only to those who are not currently enrolled in a public program and do not have access to ESI/RHI, but I presume that 90 percent of current participants in the nongroup market who are made eligible will participate in the program, and that 10 percent of those with ESI/RHI will drift over into the program either by choice or because their employers will induce or force them to.

The first policy is targeted to low-income 55- to 64-year-olds. It would provide 100 percent of the cost of a plan (presumed to cost the community rate of $3,900 in the income-related case) for all persons 55–64 who have incomes at or below poverty and who are not eligible for Medicare or Medicaid and without access to ESI or RHI.  Starting at incomes just above 100 percent of poverty, subsidies (and participation) decline along a sliding scale to 0 at 200 percent of poverty.

The second policy is targeted at those who have the greatest health needs.  It would grant a 100 percent subsidy to all persons with fair or poor health, regardless of income.  The price of coverage for each of these persons is presumed to be $6,750.  Eligibility for this kind of policy could be determined or certified by physicians, in a process similar to the individual functional assessment test now given to potentially "disabled" Medicaid enrollees.  Alternatively, and preferably from my point of view, one can imagine using a kind of underwriting process, similar to that used by nongroup insurers all the time, but in cooperation with the purchasing authority so it can be standardized across plans.  Postenrollment encounter data could be required of participating health plans to assess the accuracy of *ex ante* assessments, and this would work best if a competitive bidding process was also implemented to set the price the government pays for this population.

In essence, this option is for the government to become an organized purchaser for those between 55 and 64 and in poor health.[3]  In principle, there is no reason that moral hazard on the part of insurers should be debilitating for this scheme, and competitive bidding (and concomitant data reporting requirements just like private sector organized purchasers use) may be all that is necessary to minimize this risk and monitor the effectiveness of competition.  If insurers can define health states that we agree deserve this kind of subsidy, then we can write an RFP for covering people who possess them and competitive bidding should be able to elicit a fair price for the government to pay.  "Fair + poor" self-reported health status is merely a simplified way I can approximate a concept like "bad health" using nationally representative survey data.  Using all of those currently reporting fair and poor health in the analysis of this option probably represents an upper bound of the numbers of people that AHRQ and private insurers would declare to be possessors of the appropriately targeted health states, i.e., those that lie between current definitions of disabled and the health status level underlying the concept of "standard" risk in the insurance industry.  Competitive bidding is a powerful tool for eliciting cost-based prices of services that has typically been absent when Medicaid and Medicare disability determination were being made. At a minimum, it seems worth provoking a conversation about how this might be implemented, if people do agree that helping those with low health status is a primary goal for coverage expansion policy, especially for the 55–64 population which has a far greater percentage of members with fair + poor health status than the nonelderly age cohorts (remember Table 2).

The third policy explored is a combination income–health status subsidy. The idea is to provide 100 percent for all the low-income persons who also have fair or poor health status. Again, the subsidy would not be available to those who have public coverage or access to ESI/RHI.

Table 6 reports the bottom line results of these policy simulations.[4] No subsidy approach dominates in all dimensions, so that a case can be made for and against each of the subsidy targets. They were of course designed to illustrate certain prototypical features of each subsidy type.

The income-only subsidy covers the most people and is relatively target-efficient. The health-status-only subsidy costs more, but covers the vast majority of those with a compelling and unmet health-status-related demand for health insurance. The income + health status subsidy is cheaper and more efficient than the health-status-only subsidy alone, for it covers 55 percent of the fair + poor people at 65 percent of the cost of the health-status-only subsidy scheme. This is because the fair + poor are more numerous in the lower income ranges.

**Table 6  Simulated Results of Policy Options**

|  | Basis for subsidy | | |
|  | Income | Health | Income and health |
| --- | --- | --- | --- |
| Newly covered (millions) | 1.2 | 0.77 | 0.5 |
| % of uninsured newly covered | 34 | 23 | 15 |
| % of uninsured in fair/poor health covered | 44 | 85 | 55 |
| Total cost ($, billions) | 6.6 | 7.1 | 4.3 |
| Cost per newly insured ($) | 5,674 | 9,280 | 8,644 |

SOURCE: Author's calculations using CPS, NMES, MEPS, and other data.

The relative efficiency of income + health status–based subsidies for this population is appealing to the economist in me, but it does leave out those in poor health at higher incomes. One might infer that those who remain uninsured do so voluntarily, since their families have means, but two facts about the current nongroup market in most states give pause to reaching this conclusion. First, in most states, insurers are allowed to refuse to sell in the nongroup market except to the relatively small number of HIPAA eligibles. Pauly and Herring report that if the underwriting process leads a nongroup insurer to think that a person's health merits a premium of 3 times standard, they most often refuse to sell at all. Recall that the NMES data support the existence of a 2.7 health status multiple within the 55–64 age cohort. If nongroup insurers measure applicants' health risks relative to the population standard, as seems likely, then many of those with fair or poor health status who are uninsured despite having higher incomes may very well have had trouble finding a willing seller. Second, even if they could find a willing seller at actuarially fair prices, the $6,750 price I estimated is more than 10 percent of income until income exceeds 8 times poverty (for single individuals). And of course, some insurers may offer a price far above the actuarially fair one in order to discourage purchases by individuals who are feared to be quite sick.

This price/income fact made me think about an addition to the income + health–based subsidy, an addition that relates to a choice between subsidies and separate group purchase mechanisms on the one hand versus subsidies and a reformed nongroup market on the other.

Suppose that instead of creating a new group purchasing entity, we gave the newly eligible subsidies and sent them off into a reformed nongroup market to purchase would they could. This approach would likely include some kind of community rating (CR) requirement, at least within age cohorts. Let $h$ = the high-risk premium and $c$ = the community rate. The idea is that the unsubsidized, those with incomes above 200 percent of poverty, say, could buy a policy at $c$. In that sense, you could say they were "community rate–protected," in that they would never pay more than $c$.

Because I am wary of trying to accomplish wholesale reform of the nongroup market in today's political climate, I recommended creating the separate group purchase mechanism and the types of subsidies I have described. But we could easily create a subsidy just for the amount above the community rate, $h - c$, for those who have incomes between 200 percent of poverty and 800 percent of poverty. That way, those with fair + poor health and incomes above 200 percent would pay $c$, the exact community rate they would have paid if we had reformed the nongroup market, but we could avoid the collateral damage to those whose premiums would have been increased. Presumably, most if not all of those in fair or poor health with reasonable incomes would gladly pay $c$ to get guaranteed issue health insurance.

Table 7 reports the results of this type of subsidy. The first column is the same as column 3 from Table 6, the income + health status subsidy. The "CR Protection alone" column reports what this $h - c$ subsidy does for those with incomes between 200 and 800 percent of poverty, and the final column combines it with the income + health status subsidy we've already analyzed. There we see that the total cost is still modest, the target efficiency on those with fair or poor health is very good, and the overall target efficiency in cost per newly insured person is improved from that obtained with the income + health status subsidy without CR protection.

Finally, Table 8 compares the required net increase in average federal income tax rates necessary to finance the income + health status + CR protection subsidy (0.108 percent, that is, one-tenth of 1 percentage point) with the average premium increase in the nongroup market for 55- to 64-year-olds if the same number of subsidized purchasers entered the nongroup market with guaranteed issue and community rat-

**Table 7  Simulated Results of Community-Rating Protection**

|  | Basis for subsidy | | |
| --- | --- | --- | --- |
|  | Income + health | CR protection alone | Income + health + CR |
| Newly covered (millions) | 0.5 | 0.25 | 0.75 |
| % of uninsured newly covered | 15 | 7 | 22 |
| % of uninsured in fair/poor health covered | 55 | 28 | 83 |
| Total cost ($, billions) | 4.3 | 1.2 | 5.5 |
| Cost per newly insured ($) | 8,644 | 4,972 | 7,333 |

SOURCE: Author's calculations using CPS, NMES, MEPS, and other data.

**Table 8  Alternative "Tax" Rates from Subsidizing Low-Income + High-Risk Protection (%)**

| | |
|---|---|
| Increase in average federal income tax rate required to finance Income + Health + CR | 0.108 |
| Increase in average premium from putting same number of high risk into nongroup market with CR | 23.9 |
| Share of nongroup market that would be high risk under reform | 45.2 |

ing (23.9 percent). This large premium increase results because the fraction of nongroup purchasers who would be in fair or poor health in that cohort would basically double to 45.2 percent. I have no doubt the tiny income tax increase would cause much less disruption than this large premium increase, except perhaps in certain ideological circles which oppose all publicly financed coverage expansions.


## CONCLUSIONS

The need for health insurance policy options for the 55–64 group is compelling now and is going to intensify as the baby boomers expand that cohort in the next decade. The financial risk of going without coverage is high for members of this cohort, the health risks could be substantial (we do not know a great deal about this at the present time), and a traditional pillar of pre-Medicare coverage, employer-sponsored retiree coverage, is expected to continue to decline in prevalence.

Reasonably inexpensive and targeted subsidy programs can be devised and implemented that would go a long way toward covering the neediest near-elderly, those with low incomes and low health status. The subsidy and purchasing entity that achieves the best overall outcome, in my view, has the virtue of highlighting the fact that subsidies most efficiently eradicate need when they reflect both income and health status dimensions of people's lives.

Researching and writing this paper has forced me to reflect on many dimensions of coverage expansion options. I would like to conclude by offering the following normative principles for health insurance subsidy policy that seem particularly applicable to the 55- to 64-year-old cohort and maybe others as well.

- No poor person should pay for health insurance. (Corollary: No person who makes more than 10 times poverty should tell a person in poverty what that poor person can afford to pay.)

- No person with poor health should pay more than the actuarially fair community rate unless their income is high.

- The people of the United States can afford to offer substantial relief to 55- to 64-year-olds with low incomes who are also in bad heath, and indeed to most of those in poor health regardless of income.

- We can offer this relief with very modest income tax rate increases. This is a much less costly financing mechanism—in terms of social disruption—than forcing nongroup insurers to charge community rated premiums to all purchasers.

## Notes

I am grateful to Kathy Swartz, Rich Johnson, Karen Pollitz, Alan Monheit, Marilyn Moon, Bo Garrett, Linda Blumberg, and Frank Sammartino for many helpful conversations and to Joseph Llobrera for timely research assistance. I remain solely responsible for all errors or omissions. The views expressed herein are mine alone and not those of the Urban Institute, its Trustees, or its sponsors. My address is 2100 M Street, NW, Washington, DC, 20037; (202)261-5697; lnichols@ui.urban.org.

1. See Johnson, Davidoff, and Perese (2000) for a summary of recent and ongoing work.
2. Berk and Monheit (1992) show that the distribution of health expenditures has been remarkably stable since 1929, so that the skewness (10 percent of the population accounting for 70 percent of the spending) that was present in the 1987 data is very likely to still be present.
3. The hypothetical new program needs a name. For this cohort, all concepts are "near-something" (-Medicare, -work, -elderly, etc.). "Near" makes me think of something off in the distance, somehow better than what we have now. This all suggests Avalon, the mythical Arthurian island, shrouded in mist, where the Lady of Lake lives, where Arthur was taken after he was slain, and from whence Camelot will return, if it ever does. It could be the Avalon Purchasing Authority (APA), with apologies to the American Psychological Association.
4. In each case I assumed that a 100 percent subsidy would engender an 85 percent participation rate from the currently uninsured who were targeted, 90 percent

from current nongroup purchasers who would be eligible, and 10 percent of current ESI and RHI holders who are ineligible but expected to drift. I also assumed that participation would decline linearly as the subsidy falls to zero.

# References

BCBSA. 1999. *State Legislative Health Care and Insurance Issues.* Washington, D.C.: Blue Cross and Blue Shield Association.

Berk, Mark L., and Alan C. Monheit. 1992. "The Concentration of Health Expenditures: An Update." *Health Affairs* 11(4): 145–149.

Blau, David, and Donna Gileskie. 1997. "Retiree Health Insurance and the Labor Force Behavior of Older Men in the 1990s." Working paper no. 5948, National Bureau of Economic Research, Cambridge, Massachusetts.

Blumberg, Linda J. 1999. "Children's Health Insurance Tax Credit and Publicly Sponsored Children's Insurance Pools." In *Options for Expanding Health Insurance Coverage: What Difference Do Different Approaches Make?*, J. Feder, ed. Henry J. Kaiser Family Foundation Project on Incremental Health Reform.

Campbell, Jennifer A. 1999. *Health Insurance Coverage, 1998.* Current Population Reports P60-208, October.

Chollet D.J. 2000. "The Individual Health Insurance Market—Consumers, Insurers, and Market Behavior." *Journal of Health Politics, Policy and Law* 25(1): 127–144.

Chollet, D.J., and A.M. Kirk. 1998. *Understanding Individual Health Insurance Markets: Structure, Practices, and Products in Ten States.* Menlo Park, California: Henry J. Kaiser Family Foundation.

Communicating for Agriculture. 1999. *Comprehensive Health Insurance for High-Risk Individuals, 1998.* Fergus Falls, Minnesota.

Franks, P., C.M. Clancy, and M.R. Gold. 1993. "Health Insurance and Mortality: Evidence From a National Cohort." *Journal of the American Medical Association* 270(6): 737–741.

Franks, P., C.M. Clancy, M.R. Gold, and P.A. Nutting. 1993. "Health Insurance and Subjective Health Status." *American Journal of Public Health* 83(9): 1295–1299.

General Accounting Office. 1998. *Private Health Insurance: Declining Employer Coverage May Affect Access for 55–64 Year Olds.* Washington, D.C.: General Accounting Office.

Gruber, Jonathan, and Larry Levitt. 2000. "Tax Subsidies for Health Insurance: Costs and Benefits." *Health Affairs* 19(1): 72–85.

Gruber, Jonathan, and Brigitte C. Madrian. 1995. "Health Insurance Availability and the Retirement Decision." *American Economic Review* 84(4): 938–948.

Hall, Mark A. 1999. "The Structure and Enforcement of Health Insurance Rating Reforms." Unpublished manuscript, Wake Forest University.

_____. 2000. "An Evaluation of Vermont's Reform Law." *Journal of Health Politics, Policy and Law* 25(1): 101–131.

Johnson, Richard W., Amy J. Davidoff, and Kevin Perese. 2000. "Health Insurance Costs and Early Retirement Decisions." Presented to the Allied Social Science Associations, Boston, Massachusetts, January.

Karoly, Lynn A., and Jeanette A. Rogowski. 1998. "Retiree Health Benefits and Retirement Behavior: Implications for Health Policy." In *Health Benefits and the Workforce, v. 2*. Washington, D.C.: U.S. Department of Labor, pp. 43–71.

Kirk, Adele M. 2000. The Individual Health Insurance Market—Riding the Bull: Reform in Washington, Kentucky, and Massachusetts." *Journal of Health Politics, Policy and Law* 25(1): 133–174.

Kubik, J. 1996. "Is Disability Endogenours? The SSI Disability Program and the Health of Children." Unpublished manuscript, MIT Department of Economics.

Loprest, Pamela J., and Marilyn Moon. 1999. *Medicare Buy-In Proposal*. Menlo Park, California: Henry J. Kaiser Family Foundation.

Loprest, Pamela J., and Sheila R. Zedlewski. 1998. *Health Insurance Coverage Transitions of Older Americans*. Washington, D.C.: Urban Institute.

Marsteller, Jill A., Len M. Nichols, Adam Badawi, Beth Kessler, Shruti Rajan, and Stephen Zuckerman. 1998. *Variations in the Uninsured: State and County Level Analyses*. Urban Institute monograph, June.

McArdle, Frank, Steve Coppock, Dala Yamamoto, and Andrew Zebrak. 1999. *Retiree Health Coverage: Recent Trends and Employer Perspectives on Future Benefits*. Menlo Park, California: Henry J. Kaiser Family Foundation.

Nichols, Len M. 2000. "State Regulation: What Have We Learned So Far?" *Journal of Health Politics, Policy and Law* 25(1):175–196.

Pauly, Mark, and Bradley Herring. 1999a. *Pooling Health Insurance Risks*. AEI Press: Washington, D.C.

_____. 1999b. "Cutting Taxes for Insuring: Options and Effects of Tax Credits for Health Insurance." Presented to the Council on The Economic Impact of Health System Change conference: *Using Tax Policy to Reduce the Number of Uninsured*, Washington, D.C., December.

Pollitz, Karen. 2001. "Extending Health Insurance Coverage for Older Workers and Early Retirees: How Well Have Public Policies Worked?" In this volume, pp. 233–254.

Sloan, Frank A., and Christopher J. Conover. 1998. "Effects of State Reforms on Health Insurance Coverage of Adults." *Inquiry* 35: 280–293.

Swartz, Katherine, and Deborah W. Garnick. 2000. "Lessons from New Jersey." *Journal of Health Politics, Policy and Law* 25(1): 145–170.

Swartz, Katherine, and Betsey Stevenson. 2001. "Health Insurance Coverage of People in the Ten Years before Medicare Eligibility." In this volume, pp. 13–40.

U.S. Department of Labor. 1995. *Retirement Benefits of American Workers.* Pension and Welfare Benefits Administration. Washington, D.C.: U.S. Government Printing Office.

Zuckerman, Stephen, and Shruti Rajan. 1999. "An Alternative Approach to Measuring the Effects of Insurance Market Reforms." *Inquiry* 36: 44–56.

Filling Gaps in Health Coverage:

# Commentary

Deborah Chollet
*Mathematica Policy Research*

J16 J14 J26
I11 I18
G22

651

The fact that older women are less likely to have health insurance coverage than they were a decade ago is not surprising, but the fact that they are about half as likely to have individual coverage than a decade ago is surprising. That they are about half as likely as younger women to have health insurance coverage as a dependent is sobering, as is the fact that nearly a quarter of older working women with health problems have no health insurance at all.

From the CPS, we have evidence that small firms are more likely than large firms to employ low-wage workers. We also see persistently lower wage levels among women, and especially among older women. It shouldn't altogether surprise us that these paths converge in a way that disadvantages older women in the workforce.

So there are a couple of problems to be solved. Len was charged with solving those problems—and did indeed think outside the box— and he certainly is a good seller of his perspective. But his discussion raised at least two questions in my mind: what would be the source of coverage for this population and what would be the source of subsidies? These are low-wage individuals and low-wage families; as was mentioned in the last session, we know that these families require subsidies to buy insurance. While I wouldn't expect to dictate what an individual should pay for health insurance, I would guess it would be something less than a tithe, less than 10 percent of family income. Therefore, I would guess that virtually all families below 200 percent of poverty, and perhaps higher, would need a significant subsidy to buy health insurance.

Len raises several possibilities for pooling risk, including FEHBP and state employee plans. We have been the route of mandated employer coverage in the private sector, and we abandoned it for a couple of reasons. Groups of any size don't like to accept individuals. From an underwriting perspective, individuals are a very different cast of characters. Employee plans are groups that form not for the purpose of insurance, individuals arrive explicitly for coverage, raising significantly the potential for adverse selection. People who seek coverage when they are sick are more expensive than the population average and more expensive than a group community rate. The only question is how much more expensive will these people be? It is not a question of whether individuals would like to be pooled with employee groups, but, from an insurance perspective and from an underwriting perspective, the two are very different. We have to worry also about people dropping away and destabilizing the group when they believe that they no longer need health insurance. Pools of employees don't pose that problem to the extent that pools of individuals do in a voluntary system.

The program that Len envisions is appealing in some dimensions, but I would argue it is very unappealing in others, such as equity. Why would we want to construct yet another narrow program for a narrow subset of the deserving whomever? Why does an older woman who is sick and of low income deserve coverage more than a younger woman who is sick and of low income, or an older man who is sick and of low income? I don't understand why we would discriminate across a population on the basis of age and gender, when in fact we don't allow that discrimination in any other aspect of our civic life.

We already have some programs expressly for people who are low income and people who are sick: Medicaid and Medicare. We have additional, usually very small programs in many states. In 28 states, there are more or less well-functioning high-risk pools. I would like to spend a few minutes talking about what those high-risk pools are and why HIPAA, the Health Insurance Portability and Accountability Act that Karen Pollitz talked to you about yesterday, might be a model for helping them to work better.

As I mentioned, 28 states have high-risk pools, although in five big states—California, Florida, Louisiana, Illinois, and Utah—they are closed to new enrollment. Despite the fact that high-risk pools are struggling in these and many other states, there are only seven states in this country that have no provision at all for high-risk individuals. Among the states that provide for high-risk individuals, one requires guaranteed issue and risk adjustments. Another caps the proportion of high risk that any one insurer must accept relative to its total business. TennCare blends Tennessee's high-risk pool with its Medicaid and CHIP programs. But the most common model is a separate high-risk pool, and the most common source of funding for these high-risk pools is an assessment on commercial insurers and Blue Cross/Blue Shield plans.

Well, you see the problem. States that fund a high-risk pool with a tax on insurers in effect reward employers who are self-insured. In turn, the tax base to support high risk becomes smaller as employers remove themselves from it. Hence, without federal action helping high-risk pools, they may be a lost cause; but with federal action on the model of HIPAA, they might work quite well by reaching across group plans, individual plans, insured plans, and self-insured plans, treating them as an insurance system that would support high-risk individuals without access to group coverage.

There are other aspects of high risk that might be fixed with HIPAA-type federal legislation. Many states have narrowed insurers' rating practices, especially in the small-group market but also in the individual market. At present, six states limit rate variation for health to less than two to one in the individual market, and eight states prohibit health rating altogether in this market. The latter is the community rate that Len talked about; there are indeed problems with low-risk people dropping coverage. But if there were a high-risk pool that would readily accept and fully subsidize excess risk, the community rate could be much lower in the general market.

In fact, the literature on the effect of a community rate on coverage in the individual market is extremely meager. I have not yet seen a study only of the individual market that evaluates the impact of regulation. Nevertheless, Len's comment that some kinds of regulation depress coverage in the small-group market seems true from what we know thus far, and it is probably also the case in the individual market. Yet, if a high-risk pool accepted all extreme risks, then one would expect the standard rate in the conventional market could be significantly lower and prohibition of health rating would not depress coverage. For example, Minnesota has the largest high-risk pool in the country, with over 25,000 people participating. Minnesota is a market in which insurers underwrite aggressively, and the high-risk pool actually has a distribution of risk. Its rates are affordable because of the distribution of risk in the pool as well as the usual subsidy to the pool.

At present, 11 states limit age rating in the individual market significantly, and 3 states prohibit rating on age altogether in the individual market. Eleven states also limit composite rating: that is, all rate factors taken together cannot produce greater variation in rates than the statutory limit. Those markets have not fallen apart, and they deserve closer investigation as potential models for new federal law constraining insurer rates, especially in the presence of a state program to absorb high risk.

In closing, I would argue that a principal danger is to try to fix too much. That is especially a danger when looking at private/public combinations that rely heavily on private markets to resolve problems of noncoverage. One example of attempting to fix too much may be states' efforts to reduce the waiting period for coverage of preexisting conditions, eliminating it or making it very brief. There I would argue that HIPAA offers a reasonable model. HIPAA provides that, if you do not come from an insurance plan, you have a waiting period on preexisting conditions up to 12 months, with a 6-month look-back. It is not perfect, but it recognizes the frailties of a voluntary system. If we are not going to require coverage, either of individuals or employers, then we must deal in reasonable improvements, knowing that they assure neither seamless protection nor universal coverage, especially for people with health problems.

# Commentary

Frank McArdle
*Hewitt Associates*

I've been asked to comment on this general issue from an "employer perspective," and I would like to remind everyone that we cannot easily generalize about the employer perspective because employers are such a diverse group. Employer reactions can vary very widely depending on their business, their locale, the size of their business, their labor costs, their margins, their competition, their employee relations, and even their individual company cultures.

When you step up from individual employers to larger groups of employers—the business groups and the employer trade groups—you will find that there is somewhat more consistency across employer groups, but even at that level there are very significant differences when you are talking about employer positions on public policy. So, there is a wide diversity among the employer group, and as I speak on the employer perspective, I urge you to remember that.

## THE UNINSURED

Let me say by way of context that the problem of the uninsured is indeed viewed as an employer problem as well, in two ways. For one thing, employers intuitively realize that they are paying more for health care because the costs of uncompensated care are being reflected in what they pay providers. The second thing is that large employers also realize that they are covering more individuals than they would have to cover under their plan if other employers offered coverage. So the problem of the uninsured is recognized by most of the large employers that we at Hewitt Associates deal with, but (with some notable exceptions), employers generally don't feel, at least at the individual company level, that the problem of the uninsured is something they can do very much about.

I think that you will see some thought leadership emerging on this issue and more attention devoted to it. But you'll find that employers have not devoted a lot of thought to the uninsured in their daily operations. For example, I am meeting with a company tomorrow which has spent $1.4 billion on health care this year for retirees and active employees. When you are spending $1.4 billion, it is hard for you to relate to what is needed for the uninsured, because your population is so well insured and so well covered. And large employers generally insure their employees at a very high rate.

## TAX CREDITS

Len and others have talked about tax credits and tax incentives. In my experience, the combination of individual tax credits for the uninsured combined with a subsidy—such as an ability to buy into Medicaid or state Children's Health Insurance Programs—employers would not lose a lot of sleep over that. If there were a direct and transparent tax increase on business associated with the subsidy, then I think you would get a different and stronger reaction. As the policy realm is evolving right now, it seems the individual tax credits would be most likely considered as a way of extending coverage for the uninsured and not as a way of replacing the current employer coverage or the current federal income tax exclusion, which would be potentially a major concern for employers.

From personal experience, I would like to add one administrative caution about tax credits. Len talked about the need to have refundable tax credits and to have the money paid up front. Well, I agree, but that is also a guaranteed formula for an overpayment. And as someone who has had to work with Supplemental Security Income beneficiaries and Social Security beneficiaries, attempting to take back money from a low-income group or a barely moderate-income group is not a politically pleasant exercise, let me assure you.

## PROGRAM COORDINATION

Whenever public policy uses subsidies and tax credits and government programs in relationship to the private sector, there arises the question of coordination. It is an important question but often overlooked, particularly in the legislative developments that we see now. In my view, the idea of combining a government share of an insurance premium and an employer's share of the premium would not be well received by employers. A lot of companies that we deal with tend to want to avoid interactions with government agencies, especially when money is trading hands.

For example, in a recent study we did for the Henry J. Kaiser Family Foundation, Hewitt asked how many employers would accept the direct government subsidy under President Clinton's prescription drug proposal. About 25 percent said they would accept it, while many of the others don't want anything to do with it. There are lots of reasons for employers to do something different than accepting the subsidy, but one reason among several was their dread over docu-mentation, audits, etc., and the attendant bureaucracy when money crosses hands between the federal government and a private sector benefit sponsor.

Likewise, in the area of retiree health, whether it is extending Medicare coverage to pre-Medicare eligible retirees or reforming Medicare options for post-65 retirees, there are bigger issues of coordination because of the existence of Medicare.

## COBRA

Len also mentioned that the extension of COBRA continuation coverage is an attractive policy option, but also an option that is not free. When you talk to large employers and employers of any size, there is a real disconnect between what they think are the costs of COBRA and what the legislators think are the costs of COBRA. For example, according to the latest survey that I've seen by Charles D. Spencer & Associates, the actual average claims cost of COBRA beneficiaries is 156 percent of the cost of active employees. Because the employer can only charge a 2 percent additional premium for that COBRA coverage, what you get, in effect, is another 54 percent or so that is coming from the individual's former employer and from the employees at the individual's former company; there is that subsidy that passes back. So not only is COBRA not free, it is still subsidized to a significant degree by the individual's former employer.

Now when you talk about extending current COBRA eligibility periods( from the current 18 to 36 months available) up until age 65, you can see that the employer subsidy of COBRA would be much, much higher. Even allowing for the employer to charge 125 percent of the premium as some have proposed wouldn't come even close to covering those costs. So that proposed policy change is bound to generate opposition from employers on the matter of cost and also on a certain matter of equity for active employees.

### Mandates

Mandates are a nonstarter for businesses. They are scary for employers, conjuring up images of high costs, limited flexibility, and stiff imposition of government rules. For better or for worse, those feelings are well established and in my opinion have not evolved since the 1993–1994 debate. I think we are still there. I would not expect mandated coverage to become feasible on a large scale for employers anywhere in the near term.

### Retiree Health Coverage

On retiree health coverage, and in particular regarding pre-65 retirees, again citing the Hewitt report for the Henry J. Kaiser Family Foundation, we found a continuing decline in employer provision of retiree medical benefits. Most large companies with more than 1,000 employees are likely to provide retiree medical coverage. They are also more likely to provide coverage for pre-65 retirees than for post-65 retirees, because there is no Medicare available for pre-65 retirees. But even among this group, there has been a very significant decline. And based on questions that we asked employers about what kinds of changes they would consider over the next three to five years, we expect continued retrenchment in the employer-provider system. As many as 30 percent said they would "seriously consider" eliminating retiree health coverage on a prospective basis in the next three to five years, meaning for new hires. Current retirees and near retirees are likely to be grand-fathered under any situation.

I think the continuing decline in retiree coverage surprised some analysts who expected that after the accounting rules were adopted in the early 1990s—the FAS 106 rules, that forced such a big change among employers—a lot of people thought it was a one-time reaction to those accounting rules and that it would stabilize. Well, it hasn't, and our data shows it is not only continuing to decline, but has accelerated slightly.

I do think there are some options out there that could slow the erosion of employer-provided retiree coverage that wouldn't cost a great deal of new money and may even raise money in some ways. So, I would say in general that it is worth discussing policy measures that would slow the erosion of employer coverage. In doing so, we must also recognize that we have to be creative about how we would do that and also recognize that it may be an evolution toward a newer model—a model in which alongside the direct provision of a defined-benefit system there also might be room for a defined-contribution approach as well.

Here are some specific ideas.

1. A recent report from an ERISA Advisory Council work group suggests that it is a good idea to use pension surplus assets to fund and prefund retiree medical expenses for this same group of employees in the pension plan and with guaranteed protections for those employees in the pension plan. There is a huge wealth of surplus pension assets, particularly as a result of the recent stock market performance, and applying those assets to stabilize retiree medical is probably not a bad idea.

2. There are also some relatively small changes in the tax code that would help, such as allowing employers to take future inflation into account when prefunding retiree medical benefits through what's called a Voluntary Employee Beneficiary Association (VEBA); that's another positive change.

3. A third idea is talking about development of some kind of individual account that would allow employees and employers to save for retiree health expenses. The key to the tax treatment here

would be that the accumulated funds would be usable by the retiree for health care expenses only and without incurring taxable income for the purchase of coverage, which is not available to a broad extent in the tax treatment of 401(k) plan withdrawals right now.

So, creation of a dedicated account where employers and employees could contribute could be a meaningful contribution to meeting retiree health care expenses later on. And, it would also facilitate coordination with Medicare, in the sense that the retirees could then allocate the money to a plan of their choice for supplemental or high-option coverage that they wanted or for out-of-pocket expenses associated with that plan, without incurring taxable income.

In this sense, it really is something very compatible with what Len has talked about, but in a different setting. Len says there are two key dimensions to expand coverage policies for the near elderly: the subsidy mechanism and the range of market opportunities the beneficiary will have in which to use that subsidy. I think you could substitute for subsidy the employer and the employee contributions and the tax benefits conferred thereon. In essence, what you need is money and a place where you can buy coverage at an affordable price. We don't always need to think of employer coverage as a specific comprehensive benefit plan, and I think we should broaden our horizons to think of a combination of both defined-benefit and defined-contribution approaches, not just one traditional approach.

Speaking of saving for retiree medical expenses, I don't think that this issue gets enough publicity on the retirement side of the equation in terms of underscoring that individuals do need to factor into their target replacement ratios future retiree medical expenses. Nor do I think Social Security in its replacement ratios gets credit for the Medicare coverage that is also provided with the additional FICA payroll taxes. In other words, a 40–50 percent average replacement ratio is a lot more when the lifetime Medicare coverage is added on.

A couple of years ago, we did some very rough estimates, rough calculations that we did internally. For example, for someone without employer retiree health coverage who is age 40 and earning $25,000, we estimated that individual would need to save between 7 and 13 percent of pay at age 40 for retiree health expenses if they were to retire at age 62. Naturally the amount required as a percentage of pay goes down with income, but it rises with age. At age 50, a worker making $25,000 would have to save between 15 and 25 percent of pay if he/she had no employer retiree health coverage.

## CLOSING

I would like to close with a couple of comments. Len talked about his preferred option of creating a new group purchasing entity to facilitate group market conditions, and Deborah has commented on that too. I have to tell you that from an employer perspective, "Avalon" sounds like the 1993–1994 HIPCs (health insurance purchasing cooperatives). It conjures up this image that, if it is government-initiated, it is going to be unwieldy, expansive, and bureaucratic, and employers are going to be nervous about it as a group.

I also think we may be at the beginning of a stage where we are going to see some new intermediaries emerge in the marketplace who may be able to create some of these markets on their own. For example, with the use of the Internet, some of the relatively big administrative loads that Len and also Deborah talked about, there is a potential for those administrative costs to come way down in a highly electronic Internet environment. We can also foresee the development of new intermediaries that would create a virtual marketplace where the money could be applied and also reduce administrative costs substantially by using the Internet and other means, such as standardization of health plan offerings to increase efficiencies and lower costs.

Finally, in Len's simulations, the cost of the insurance premium modeled reflects a premium for fairly comprehensive health care coverage. Comprehensive coverage has traditionally been the standard of coverage advocated by most policy analysts, and it certainly remains a viable policy option for the future.

# Commentary

Diane Rowland
*Kaiser Commission on Medicaid and the Uninsured*

Well, this has been a good panel, and I have learned a lot from all the presentations.

From Len Nichols, I have learned that when you go and think outside the box, sometimes you come back to the box as the best option. And that is what I am going to talk about: the box of public programs and where they fit into the solution. What I have been listening to today has convinced me that we ought not to throw out the good in our public programs, since we seem to encounter even more problems when we try to replace them with new strategies—when we go outside the box.

Before I begin to explain why I feel this is true, I would like to mention a few issues that we shoulda bear in mind. First, people without health insurance at any age are vulnerable, and our health insurance agenda for the uninsured should not segment people by age. It should segment them by need, and need is the greatest among the lowest income people at all ages. Today we are focusing on a group of particularly vulnerable people within the low-income population, because we know that uninsured children are healthier than their older counterparts—the non-elderly group that we are talking about today. This group also merits special attention because, while we have made political advances in coverage of children (because they are popular and cheap to cover), we have not done so for the population we are talking about today, a group that is more expensive to cover because they have greater health needs.

Second, in focusing on the most vulnerable populations, I think it is very important to go beyond the work that John Eisenberg and his colleagues at AHCPR did in looking at workers in the near-elderly age group and look at those in that age group that are outside of the workforce, as they may in fact be among the most vulnerable. The non-workers may in fact be those who have higher health needs, contributing to their departure from the workforce. Most importantly, I think we need to look at the fact that there are some significant differ-

489

ences in this group and the general population in terms of the duration of periods without insurance. These individuals often tend to be out of the workplace if they are uninsured. Therefore, they are more likely to have long and extended stays of uninsurance instead of being in the transitions from one job to another, which is the case with many of the younger uninsured.

Finally, I would like to remind you of some of the problems with retiree benefits. Frank McArdle talked a little bit about the work he did for the Kaiser Family Foundation on this topic. Deborah Chollet also did some related work for the Kaiser Foundation on the individual market, which I think really points out the vulnerability of the people in the near-elderly age group in terms of access to the individual market and affordable insurance. Her work highlights that states don't absolutely protect older Americans from being excluded from insurance coverage because of preexisting conditions and shows that the cost of coverage can be as high as a $1,000 a month for a 60-year-old male without preexisting conditions in a high-cost state.

With those issues in mind—the need to help the most vulnerable groups, the problems with access to employer coverage, and the barriers in the individual market—we can turn to understanding this population. We did some work back in 1996 looking at the very low-income population, those under 200 percent of poverty, in the 50- to 64-year-old age group. We found some striking differences in health status between younger and older uninsured low-income people. Nearly half (46 percent) of those age 50 to 64 in our survey reported fair or poor health, compared with 18 percent of those 18 to 24 and 24 percent of those 25 to 49. Health status has been shown to be a solid indicator of health needs. So that as hard as the problem is and will remain helping low-income people to gain access to insurance, low-income older people have some greater health needs that magnify the challenge.

In addition, differences in access to care between low-income people without insurance and low-income people with insurance is striking. When we looked at access to care for uninsured people who were sick—people reporting their health status as fair or poor in the age 50 to 64 group with incomes under 200 percent of poverty—29 percent of that group said they had no physician visits in the prior year, and 22 percent reported that they had no usual source of care. These figures contrast sharply with those for individuals with Medicaid or private insurance who are equally low income and equally in poor health, only 8 percent of whom report any of these difficulties.

Clearly all of the evidence on health needs and insurance differentials with the pre-elderly group makes a strong case for helping this age group as well as for the younger uninsured. And when we look at how Medicaid performs against private insurance for this age group—they are typically not eligible yet for Medicare—we see that Medicaid is performing as well as private coverage in guaranteeing access and improving coverage.

So, what that leads me to conclude is that we should really look at the public programs, both Medicare and Medicaid, as a strategy for protecting this population. First, I think we really need to look very carefully at Medicare. It hasn't been discussed much here today, but we have some policymakers proposing raising the age of eligibility for Medicare. That clearly is a totally counterproductive policy to the needs of this near-elderly group we are talking about. I did a call-in show in New Hampshire, and I had about seven uninsured people call in, of whom five were in the age 60- to 65-year-old group saying, "I am uninsured and I am waiting for Medicare. I am trying to do all these things to keep my health going or I am postponing different tests because I need to wait until I am eligible for Medicare." So, one strategy that I would strongly recommend is looking at ways to let people gain Medicare coverage on a buy-in basis earlier than age 65, with subsidies for the lower income. Clearly, raising the age of eligibility of Medicare would be a counterproductive step.

I would also urge that for people who retire early and take Social Security benefits at 62, their ability to access Medicare at that point be changed to allow them to be able to gain Medicare coverage along with their retirement coverage. We know that workers who retire early tend to be people who have health problems, so this is a particularly vulnerable group that may in fact not have any access to the individual insurance market when they retire if they can't gain access to Medicare.

Second, I would also urge that we really take a harder look at the policies we have today for coverage of adults under the Medicaid program. Medicaid has increasingly become—with its decoupling from welfare—a program for children and pregnant women. We are now talking about extending coverage to the parents of children who are covered by Medicaid, but we are not talking about what happens to single adults and childless couples, who no matter how poor now are ineligible in almost every state for the Medicaid program.

If we want to look at a direct, cost-effective, and efficient way to cover low-income adults, we really need to look at decategorizing Medicaid and making it an insurance program by income, not by category, and really begin to focus on bringing in low-income adults below the poverty level. That would help a substantial number of the people in this age group. We can overcome the state variations in Medicaid coverage that Len Nichols noted by doing the unpopular thing of mandating coverage across states at a specific income level, as we have done for children.

The experience with children has shown that public coverage at the lowest incomes work. But regardless of the specifics of the policy, we really need to take a much harder look across the age spectrum at how our low-income program, Medicaid, and its companion CHIP, are covering not just children, but the adults in those states.

And, finally, I would urge that as we look at all of this, we have the ability to afford coverage as our main criteria, and we do not try to link any of these efforts to the health status of individuals. I have looked at Len Nichols' proposal several times, and I know it is fairly attractive to say we would provide coverage to those who are in fair or poor health. However, I don't think we are quite ready to develop the instruments and measures that would enable us to do so. What we see especially in this age group is that health status can change quite dramatically from one day to another, and we really don't want to link your ability to get health coverage to whether you were sick yesterday or are sick today.

In conclusion, I think that as we look forward to trying to provide better coverage for all Americans, we ought to focus not just on children and not just on their parents, but on people of all ages that are without health insurance. It doesn't matter what your risk is. If you are uninsured, you face problems. And we ought to really look at building upon the Medicare program and the Medicaid program as strategies to provide that protection quite efficiently and with help to those most in need among the low income through the Medicaid program.

# Cited Author Index

The italic letters *f*, *n*, and *t* following a page number indicate that the cited name is within a figure, note, or table, respectively, on that page.

# Subject Index

The italic letters *f*, *n*, and *t* following a page number indicate that the subject information is within a figure, note, or table, respectively, on that page.

504

518

# About the Institute

The W.E. Upjohn Institute for Employment Research is a nonprofit research organization devoted to finding and promoting solutions to employment-related problems at the national, state, and local levels. It is an activity of the W.E. Upjohn Unemployment Trustee Corporation, which was established in 1932 to administer a fund set aside by the late Dr. W.E. Upjohn, founder of The Upjohn Company, to seek ways to counteract the loss of employment income during economic downturns.

The Institute is funded largely by income from the W.E. Upjohn Unemployment Trust, supplemented by outside grants, contracts, and sales of publications. Activities of the Institute comprise the following elements: 1) a research program conducted by a resident staff of professional social scientists; 2) a competitive grant program, which expands and complements the internal research program by providing financial support to researchers outside the Institute; 3) a publications program, which provides the major vehicle for disseminating the research of staff and grantees, as well as other selected works in the field; and 4) an Employment Management Services division, which manages most of the publicly funded employment and training programs in the local area.

The broad objectives of the Institute's research, grant, and publication programs are to 1) promote scholarship and experimentation on issues of public and private employment and unemployment policy, and 2) make knowledge and scholarship relevant and useful to policymakers in their pursuit of solutions to employment and unemployment problems.

Current areas of concentration for these programs include causes, consequences, and measures to alleviate unemployment; social insurance and income maintenance programs; compensation; workforce quality; work arrangements; family labor issues; labor-management relations; and regional economic development and local labor markets.